OXFORD STUDIES IN ROMAN SOCIETY AND LAW

General Editors

PAUL DU PLESSIS   THOMAS A. J. MCGINN

OXFORD STUDIES IN ROMAN SOCIETY AND LAW

The aim of this monograph series is to create an interdisciplinary forum devoted to the interaction between legal history and ancient history, in the context of the study of Roman law. Focusing on the relationship of law to society, the volumes will cover the most significant periods of Roman law (up to the death of Justinian in 565) so as to provide a balanced view of growth, decline, and resurgence. Most importantly, the series will provoke general debate over the extent to which legal rules should be examined in light of the society which produced them in order to understand their purpose and efficacy.

Roman Law and Economics
Volume I

Institutions and Organizations

Edited by
GIUSEPPE DARI-MATTIACCI
AND DENNIS P. KEHOE

OXFORD
UNIVERSITY PRESS

OXFORD
UNIVERSITY PRESS

Great Clarendon Street, Oxford, OX2 6DP,
United Kingdom

Oxford University Press is a department of the University of Oxford.
It furthers the University's objective of excellence in research, scholarship,
and education by publishing worldwide. Oxford is a registered trade mark of
Oxford University Press in the UK and in certain other countries

First Edition published in 2020

Published in the United States of America by Oxford University Press
198 Madison Avenue, New York, NY 10016, United States of America

British Library Cataloguing in Publication Data
Data available

Library of Congress Control Number: 2020934649

ISBN 978-0-19-878720-4

Preface

In recent years, historians of Roman law and the Roman economy have increasingly turned toward insights from economic theory to come to a better understanding of the relationship between Roman law and institutions and the economy of the Roman world. The research of such scholars has borrowed tools mainly from the fields of law and economics and new institutional economics, and the result has been very fruitful, with an increasing number of Roman historians pursuing genuine interdisciplinary work that applies modern theoretical perspectives to understanding the development of Roman jurisprudence and legal institutions in numerous areas of the law that were important to the economy, such as contracts of sale and lease and hire, markets, credit, agency, and banking, not to mention the vast field of Roman slavery. At the same time, modern legal scholars and economists have found the ancient world, particularly the Roman Empire, to be an intriguing test case to trace the role of law and legal institutions in a pre-industrial society. The Roman Empire provides a fitting test case for theories about the relationship between law and the economy because its legal institutions are relatively well documented, while at the same time the economic performance of the Roman world has been an area of intensive study and debate among economic historians. One of the principal questions that historians of the Roman economy have been addressing in recent years concerns the performance of the economy of the Roman Empire: given the favorable conditions resulting from relative peace, political unification, and a more uniform and predictable system of courts and enforcement of contracts, to what extent did the Roman Empire experience economic growth, and, if so, how were the fruits of economic growth shared across society and to what extent did the legal institutions in place contribute and change in response to it? Roman economic historians have also focused on many other questions related to these overarching issues, such as the effects of demographic change on the economy, economic planning by Roman property owners, and the role of the state in the economy, not to mention the actual effectiveness of Roman legal institutions and the degree to which people in the empire relied on them as they sought to protect their own most important economic interests.

The rich debate over these and many other issues provides a very favorable climate for genuine interdisciplinary research on the Roman world. This collection of essays endeavors to make an important contribution to bringing together scholars with diverse research backgrounds and thus to consolidate a new field of research, the economic analysis of Roman law (or Roman law and economics). The collection does so by drawing together scholars from a variety of fields both ancient and modern, and integrating insights from legal history, economic history, and the social sciences and, in particular, economic theory and econometrics. We hope to achieve two sets of goals.

First, this collection provides a novel perspective on the function, evolution, and, possibly, rationale of Roman legal institutions. While we have no ambition to provide a systematic analysis, the various chapters offer a wide coverage of the law and institutions of ancient Rome and provide an innovative perspective of often long-studied issues.

Second, this collection contributes a radically interdisciplinary methodological toolbox to the analysis of Roman legal institutions (and ancient legal institutions, more generally). Through the various chapters, the reader is exposed to a rich array of methodological approaches. Careful historical analysis of both legal and economic institutions is combined with cutting-edge theoretical and empirical examination.

Next to those who, like us, are fascinated by the law and institutions of ancient Rome, we hope to interest a broader community of historians (both legal and economic), legal scholars, and social scientists. On the one hand, the set of methods that are used in this book can be applied to many more issues than we could cover in two volumes. Students of Roman legal and economic institutions will hopefully find some of these methods useful. On the other hand, we hope to have demonstrated that the information available on about one thousand years of Roman history offers an interesting natural laboratory to test the explanatory power of modern theoretical approaches.

This project would have not been possible without invaluable advice, support, and encouragement we received from Barbara Abatino, Erasmo Giambona, Henry Hansmann, Elio Lo Cascio, and

Peter Temin at many crucial junctures. We are also deeply indebted to the series editors, Paul du Plessis and Thomas A. J. McGinn, and two anonymous reviewers, who guided and advised us throughout a long and intense process of revision. Georgina Leighton has been extraordinarily supportive and patient as we have worked to bring the collection into its final form. We would also like to thank Tim Beck for his energetic work in copyediting, and Chandrakala Chandrasekaran for managing production. In addition, we are grateful to Claudia Kassner and Aparna Sundaram of Columbia Law School for preparing the index. Needless to say, the greatest share of efforts has been exerted by the authors of the chapters in this book; we are extremely grateful to them all.

Giuseppe Dari-Mattiacci
Dennis P. Kehoe

Contents

VOLUME I

III. ORGANIZING BUSINESS

VOLUME II

IV. SLAVERY AND THE ROMAN ECONOMY

V. CREDIT

List of Figures

Whilst every effort has been made to secure permissions, we may have failed in a few cases to trace the copyright holders. If contacted, the publisher will be pleased to rectify any omissions at the earliest opportunity.

List of Tables

List of Contributors

Barbara Abatino, Research Fellow in the Faculty of Law at the University of Amsterdam, the Netherlands.

Jean Andreau, Director of Studies at the School for Advanced Studies in the Social Sciences (EHESS), France.

Benito Arruñada, Professor of Business Organization at Pompeu Fabra University, Spain.

Giuseppe Dari-Mattiacci, Alfred W. Bressler Professor of Law at Columbia Law School, USA.

Luuk de Ligt, Professor of Ancient History at Leiden University, the Netherlands.

Robert C. Ellickson, Walter E. Meyer Professor Emeritus of Property and Urban Law and Professorial Lecturer in Law at Yale Law School, USA.

Richard A. Epstein, Laurence A. Tisch Professor of Law at NYU School of Law, the Peter and Kirsten Bedford Senior Fellow at the Hoover Institution, and the James Parker Hall Distinguished Service Professor Emeritus of Law at the University of Chicago Law School, USA.

Iole Fargnoli, Professor of Roman Law at the University of Bern, Switzerland, and the University of Milan, Italy.

Robert K. Fleck, Professor, John E. Walker Department of Economics, Clemson University, USA.

Andreas Martin Fleckner, Professor of Private Law, Roman Law, and Commercial Law at Humboldt University of Berlin, Germany.

David Friedman, Professor of Law at the Santa Clara University School of Law, USA.

Henry Hansmann, Oscar M. Ruebhausen Professor of Law at Yale Law School, USA.

F. Andrew Hanssen, Professor, John E. Walker Department of Economics, Clemson University, USA.

Ron Harris, Kalman Lubowsky Professor of Law and History at Tel Aviv University, Israel.

Dennis P. Kehoe, Professor, Department of Classical Studies and Andrew W. Mellon Professor in the Humanities (2010–13) at Tulane University, USA.

Egbert Koops, Professor of Legal History at Leiden University, the Netherlands.

Reinier Kraakman, Ezra Ripley Thayer Professor of Law at Harvard Law School, USA.

Gary D. Libecap, Distinguished Emeritus Professor of Economics at the University of California, Santa Barbara and a Research Associate at the National Bureau of Economic Research, USA.

Elio Lo Cascio, Professor Emeritus of Roman History at the Sapienza University of Rome, Italy.

Dean Lueck, Director of the Program on Natural Resource Governance at the Ostrom Workshop, Professor of Economics and Affiliate Professor of Law at Indiana University Bloomington, USA.

Barbara Luppi, Assistant Professor of Economics at the University of Modena and Reggio Emilia and Adjunct Professor of International Economics at the Bologna Institute for Policy Research, Italy.

Thomas J. Miceli, Professor of Economics at the University of Connecticut, USA.

Geoffrey Parsons Miller, Stuyvesant P. Comfort Professor of Law at NYU School of Law, USA.

Francesco Parisi, Oppenheimer Wolff and Donnelly Professor of Law at University of Minnesota Law School, USA, and Professor of Economics at the University of Bologna, Italy.

Daniel Pi, Visiting Professor of Law at Mitchell Hamline School of Law, USA.

Eric A. Posner, Kirkland and Ellis Distinguished Service Professor of Law at the University of Chicago Law School, USA.

Aldo Schiavone, Professor of Roman Law at the Università di Roma La Sapienza, Italy.

Richard Squire, Alpin J. Cameron Professor of Law at Fordham University School of Law, USA.

Peter Temin, Elisha Gray II Professor Emeritus of Economics at MIT, USA.

Hendrik L. E. Verhagen, Professor of Private International Law, Comparative Law and Roman Law and Society at Radboud University, the Netherlands, and attorney-at-law at Clifford Chance (Financial Markets, Amsterdam).

List of Abbreviations

C.	*Codex of Justinian*
CIL	*Corpus Inscriptionum Latinarum*
C.Th.	*Theodosian Code*
D.	*Digest of Justinian*
FIRA	*Fontes Iuris Romani Antejustiniani*
Gai., *Inst.*	Gaius, *Institutes*
Iust., *Inst.*	Justinian, *Institutes*

Standard abbreviations are used for inscriptions, papyri, and other legal texts are used, as well as for ancient literary sources.

1

Rome and the Economics of Ancient Law I

Geoffrey Parsons Miller

Ancient Rome can boast many achievements—in social organization, engineering, the arts, military strategy, and more—but perhaps none has had such a lasting influence as its legal system. Roman law was a pillar of the ancient world, and for more than a thousand years continued to exert a powerful influence over civil law systems across the globe. Even common law countries owe much to Roman antecedents. Terms such as *bona fide*, *contra proferentem*, rights *in rem* and *in personam*, *in solidum*, *ne bis in idem*, and *restitutio in integrum* reflect the influence of Roman legal concepts on the common law world. The early American legal commentators James Kent and Joseph Story were familiar with the *Institutes* of Justinian and highly esteemed the principles of private law found therein (Radin 1924). Roman law was standard fare in legal education in the United States and elsewhere (Reed 1921: 51). Erudite lawyers were familiar with the *jus civile* and *jus gentium*, with the *Digest*, *Institutes*, and *Corpus Juris Civilis*, with quasi-contract, usufruct, and servitude. Legal scholars considered Roman law to be a fitting subject of research: Max Radin's *Handbook of Roman Law* (1927) offered an introduction to the topic for generations of American law students and legal scholars. The work of A. Arthur Schiller at Columbia University maintained Roman law as an area of research in American schools of law and established important links between the fields of law and classics and ancient history. An important indication of the importance of Schiller's contribution in this regard is the volume *Studies in Roman*

Geoffrey Parsons Miller, *Rome and the Economics of Ancient Law I* In: *Roman Law and Economics: Institutions and Organizations, Volume I*. Edited by: Giuseppe Dari-Mattiacci and Dennis P. Kehoe, Oxford University Press (2020).

DOI: 10.1093/oso/9780198787204.003.0001

Law in Memory of A. Arthur Schiller (1986), which was edited by two colleagues from Columbia: papyrologist Roger Bagnall and William Harris, an ancient historian. The volume includes contributions from both legal historians and classicists.

Over more recent decades, however, Roman law fell decidedly out of fashion in American law schools. Few American law students view Roman law as a pathway to success in practice; and, although the class is taught at some law schools, it has moved to the margins of American legal education. Roman law, however, remains an essential topic in many European law faculties. If few law faculty in the United States specialize in ancient law, the situation is much different in the field of classical studies, where ancient law has gained increased prominence as a field of study both in the United States and Europe, contributing in particular to scholarship on the family, women, the economy, and slavery. In addition, Roman law classes are a very popular component of many undergraduate classics programs in the United States.

In recent years, scholars from law schools and economics departments have increasingly focused attention on the ancient world. At the same time, classicists and ancient historians have sought to apply lessons from the modern theoretical debates in economics and law in their understanding the ancient world. This approach has been particularly fruitful in the study of the ancient economy. To cite one major example, many of the essays in *The Cambridge Economic History of the Greco-Roman World* (2007) apply perspectives from the new institutional economics to examine the interplay between political and legal institutions and the economies of Greece and Rome. The present collection of essays represents an effort to bring together the perspectives of ancient historians interested in using modern theoretical perspectives to ask new questions about the ancient economy with those of lawyers and economists who, while sharing this goal, are interested in using the ancient world as a testing ground for theories about institutions and their effects on economic performance. It is hoped that such an effort will contribute to the ongoing debates in the fields of Roman law and ancient economic history. The contributions to this collection bring a variety of perspectives to this scholarly agenda.

Not everyone, of course, would accept that economic analysis in the modern sense has much to say about an ancient culture. To cite a prominent criticism of such an approach, as argued by Francesco

Boldizzoni (2011), an historian of early modern Europe, it is inappropriate to apply models drawn from the fields of law and economics in analyzing pre-modern economies, since such models are based on anachronistic assumptions about economic preferences. For the ancient economy, Boldizzoni endorses the view of Moses Finley, who in his masterwork, *The Ancient Economy* (1973), presented the principal determinants of behavior in ancient times as social rather than economic in nature. People were more driven by striving for prestige and status than by a wish to amass wealth. By implication, the standard techniques of conventional economic modeling will not be effective at describing ancient legal institutions.

To be sure, Boldizzoni argues convincingly that fully understanding the ancient economy requires taking into account the social factors affecting economic institutions, but this recognition does not rule out examining the ancient economy in terms of the incentives created by various property regimes, and seeing economic actors as rationally seeking to promote their own welfare within broad overall constraints. These include social and political institutions, as well as population and technology; a common theme is that population and technology established basic parameters within which a pre-industrial economy could develop. An economist who led the way in applying modern economic theory to understand an ancient economy is Morris Silver. In his *Economic Structures of the Ancient Near East* (1985), Silver argues that prices in the ancient Near East were determined by supply and demand; that reasonably well-developed markets for capital, labor, and goods existed in ancient times; that money was widely used to facilitate trade; and that people in ancient times, as today, were diligent at promoting and protecting their self-interest.[1] For some years now, ancient historians have applied methodologies drawn from law and the social sciences to understand better the performances of ancient economies, including those of the Near East, Egypt, Greece, and the Roman world. These approaches include studying, to the extent possible given the limitations of the evidence, the development of wages and prices over time, the organization of commercial enterprises, the role of financial institutions, and land tenure.

The papers in this volume generally share Silver's functionalist view that conventional economic analysis can explain features of

[1] For an updated perspective see Silver (1995).

the ancient world.[2] Underlying this consensus are two fundamental premises. First, the basic structures that separate ancient societies from our own notwithstanding, economic models provide a useful method to analyze economic activity. Underlying this approach is the assumption that people in the ancient world tended to behave in ways that rationally enhanced their prospects of achieving security, prestige, prosperity, enjoyment, and opportunities for their children to have an even better life. Second, the problems addressed by Roman law are not fundamentally dissimilar to those addressed by modern law. There are, to be sure, many contrasts between the social world of the Roman period and society today: differences in the amount and distribution of wealth; in social practices, religious beliefs, language, and politics; in life expectancy, technology, science, and information storage, analysis, and transmission; and much else besides. But the essential challenge remains the same: to establish stable institutions that achieve the benefits of cooperation without creating undue potential for oppression, facilitate value-enhancing transactions, provide opportunities for reducing or limiting risk, and allow at least some people the means to live a good and decent life. Together, these assumptions suggest that, to achieve its objectives, any legal system will seek to create incentives for people to act in value-enhancing ways and to refrain from acting in harmful ways.

It is, therefore, a goal of these volumes to employ economic analysis to further our understanding of the past. As discussed below, the contributions found in these pages fulfill that promise: they are uniformly intriguing and, at times, offer illumination on topics that heretofore were cloaked in obscurity. But these papers offer other benefits as well. Economic analysis can aid in tracing the path of legal history—in understanding the patterns of influence and change and in analyzing how ideas derived from Roman law are precursors to modern legal rules. The study of Roman legal institutions can contribute to the analysis of public policy by providing a menu of potential approaches to problems of economic organization. In some cases, economic analysis of Roman law may enhance our understanding of economics itself by presenting examples of unusual forms of economic organization and engaging in original economic theorizing to explain them.

[2] Several chapters suggest alternative explanations when functional ones do not appear to explain the phenomenon at issue.

Roman Law and Economics makes a valuable contribution to our understanding of the laws and legal institutions of ancient Rome. The materials on public law illustrate the potential of the economic approach. For example, Robert K. Fleck, F. Andrew Hanssen, and Dennis P. Kehoe focus on the role of the Roman state in promoting private property rights in agriculture, which was by far the most important sector in the Roman economy, as in all pre-industrial economies. They approach this issue from the perspective of recent literature on the economic role of endogenous institutions. They argue that although as a general principle the Roman government promoted private rights to land as the empire expanded in Italy and across the Mediterranean, this policy ran up against constraints imposed by local land tenure systems and the imperial government's own fiscal interests.

Eric A. Posner's chapter also considers the puzzle of why the political organization of the Roman Republic gave way to the less democratic system of the Empire. Posner applies agency theory to examine how the strong system of checks and balances built into the constitution of the Republic, appropriate for a small polity and a homogenous political class, proved unworkable when Rome acquired a vast empire. Posner's treatment of the Roman republican constitution and its eventual transformation into the monarchy of the Principate is especially interesting because the American founding fathers, in writing the American constitution, were greatly influenced by their understanding of Roman institutions. The Roman experience with the passage from a republic to monarchy thus can enhance our own understanding of the development of American political life.

Luuk de Ligt's chapter, "Law-Making and Economic Change During the Republic and Early Empire," adopts a more conventional approach. In his view, while the law-makers clearly responded to changing economic conditions, their focus and intent was not so much to align the law with principles of economic efficiency but rather to develop Roman law as an autonomous juridical discipline. Although de Ligt's chapter counsels caution in the use of economic reasoning, his analysis nevertheless recognizes that legal innovation did adapt and respond over time to changing economic circumstances.

Economic analysis also takes center stage in the chapters dealing with markets and trade. Elio Lo Cascio's chapter, "Setting the Rules of the Game: The Market and Its Working in the Roman Empire," employs the techniques and insights of new institutional economics to investigate the functioning of Roman economic markets. Lo Cascio concludes that throughout its history—and regardless of changing political arrangements—the legal system of ancient Rome privileged the operation of market forces and sought to protect the institutions of competitive markets. Roman authorities generally avoided attempts to regulate prices, but sought instead to regulate markets to ensure the efficiency of prices.

Peter Temin offers a complementary account of the Roman economic system in his chapter, "Statistics in Ancient History: Prices and Trade in the *Pax Romana.*" Rather than examining legal institutions at the level of abstract description, Temin engages in a detailed analysis of prices in the market for wheat in the late Republic and early Empire. Temin's work is to be commended for its effort to employ statistical analysis in an effort to understand the functioning and regulation of market in an ancient society. His remarkable claim is that the market for wheat in ancient Rome was sufficiently deep and well developed as to establish essentially a single price for the commodity throughout the Roman Mediterranean. Temin's work is not only instructive in its own right—illustrating the undeniable impact of market forces on wheat prices in the period under study—but is also important at the level of theory insofar as it addresses methodological problems inherent in the analysis of data sets containing limited information and significant uncertainty. Temin's work is exemplary for the value of empirical research in the study of ancient economic and legal institutions.[3]

The value of analyzing particular markets and institutions is also reflected in Ron Harris's chapter, "The Organization of India-to-Rome Trade: Loans and Agents in the Muziris Papyrus." Long-distance trade in ancient times was highly profitable but also risky—plagued by agency costs, difficulties of contract enforcement, potential expropriation, and informational asymmetry. Harris's study examines the Muziris Papyrus, the only extant document evidencing how merchants dealt with the transaction costs of long-distance trade between Rome and India. The document deals with the sort of issues that any contract for the conveyance of traded goods across distance contains today: the financing of the deal, the security for credit advanced, the scope of agency accorded to the custodian, and the

[3] For further detailed analysis of economic conditions in ancient Rome, see Temin (2013).

risk of loss or damage to the cargo. Harris demonstrates that the contract drafters adapted conventional legal forms to deal in an economically sensible way with the particular features of the enterprise.

The legal organization of business activities—a focus of contemporary business law scholarship—was also a significant issue in ancient Rome. Henry Hansmann, Reinier Kraakman, and Richard Squire, individually and in collaboration, have been at the forefront of contemporary scholarship that has sought to rethink our understanding of the nature and functioning of business organizations.[4] Their chapter, "Incomplete Organizations: Legal Entities and Asset Partitioning in Roman Commerce," applies the concept of asset partitioning to Roman business organizations. Asset partitioning, in the authors' terminology, refers to a legal structure that limits creditor collection rights as between personal and business assets. Asset partitioning in modern business forms helps simplify the assessment of credit risk and expedite insolvency proceedings. The same advantages could be expected for asset partitioning in ancient Rome. However, despite the impressive development of the Roman economy and the sophistication of the Roman legal system, the authors conclude that asset partitioning in the modern sense was not a dominant feature of Roman business organizations. They conjecture—in a mode of thinking more reminiscent of Francesco Boldizzoni and Moses Finley than of the approaches taken by the writers in this collection—that Rome's failure to develop asset partitioning may have reflected non-economic factors such as the aristocracy's disparagement of commerce, the emperor's distrust of strong non-state institutions, or Roman society's reliance on family organization.

Andreas Martin Fleckner's chapter, "Roman Business Associations," also addresses the legal structure of Roman enterprise. Like Hansmann, Kraakman, and Squire, Fleckner observes that Roman business associations did not develop into forms familiar today. In particular, Roman firms did not grow to large size or issue publicly traded shares. Fleckner argues that Roman law made it easy to dissolve or terminate business enterprises, thus reducing the utility or feasibility of public firms in the modern sense. Further, Rome never developed other essential features that undergird the modern business enterprise: a robust law of agency and strong protections for

[4] See e.g. Hansmann, Kraakman, and Squire (2006).

personal assets. Fleckner suggests that the lack of stable share financing for large-scale Roman enterprise traces ultimately to social phenomena: the unwillingness of Roman elites to enter into legally binding contracts and the familial roots of Roman business firms. While these explanations may provide part of the answer, it remains puzzling why the economic advantages of more effective rules for facilitating finance were not potent enough to overcome objections based on social norms and values.

Barbara Abatino and Giuseppe Dari-Mattiacci's "Agency Problems and Organizational Costs in Slave-Run Businesses" focuses on the central issue of agency in the design of business firms between the second century BCE and the second century CE. Roman law recognized the *peculium servi communis*, a form of business organization managed by slaves. This institution offered legal advantages, notably a form of indirect limited liability for their owners. Economic theory might predict, therefore, that the *peculium servi communis* would evolve to significant size. The evidence suggests, however, that these firms were small- to medium-sized organizations. Why did they remain small? The authors suggest that complex agency problems constrained the growth of these institutions, limiting the number of individuals involved as well as the amount of capital invested. Abatino and Dari-Mattiacci's analysis is exemplary of the results that can be obtained when conventional economic ideas (agency cost theory) are applied to unconventional topics (slave-run businesses in ancient Rome).

Dennis P. Kehoe expands the analysis of agency in the Roman economy in his chapter, "Mandate and the Management of Business in the Roman Empire." Despite the lack of a provision for direct agency, Roman law developed sophisticated forms of agency through the use of slaves and other social dependents. However, certain beneficial economic arrangements required direct undertakings of a principal, and thus required the involvement of a social equal. Roman law's response to this problem was the contract of mandate. Mandate was by definition a gratuitous contract—the agent was obligated to perform on his promise but had no legal entitlement to compensation for his services. Although the gratuitous feature of the mandate may have addressed certain social or cultural issues, it created obvious incentive problems because it placed the principal in an advantageous position vis-à-vis the agent. Kehoe advances the idea that incentive-compatible arrangements were achieved under the mandate, notwithstanding its gratuitous character, because of complex webs of reciprocal favors that property owners and business people performed for one another. The theory is interesting and plausible, although it leaves open the deeper question of why Roman law did not develop what appear, by today's standards, to be a simpler and more efficient regime for the management of agency relationships.

Overall, these investigations enhance our understanding of Roman law and economic practice, identify interesting puzzles and problems for analysis, and illustrate the potential of economic reasoning to deepen and enrich the analysis of ancient legal systems.

REFERENCES

Bagnall, Roger S., and William V. Harris, eds. 1986. *Studies in Roman Law in Memory of A. Arthur Schiller*. Leiden: Brill.

Boldizzoni, Francesco. 2011. *The Poverty of Clio: Resurrecting Economic History*. Princeton: Princeton University Press.

Finley, Moses I. 1973. *The Ancient Economy*. Revised edition 1999, edited with introduction by Ian Morris. Berkeley: University of California Press.

Hansmann, Henry, Reinier Kraakman, and Richard Squire. 2006. "Law and the Rise of the Firm." 119 *Harvard Law Review* 1333–1403.

Radin, Max. 1924. "Fundamental Concepts of the Roman Law." 12 *California Law Review* 393–410.

Radin, Max. 1927. *Handbook of Roman Law*. St. Paul: West Publishing Co.

Reed, Alfred Zantzinger. 1921. *Training for the Public Profession of the Law: Historical Development and Principal Contemporary Problems of Legal Education in the United States with Some Account of Conditions in England and Canada*. New York: The Carnegie Foundation for the Advancement of Teaching, Bulletin No. 15.

Scheidel, Walter, Ian Morris, and Richard Saller, eds. 2007. *The Cambridge Economic History of the Greco-Roman World*. Cambridge: Cambridge University Press.

Silver, Morris. 1985. *Economic Structures of the Ancient Near East*. London: Croom Helm.

Silver, Morris. 1995. *Economic Structures of Antiquity*. Westport and London: Greenwood.

Temin, Peter. 2013. *The Roman Market Economy*. Princeton: Princeton University Press.

Part I

Institutions

2

What Can the Endogenous Institutions Literature Tell Us About Ancient Rome?

Robert K. Fleck, F. Andrew Hanssen, and Dennis P. Kehoe

2.1. INTRODUCTION

A major issue in Roman history concerns the effects that the empire's political and legal institutions had on the broader economy, whether they promoted broad economic prosperity and benefited society as a whole, or whether, rather, they tended primarily to enrich a well-connected elite, even at the expense of society as a whole. In this paper, we address this issue by focusing on the most important political and legal institutions that surrounded the Roman agrarian economy. This is appropriate because, as in other pre-industrial societies, agriculture was the basis of the Roman economy. It employed the vast majority of the empire's population, and at the same time landownership underpinned the empire's political economy. The wealth of the Roman elite, the senatorial and equestrian classes, was largely based in agriculture, and the Roman imperial government fostered the development of an elite class of landowners in the cities throughout the empire. These landowners served on city councils, and the imperial government depended on them to perform most of the day to day functions in governing the empire, most crucially, the collection of taxes. Moreover, agriculture represented by far the most important source of tax revenue for the imperial government. In addition, the emperor was the pre-eminent

Robert K. Fleck, F. Andrew Hanssen, and Dennis P. Kehoe, *What Can the Endogenous Institutions Literature Tell Us About Ancient Rome?* In: *Roman Law and Economics: Institutions and Organizations, Volume I.*
Edited by: Giuseppe Dari-Mattiacci and Dennis P. Kehoe, Oxford University Press (2020).
DOI: 10.1093/oso/9780198787204.003.0002

landowner in the empire, and imperial estates, along with mines and quarries, formed part of a network of properties under the management of the imperial treasury, or Fiscus, that provided a major source of revenues supplementing those achieved through taxation. The emperor's capacity to take land from opponents and bestow it on supporters was an important aspect of his power over the senatorial order.[1]

The focus of this paper will be to come to a better understanding of the role that legal institutions played in shaping the Roman economy by examining the long-term policies of the Roman imperial government over land in terms of recent literature on endogenous institutions. The purpose of this project is twofold. First, analyzing property rights in the Roman Empire from the perspective of contemporary debates about institutions helps to clarify the relationships between Roman institutions and the empire's economic performance, and to place the Roman economic experience in a broader historical perspective. Thus the theoretical perspectives on property rights to be examined below will offer insights into the Roman government's fostering of private property rights over land by clarifying the incentives they created for investment as well as the limits on the Roman government's ability to maintain long-term policies. At the same time, it is hoped, such an analysis will make scholars from diverse fields in legal and economic history aware of the relevance of ancient history to the basic issues that they confront.

To put the role of agriculture in the Roman economy in perspective, the Roman agrarian economy supported the empire's flourishing urban culture, which has left behind striking material remains. Although there is no certainty about the size of any city in the ancient world, scholars generally agree that the Roman Empire achieved a degree of urbanization not matched in most areas of Europe until the early modern period. Thus in a detailed analysis of the likely populations of Roman cities, Andrew Wilson (2011: 161–95) argues that the empire supported an urban population (in cities of 5,000 or more) of about seven million (7,388,500). At the lower range of conventional estimates of the population of the Roman Empire at its peak in 165 CE (when the Antonine plague apparently reduced the population dramatically), which range from 60 to 110 million, this would have

[1] Mauiro (2012).

represented an urbanization rate of about 10 to 12 percent, a much higher rate than in England and Wales in 1600, and about the same as in Spain in the same period, but much lower than the Netherlands.[2] The Roman Empire had a handful of giant cities: Rome, with a population of about one million at the time of Augustus leads the way, followed by Alexandria, which may have had as many as 500,000 residents at its peak. Antioch in Syria had on the order of 250,000 people, and a few other cities, including Carthage in North Africa, had populations over 100,000 or at least approached this size. There were numerous cities with populations in the tens of thousands. Some parts of the Roman Empire were heavily urbanized, led by Egypt and Italy, with urban populations of 20 percent or more, followed by Africa and Asia Minor.

Many scholars, most notably Wilson, have seen urbanism in the Roman Empire as proxy evidence for economic growth, but the nature of this growth remains in dispute.[3] As emphasized in *The Cambridge Economic History of the Greco-Roman World* (2007), population and technology established basic parameters within which a pre-industrial agrarian economy could change. In the most pessimist assessment, the Roman economy would always be subject to Malthusian constraints, so that the expansion of cities would result mainly from a growing overall population, with an elite able to capture an ever larger portion of the surplus produced by a vast class of farmers facing increasing competition for land.[4] In a more optimistic scenario, the Roman economy, like other pre-industrial economies, never reached full capacity, so that the right mix of institutions could promote positive economic change and even growth.[5] We will investigate how the Roman imperial government struggled to maintain institutions that promoted the private ownership of land at the center of the empire's political economy. The Roman policy to define private property rights precisely and to foster authoritative legal institutions to protect them represents a credible commitment on the part of the imperial government to the coalition of landowners. The Roman government's credible commitment to

[2] Maddison (2007: 40–3); de Vries (1984: 39).

[3] Wilson (2009); more skeptical, Morley (2011).

[4] For the demographic factors surrounding the Roman economy, see Scheidel (2007).

[5] See especially Erdkamp (2015: 18–39).

private property rights promoted the interests of a coalition of landowners throughout the empire, providing important incentives for investments in agriculture. But imperial government's efforts to promote private property rights and promote investment ran up against some basic constraints. One was that Roman property owners had a restricted range of options in investing large amounts of wealth, and this meant that many simply relied on exacting some share of the surplus produced by tenants and other workers, a situation that required policy adjustments on the part of the Roman legal authorities that compromised private property rights. Fiscal considerations also limited the credibility of the Roman government's commitment to the empire's landowning class. The Roman government tended to protect the tenure rights of tenants and other small farmers, because their ability to produce a surplus was the key to stable tax revenues. In addition, to make sure that administrative posts throughout the empire could be filled, the Roman government restricted the rights of key social groups to dispose over their land. The Roman government thus faced the difficult task of balancing these competing concerns as it sought to maintain the private landownership of as the basis of the empire's political order.

2.1.1. Endogenous Institutions Literature

A large and growing literature on "endogenous" institutions seeks to understand the circumstances under which institutions of particular types arise. One of the literature's guiding principles is that, because institutions structure the incentives that members of a society face, if institutions are not well matched to a society's circumstances—that is to say, not designed to inspire productive activities, broadly defined—the society will not thrive. An important purpose of political institutions is to promote a government's ability to commit to policy promises.[6] The models we will discuss emphasize how the expansion or contraction of political rights can help promote commitment. Treating political rights as endogenous appears a particularly promising approach to apply to ancient Rome, albeit with certain caveats.

[6] As James Madison famously wrote, "In framing a government that is to be administered by men over men, the great difficulty lies in this: You must first enable the government to control the governed; and in the next place, oblige it to control itself" (*The Federalist*, No. 51, p. 349).

If one considers simply Roman citizens resident in Italy, one could posit that: (1) Rome expanded rights during the Republic; (2) this expansion was gradual (occurring over centuries) rather than all at once; (3) the expansion was eventually reversed, with a contraction of rights accompanying the transition to Empire; and (4) the Empire's institutional structure was very durable (not a simple "mistake").

In applying these ideas to the Roman Empire, however, it is necessary to consider what kinds of "rights" to focus on. The endogenous institutions literature tends to focus on the expansion of rights in attempts to understand the establishment of "democracy." In the Roman Empire, it is clear that people across the empire had few political rights that we might associate with modern democracies, but it is also doubtful whether it would be meaningful to speak of such rights for most people when Rome was ruled by the Republic. It seems more useful to analyze the Roman Empire in terms of the rule of law, and, although there remains a great deal of debate on this subject, it is clear that the Roman imperial government over the long-term fostered the development of a more uniform legal system that helped to define property rights and that, at the same time, it maintained authoritative legal institutions to resolve disputes in a predictable and open manner. This effort to promote more uniform legal institutions involved establishing Roman law as the basis for private law in the west, as documented in numerous municipal charters from Spain.[7] Moreover, as Aldo Schiavone (2012) has recently argued in his magisterial book on the Roman jurists, Roman law was the creation of an intellectual tradition to a large degree independent of immediate political pressures, but the late classical jurists played a substantial role in Rome's imperial project that was much more complicated: in the late Principate, beginning in the Antonine age, the most important Roman jurists served in the imperial administration, and thus had the task of administering the law in an empire with increasing numbers of Roman citizens. This process culminated in the Severan age with the grant of universal citizenship by Caracalla in 212, and the service of the great jurists like Paul, Papinian, and Ulpian in the highest levels of imperial administration, including the offices of the *a libellis*, responsible for responding to petitions, and the praetorian prefecture. In recent years, scholars have focused on the

[7] See Gonzalez and Crawford (1986).

role of the emperor as judge.[8] From another perspective, some important new scholarship has enriched our perspectives on the ways in which the law functioned among ordinary people in the Roman Empire. Thus Serena Connolly's study (2010) of petitions to the emperor Diocletian in the years 293–4 suggests that people outside of the elite, belonging to what she describes as a "middling class," were able to make use of the legal protections provided by Roman law to resolve disputes. Benjamin Kelly (2011) and Ari Bryen (2013) have shown how important the process of petitioning various officials, including the governor, was to the efforts of ordinary people in Roman Egypt to protect their interests. The petitions to the emperor that Connolly examines were part of a broad transformation of the legal culture in the Roman Empire, in which one of the principal functions of the emperor became the adjudication of legal questions and in this function supervising the orderly administration of law across the empire. So important was this function that, beginning in the Severan period, emperors appointed deputies, *iudices vice Caesaris*, who had the authority to administer justice in the emperor's name.[9] All of this suggests a very vigorous legal culture in the Roman Empire, in which litigants had the capacity to learn of legal rights that might protect them. To cite one especially noteworthy example, the second-century Babatha archive from Judaea indicates that a Jewish woman from the provinces could use both Nabataean and Roman law to safeguard her interests and those of her son.[10] Moreover, in Egypt, as Keenan, Manning, and Yiftach-Firanko (2014) argue, much of the knowledge of the law resided with scribes, who knew how to formulate contracts to secure the legal interests of their clients, and were able to alter and adapt contractual forms to meet the changing needs of society.[11]

To return to the endogenous institutions literature, one important lesson is that, because institutions structure the incentives that members of a society face, successful societies will be those that match institutions to circumstances. If a society's institutions are not designed to inspire productive activities, broadly defined—economic, military—the society will not thrive. Rome was a thriving society.

[8] For ancient perceptions of the role of the emperor as judge, see Tuori (2016).
[9] See Peachin (1996).
[10] See Czajkowski (2017); as well as Cotton (1993).
[11] For a survey of Roman legal institutions, see du Plessis, Ando, and Tuori (2016).

Investigating its match of institutions and circumstances can help us understand why. By viewing the history of ancient Rome through the lens of endogenous institutions, we hope to gain insight both into Rome's institutional history, and into the broader applicability of the endogenous institutions literature.

2.2. MODELS OF ENDOGENOUS INSTITUTIONS

As noted, we will give primary emphasis to scholars who have modeled political institutions as commitment devices. The critical nature of establishing commitment to future policy has been demonstrated in various domains.[12] Perhaps most famously, Kydland and Prescott (KP) (1977, 1980) won a Nobel Prize for work in which they emphasize the importance of "time inconsistency" for understanding optimal policy. KP explain that the ex ante wishes of policymakers (be they rulers or voters) may differ in predictable ways from the ex post wishes. When that occurs, the policymakers may benefit if they can find ways to commit themselves. Consider, for example, a ruler who promises low tax rates on capital gains in order to encourage investment. Everyone knows (including the ruler) that once the investment is sunk, the ruler's incentives change completely: the ruler will then want to impose a high tax rate. But because everyone knows that, little investment occurs, and all parties—including the ruler—end up worse off than they would be if the ruler could commit ex ante to low tax rates.[13]

The endogenous institutions literature models actors as rational decision makers, weighing the costs and benefits of changing the distribution of rights, or reacting to changes in those rights. The maintained assumption is that political institutions are more difficult to alter or evade than are individual policies. The models differ in the *type*

[12] The idea has a long pedigree, as Juvenal's question (*Sat.* 6.347–8: *Quis custodiet ipsos custodes*) suggests.

[13] Time inconsistency problems need not involve one group taking from another; the same logic applies if policy is set by a homogeneous set of voters. Even if endowments of capital and labor do not differ between voters, all may desire ex ante to commit to taxing labor (so as not to discourage investment), but then after investments are made prefer to tax capital.

of commitment achieved by altering the number "enfranchised" (i.e. empowered to participate in the policymaking process): commitment to redistribution, commitment to property rights, and commitment to a policy platform.

2.2.1. Committing to Redistribution

The quasi-romantic idea of the dispossessed rising up to overthrow oppressive elites has lost some of its appeal post–Soviet Union and Chairman Mao, but unrest among the masses remains an important consideration in explanations of democratization. As a mechanism for establishing durable democracy, the responses of rulers to threats of violence surely play a more important role than do violent revolutions won by pro-democracy rebels. Acemoglu and Robinson (AR) emphasize this point. In the AR (2000) model, the elite can forestall threatened revolution by promising to redistribute (some of) their wealth. However, for the promised redistribution to convince the masses to lay down their pitchforks, the elite must overcome a time-inconsistency problem: the elite will have the incentive to renege on the promise once transitory (by assumption) revolutionary fervor has passed. As a means of committing, the elite expands political rights to the rebelling masses—once the masses are enfranchised, they can ensure that the promise to redistribute wealth is kept. The threat of revolution thus leads to expanded political rights, as a means of committing to redistribute wealth.

How commonly political rights have been expanded via threats of revolution is difficult to gauge. Yet it is clear that some of the most famous examples of increased enfranchisement have been undertaken without the threat. For example, the United States gradually granted rights to disenfranchised segments of its population (the landless, women) with remarkably little violence—and in the war that ended slavery, the main force for emancipation came from the more widely enfranchised North, which imposed emancipation on the South against the will of enfranchised southerners. Nor did violence (or threats of violence) play much of a role in the first major wave of democratization—the one that occurred among the city-states of ancient Greece. These examples suggest the importance of examining factors that inspire those initially holding political rights to expand set of individuals holding rights.

2.2.2. Committing to Property Rights

Although the expansion of rights will generally help some groups and harm others, there may be large social gains accruing to the elite as well as to the masses. Note that if making a credible commitment to growth-enhancing policies becomes sufficiently valuable, the elite may choose to give up power voluntarily, as a means of achieving commitment. In a seminal article on credible commitment, North and Weingast (NW) (1989) examine Great Britain's "Glorious Revolution" of 1688. NW recount how many British sovereigns borrowed to pay for wars, and subsequently reneged on the debts. Creditors increasingly refused to lend, presenting the kings (whose appetites for war were unabated) with a problem. The kings turned to Parliament, and Parliament agreed to help raise funds in return for limitations on the powers of the monarch. The process culminated with the Glorious Revolution, which placed taxing power squarely with Parliament, and thereby made the sovereign better off in at least one dimension—he could commit to obey rules and abide by contracts.

Many scholars have used these ideas to explain the distribution of political rights.[14] Fleck and Hanssen (FH) (2006) develop a model in which the expansion of the franchise will—under some but not all conditions—benefit those initially in power as well as the newly enfranchised. In FH's model, a representative aristocrat decides whether or not to relinquish control of tax rates to a representative *demos* ("people"). Taxes are used to finance a public good that both the aristocrat and the *demos* value; however, the *demos* prefers lower tax rates than does the aristocrat, because the *demos* also values its own consumption. If the aristocrat relinquishes control of tax rates, the *demos* will undertake a wealth-enhancing investment that it would not otherwise undertake (because the aristocrat would tax away the gains). The investment is costly to monitor, so the aristocrat cannot simply order the *demos* to invest. The aristocrat is faced with the following choice: cede control of tax rates and inspire investment, or maintain control of tax rates and discourage investment. If the aristocrat chooses the former, a higher level of income is earned, but a

[14] See, for example, North (1990, 1993); Kiser and Barzel (1991); Barzel (1992, 2000); Greif (1993, 1994); Weingast (1993, 1995, 1997); Greif, Milgrom, and Weingast (1994); Levy and Spiller (1994); Anderson (1995); Alston, Libecap, and Schneider (1996); Knack and Keefer (1997a, 1997b); Fleck (2000); Wittman (2000); and Hanssen (2004).

lower tax rate is applied to it. If the aristocrat chooses the latter, income is lower but tax rates are higher. The model predicts a greater likelihood of democracy where output without investment is low and returns to investment are high, and a lower likelihood of democracy when those conditions are reversed.

2.2.3. Committing to Policy

The models we have discussed so far (such as AR and FH) treat the elite as a single actor, in effect, homogenous in its interests. Divided elite models are based on the assumption that different segments of the elite have different interests, and thus desire different public policies. These differences may inspire segments of the elite to seek allies from the outside. Lizzeri and Persico (LP) (2004) model and apply this idea to Britain's nineteenth-century extension of the franchise. LP argue that the extension was promoted by commercial elements among the enfranchised, who subsequently allied themselves with newly enfranchised urban voters to enact spending on public health infrastructure (sewers, filtered water). This investment benefitted rapidly growing urban populations and promoted trade and commerce, but was opposed by rural landed interests among the elite. Llavador and Oxoby (2005) develop a related model and apply it to a number of countries in Europe and Latin America. Jack and Lagunoff (2006) provide a model of dynamic enfranchisement, in which the current median voter seeks to change the identity of the future median voter through changes in enfranchisement, thereby inducing credible changes in future policy choices.

FH's (2013) exploration of archaic period tyranny in ancient Greece is one of the few works to focus on the *contraction* of political rights. Both FH and LP posit that an alteration in the franchise that alters the identity of the decisive voter can increase commitment to a policy platform. LP argue that by expanding the franchise in nineteenth-century Britain, a pro-infrastructure investment decisive voter was ensured. FH argue that by (in effect) contracting the franchise to a single voter—the tyrant—archaic Greek *poleis* also ensured a pro-infrastructure investment vote. FH argue that although members of the commercial elite stood to gain on average from investments in infrastructure (port facilities, water supplies, and so forth), so that all supported such investment ex ante, ex post, there would be losers among them (as with any business endeavor). Rather than facing the threat of disruption as ex post losers withdrew from the coalition (investment programs of that type took years to complete), the commercial elite empowered one of their own to make the decisions for them.[15] The Greek tyrants of the archaic period were thus not the despots that later usage of the term would signify—they took power with the support of previously ruling elites, and ruled with the support of the broad mass of the citizenry. Indeed, Aristotle, writing late in the classical period (in the fourth century BCE), distinguished between the "all bad" tyrants of his own day, and the "half bad" tyrants of the archaic period, who contributed to the public good. FH (2013) argue that tyranny was a means by which segments of the elite committed to policies such as infrastructure investment that took time to put into effect. In other words, FH argue that ancient Greek tyrants achieved commitment through contraction of the franchise to the same types of policies that LP argue was achieved via expansion of the franchise. By assigning decision power to a single man with incentives aligned with theirs (the tyrant was typically one of the commercial elite), the elite locked in desired policies.[16]

In sum, either expanding or contracting political rights, depending upon the circumstances, may help a government commit to its promises. We now turn to applying this idea to ancient Rome.

2.3. APPLYING THE ENDOGENOUS INSTITUTIONS LITERATURE TO ANCIENT ROME

The long historical process by which Rome created private rights over land can usefully be interpreted in terms of several of the concepts arising in the preceding discussion. If the goal of the Roman ruling

[15] Tyrants were so common that the archaic period (800–480 BCE) has been termed "the age of the tyrant" (Andrewes 1956: 8; Raaflaub and Wallace 2007: 43). The word tyrant is not of Greek origin, and its precise early meaning has been lost. However, it appears to have referred to a ruler who was a strong executive, possibly an autocrat, but not necessarily a "tyrant" in the modern sense of the world.

[16] Fleck and Hanssen (2013) analyze a dataset of forty-six *poleis*, and find that tyrannies arose predominantly in coastal *poleis* (which had the most to gain from trade), and were followed by democracy with much greater frequency than states that did not host tyrannies, controlling for coastal location.

elite, the senatorial oligarchy in the Republic and the emperor and the court in the Principate, was to maintain itself in power, the creation of private rights over land represented a commitment strategy to secure the loyalty of the municipal elites in Italy and ultimately across the empire. At the same time, especially in the imperial period, the Roman government can be seen as securing the loyalty of a broader class of the population by making commitments to redistribution. It did so by protecting the tenure of small landowners and tenants, a commitment in part followed by large private landowners, who accorded security of tenure as a means to incentivize tenants to make investments in the continued productivity of their land.

To take the case of Italy during the Republican period first, we can see the process of the Roman elite making credible commitments in the changes involving the status of public land, or *ager publicus*. The Roman state greatly increased its holdings in public land as it confiscated land from cities that it conquered in Italy. Often public land was left in the hands of the people of the cities that were brought under Roman hegemony, with the possessors' title to the land subject to being revoked by Rome.[17] But public land also included a great deal of communal land that could be used as pasture. In her analysis of the status of public land in the Roman Republic, Saskia Roselaar (2010: 146–289) argues convincingly that, over time, and especially in the second century BCE, the Roman state converted much of this land, both what was occupied by individuals and communally owned land, into land over which the occupiers exercised private and exclusive rights. This process reached its culmination under the Gracchi (133–121 BCE) and in the decades immediately following, when agrarian reforms led to the full privatization of public land.

In Roselaar's view, this process had important consequences for the economy of Italy, since the creation of private rights over land created incentives for investment in agriculture precisely in the period in which the Roman upper classes were bringing large amounts of wealth from abroad into Italy. The increasingly wealthy Roman elite used their new-found wealth to acquire land, although they certainly had other types of investments that provided them with incomes, notably urban real estate, particularly in Rome but probably also in other cities in Italy (Rosenstein 2008). The growing opportunities for commercial

[17] For a broad discussion of the institutional and legal changes in the Roman Republic, see Capogrossi Colognesi (2014).

agriculture in the Roman Republic tended to affect investment on private land rather than public land. The latter category of land, whether in the territories of towns that had seen land confiscated by the Romans or in the territory in northern Italy added to the empire in the third century BCE, was often occupied by local landowners, but without a firm title. When the occupiers of this land were relatively wealthy, they would have had little incentive to invest in viticulture and other forms of more intensive agriculture, since their ability to profit from their investment for the long-term was uncertain. Rather, as archaeological evidence indicates, the focal point for the growth of the villa economy of Republican Italy was in central Italy and on the western coast, which had the most direct access to the Roman market.[18] In this region, most land had long been established in private hands before the growth of the villa economy in the second century BCE.

In the last century of the Republic, it is likely that the consolidation of land that took place in this region came at the expense of small-scale private landowners, rather than as a result of large landowners' taking over public land.[19] Some small landowners may have been attracted by rising land prices and sold their land to larger landowners. Although it has long been argued that the free rural population of Italy declined in the late Republic, it now seems likely that the rural population increased, although some of the pressure on the free rural population would have been relieved by migration to Rome and other cities.[20] When the public land in the peripheries of Italy became privatized as a result of the Gracchan legislation and subsequent land laws, it seems to be a likely hypothesis that the owners of this land had a much greater incentive to invest in more intensive forms of agriculture, so that this land could also have experienced the same type of consolidation that characterized central Italy and the Tyrrhenian coast.[21] From a long-term perspective, then, it could be argued that Roman policy both in Italy adapted to changing demographic conditions by privatizing communally held lands. Such a policy would produce winners and losers, with a more complex economy, the growth of cities, greater stratification of wealth, and large numbers of people excluded from

[18] Marzano (2007). [19] Roselaar (2010: 146–220).

[20] Roselaar (2010: 199–200). See Launaro (2011: 25–50) for the debate about Roman Italy's population, as well as de Ligt (2012).

[21] See Launaro (2011).

landownership. This situation produced a backlash on many occasions, as the repeated efforts at land re-distribution from the period of the Gracchi to the Triumvirate (43–31 BCE) indicate.[22]

2.3.1. Privatization of Land in the Provinces

The process of privatizing land in late Republican Italy was the result of a complex historical process that involved many competing interests, including the Roman government's efforts to assure itself of an adequate recruitment base for the army and pressure from poorer Romans for land reform. However, notwithstanding the disorders of the Sullan (82–79 BCE) and Triumviral periods, which saw massive confiscations in Italy and the redistribution of land to veterans, the long-term trend in late Republican and early imperial Italy was to safeguard private rights to land. The spotty nature of the evidence makes it more difficult to trace the development of land policies in the provinces, but the overall trend seems unmistakable: the Romans promoted private landownership as the economic basis for a political system relying on local councils to carry out much of the work of local government. Formally, land in the provinces remained the property of the Roman people, thus subject to a land tax, and so was distinct from Italy, where land since the second century BCE had been exempt from taxation. On occasion, provincial *coloniae*, towns in which all citizens enjoyed Roman citizenship, were also accorded the *ius Italicum*, or Italic right, which involved immunity from the land tax. The emperor Diocletian (r. 284–305), as part of a sweeping financial reform, removed the distinction between Italic and provincial land as well as the special tax immunities of Italy. However, if provincials outside of colonies with the Italic right did not have full rights of ownership of their land, the Roman government recognized de facto ownership rights that were protected in the law (Jördens 2016). The results of this process can be seen from Julia Hoffmann-Salz's (2011) study of the economic changes resulting from Roman rule in Spain, Africa, and Syria. In each of the regions she studies, Roman rule brought substantial changes in the rural economy, with the

[22] On the connection between the privatization of land and population pressure, see Monson (2012: 33–69).

emergence of estates oriented toward the production of agricultural surpluses for market economies.

The growth of private estates in Spain and Africa is closely connected with the development of a municipal system in both regions. An essential feature of this municipal system, as documented by the municipal charters from Spain, is the adoption of Roman private law.[23] Private investment in land, moreover, made possible the rise of an elite class from the provinces, which over the course of the empire represented a substantial portion of the senatorial and equestrian orders. To cite the case of Africa, David Mattingly sees the rise of the Severan dynasty in the late second-century Lepcis Magna (in modern-day Libya) as part of a long-term emergence of a landowning aristocracy that derived much of its wealth from the production of olive oil for export. Similar arguments can be made for Spain, especially in the Guadalquivir valley in the province of Baetica. This region in the early empire saw the rise of intensively exploited estates that produced wine and olive oil for export, particularly to Rome. Finally, Gaul in the early imperial period saw the development of Roman-style villae or rural estates that engaged in market-oriented agriculture.[24]

It would be an overstatement to claim that development of market-oriented agriculture in Spain, Gaul, and Africa was simply the result of the imposition of Roman concepts of property rights, but at the same time it is reasonable to conclude that Roman forms of ownership provided incentives for landowners to invest in intensive forms of agriculture such as olive cultivation and viticulture. We can trace how changes in the status of land affected such incentives most clearly in the case of Egypt, as analyzed recently by Andrew Monson (2012). There, the Romans inherited a land regime from the Ptolemies that involved communal control over land and a fiscal system that discouraged investment. In Ptolemaic Egypt, the land under the control of the monarchy, termed royal land, or *basilike ge*, tended to be occupied by small-scale farmers, who enjoyed substantial security of tenure. Much of this land was under the control of village authorities, who were permitted to exercise some discretion in allocating it among

[23] See above, p. 17.

[24] For Africa, see especially Mattingly (1988, 1994: 138–59); and Hobson (2015); for Spain, see Haley (2003); for Gaul, see Woolf (1998); as well as Leveau (2014). For more general discussion of the Roman government's approach to private property rights in the provinces, see Kehoe (2015).

villagers. Other land, particularly in the relatively densely populated Nile valley, was in private hands, nominally under the control of the powerful temples that were characteristic of pre-Roman Egypt. The holders of this land, who generally had some connection with the temple, could freely alienate it, at least among other people sharing their status with the temple.[25] The major innovation of the Ptolemies was the creation of cleruchic or catoecic grants as a form of private land. This land was originally assigned to Greek and then eventually to Egyptian soldiers under revocable grants; the land provided the income that allowed its holders to serve the monarchy, particularly as cavalry. Over time, however, the direct link between being a catoecic possessor and military service blurred, and by Roman times it no longer existed. As a result, the rights of catoecic possessors to their land became more secure, so that they could bequeath it or sell it.

The most important innovation that the Romans brought to Egypt was a fiscal one. Under the Ptolemies, both royal land and nominally private land provided a harvest tax, consisting of fixed assessments of wheat for each unit of land that might be readjusted periodically to account for anticipated changes in productivity. In Monson's analysis, this form of taxation diminished incentives to invest in improvements on the land, since any gains from higher productivity would be eaten up by increased taxation. One consequence of this situation is that well-connected people in Ptolemaic Egypt would not tend to invest their wealth in land, but instead would seek to hold the many profitable offices that were involved in the collection of taxes and other fees connected with state revenues. The Romans gradually implemented two major reforms in the first two centuries CE. The first was to eliminate many of the offices that profited from the collection of revenues for the state, and instead to impose these services on private individuals as uncompensated services, or liturgies. In so doing, the Romans were establishing a municipal system in Egypt comparable to the practice in most other parts of the empire, particularly in the Greek east.[26] But the development of the liturgical system throughout the empire depended on the existence of a class of landowners with sufficient wealth to guarantee their performance of their liturgical duties, such as making good shortfalls in tax assessments. Thus a key element in the Romans' policy in Egypt was

[25] Manning (2003, 2007).

[26] See Bowman and Rathbone (1992).

implementing a tax system similar to those that existed in other parts of the empire (in the early imperial period, there was no uniform tax system for land). Consequently, the Romans, in the Julio-Claudian period, abolished the harvest-tax inherited from the Ptolemies, and instituted instead a fixed assessment of wheat for most categories of land. The tax, called the *artabeia*, generally 1 or 1.5 artabs per aroura, represented about one-tenth or less of a typical wheat harvest. The previous harvest taxes had been much higher, on the order of five–six artabs/aroura. The lower tax rate meant that owners of land could profit by leasing it out to tenants.[27]

The changes initiated by the Roman administration in the Julio-Claudian period had long-lasting consequences. Beginning in the second century, Egypt saw the development of large estates under the control of private owners, and in the third century this process culminated in the emergence of a landowning elite in the province whose properties could be found in many nomes (administrative divisions). The best illustration of this trend is landowner Aurelius Appianus, the management of whose estate is richly documented in the Heroninos archive, a collection of accounts and letters associated with the manager of an individual division of the estate.[28] Under the emperor Septimius Severus, moreover, the major cities (*metropoleis*) of the nomes were reorganized as municipalities comparable to those in the rest of the empire, with city councils; Aurelius Appianus was councilor at Alexandria. The emergence of city councils in Egypt would not have been possible without the creation of a stable class of landowners capable of handling the financial obligations connected with liturgical service. One sign of the changing landscape for investment in agriculture in Egypt was the growing importance of viticulture. The Roman period saw increased investment in viticulture, especially in the Fayum, where perennial irrigation was possible. It represented the major source of revenue on the estate of Aurelius Appianus, as it would on the estate of the Apiones, wealthy landowners in late antique Egypt.[29]

The Roman administration protected property rights of landowners in other ways as well. One important reform was a strict

[27] Monson (2012: 159–208). [28] Rathbone (1991).

[29] There is a large literature on the estate of the Apiones; see most recently Hickey (2012). For investment in viticulture more broadly in Roman Egypt, see Rathbone (2007: 700–5).

policy of maintaining the "property registry" or "bureau of acquisitions," two translations for the Greek *βιβλιοθήκη ἐγκτήσεων*, whose administration the prefect Mettius Rufus sought to reform through an edict of 89 CE (*Sel.Pap.* II 219). This office, organized at the level of the nome, was designed to maintain accurate records concerning landed property, including the identities of owners and any liens that might be connected with it. Maintaining such records, as François Lerouxel argues, was an important component to the Roman liturgy system, which tied the performance of many liturgies to the ownership of land. A significant by-product of this administrative reform would have been to lower the transaction costs for any business involving real estate, including buying, selling, and mortgaging property, making it easier for people to use their landed property as collateral for credit.[30]

2.3.2. Constraints on Private Property

Granted that there was an inexorable trend in the Roman Empire for the development of large estates and an increased stratification in land ownership, this trend was to some extent countered by policies that the imperial government pursued to limit the power of large landowners. These policies did not directly undermine the empire's commitment to property rights, but they did have implications for the distribution of wealth. The policies to be discussed below can thus be seen as a commitment to a redistribution that preserved stability. The emperor to some extent restrained the power of the wealthiest landowners from the senatorial and equestrian orders, and, within limits, sought to maintain the economic viability of the vast class of cultivators on whose production the imperial taxes ultimately depended. At the same time, the state established favorable terms of land tenure on imperial estates, offering its tenants security of tenure as an incentive to encourage investment for the long term. Many private landowners, whose incomes also depended on the production of small-scale tenants, offered similar terms of tenure.

The emperor, although ruling in conjunction with the landowning elite, was also in many respects in competition with them. As discussed below, the emperor was by far the largest landowner in the

[30] See Lerouxel (2015).

Roman Empire, and the ability to give away land to supporters, not to mention to confiscate it from opponents, represented an enormous part of his power.[31] The most extreme case of this came when the emperor Septimius Severus took power in the 190s after defeating two rivals; one result of his victory was the confiscation of the estates of many of his political opponents, and a considerable expansion of the property under the control of the Fiscus. Occasional actions against political opponents could increase the extent of imperial property, but the emperor also acquired property on a regular basis from a number of sources.[32] These included bequests from senators and other members of the elite, as well as confiscations resulting from condemnations for serious crimes, the seizure of property of people defaulting on tax and liturgical obligations, and the assumption of property of the deceased without lawful successors. This last category is likely to have provided a considerable source of property because the Augustan marriage legislation restricted the rights to receive bequests of people who were unmarried or childless. As Maiuro argues, most of the property that passed to the Fiscus in this way was sold off to private owners, but some was retained, particularly when it was in locations with existing imperial properties.

The practice of the Fiscus to sell much of the property that passed to it presupposes that there was a market for land, one in which private people could participate as buyers and sellers. The Fiscus itself would observe the rules of Roman private law in conducting sales and in engaging in other contractual relationships with private individuals. The main advantage that the Fiscus enjoyed was that its claims against a debtor or property had to be satisfied ahead of those of any other creditor. In view of the importance that the imperial government placed on making sure that decurions and other people responsible to perform civic liturgies had sufficient property to cover the potential costs of their defaulting, sales by Fiscus of confiscated property were common, and there was a body of law to make sure that such sales were carried out in a predictable and transparent fashion. This was clearly an area of concern for the imperial government, since from the time of Diocletian (r. 284–305) emperors took

[31] See Maiuro (2012: 11, 230–9). For the emperor's economic competition with members of the upper classes, see Hopkins (2009: 180–1, 187–90).

[32] On what follows see especially Maiuro (2012: 17–145).

repeated measures to curtail corruption on the part of imperial agents supervising such sales.[33] Likewise, sales of private land to enforce debts were also common, and the Roman government, especially from the time of Marcus Aurelius, strove to limit the capacity of creditors to exercise self-help by seizing the property of debtors; instead, the Roman legal authorities required such sales to be carried out under the authority of a court.[34] The imperial government's policies on the enforcement of private debts provided some protection for the economically vulnerable, thus anchoring property rights in the law rather than in the strength of a party to a contract.

2.3.3. Distributional Constraints

The Fiscus played a considerable role as an economic actor in the Roman Empire, and this situation had important distributive effects that affected private property rights.[35] It is not possible to provide much more than a guess about the portion of productive land in the empire that the Fiscus controlled. Maiuro (2012–13: 143–4) suggests that the Fiscus could not have controlled more than the aggregate landholdings of the entire senatorial order, whose share he estimates at about 8 to 10 percent of the empire's land in 165 CE, when the empire's population was at its height, just before the onset of the devastating Antonine plague. Whatever the overall share of the Fiscus in the empire's agricultural economy, it is clear that it owned vast estates in several areas, including in the northern part of the province of Africa, which was one of the empire's most important producers of wheat and olive oil—wheat from North African imperial estates supported the grain distributions at Rome, and North Africa was also one of the principal suppliers, along with Spain, of oil for the Roman market. We are well informed about the conditions under which imperial estates in North Africa were cultivated from a series of inscriptions from the second century CE; these, associated with the fertile Medjerda (ancient Bagradas) valley in northern Tunisia inform

[33] See. e.g. C. 10.1.5 (Diocletian), a rescript aimed at restraining the power of imperial officials called *Caesariani* in seizing and selling property.

[34] Discussed in Kehoe (2007: 148–60; 2013b: 45–6).

[35] For this formulation, see Lo Cascio (2007: 642–6). Lo Cascio (2015) emphasizes that the emperor as an economic actor organized and exploited land much as a private landowner would, but on a vastly larger scale.

us both about the terms of land tenure that the Fiscus maintained on its estates and the conflicts that often arose in connection with them.[36] The Fiscus exploited its estates by granting it land in perpetual leaseholds to small-scale farmers, *coloni*. The *coloni* generally paid shares of their crops, usually one-third, to middlemen, or *conductores*, who held short-term leases on the estates. In addition to the share rent, the *conductores* could exact labor services from the *coloni* as well as the use of their draft animals to cultivate certain lands within the estates. It seems clear that the Fiscus saw the continued capacity of the *coloni* to invest in their own land and cultivate it productively as the best way to achieve stable long-term revenues from its estates. Accordingly, the Fiscus offered the *coloni* incentives to invest in their land, including rent-free seasons and perpetual leaseholds if they cultivated olives, other fruit trees, and vines; the Fiscus's revenues would come from the shares of their crops that the *coloni* paid as rent, including olive oil and other tree crops, but also the grain that the *coloni* cultivated among their olive trees and vines. Thus when inevitable conflicts arose between the *coloni* and *conductores*, the Fiscus consistently sided with the *coloni*, maintaining their traditional tenure rights. In Asia Minor, imperial estates were organized in a comparable way, with tenants who exercised perpetual tenure rights and lived and cultivated land on the same estates for many generations (Hauken 1998).

The method that the Fiscus adapted in exploiting its estates points to a complex relationship between the imperial government's policies in promoting the ownership of private property and incentives to invest in agriculture. To consider again the case of Egypt, as we have seen, the Roman reforms of the tax system on agricultural lands tended to promote private investment in land; landowners could expect to keep the gains from investments that they made, and, perhaps more important, they could profit by leasing land out. It is not possible to calculate how such a fiscal system affected revenues, whether the older communal system of allocating royal land actually produced more or less revenue than the reformed Roman system did. In any case, the cultivators themselves benefited from the Ptolemaic system, since communal leasing and security of tenure provided as much assurance as possible of their being able to meet their

[36] See most recently Kehoe (2007: 56–79); Hobson (2015: 54–61); and now González Bordas and France (2017).

subsistence needs. This system in all likelihood kept much of the wealth generated from agriculture in the villages. To consider the North African imperial estates, the imperial government, to secure its revenues, created a large class of farmers with security of tenure and close ties to the emperor rather than to a private landlord. The terms of tenure on imperial estates were far more favorable to the tenant than the conventional private lease terms in Roman law, which were short-term and imposed the risk for the harvest and market price of the crops on the tenant.[37] It stands to reason that the rights that the Roman administration created on imperial estates affected tenure conditions on private estates, which were often in close proximity to imperial properties. Because of this proximity, the local towns often competed for the services of local farmers with imperial estates. Thus a series of inscriptions from Asia Minor in the third century records conflicts between towns and imperial estates: towns often tried to impose fiscal and liturgical obligations on imperial tenants in or adjacent to their territories, while the imperial tenants themselves petitioned to the imperial government to defend their favorable terms of tenure.[38]

In its efforts to safeguard its tax base, moreover, the Roman government in the fourth century accorded small private landowners and tenants some protection by imposing severe punishments on officials seizing slaves or livestock from farmers (C.Th. 2.30.1, C. 8.167.7, 315); later, it was forbidden to extend credit to farmers against such security (C. 8.16.8, 414).[39] It also seems likely that many private estate owners derived their incomes from their land in much the same way as the imperial Fiscus, that is, by skimming a portion of the surplus produced by farmers occupying their land on the long term. Such landowners, in effect, placed voluntary limitations on their own exercise of property rights by assuring their tenants security of tenure so as to profit from the tenants' investment. A private estate organized in this way is documented by inscriptional evidence in southwest Asia Minor in the third century. This estate was owned by a senatorial family, the Ummidii, and it included villages inhabited by an ethic group called the Ormeleis (Corsten 2005). This relationship between landowners and tenants explains the law of the emperor

[37] On Roman leasing, see Kehoe (2016).
[38] See Hauken (1998), discussed in Kehoe (2007: 79–89).
[39] Discussed in Kehoe (2007: 45).

Constantine that prohibited landowners from raising customary rents and established a remedy for tenants whose landlords tried to do this (C. 11.50.1, 325). Constantine's legislation defined the customary rents, such as those paid by the tenants on the estate of the Ummidii, as enforceable in Roman law.

In an agricultural economy in which much of the land was cultivated by tenants with de facto possession rights to their land, the line between being a landowner and a tenant might become blurred. This was a problem that the imperial government confronted in interpreting the long-term prescription (*longi temporis praescriptio*), a principle established in the second century, arguably in response to the disruptions caused by the Antonine plague, to safeguard the ownership of property against people, often creditors, bringing claims after a long passage of time. According to this principle, whoever occupied provincial land undisturbed was protected against any claim against it after ten years from a person in the same city, and after twenty years against a claim from a person in a different city. To judge by a number of imperial rescripts on the issue, the Roman legal authorities confronted disputes between cultivators and landlords over ownership rights.[40] The consistent interpretation of the Roman legal authorities was that, in terms of the law, no tenant could claim ownership rights over his land, so that he could not dispose of his cultivation rights as a landowner might, by selling or pledging them. In practice, it seems likely that some cultivators on private estates had rights to their land that far exceeded those of conventional tenants.

2.3.4. Policy Constraints

To consider again its support for the local landowning elite that comprised town councils throughout the empire, the imperial government's pursuit of its long-term strategy on governing the empire resulted in significant restrictions on the private property rights of the very groups it protected. These policy considerations can be seen as the Roman legal authorities' understanding of the basic constraints imposed by economic conditions in the ancient world: land represented the pre-eminent form of economic security, and the only resource that could be relied upon to produce stable incomes for

[40] Discussed in Kehoe (2007: 135–43).

the long term. This understanding of the value of land as a resource is consistent with the ways in which many landowners derived revenues from their holdings, as sketched out in the previous section. Consequently, the imperial government viewed the loss of land as the most significant threat to economic security, and so in cases in which the economic viability of certain classes of people was at issue, it imposed restrictions on their capacity to alienate their land.

Such restrictions were a key component of Roman legal policy toward underage persons who were considered incapable of managing their own finances. In Roman law, the property of all fatherless children was subject to management by guardians, or tutors, until the age of puberty. Tutors were responsible for all aspects of the upbringing of their wards, or pupils, including authorizing all expenses connected with their upbringing as well as managing their property. In this latter responsibility, a tutor was not to allow his pupil's wealth to remain idle, but was instead expected to use any funds available to purchase land, and only when this was not possible was it permissible to lend the pupil's money out at interest, the major investment alternative to investing in land.[41] A tutor who failed in his fiduciary duty toward his pupil could be sued at the end of his service, and in some cases a tutor suspected of corruption could be removed from his post and be subject to severe penalties. In addition, Roman law extended certain legal protections to minors, males and females who had reached puberty but had not yet turned twenty-five, the age of full majority in Roman law. A minor who felt cheated in a contract could seek legal relief, and the judge might restore all existing rights (*restitutio in integrum*), cancelling the transaction that was deemed disadvantageous to the minor. To avoid this possibility, it was common for minors to be represented in business dealings by curators; a transaction approved by a curator was not subject to *restitutio in integrum*. Over the course of the third century, it became increasingly expected and eventually mandatory that a minor be represented by a curator.[42]

If the tutor was expected to invest the pupil's wealth in land, it follows that he was also discouraged from alienating land. This policy received its fullest expression when, in 195 CE, the emperor Septimius Severus enacted legislation, the *Oratio Severi*, that prohibited the

[41] See Kehoe (1997: 22–76; 2013a).

[42] Cervenca (1979).

alienation of land belonging to pupils, with the sole exception to pay off debt. Even to alienate land in this circumstance, the tutor was required to obtain a degree from the praetor or provincial governor, after he had shown that the pupil had no other resources available to repay an existing debt (often one that was inherited). The Severan restrictions on alienating the pupil's property were soon applied to curators managing the property of minors; any unsanctioned alienation would be null and void, and the pupil (or minor) would regain ownership of the land in question. In view of Roman demographic conditions, the large number of fatherless people under the age of twenty-five, the Severan restrictions are likely to have affected a considerable portion of the empire's property.[43]

The reasons for overall legal policy toward pupils and minors and the Severan legislation are complex: the law protected people incapable of looking out for their own interests against fraud while maintaining inheritance rights within families. At the same time, in the late second and especially in the third centuries, maintaining the integrity of city councils became an increasingly urgent matter as the empire faced a continuing series of military challenges that caused significant fiscal issues. Over the course of the third century, membership on city councils became a hereditary obligation. Moreover, city councils faced, in theory at least, significant new obligations, including liability for the tax obligations of unoccupied lands within their towns' territories, a duty imposed by the emperor Aurelian (r. 270–5; C. 11.59.1). Later emperors extended this responsibility beyond the class of decurions, requiring other landowners to be responsible for the taxes for uncultivated lands in their towns' territories.[44] The Roman government saw any threat to the financial stability of the empire's landowning class as a threat to the social and political order that it sought to maintain throughout the empire. It is a reasonable hypothesis that the imperial administration saw the protection of pupils and minors as key to making sure that new generations of decurions would be able to take up their roles on town councils throughout the empire.

In the fourth century and later, the Roman government continued to display great urgency in assuring both that town councils were staffed and that individual decurions, as well as the councils themselves, had access to the property needed to meet fiscal and liturgical

[43] Saller (1994: 181–203).

[44] The imperial constitutions on this issue are collected in C. 11.59 and C.Th. 11.1.

obligations. The imperial government's policies toward decurions were consistent with those toward other important occupations, which increasingly became hereditary, for example, arms makers, moneyers, and bakers; one important aspect of the imperial government's efforts to safeguard revenues was to bind certain classes of farmers, particularly those not recorded on the census rolls as landowners in their own right, to the land that they cultivated, and to make their landlords responsible for their tax obligations.[45] To return to the town councils, one problem was that, to avoid the costs of service on them, some decurions might simply flee. Like other small landowners seeking protection from tax and liturgical obligations, they might place themselves under the control of more powerful patrons. They would cede control of their land to such patrons, who could often defy the demands of local councils for the services of people under their protection.[46] The imperial government addressed this situation with frequent laws against rural patronage, or *patrocinium*; and these measures were also directed at decurions. Thus the emperors Valentinian, Valens, and Gratian threatened those who harbored people obligated to service as decurions with the loss of their property (C. 10.32.31, C.Th. 12.1.76, 371). The imperial government also enacted restrictions on the ability of decurions to alienate their land (C. 10.34.1, C.Th. 12.3.1, 386; C.Th. 12.3.2, 432).[47] To be able to alienate land, a decurion had first to obtain a degree from a judge or eventually the provincial governor. One purpose of these laws was to prevent extreme stratification among local elites, since it was feared that the wealthiest landowners could buy out their more humble counterparts, depriving the council of its membership.

Another major problem was that councils might lose their members to other offices, whether in the military, in imperial service, or the senate (including that of Constantinople). Over the course of the fourth and fifth centuries, the emperors issued repeated decrees requiring people who avoided local service by taking up military or administrative posts, or even by joining the clergy or religious orders,

[45] The late antique colonate is a complex subject with an enormous bibliography; for discussion, see Kehoe (2007: 165–73).

[46] Kehoe (2007: 182–3, 187–9); more general, Krause (1987); Sarris (2006: 183–93); Grey (2011).

[47] Discussed in Kehoe (2007: 169–70).

to return to their town council (C. 10.32, C.Th. 12.1). Likewise, if people who otherwise might be bound to the council had achieved a promotion to the senate, nonetheless their sons would remain bound to the local council, along with their property. In the formulation of the late imperial government, the local council had a claim on the property of its members. Thus the emperors Valentinian and Valens criticize "followers of idleness [who], having abandoned the services (owed) to their cities, long for the deserts and out-of-the-way places and, under the pretext of religion, join up with communities of monks" (C. 10.32.26 pr., 373; C.Th. 12.163).[48] Such people who refused to return to their hometowns were to be deprived of their property, which would be set at the disposal of people willing to perform public services (ibid. §1). Other laws aimed at decurions who sought to avoid services repeatedly included the provision that the recalcitrant decurion's property was subject to being confiscated and claimed for the local council. Finally, beginning in the fifth century, when a decurion died without a male heir to succeed him on the council, and without a daughter married to a decurion, the local council would have a claim on one-fourth of the estate (C. 10.35.1, 428). In a subsequent law (C. 10.35.2, 443), the emperors Theodosius II and Valentinian III specified that the proceeds from property acquired in this way, like funds from debts repaid to the town, were to be used to purchase land, the rents from which would support the town. Earlier, the emperor Theodosius I had established a tax on property that passed from decurions to non-decurions (C.Th. 12.1.107, 12.1.123, 391 CE).[49]

The restrictions on the alienation of land in late antiquity point to the difficulties that the imperial government faced in maintaining a political order based on fostering the private property rights of a landowning class throughout the provinces that would share in the burdens of governing the empire. The development of this class, as the history of landownership in Egypt suggests, depended on a commitment on the part of the imperial government to define property rights carefully and to maintain legal institutions that would defend them. But the reality of its fiscal requirements meant that

[48] C. 10.32.26 pr.: *Quidam ignaviae sectatores desertis civitatum muneribus captant solitudines ac secreta et specie religionis cum coetibus monozanton congregantur.*

[49] See the views of Blume, discussed at C. 10.36.1, n. 204.

the Roman government had to interfere frequently with the property rights it maintained, by confiscating land that found no legal owners through succession, or that belonged to liturgists defaulting on their obligations. But perhaps the most important intervention on the part of the imperial government stemmed from its control over so much of the empire's land. One aspect of this control was that the emperor could reward supporters with gifts of land, and thus use the property rights regime that Roman rule supported as an expression of power. At the same time, fiscal exigencies required the imperial government to intervene in the rural economy by restricting the ways in which the very people whose privileges it was its policy to foster could dispose of their land.

2.4. CONCLUSION

In this paper, we have presented a sketch of the history of land ownership in the Roman world, using the endogenous institutions literature to guide our discussion. The endogenous institutions literature seeks to explain the circumstances under which institutions of particular types arise. One of the literature's central principles is that, because institutions structure the incentives that members of a society face (for wealth creation, for defense), if institutions are not well-matched to a society's circumstances—that is to say, not designed to inspire productive activities, broadly defined—the society will not thrive, and indeed, may be wiped out by competing states.

Rome provides a promising case for analysis. Rome began as a monarchy, evolved through aristocracy to near-democracy, and then contracted rights under the institutions of empire. We suggest that both the expansions of and the contractions of political rights can be understood as responses to the imperatives created by the process of wealth creation and corresponding military needs. By matching its institutions to its circumstances, Rome prospered for many centuries.

Today, there is a tendency to classify a certain set of institutions as "good"—for example, democracies that support the rule of law—and another type as "bad"—for example, extractive regimes run by an elite free to ignore rules and laws. And there is good reason for the classifications: in today's circumstances, the institutions that embody the rule of law can attract investment, support economic development, and deliver a high quality of life for their citizens. But a message of this chapter is that a society will only thrive if its institutions match its circumstances, and create the incentives for productive action, *whatever that may be*. The Roman Republic is often more admired than the empire, because it employed institutions that were more broadly representative. But a reading of the endogenous institutions literature suggests that more broadly representative institutions are not inherently preferable for all times and places. In other words, the institutions of the Republic were not "good" in an absolute sense, but rather good at creating incentives conducive to the Republic's survival and growth. And when the circumstances faced by Rome changed, Rome changed its institutions. If it had not, fewer people might be writing about it today.

REFERENCES

Acemoglu, Daron, and James A. Robinson. 2000. "Why Did the West Extend the Franchise? Democracy, Inequality and Growth in Historical Perspective." 115 *Quarterly Journal of Economics* 1167–99.

Alston, Lee J., Gary D. Libecap, and Robert Schneider. 1996. "The Determinants and Impact of Property Rights: Land Titles on the Brazilian Frontier." 12 *Journal of Law, Economics, & Organization* 25–61.

Anderson, Terry L. 1995. *Sovereign Nations or Reservations*. San Francisco: Pacific Research Institute for Public Policy.

Andrewes, A. 1956. *The Greek Tyrants*. London: Hutchinson's University Library.

Barzel, Yoram. 1992. "Confiscation by the Ruler: The Rise and Fall of Jewish Lending in the Middle Ages." 35 *Journal of Law and Economics* 1–13.

Barzel, Yoram. 2000. "Property Rights and the Evolution of the State." 1 *Economics of Governance* 25–51.

Bowman, Alan K., and Dominic Rathbone. 1992. "Cities and Administration in Roman Egypt." 82 *Journal of Roman Studies* 107–27.

Bowman, Alan K., and Andrew I. Wilson, eds. 2011. *Settlement, Urbanization, and Population* (Oxford Studies on the Roman Economy). Oxford: Oxford University Press.

Bryen, Ari Z. 2013. *Violence in Roman Egypt: A Study in Legal Interpretation*. Philadelphia: University of Pennsylvania Press.

Capogrossi Colognesi, Luigi. 2014. *Law and Power in the Making of the Roman Commonwealth*. Trans. Laura Kopp. Cambridge: Cambridge University Press.

Cervenca, Giuliano. 1979 "Studi sulla '*cura minorum*,' 3. L'estensione ai minori del regime dell'*Oratio Severi*." n.s. 21 *Bulletino dell'Istituto di Diritto Romano* 41–94.

Connolly, Serena. 2010. *Lives behind the Laws: The World of the Codex Hermoginianus*. Bloomington: Indiana University Press.

Corsten, Thomas. 2005. "Estates in Roman Asia Minor: The Case of Kibyratis," in S. Mitchell and C. Katsari, eds, *Patterns in the Economy of Roman Asia Minor*. Swansea: Classical Press of Wales, 1–52.

Cotton, Hannah. "The Guardianship of Jesus Son of Babatha: Roman and Local Law in the Province of Arabia." 94 *Journal of Roman Studies* 94–108.

Czajkowski, Kimberly. 2017. *Localized Law: The Babatha and Salome Komaise Archives*. Oxford: Oxford University Press.

Dahl, Robert A. 1971. *Polyarchy: Participation and Opposition*. New Haven: Yale University Press.

de Ligt, Luuk. 2012. *Peasants, Citizens and Soldiers: Studies in the Roman Demographic History of Roman Italy 225 BC–AD 100*. Cambridge: Cambridge University Press.

de Vries, Jan. 1984. *European Urbanization 1500–1800*. Cambridge, MA: Harvard University Press.

du Plessis, Paul J., Clifford Ando, and Kaius Tuori, eds. 2016. *Oxford Handbook of Roman Law and Society*. Oxford: Oxford University Press.

Erdkamp, Paul. 2015. "Agriculture, Division of Labour, and the Paths to Economic Growth," in Erdkamp et al., eds, 18–39.

Erdkamp, Paul, Koenraad Verboven, and Arjam Zuiderhoek, eds. 2015. *Ownership and Exploitation of Land and Natural Resources in the Roman World*. Oxford: Oxford University Press.

Fleck, Robert K. 2000. "When Should Market-Supporting Institutions Be Established?" 16 *Journal of Law, Economics, & Organization* 129–54.

Fleck, Robert K., and F. Andrew Hanssen. 2006. "The Origins of Democracy: A Model with Application to Ancient Greece." 49 *Journal of Law and Economics* 115–46.

Fleck, Robert K., and F. Andrew Hanssen. 2012. "On the Benefits and Costs of Legal Expertise: Adjudication in Ancient Athens." 8 *Review of Law and Economics* 367–99.

Fleck, Robert K., and F. Andrew Hanssen. 2013. "How Tyranny Paved the Way to Democracy: The Democratic Transition in Ancient Greece." 56 *Journal of Law and Economics* 389–416.

González Bordas, Hernán, and Jérôme France. 2017. "A New Edition of the Imperial Regulation from the Lella Drebblia Shrine near Dougga (*AE* 2001, 2083)." 30 *Journal of Roman Archaeology* 407–28.

Greif, Avner. 1993. "Contract Enforceability and Economic Institutions in Early Trade: The Maghribi Traders' Coalition." 83 *American Economic Review* 525–48.

Greif, Avner. 1994. "On the Political Foundations of the Late Medieval Commercial Revolution: Genoa during the Twelfth and Thirteenth Centuries." 54 *Journal of Economic History* 271–87.

Greif, Avner, Paul Milgrom, and Barry R. Weingast. 1994. "Coordination, Commitment, and Enforcement: The Case of the Merchant Guild." 102 *Journal of Political Economy* 745–76.

Grey, Cameron. 2011. *Constructing Communities in the Late Roman Countryside*. Cambridge: Cambridge University Press.

Haley, Evan W. 2003. Baetica Felix*: People and Prosperity in Southern Spain from Caesar to Septimius Severus*. Austin: University of Texas Press.

Hanssen, F. Andrew. 2004. "Is There a Politically Optimal Level of Judicial Independence?" 94 *American Economic Review* 712–29.

Hauken, Tor. 1998. *Petition and Response: An Epigraphic Study of Petitions to Roman Emperors 181–249* (Monographs from the Norwegian Institute at Athens, vol. 2). Bergen: Norwegian Institute at Athens.

Hickey, Todd M. 2012. *Wine, Wealth, and the State in Late Antique Egypt: The House of Apion at Oxyrhynchus*. Ann Arbor: University of Michigan Press.

Hobson, Matthew S. 2015. *The North Africa Boom: Evaluating Economic Growth in the Roman Province of* Africa Proconsularis (*146 B.C. – A.D. 439*), *JRA* Suppl. 100. Portsmouth, RI.

Hoffmann-Salz, J. 2011. *Die wirtschaftlichen Auswirkungen der römischen Eroberung: Vergleichende Untersuchungen der Provinz Hispania Tarraconensis, Africa Proconsularis und Syria* (Historia Einzelschriften 218). Stuttgart: Steiner.

Hopkins, Keith 2009. "The Political Economy of the Roman Empire," in Ian Morris and Walter Scheidel, eds. *The Dynamics of Ancient Empires: State Power from Assyria to Byzantium*. New York: Oxford University Press, 178–204.

Jack, William, and Roger Lagunoff. 2006. "Dynamic Enfranchisement." 90 *Journal of Public Economics* 551–72.

Jördens, Andrea. 2016. "Possession and Provincial Practice," in du Plessis, et al., eds, 553–65.

Keenan, James G., Joseph G. Manning, and Uri Yiftach-Firanko, eds. 2014. *Law and Legal Practice in Egypt from Alexander to the Arab Conquest: A Selection of Papyrological Sources in Translation, with Introductions and Commentary*. Cambridge: Cambridge University Press.

Kehoe, Dennis P. 1997. *Investment, Profit, and Tenancy: The Jurists and the Roman Agrarian Economy*. Ann Arbor: University of Michigan Press.

Kehoe, Dennis P. 2007. *Law and the Rural Economy in the Roman Empire*. Ann Arbor: University of Michigan Press.

Kehoe, Dennis P. 2013a. "Law, Agency, and Growth in the Roman Economy," in Paul J. du Plessis, ed., *New Frontiers: Law and Society in the Roman World*. Edinburgh: University of Edinburgh Press, 177–91.

Kehoe, Dennis P. 2013b. "The State and Production in the Roman Agrarian Economy," in Alan K. Bowman and Andrew I. Wilson, eds, *The Agricultural Economy: Production and Consumption*. Oxford: Oxford University Press, 33–53.

Kehoe, Dennis P. 2015. "Property Rights over Land and Economic Growth in the Roman Empire," in Erdkamp et al., eds, 88–106.

Kehoe, Dennis P. 2016. "Tenure of Land and Agricultural Regulation," in du Plessis et al., eds, 646–59.

Kelly, Benjamin. 2011. *Petitions, Litigation, and Social Control in Roman Egypt*. Oxford: Oxford University Press.

Kiser, Edgar, and Yoram Barzel. 1991. "The Origins of Democracy in England." 3 *Rationality and Society* 396–422.

Knack, Stephen, and Philip Keefer. 1997a. "Does Social Capital Have an Economic Payoff? A Cross-Country Investigation." 112 *Quarterly Journal of Economics* 1251–88.

Knack, Stephen, and Philip Keefer. 1997b. "Why Don't Poor Countries Catch Up? A Cross-National Test of Institutional Explanation." 35 *Economic Inquiry* 590–602.

Krause, Jens-Uwe 1987. *Spätantike Patronatsformen im Westen des römischen Reiches*. Munich: Beck.

Kydland, Finn E. and Edward C. Prescott. 1977. "Rules Rather than Discretion: The Inconsistency of Optimal Plans." 85 *Journal of Political Economy* 473–91.

Kydland, Finn E. and Edward C. Prescott. 1980. "Dynamic Optimal Taxation, Rational Expectations and Optimal Control." 2 *Journal of Economic Dynamics and Control* 79–91.

Launaro, Alessandro. 2011. *Peasants and Slaves: The Rural Population of Roman Italy (200 BC to AD 100)*. Cambridge: Cambridge University Press.

Lerouxel, François. 2015. "The *βιβλιοθήκη ἐγκτήσεων* and Transaction Costs in the Credit Market of Roman Egypt (30 B.C.E. – ca. 170 C.E.)," in Dennis P. Kehoe, David M. Ratzan, and Uri Yiftach-Firanko, eds, *Law and Transaction Costs in the Ancient Economy*. Ann Arbor: University of Michigan Press, 162–84.

Leveau, Philippe 2014. "Villa, romanisation, développement économique entre idéal-type wéberien et modelisation territorial," in Catherine Apicella, Marie-Laurence Haack, and François Lerouxel, eds, *Les affaires de Monsieur Andreau: économie et société du monde romain*. Scripta antiqua, 61. Bordeaux: Ausonius Éditions, 97–106.

Levy, Brian, and Pablo T. Spiller. 1994. "The Institutional Foundations of Regulatory Commitment: A Comparative Analysis of Telecommunications Regulation." 10 *Journal of Law, Economics, and Organization* 201–46.

Lizzeri, Alessandro, and Nicola Persico. 2004. "Why Did the Elites Extend the Suffrage? Democracy and the Scope of Government, with an Application to Britain's 'Age of Reform.'" 119 *Quarterly Journal of Economics* 707–65.

Llavador, Humberto, and Robert J. Oxoby. 2005. "Partisan Competition, Growth, and the Franchise." 120 *Quarterly Journal of Economics* 1155–89.

Lo Cascio, Elio 2007. "The Early Empire: The State and the Economy," in Scheidel et al. eds, 619–47.

Lo Cascio, Elio 2015. "The Imperial Property and Its Development," in Erdkamp et al., eds, 62–71.

Maddison, A. 2007. *Contours of the World Economy 1–2030 AD: Essays in Macro-Economic History*. Oxford: Oxford University Press.

Maiuro, Marco. 2012. *Res Caesaris. Ricerche sulla proprietà imperiale nel Principato*. Bari: Edipuglia.

Manning, Joseph G. 2003. *Land and Power in Ptolemaic Egypt: The Structure of Land Tenure*, Cambridge: Cambridge University Press.

Manning, Joseph G. 2007. "Hellenistic Egypt," in Scheidel et al. eds, 434–49.

Marzano, Annalisa. 2007. *Roman Villas in Central Italy: A Social and Economic History*. Leiden: Brill.

Mattingly, David. J. 1988. "The Olive Boom. Oil Surpluses, Wealth and Power in Roman Tripolitania." 19 *Libyan Studies* 21–41.

Mattingly, David J. 1994. *Tripolitania*. Ann Arbor: University of Michigan Press.

Monson, Andrew. 2012. *From the Ptolemies to the Romans: Political and Economic Change in Egypt*. Cambridge: Cambridge University Press.

Morley, Neville. 2011. "Cities and Economic Development in the Roman Empire," in Bowman and Wilson, eds, 143–60.

North, Douglass C. 1990. *Institutions, Institutional Change and Economic Performance*. Cambridge: Cambridge University Press.

North, Douglass C. 1993. "Institutions and Credible Commitment." 149 *Journal of Institutional and Theoretical Economics* 11–23.

North, Douglass C., and Barry R. Weingast. 1989. "Constitutions and Commitment: The Evolution of Institutions Governing Public Choice in Seventeenth Century England." 49 *Journal of Economic History* 803–32.

Peachin, Michael. 1996. *Iudex vice Caesaris: Deputy Emperors and the Administration of Justice during the Principate* (Heidelberger Althistorische und Epigraphische Beiträge 21). Stuttgart: Steiner.

Raaflaub, Kurt A., and Robert W. Wallace. 2007. "'People's Power' and Egalitarian Trends in Archaic Greece," in Kurt A. Raaflaub, Josiah Ober, and Robert W. Wallace, eds, *Origins of Democracy in Ancient Greece*. Berkeley: University of California Press, 22–48.

Rathbone, Dominic. 1991. *Economic Rationalism and Rural Society in Third-Century AD Egypt: The Heroninos Archive and the Appianus Estate*. Cambridge: Cambridge University Press.

Rathbone, Dominic. 2007. "Roman Egypt." in Scheidel et al., eds, 698–719.

Roselaar, Saskia T. 2010. *Public Land in the Roman Republic: A Social and Economic History of* ager publicus *in Italy, 396–89 BC*. Oxford: Oxford University Press.

Rosenstein, Nathan. 2008. "Agriculture and Aristocrats in the Middle and Late Republic." 98 *Journal of Roman Studies* 1–26.

Saller, Richard P. 1994. *Patriarch, Property and Death in the Roman Family*. Cambridge: Cambridge University Press.

Sarris, Peter. 2006. *Economy and Society in the Age of Justinian*. Cambridge: Cambridge University Press.

Scheidel, Walter, Ian Morris, and Richard Saller, eds. 2007. *The Cambridge Economic History of the Greco-Roman World*. Cambridge: Cambridge University Press.

Scheidel, Walter. 2007. "Demography," in Scheidel et al., eds, 38–86.

Schiavone, Aldo. 2012. *The Invention of Law in the West*. Trans. Jeremy Carden and Antony Shugaar. Cambridge and London: Harvard University Press.

Tuori, Kaius. 2016. *The Emperor of Law: The Emergence of Roman Imperial Adjudication*. Oxford: Oxford University Press.

Weingast, Barry R. 1993. "Constitutions as Governance Structures: The Political Foundations of Secure Markets." 149 *Journal of Institutional and Theoretical Economics* 286–311.

Weingast, Barry R. 1995. "The Economic Role of Political Institutions: Market Preserving Federalism and Economic Development." 11 *The Journal of Law, Economics, and Organization* 1–31.

Weingast, Barry R. 1997. "The Political Foundations of Democracy and the Rule of Law." 91 *American Political Science Review* 245–63.

Wilson, Andrew I. 2009. "Indicators for Roman Economic Growth: A Response to Walter Scheidel." 22 *Journal of Roman Archaeology* 71–82.

Wilson, Andrew I. 2011. "City Sizes and Urbanization in the Roman Empire," in Bowman and Wilson, eds, 2011, 161–95.

Wittman, Donald. 2000. "The Wealth and Size of Nations." 44 *Journal of Conflict Resolution* 868–84.

Woolf, Greg. 1998. *Becoming Roman: The Origins of Provincial Civilization in Gaul*. Cambridge: Cambridge University Press.

3

The Constitution of the Roman Republic

Eric A. Posner

The constitution of the Roman Republic (509 to 27 BCE)[1] was well known to the founders of the United States. They admired Roman civilization, and accepted the theory of checks and balances, which was reflected in the Roman constitution, but they disapproved of the way that the Roman constitution embodied that theory, believing that the Romans had put excessive constraints on the executive and spread power too thinly among the various offices and bodies. Treating the Roman constitution as a negative model, the founders designed a constitutional system that was significantly simpler, creating, for example, a single executive branch where in Rome executive power was shared among a number of magistrates. But were the founders correct in rejecting the Roman model? The Romans, after all, flourished under constitutional rule for almost five hundred years, in conditions far less auspicious to the rule of law than existed during the Enlightenment. In this essay, I use the modern political economy framework developed in economics and political science to reconstruct and evaluate the possible reasons the founders might have had for disapproving of the Roman constitution, and to ask whether that constitution was as dysfunctional as they assumed.

The modern scholarship on the Roman constitution is mainly descriptive and historical, with some speculation about how particular

[1] Historians disagree about the precise dates. Augustus became emperor in 27 BC, but the end of the Republic could be dated as early as the unconstitutional dictatorship of Sulla in 81, or the dictatorships of Caesar in the 40s.

Eric A. Posner, *The Constitution of the Roman Republic* In: *Roman Law and Economics: Institutions and Organizations, Volume I.* Edited by: Giuseppe Dari-Mattiacci and Dennis P. Kehoe, Oxford University Press (2020).

DOI: 10.1093/oso/9780198787204.003.0003

norms may have contributed to the prosperity and stability of the Republic, and others may have contributed to its collapse. Historians generally observe that Roman constitutional norms mediated between an upper class and the masses, and distributed executive power among multiple offices in order to forestall a return to the monarchical system that existed in the sixth century BCE. No one has tried to analyze the Roman constitution within a modern political economy framework, however, and the purpose of this chapter is to develop such an analysis.

The central idea of this framework is that of agency costs. Constitutions do many things but all constitutions manage agency costs. The people (the principal) assign government officials (the agents) the task of supplying public goods and redistributing wealth. The agents have interests that are not fully aligned with those of the people; the purpose of a constitution is to give agents incentives to act in the interests of the people, that is, to minimize agency costs. A large literature discusses the way that elections, judicial review, separation of powers, and other modern political institutions may (or may not) minimize agency costs (Mueller 2003). I address the Roman constitution from this perspective, examining ways that Roman institutions might have minimized agency costs that existed in the ancient world. I do not claim that the Roman constitutional system was optimal or efficient; my more modest goal is to describe ways in which the system may have addressed the problem of agency costs, albeit frequently in imperfect or questionable ways.

The most notable feature of the Roman system from a modern perspective was the elaborate set of precautions against the accumulation of executive power in a single person. The goal was to prevent the recurrence of monarchy, but the risk of checks and balances is that they paralyze governance. I argue that gridlock did not pose an insurmountable obstacle to effective governance during the Republic's first four centuries because the population was relatively small and homogenous, so political agents could bargain around the institutional checks and balances when necessary for the sake of public security. But as conquered foreign populations streamed into the city, the population became large and heterogeneous. Most of the fabulous wealth resulting from conquest enriched the elites, not ordinary people, resulting in divergence of interests between the upper and lower classes. Governance became subject to gridlock, setting the stage for extra-constitutional behavior in the last century and eventually dictatorship.

There are three reasons why such an analysis contributes to the literature. First, classicists have been cautious about speculating about the functions of the Roman constitution because of the paucity of sources. Nonetheless, they have tried to make inferences which reflect informal rational choice reasoning but without, as far as I can tell, any knowledge of the vast modern literature on political economy. One purpose of this chapter is to bring to bear recent ideas from one discipline on the discussions of specialists in another.

Second, the Roman constitution has influenced modern political institutions. American revolutionaries (and, subsequently, French revolutionaries) were obsessed with ancient Rome (Richard 1994: 12–38). References to the heroes and villains of ancient Rome are ubiquitous in founding-era pamphlets, letters, orations, and books. Publius wrote the Federalist Papers, the veterans of the Revolutionary War created the Society of Cincinnatus, etc., etc. A more fine-grained understanding of the Roman constitution will contribute to our understanding of the founders' constitutional thinking and to constitutional theory in general.

Third, modern constitutional legal theory has taken a comparative turn, and a new, rich literature has produced rigorous accounts of foreign constitutions, often from the perspective of rational choice (Elkins et al. 2009; Voigt, ed. 2005; Law and Versteeg 2011; Jackson and Tushnet 1999). One benefit of this approach is that it helps stimulate ideas for constitutional design and development in modern countries. The Roman constitution provides a fresh example, which is notable because of its stark differences from modern constitutional systems.

Before I turn to the analysis, I need to offer a number of cautions. The secondary literature contains many internal disagreements about the meaning of sources, which are themselves extremely sparse and not always to be trusted. Only the final years of the Republic are well-documented, thanks in large part to Cicero's private letters to his friends, and the survival of speeches and other contemporary materials. For earlier periods, historians rely mainly on Polybius, who was a foreigner with a foreign perspective and a particular ideological and philosophical agenda; Livy, who relied on earlier historical sources that are now lost and, writing in the Augustan age, needed to avoid making claims that would have displeased Augustus; and mostly ambiguous archeological evidence. Augustus, Rome's first emperor, and late republicans like Cicero idealized the old days and emphasized the decadence of the late republican period—Cicero to justify a return to an era supposedly dominated by the elites, Augustus to justify his own broad political program.

In order to make progress with a political economy analysis, I will have to engage in simplification, based on my reading of the modern literature. My claims about Roman constitutional norms should all be taken in this spirit; because I will not reproduce the controversies in the literature, interested readers will need to consult the sources.

On top of the problem of interpreting old sources that could be self-serving and that are rife with gaps, there is the problem of interpreting an unwritten constitution. Even with a modern system such as Britain's, it is never entirely clear when a norm is constitutional or merely legal or political. In such cases, claims about the meaning of the constitution are hard to separate from ideological or self-interested wishful thinking—as is, of course, even the case with written constitutions. However, that Rome did have a constitution, and that Romans themselves believed themselves to have a constitution, is not open to serious doubt (Brennan 2004: 31). That is, at least, until the last century of its existence (Syme 1952: 15).

In addition, it is impossible to identify a single Roman constitution over the five-hundred-year period of the Roman Republic (Flower 2010). There was significant change and disruption throughout this period. During its last century, the Republic was in a state of nearly continuous crisis and sometimes civil war. The secondary sources that describe the Roman constitution focus on the third and second centuries BCE, when the political order was relatively stable, while also identifying norms that persisted over time and some historical variation during other periods, especially the final fifty years. I follow them but deemphasize the historical variation, which is complex and elusive (Lintott 1999).

3.1. A THUMBNAIL SKETCH OF THE ROMAN CONSTITUTION

The U.S. constitution embodies a system of separation of powers, with a presidency that executes the laws, a Congress that legislates, and a judiciary that interprets the laws. Federalist structures guarantee some autonomy for states. The source of authority is the people, who can amend the constitution by following prescribed procedures. The Roman system is quite different. Most scholarly discussions divide it into three main elements: the senate, the magistrates, and the assemblies. The senate is politically important as the locus for political discussion but has mainly advisory powers in a formal sense. The magistrates have the major executive and administrative powers, but also serve as judges, and initiate legislation by summoning assemblies of the people and submitting bills to them for their approval. The people, acting in assemblies, pass bills, elect magistrates, and serve certain judicial functions. Roman provinces had no autonomy but were governed by delegates of the government. Table 3.1 provides an overview of the Roman Constitution as it existed in the mid- to late Republic. The information provided is approximate, and will be discussed in more detail in the text below.[2]

3.1.1. The Senate

The senate was the central institution in Roman politics, but its formal powers were few. It did not pass legislation or appoint magistrates, for example. As a matter of formal constitutional law, the senate was mainly an advisory institution whose members received delegations, digested reports, debated, and issued decrees, which were not legally binding (Lintott 1999: 66). Nonetheless, in practice the senate had a considerable degree of authority during most of its existence. Over the last one hundred years of the Republic, the senate lost power to magistrates with popular followings (Boatwright et al. 2004: 136).

The senate's decrees did not have formal legal force, but they frequently guided subsequent legislation enacted by the plebeian assembly, which was the main legislative body. Senatorial decrees also guided the magistrates, who were generally senators themselves. The senate also provided a forum in which the magistrates divided authority among each other so as to avoid jurisdictional conflicts (Lintott 1999: 100–1). The senate received delegations from foreign

[2] The following account relies mainly on Lintott 1999. I also consulted Nicolet 1980; Mousourakis 2003; Williamson 2005; Flower 2010; Beck et al. 2011; and other sources as noted. Capogrossi Colognesi (2014) provides a thorough discussion of the institutional and legal changes of early Rome and the Republic.

Table 3.1. The Roman constitution.

Institution		Eligibility	Term	Powers
Senate		Former magistrate; good character	Lifetime	Advisory; finances
Magistrates (number by end of Republic)	Consul (2)	Former praetor	One year	Military command; head of state; power to convene assemblies and propose legislation
	Praetor (16)	Former quaestor	One year	Military command; judicial authority; power to convene assemblies and propose legislation
	Quaestor (40)	Citizen	One year	Public finances; assistants to other magistrates; power to convene assemblies and propose legislation; public prosecutors
	Tribune (10)	Plebeian	One year	Power to convene assemblies and propose legislation; *intercessio*
	Plebeian Aedile (2)	Plebeian	One year	Public infrastructure, games
	Curule Aedile (2)	Citizen	One year	Public infrastructure, games
	Censor (2)	Citizen	Five years	Maintaining census; enrolling senate; public contracts
	Dictator	Citizen	Six months	Maintaining order in emergencies; appointed on an ad hoc basis
Assemblies	Centuriate	Citizen	Ad hoc	General legislation; elected consuls, praetors, and censors; capital trials
	Tribal	Citizen	Ad hoc	General legislation; elected other magistrates; trials
	Plebeian	Plebeian	Ad hoc	General legislation; trials

countries and negotiated treaties with them, and had a significant role in public finances. The membership of the senate varied over time, but it was always in the hundreds. Apart from being subject to removal by the censors for moral turpitude, senators served for life (Lintott 1999: 71–2).

3.1.2. The Magistrates

Day-to-day governance occurred through the magistrates. The major magistrates were the consuls, praetors, tribunes, aediles, and censors. Each office had more than one occupant. Each type of magistrate possessed authority over a different area of life; their authority included executive, legislative, and judicial powers, as we understand them today (Lintott 1999: 100). The consulships and praetorship gave their occupants *imperium*, broad authority to engage in military action and maintain civil order. In times of emergency, a dictator could be appointed to defend the Republic; the dictator's office, unlike the others, was not recurring. The quaestors managed public finances. The plebeian and curule aediles maintained public infrastructure and arranged for the games. The censors conducted a census of all Roman citizens, determined the membership of the senate, and supervised public contracts and taxation (Abbott 1901: 115–20; Stewart 2010: 130). The *pontifex maximus* was the head of the college of pontiffs, the most important religious body in ancient Rome, which had control over sacred spaces, public religious rituals, aspects of family law, and the calendar (Lintott 1999: 183–5, 189).

The function of the tribune was originally to protect plebeians, who elected the tribunes, against actions by the other magistrates, who almost always hailed from the patrician class. Tribunes could, under certain conditions, block the magistrates from executing a sentence against a person. In the later Republic, it became common for tribunes to propose legislation, which would be enacted by the plebeian assembly.

The magistrates were mostly elected (except the dictator, who was typically appointed by the senate and a consul). Consuls, praetors, quaestors, aediles, and tribunes served terms of one year; the censors enjoyed five-year terms. The magistracies were, in effect, shared. There were two consuls, for example. The two consuls could veto one another's actions but in principle chose to cooperate (Lintott

1999: 114–15). The numbers for the other magistracies varied over time; by the end of the Republic, there were sixteen praetors, forty quaestors, ten tribunes, and four aediles. Only the dictator was a single person. In emergencies, the dictator had supreme power. Otherwise, the consuls were the leading magistrates; the praetors were their subordinates.

Madison, following Montesquieu, warned that breach of separation of powers was a recipe for tyranny (Wills, ed. 1982: Federalist No. 10). But the Roman magistrates were subject to significant checks. Their terms were short; they were elected by the people (in most cases); they had to obtain the approval of the people for certain actions such as legislation; they could be tried and punished for abuse of their office after their term expired; and they were constantly subject to public scrutiny because they had to act publicly in most cases. They could act independently but some amount of cooperation was necessary so that they did not undermine each other's actions; in addition, magistrates could veto actions of other magistrates of equal or lower rank as long as the vetoing magistrate was present (Boatwright et al. 2004: 137). All of the magistracies were open to plebeians as well as patricians by the mid-Republic.

3.1.3. Assemblies, Elections, and Legislation

Laws were enacted through the joint action of a magistrate and an assembly. Magistrates—consuls, praetors, aediles, tribunes, or dictators—summoned assemblies and proposed bills. In the middle and late Republic, there were two major assemblies, or *comitia*: the *comitia centuriata* (the centuriate assembly) and the *comitia tributa* (the tribal assembly). The centuriate assembly was organized into centuries, groups ranked by wealth (Lintott 1999: 55). The members of each century determined the vote of the century as a whole; then the voting on the bill took place by century: a bill passed if a majority of the centuries supported it. The centuries were originally based on military structure, but effectively they were groups based on wealth, with the wealthier people allotted to smaller centuries so that they exercised greater political influence. The poor, termed *capite censi* or *proletarii*, were restricted to just a single century (Taylor 1966: 84–7), and thus could almost always be outvoted. In the *comitia tributa*, voting was carried out by Rome's tribes (of which there were thirty-five in the late Republic). All citizens were allotted into tribes, which were originally based on kinship or geography (Lintott 1999: 50–1). Voting took place by tribes. In the tribal assembly, a measure passed if a majority of tribes supported it. In both assemblies, voters divided themselves into their tribes or centuries and marched forward to cast votes orally or (later) by using ballots (Lintott 1999: 42–3; Taylor 1966: 3–8, 111). The plebeian assembly was also organized in tribes and voted in the same way, and so it was like the *comitia tributa*, except that it included only plebeians and was presided over by the tribunes (Taylor 1966: 3–8). The centuriate assembly elected consuls, praetors, and censors. The tribal assembly voted on general legislation and elected other magistrates.

The account so far might give a misleading impression that the system for enacting legislation was highly democratic, even biased in favor of the lower classes. As noted, much legislation was enacted by plebeian assembly, from which patricians were excluded; and the plebeian tribune, acting on behalf of the plebeians, could veto legislation in the centuriate and tribal assemblies where the patricians could vote.

However, several factors favored the senate. First, the senate and the chief magistrates, at least until the late second century CE, set the legislative agenda. Second, the interests of many tribunes were surely aligned with those of powerful senators, who sought to conserve Roman traditions and maintain the existing distribution of property. Third, the assemblies were not entirely democratic in character. In the centuriate assembly, people were assigned to centuries on the basis of wealth, and the wealthier citizens were distributed among many more centuries than their poorer counterparts. In the tribal assembly, the urban tribes were overpopulated with the poor (including recently freed slaves) (Taylor 1966: 64–5). Thus, the urban tribes could be outvoted by the less populated rural tribes, which were dominated by landowners. On the other hand, members of the urban tribes were more likely to be present, and sheer numbers and the ever-present threat of mob violence must have made a difference (Taylor 1966: 54). Many patricians, notably Clodius (who actually transformed himself into a plebeian by engineering his “adoption” by a plebeian), came to power by promising to redistribute wealth to the poor, and used the mob effectively. Fourth, as a practical matter, only wealthy people could afford to be magistrates. Other wealthy Romans, including members of the equestrian class, served on the permanent courts in the late Republic. Fifth, the voting population excluded women and slaves, and slaves presented a substantial portion of the population of the city of Rome. It also excluded conquered peoples up until the Social War of 91–89 BCE, after which people living on the Italian peninsula (but by no means all conquered people) gradually were granted Roman citizenship (Nicolet 1980: 23).

3.1.4. Rights and Constitutional Change

Roman constitutional law did not contain judicially enforceable individual rights in a modern sense. Nonetheless, there were recognizable rights, which might be called constitutional or political rights. One such right, which can be found in the Twelve Tables, was that a Roman citizen could not be executed without a trial before the people (Lintott 1999: 149). This right seems to have been taken very seriously. Roman citizens were rarely punished by execution at all. Cicero, as consul in 63 BCE, did order the execution of several members of the Catilinarian conspiracy without a trial. Cicero acted on the authority of a senatorial decree, but his legal capacity to do so was disputed (Abbott 1901: 103).

3.2. ANALYSIS

3.2.1. The Literature on Roman Constitutionalism

In trying to explain the development of the Roman constitution, historians emphasize two themes: Romans' fear of executive power, and the conflict between the elites and the masses. The fear of executive power explains the multitude of checks and balances in the Roman constitution. The conflict between the elites and the masses explains why certain institutions were oriented toward one group or the other.

The Republic emerged from a rebellion against a monarchical system, and Romans sought to prevent a relapse. It was for this reason that the Roman constitution established such a weak executive. Two consuls shared power with each other, and with lesser magistrates who had independent sources of power. The consuls could not make laws without popular approval; in the city of Rome they could not punish people without a trial before the people. They could serve only one-year terms, which prevented them from consolidating power and establishing permanent dictatorships. They were subject to oversight by the senate, of which the consuls themselves were members, and to interference from religious figures. These urgent constitutional efforts to check executive power lend poignancy to the collapse of republican institutions and their replacement with an absolute monarchy in the first century BCE.

The other theme is the conflict between the elites and the masses—or to be more precise, the conflict between conservative members of the senate and their wealthy supporters (often *equites*) who sought to maintain the status quo and the ordinary plebeians and their occasional popular leaders (sometimes patricians) who sought to redistribute wealth and power to the people. The first group came to be known as the *optimates*, the second as the *populares*. In the early centuries of the Republic, most offices were open only to patricians, but over the centuries, the patricians yielded more and more rights to the plebeians, and most offices, including the consulship, were open to plebeians. As mentioned previously, by the third century BCE, measures passed by the plebeian assembly were binding on the entire citizen body. In the late Republic, the senatorial elite consisted of a patrician and plebeian aristocracy; families with an ancestor who served as consul were considered "noble."

That class conflict was central to Roman politics is the settled wisdom among historians (De Ste. Croix 1981). The ancient sources suggest a long-term trend in favor of the people. However, how much power the senatorial elite actually yielded to the lower classes over time is the subject of considerable dispute. On the one hand, members of the senatorial elite enjoyed wealth and significant social and institutional advantages. Patron-client relationships persisted throughout the entire period: if ordinary people depended on the nobles for subsidies, contacts, advice, and other benefits, they might not have been able to exercise much political independence (Gilbert 1978: 70–1). It took a vast amount of wealth to conduct election campaigns (which frequently involved bribery) and hold offices. It was not just that magistrates were unpaid; they also were expected to use their own funds for the public good. A small number of noble families dominated the governing class for centuries; families maintained their political power by entering alliances with each other, often ratified through the marriage of their children. These families also dominated the religious cults, which had a great deal of influence over political life (Grant 1971: 71). Plebeians wealthy enough to win office often had the conservative outlook of the patricians (Finer 1997: 387). Cicero frequently gives the impression that the tribuneship and other institutions that favored the plebeians were granted to them in response to popular pressure but did not actually matter. The public was happy with the constitutional forms of political power, which could cause annoyance but not affect political outcomes in a substantial way (Cicero, *The Laws* 154–8).

On the other hand, the common people enjoyed the significant advantage of numbers. And, indeed, the poorest of the plebeians exercised disproportionate influence through the threat of street violence: only a fraction of Roman citizens actually lived in Rome and those citizens were among the very poorest (Finer 1997: 426–7). The senatorial elite needed the support of the common people for a variety of reasons, including the fact that they supplied the soldiers so important for Rome's defense and imperial glory. Both plebeian and patrician politicians rose to power by appealing to plebeian interests. Elections were meaningful; assemblies mattered. Aside from the changes in the Roman constitution that progressively favored the plebeians, significant substantive laws were enacted that benefited common people—from land reform to the distribution of free food. Patron-client relationships, bribery, and private financing of public goods can also be reinterpreted as reflections of popular power. Why would elite politicians risk bankruptcy to pay off rank-and-file voters if this group lacked political power (Millar 2002: 109–62)? The fact that ordinary citizens secured substantive laws that benefited them, and that their efforts to secure these laws usually respected constitutional forms, suggests that the Roman political system was not a pure oligarchy. One might call it democratic republic that heavily favored an aristocracy or an oligarchy with significant democratic elements.

The two themes—fear of executive power and the conflict between the elites and the masses—are closely linked in Roman history. Roman elites feared popular demagogues from their own class—individuals who could amass power by promising to redistribute wealth from the nobles to the common people and hence securing their support in the assemblies. It seems clear that this fear lay behind many of the constitutional norms. If those norms were respected, it would be impossible even for a successful general or charismatic demagogue to establish a personal dictatorship. He could not be consul for more than one year; he would have to share power with others; as a member of the senate, he had just one vote; and so forth. The problem turned out to be that constitutional traditions were not powerful enough to prevent this from happening. People could obtain power through extra-constitutional means—for example, by relying on soldiers and other supporters to threaten violence. This is what eventually happened, starting with Sulla in 82 and culminating with Caesar. But only after more than four hundred years of extraordinary political achievement.

3.2.2. A Political Economy Perspective

3.2.2.1. The Agency Model

Agency models are extremely abstract, and can be applied to any case where one person (the agent) acts in a way that benefits another person (the principal). Typically, scholars study cases where the principal has some way to control the agent, so then the analysis focuses on methods the principal can use to control the agent at least cost, that is, to minimize agency costs. In the simplest models, there is a single agent and a single principal; but the models have been extended to cases where there are multiple agents and multiple principals.

Political economy models typically simplify by treating the "government" as a single agent and the "people" as a single principal, but of course these are abstractions, and these assumptions are frequently relaxed. A government consists of multiple offices and institutions, and these can be treated as separate agents; the principal might sometimes be the people or a subset of the people or an institution like a political party or a branch of government.

In the case of Rome, the initial impulse is to treat the Roman "government" as the agent, and the Roman "people" as the principal. The people control the government through the constitution which is a set of self-enforcing norms that dictate what the government can do (Mittal and Weingast 2013). I will generally rely on this simplification in my discussion of the Roman constitution, but I must start by noting the many ways in which it is inaccurate.

The question of who the principal is in the Roman Republic turns out to be more difficult than it first appears. The vast majority of people living in Rome and its territories were women (citizen women had no voting rights), conquered people who had not been given citizenship, and also slaves. It might be more accurate to say that the government was the agent of Roman citizens. But even this claim might not be sustainable. Most of the people were poorly educated and impoverished; it might be doubted whether they could wield much control over the sophisticated and vastly wealthy elites, many of whom exerted power through patronage and private guards and gangs. Still, the masses clearly influenced political outcomes. As so often happens with the upper classes, members of the senatorial elite were in many cases reluctant to engage in commercial activity, and in the late Republic, wealthy equestrians, especially those who held public contracts to collect taxes in the provinces, gained a great deal of political influence. Some members of the equestrian class could enter the senate, such as Cicero, a "new man," who gained semi-aristocratic status by becoming consul. Slaves were at the very bottom, but many managed to buy themselves out of slavery or were granted freedom by their masters. Freedmen had lower status than the free born, but some became immensely wealthy and influential nonetheless. People from the provinces form yet another group; they had few rights at home, when ruled by provincial governors, but brought a different perspective and often acquired citizenship when they came to Rome. For a class system, ordinary notions of the principal's "ideal point" might be inappropriate.

If, as is often claimed, Rome was an oligarchy, the proper assumption is that the government served as an agent for the upper class or some segment of it—the senatorial elite and wealthy *equites*, the *optimates*, or perhaps a few great families. That is the impression one gets, for example, from Cicero, who sometimes writes as though ordinary people are a hostile force that must be propitiated by the government for the sake of the nobility; at other times, however, he treats the people as the principal albeit one that does not, and should not, have any control over the agent, which is wiser than they are (Cicero, *Of the Laws*). On the oligarchic view, the principal consists of the relevant oligarchy; the government maximizes the utility of its members but also must pay other members of society whatever the minimum is necessary to prevent them from engaging in civil war or causing a domestic disturbance (compare Alesina and Spolaore (2003)).

The Romans themselves appeared to have yet another view of the principal: the senate and populace of Rome—the Latin acronym is

SPQR.[3] This name implies two principals—the senate and the people. These two principals are separate yet share sovereignty; compare "we the people" in the United States and the Athenian demos, which imply a single principal. One suspects that "senate" stands in for the upper class—the patrician and wealthy plebeian families that dominated Rome. Imagine, then, that two principals form a joint venture and expect the governmental agents to serve their joint interests. This again suggests a state with a form of government that lies somewhere between oligarchy and democracy.

Similar complications arise when we turn our attention to the agent. It is at best a rough approximation to say that Rome had a "government." It lacked the enormous, permanent, hierarchical bureaucracy that is the essential character of government in modern states. (It did, however, have a large army, albeit sometimes supplemented by forces paid out of the personal funds of individuals like Crassus during the slave revolt of 71 BCE, and toward the end of the Republic, mainly loyal to its commanders, who rewarded soldiers with booty.) As we have seen, the government comprised officials who were not required to cooperate with each other and were not subject to the control of a single person or institution. Magistrates could not rely on a police force to keep order, and often resorted to private guards, private gangs, and even private armies. Still, it seems fair to say that over time the Roman government acted in a largely consistent and coherent way, thanks in large part to the senate and perhaps the small size of the elite.

The Roman government, like governments at all times and places, did two things: it supplied public goods and it redistributed wealth. The public goods included security against external enemies; the rewards of conquest, including loot, tribute, and taxation; suppression of rebellion; public order; the construction and maintenance of roads, sewer systems, viaducts, and other infrastructure; adjudication of private disputes; and enforcement of property and contract rights. This type of public-good provision fits easily into the principal-agent model. The various cleavages among the population manifested themselves mainly in distributional conflict. Everyone agreed on the need for security; they disagreed about who should pay for it. Everyone welcomed conquest, but disagreed about how the spoils should be distributed. These distributional conflicts led to constitutional

[3] "SPQR" can be seen on public infrastructure throughout the modern city of Rome.

controversies because when ordinary people did not get what they regarded as their fair share, they sought more representation in government or stronger roles for their representatives. Nonetheless, everyone had an interest in a government that would maximize the social surplus.

My focus, however, will be agency costs. The political economy literature identifies a number of ways of reducing agency costs. I will focus on (1) methods for selecting government officials; (2) division of powers among offices and institutions; and (3) rewarding and sanctioning government officials.

3.2.2.2. Selection of Government Officials

Government agents such as magistrates may make decisions that are contrary to the public interest because they lack competence or because they have preferences that deviate from those of the principal. The Roman constitution addressed this problem in three ways: qualification rules for office; elections; and screening by the censors.

The major qualification rules were the age restrictions and the *cursus honorum*, which typically required that a person be of a certain age before occupying a magistracy, and that a person have held a lower magistracy before ascending to a higher one—though these rules were in flux and frequently violated in the last century of the Republic. These rules ensured that young, inexperienced people could not hold high office, and thus reduced the risk that an incompetent person might be elected. The *cursus honorum* ensured that people with mainstream preferences became consul, for people with idiosyncratic preferences were unlikely to win multiple elections.

Likewise, elections are a straightforward method for aggregating information and preferences. Suppose that the competence and political preferences of candidates are private information, but individuals can make inferences about this information on the basis of their prior behavior. Elections are efficient mechanisms for aggregating this information as long as people vote independently. One feature of Roman elections that may have worked against this function, however, was that voting was public and often sequential rather than simultaneous: one tribe or century votes first; its vote is publicly recorded as a yea or nay for a particular candidate; then another tribe or century votes. The later voters might rationally herd (Banergee 1992: 798). Indeed, herding was encouraged by the perverse superstition in tribal assemblies that the first tribe, which was selected by lot, reflected the will of the gods, and so subsequent tribes should follow it (Nicolet 1980). In later years, the secret ballot was introduced, so that voters could not be intimidated by the powerful; this may also have dampened herd behavior.

Qualification rules and elections are in tension. If qualification rules restrict who can be elected, the people do not have unfettered choice. From time to time, voters suspended qualification rules so that exceptionally talented individuals could be appointed at an early age or without previously occupying an office in the *cursus honorum*. However, usually the qualification rules were respected. Senators were *indirectly* elected. Although appointed by the censors, they were not eligible for appointment unless they had served as a magistrate in the past, which means that they had won an election. This is one way of reconciling the tension between popular sovereignty and the republican principle that only virtuous people should hold office. In the United States, this tension was resolved in another way: Americans could not vote directly for senators or the president—state legislatures and the electoral college served as mediating institutions.

Fears that elections would result in bad choices also may have accounted for the voting structure. Both the centuriate and tribal assemblies were biased in favor of the wealthy. One might believe that the wealthy, educated class selects magistrates more wisely than the illiterate masses do. On the other hand, the elites are not likely to choose magistrates who serve the interests of the masses, and they might not understand those interests in any event. And not all common people were illiterate; many (including slaves) were highly educated. The Roman voting system was a compromise, weighted in favor of the wealthy but permitting the masses to have influence when the wealthy were divided.

The American constitution has many fewer eligibility requirements—the most notable one is the rule that the president must be a natural born citizen and at least the age of 35. One could imagine a *cursus honorum*, one requiring, for example, that a person serve as governor (or senator) before becoming president, and member of the House (or mayor or alderman) before becoming governor or senator. Such a rule would reduce the risk that unqualified people reach high office, but it would also limit democratic choice in a way that surely would be considered unacceptable.

The difference can be attributed to the more fluid political environment that existed in ancient times. Then, it was possible for a talented young man from a prominent family to achieve military success early in his career and amass wealth and influence while still in his twenties (or even teens). Such a person might harbor dictatorial ambitions and possess the means to achieve them, while lacking the temperament and experience for republican politics. By contrast, wealth and military glory are not straightforward paths to the presidency in the United States. Unlike in ancient Rome, no one is wealthy enough to finance whole armies (as Crassus, Pompey, and Caesar could); and military glory is rare and usually comes only to elderly generals who have gradually moved up the ranks over the course of a long career. As a result, American politics are dominated by civilian career politicians who obtain prominence through compromise and consensus-building. Eligibility rules that emphasize age and experience are unnecessary.

3.2.2.3. Division and Limitation of Powers

Governance can be divided along two dimensions: policy domain (war, public order, games, and so forth) and type of power (legislative, executive, judicial). The U.S. founders divided the government by power—Congress has the legislative power, the president has executive power, and the judiciary has the judicial power—while also assigning some duplicative powers and imposing some restrictions on policy domain. The Roman constitution, by contrast, is divided (roughly) by policy domain. Consuls and praetors had authority over war and public security; quaestors over finances; censors over the census; aediles over public infrastructure and games; and so forth. Again, there was some overlap. But the Roman constitution did not make a fetish of separation of powers. Most of the magistrates had legislative, executive, and judicial powers: they made policy within broad legal constraints, executed it, and interpreted the law.

The Roman system had a number of advantages (Berry and Gersen 2008; Gersen 2010). First, the structure of the magistracies limited the amount of mischief that a single officeholder could do. If an incompetent or preference-outlier is elected to an office, he can produce problems only within his jurisdiction. Having no authority over games, an incompetent praetor cannot put on bad games. If some fraction of elected magistrates is incompetent, then the effect of distributing power over multiple magistrates is to reduce the *variance* of policy outcomes. By contrast, a single executive office produces consistently good outcomes when a competent person holds the office and consistently bad outcomes when an incompetent person holds the office.

Second, the Roman system established relatively clear lines of authority, in this way easing the burden on the public to monitor and sanction officeholders. Because the aedile is responsible for games, the public can evaluate an aedile on the basis of the success of the games. As a result, the public learns about the abilities of the aedile, and can reward him with future offices, or sanction him by denying him future offices. A consul responsible for defense of the city will be judged on the basis of whether the defense fails or succeeds. By contrast, in the American system lines of responsibility are not always so clear (Bueno de Mesquita and Landa 2007). When crime increases, it is hard to know whether to blame the executive for inadequate enforcement, the legislature for insufficiently tough laws, or the judiciary for excessive protection of procedural rights. Thus, in the Roman system, it was easier for the people to evaluate, and hence to reward and punish, officeholders on the basis of their public acts.[4]

Third, the Roman system nonetheless did provide for checks that ensured that projects went ahead only if they had sufficient political support. If a consul is tempted to enact a law that favors the elites, then a tribune or the other consul can veto it, and indeed a popular assembly can refuse to approve it. As a result, an implicit supermajoritarian rule holds: policies will be implemented only if officeholders representing a broad array of interests favors it. Supermajoritarian rules can be justified on the ground that they prevent redistributive politics while permitting government to produce public goods when decision costs are low (Buchanan and Tullock 1962). It is impossible to know whether supermajoritarian rules served this purpose in Rome or merely entrenched the status quo—a question to which I will return. For now, the interesting comparison is between the Roman and American systems of checking. In the American system, a branch of government cannot check another branch when that branch acts solely within its domain. So, for example, the judiciary does not try to check prosecutorial discretion. In the Roman system, such checking is possible. If the purpose of checks and balances is to ensure that a supermajoritarian

[4] However, the unbundling of powers was not pure; for example, magistrates usually had to rely on the senate for financing.

element exists in policymaking, then the American system is hard to justify. There is no particular reason to limit checking to cases where the three different types of powers must come into play in order for political outcomes to be achieved.

While Madison and Montesquieu complained that the failure to separate legislative, executive, and judicial power results in "tyranny," the usual complaint about the Roman system is that the division of powers caused gridlock (Wills, ed. 1982: Federalist No. 10). Again, let us compare the American and the Roman system. Simplifying greatly, the American president can respond to an emergency by either drawing on existing statutory authority or obtaining a single authorization from Congress, and then taking whatever actions seem necessary, subject only to a judicial check against arbitrary arrests and similar police actions. A Roman consul could respond to an emergency without senate authorization (though senate authorization would be prudent), and could, in principle, establish policy and use coercion in order to achieve it. Yet at all times, he would need to contend with objections from the other consul and the ten tribunes, and eventually he would be required to grant people trials. It seems that, on the whole, the American executive has more freedom of action than the Roman consul did. Rules restricting consuls to one-year terms and limiting the frequency with which an individual could hold consulships and other offices further weakened the executive in the Republic by preventing talented individuals from accumulating political power.

Brennan and Hamlin (1994) note that American-style separation of powers reproduces at the political level the dual monopoly problem analyzed in the industrial organization literature.[5] Suppose the government produces a public good but charges a "price" in the form of taxes. A single government official would set a monopoly price; but if two government officials must agree to the project, then the first (akin to a supplier) will charge a monopoly price to the second (akin to a distributor) who will then treat the first official's consent as, in effect, a costly input, and pass the cost along to the taxpayer plus an additional markup reflecting the second official's monopoly power. Because of the principle of collegiality in the Roman constitution, this

[5] Persson et al. (1997) offer an alternative view, which points out that separation of powers may produce optimal outcomes as long as the legislature and executive trade agenda-setting power. For criticisms of this model, see Posner and Vermeule (2011).

problem might seem even more significant than in the American constitution. A consul who seeks to implement a project must bribe the other consul not to veto it. However, there are two competing factors. First, the consuls were individuals and could bargain very easily with each other—much more easily than the president can bargain with Congress, which consists of two houses, each with a multitude of members. Second, the consuls typically came from the same class, and often were bound by family and clan alliances. From the standpoint of the Brennan/Hamlin model, separation of powers in Rome appears less damaging than it is in the United States. Gridlock and the other pathologies of separation of powers could be avoided through bargaining in a small, homogenous political class.

The Roman constitution also addressed the weakness of executive power in more direct ways. Magistrates such as consuls, proconsuls, and praetors enjoyed broadest powers when outside Rome, while on campaigns or when administering provinces. In these situations, there were relatively fewer concerns that the magistrates would abuse their powers because they had less authority over Romans (aside from soldiers, travelers, and administrators). For that reason, they could be subject to fewer limits.

In addition, magistrates could not be everywhere at once, and a magistrate could not veto the action of another magistrate unless in his presence. The constraints of time and space thus could facilitate governance, albeit only as a result of contingency. Magistrates in the same college also divided up responsibilities temporally and by domain, in this way avoiding direct conflict but possibly interfering with continuity of governance.

Further, the senate played an important role in coordinating the magistrates. However, the senate was not an elected body; as a result, senators, who surely reflected the interests of the wealthy, had an impact on policy outcomes through their influence on the assignment of roles to magistrates and their resolution of disputes between them.

Finally, the Roman constitution had a safety valve in the office of the dictator. The dictator did not have to coordinate with other magistrates; unlike the consul, the dictator did not have to contend with another person simultaneously holding the same office. Of course, such unbridled authority could be abused. The further solution to this problem was that dictators could hold office for only six months. Abuse was therefore time-limited. And because the dictator was selected by the consuls (after senate authorization) who were broadly responsible for the security of the Republic, the dictator would likely be a person who was experienced and enjoyed a fair amount of trust. However, even these protections may not have been enough. From the second century BCE through Sulla, the political class avoided reliance on dictators and instead the senate authorized a consul to take extraordinary actions during times of emergency. As an elected official, the consul may have had more trust among the public.

3.2.2.4. Term Limits

The magistrates suffered under severe term limits of, in most cases, one year. They could not run for reelection (although this tradition was not always observed), and there seemed to have been a presumption, on occasion disregarded, that a Roman could hold an office he had held before only after a long interval. In the United States, most officeholders enjoy longer terms—two or more years. In the national government, only the president faces a term limit.

Scholars are generally critical of term limits because they prevent competent officeholders from staying in office and reduce the incentive of individuals to run for office in the first place (Besley and Case 1995). In Rome, term limits may have been attractive for several reasons. First, term limits prevented consuls from acquiring monarchical powers. They had to share power over time, which meant that abusive acts undertaken during their term of office could be reversed. Second, term limits also prevented officeholders from accumulating political capital, which would enable them to acquire excessive power. A person who held office for only one year would be quickly forgotten.

The Roman system may have worked well enough for a period of time, but its chief flaw became apparent in the last century of the Republic. Because no civilian politician could amass much power through office, and perhaps because none had strong incentives to discharge their official duties competently, none could stand up to the military leaders who earned glory at battle and shared loot with soldiers and civilians who supported them. Military posts were not term-limited; and so successful generals could earn a popular following over a long period of time. These military leaders included Marius, Sulla, Pompey, and Caesar, and they were the dominant figures during the last century of the Republic's existence. By contrast, most of the consuls of that era—aside from these figures and Cicero—were undistinguished.

3.2.2.5. Rewarding and Sanctioning Government Officials

Principals cannot reward and sanction agents unless they can observe either the agent's performance or the outcome (payoff) of the agent's performance. Roman constitutional norms provided plenty of opportunities for such observation. Senatorial debates, assembly meetings, and judicial proceedings were all public and seem to have been attended by a great many people. However, physical structure put limits on the extent of public monitoring. Rome had a population in the hundreds of thousands but in certain public spaces, only tens of thousands of people could have been present (Boatwright et al. 2004: 138).

The division of powers by policy domain also lent itself to public monitoring. If the games were unsatisfactory, then everyone knew to blame the aedile with the responsibility for them. If a military campaign ended in failure, then the relevant consul or praetor could be held accountable. In addition, intense competition for political offices gave candidates with access to private information incentives to disclose such information when it harmed opponents. Finally, the requirement that citizens be out of office for two years between magistracies ensured that the medium-term consequences of their actions could be observed before they were elected to a new office.

But what were the rewards and sanctions, concretely? Roman politicians sought honor and wealth. Many politicians inherited a distinguished family name that imposed burdens and conferred opportunities. A family name is a form of human capital that one inherits rather than earns. Because Romans gave some deference to people from old families, a distinguished family name provided its bearer with political opportunities but also subjected him to a kind of bond. If he ended up a political failure, he disgraced his ancestors and deprived his descendants of the opportunities that he enjoyed. Maybe, these psychological factors gave Roman politicians longer time-horizons than those of American politicians.

To obtain honor, a Roman politician must contribute to the glory and prosperity of Rome. If he is an aedile, he must stage impressive games. If he is a consul, he must win military victories or keep the peace. Cicero won honor by suppressing the Catilinarian conspiracy. The highest honor was the triumph, a spectacular victory parade that enhanced the leader's prestige among the public, which one could earn only by being a military leader. Most (but not all) military leaders had obtained the rank of consul (or praetor). But one could become a consul or praetor only if one first was a quaestor (Pompey represents an exception to this rule). Thus, the Roman system harnessed the thirst for military glory to more mundane civic needs such as the management of public finances.

Money also played an important role in Roman politics. Officeholders were not paid, and were often expected to finance projects out of their own wealth. Many ambitious politicians resorted to borrowing; if they did not repay their debts, they could be ruined. At the same time, offices presented opportunities for gain. A consul who was given command of an army received a large share of the booty if he gained victory, and provincial governorships—the reward to consuls after their term of office expired—tendered semi-legal opportunities for their occupants to enrich themselves at the expense of the governed. In these ways, high offices offered pecuniary awards as well as honors, aligning politician's incentives to do well with the self-interest of the Roman people.

But only partially. A magistrate who borrowed in order to win an election, and could only repay those debts by winning a military victory, had strong incentives to win a military victory. But he might also plan and execute his military campaign in a way that yields the highest gain for himself rather than for Rome—for example, targeting a weak but wealthy enemy rather than a powerful enemy that posed more of a threat. Similarly, governors who milked the provinces for their own benefit set the stage for civil strife in the future.

The Romans were aware of these problems. Consuls sought triumphs—the highest political honor—by winning battles, and this might cause the distortion in incentives noted above, but the senate had the authority to confer or deny them, and it could have used that authority to dissuade consuls from pursuing military victories of no value for the Roman Republic (Beard 2007). Magistrates and governors who abused their office could be prosecuted after the term of office expired (Boatwright et al. 2004: 139). However, many prosecutions were thought to be politically motivated, the result of private feuds. Thus, whether the availability of prosecution reduced rather than increased agency costs depends on how impartial the judicial system was. If jurors could be persuaded to convict only when the magistrate abused the office, then prosecution would have improved magistrates' incentives. But if jurors could be bribed, or swayed by temporary political passions, then magistrates would have regarded the prospect of trial as a cost of doing business, but would have not have changed their behavior in response to it.

Censors could remove senators who committed crimes, became bankrupt, or violated serious moral norms. In the U.S. system, the Senate (and the House) have the responsibility for policing their members. Both institutions resolve one set of agency problems but create new ones. The prospect of removal might cause agents to act in the public interest, but the people with the power to remove do not necessarily want them to act in the public interest. Elections of censors helped mitigate the latter problem but would not have been sufficient. Perhaps for this reason, the Romans seem to have been nervous about the powers of the censors, and their terms, although nominally five years, were shortened from time to time.

Compared to the American system, Roman politicians had a great deal more at stake in politics. A successful political career resulted in fame, riches, and respect. A failed political career could result in death (at the hands of mobs and even political competitors) or exile (after a politically motivated prosecution), and certainly bankruptcy and disgrace. The high stakes must have given Roman politicians very strong incentives to perform well. However, they also had perverse consequences. Because one could be prosecuted only after leaving office, magistrates had incentives to forestall such prosecutions by taking legal action against their enemies, (in the case of Caesar) refusing to leave office, or (in the case of Catiline) fomenting rebellion. These perverse incentives were held in check for most of the Republic's history, but they contributed to its collapse.

In the United States, politics is not a life and death struggle. The low stakes ensure that power is given up voluntarily and transfers of power are peaceful. Elected officials have weaker incentives to rig the game in the incumbent's favor. If incentives to perform well are less strong, by the same token the incentives to challenge the constitutional system are weaker, and so political stability is greater.

3.2.2.6. The Role of the Senate

The system of independent magistrates creates a problem of coordination. If there are multiple aediles, which aedile is responsible for the games? If there are two consuls, which one will take command in the east and which will take command in the west? These are problems of coordination which are characteristic of unbundled executives (Gersen 2010). The senate helped coordinate magistrates.

Sometimes, the senate presided while magistrates drew lots. At other times, the senate directly appointed magistrates to undertake particular tasks. By issuing decrees that reflected general policies, the senate also provided a means for magistrates to coordinate their actions. But in the late Republic, the efforts of the senate to control the assignments of the consuls were hampered by generals who relied on laws proposed by tribunes that assigned provinces, such as Pompey in his commands against the pirates and Mithradates, Caesar in Gaul, and Marcus Antonius in Cisalpine Gaul.

The senate also played an important role in maintaining the continuity of government. Because most magistrates had one-year terms, they might have taken a short-term view toward Rome's interests.[6] The influence of the senate assured people that policies adopted by magistrates extended for greater than one year. For example, creditors want assurance that debts undertaken in one year will be repaid in a later year. By endorsing the actions of magistrates in one period, the senate led people to expect that those actions would not be repudiated by subsequent magistrates.

For the senate to serve these functions, it would need to be able to control the magistrates. It had several methods for doing this. First, the senate bestowed honors on magistrates. For example, the senate determined whether a military leader received a triumph. Second, the senate initiated criminal proceedings against magistrates who abused their office (people in the provinces could also initiate proceedings against governors for corruption). Third, the senate had control over public finances, and could penalize magistrates by refusing to fund them. Fourth, senators were rich and influential, and magistrates, as fellow-senators, would have wanted to maintain good relationships with them for personal as well as political reasons. Fifth, the senate had power to influence the allocation of tasks among magistrates, so magistrates who acted badly could be deprived of appealing (and often lucrative) posts and projects (Boatwright et al. 2004: 138). To be sure, it is possible that magistrates could ignore these assignments. But the magistrates faced a coordination game where they could end up with very low payoffs if they engaged in the same tasks as other magistrates. Tradition gave the senate the role of coordinator,

[6] But also recall that their concern for their family name might have enhanced their time horizons.

and it would have been difficult for magistrates to break out of this equilibrium.

In performing these functions, the senate diluted the control of the people over the magistrate through elections and popular approval of legislation. We might imagine a model, then, in which the people are the principal, and the principal controls the agents (the magistrates) both directly and through the senate. Modern business corporations have a roughly analogous structure. Shareholders control corporate policy both directly (certain actions like mergers must be approved by shareholders) and through an independent institution, the board of directors. Both the Roman senate and the board of directors enjoy a certain level of independence from the ultimate stakeholders. Senators are selected by censors; directors are selected by CEOs subject to a rubber stamp by shareholders. These forms of indirect representation raise agency costs. Censors do not necessarily act in the interest of the people (though they are elected themselves), and directors do not necessarily act in the interest of shareholders. The de facto and de jure qualifications for the senate also ensured that it was not a representative body. On the other hand, because senators were drawn from ex-magistrates, they were politicians who had in the past proven that they were acceptable to the people in elections.

Another feature of the senate was that it was a large body—generally in the neighborhood of three hundred people, or many more in the late Republic—and hence subject to all the problems of collective decision making. Senators had an incentive to free-ride on information-gathering and deliberation, and were vulnerable to agenda-setting by the magistrates, who could introduce bills or proposals and make take-it-or-leave-it offers. These factors suggest a weak and passive body. However, some historians argue that the senate was controlled by a core group of old and powerful families (Gilbert 1978: 146–9). If that was the case, then the senate served a more effective coordinating and disciplinary role, but was less representative of the interests of the people.

The U.S. Senate is often called a millionaire's club, but it hardly resembles the Roman senate at all. It does not serve the interests of the elites in any clear sense; it is certainly not understood to have that function, as the senate in Rome was. The United States has a single principal ("we the people") rather than a dual principal (SPQR). This is surely the result of the fact that the United States does not have clearly demarcated classes; as a result, it would make little sense to give different government institutions the responsibility of advancing the interests of one class or the other.

3.2.2.7. Judicial Process

From a modern perspective, it is strange that a magistrate, who has executive and legislative power, could also serve as a judge. As judge, the magistrate would have strong incentives to favor political allies and harm political adversaries rather than respect the rule of law.

Although the details of judicial procedure in public law cases are murky, there appear to have been a number of checks on this type of behavior. It appears that magistrates never or rarely initiated the cases in which they served as judges. Cases were initiated by the senate and the popular assemblies, by different magistrates, or by provincials in the case of alleged corruption on the part of a Roman official. The jury was an important check as well. Not only would acquittal protect the defendant; it would also give rise to an inference that the magistrate had wasted public resources pursuing a politically vindictive case. It also does not appear that Roman judges had as much power as modern judges do. The law was mostly customary and the jury had a great deal of discretion to decide cases as it saw fit. However, because jurors were selected from the upper classes, the system as a whole is likely to have worked in favor of the wealthier and better connected.

3.2.2.8. Popular Sovereignty

Rome had a mixed system of representative and direct democracy. People voted for magistrates, who conducted the government's business; but they also voted on bills proposed by the magistrates. The system is in many ways appealing. The people appoint agents to draft and propose bills but retain the right to veto bills that are contrary to their interests.

The U.S. founders rejected direct democracy in favor of a system of representative democracy, where people vote for representatives who both propose and vote on bills. Such a system would appear to increase agency costs; why then was it selected?

There are a number of problems with the Roman system. First, the direct democracy component of it did not really eliminate agency costs. Magistrates still had agenda-setting power, enabling them to propose bills that the public preferred to the status quo but not to any number of possible alternative bills. A small and collegial body, by contrast, can set up rules to mitigate agenda-setting. Second, most Romans were illiterate, and the bills had to be read to them. It is hard to believe that the public was able to understand complex laws, which means that magistrates could not propose complex but important laws or (more likely) that people voted on laws the details of which they did not understand. Debate involving thousands of people was also impossible, so the political contribution of the people was limited. Third, people could not be, and were not, compelled to attend assemblies. This probably meant that only people with low opportunity costs or a special interest in proposed bills attended assemblies. These people were not necessarily representative of the population as a whole, which means that many laws were enacted that served special interests rather than the public interest.

Direct democracy today can be found in some states like California. Systems of direct democracy have a poor reputation for reasons related to the problems with direct democracy in Rome. People often do not understand the proposals they vote on, and may not think carefully about how they interact with existing legislation.

3.2.3. The Fall of the Roman Republic

Republican institutions decayed over the last century BCE. A series of dictatorships interspersed with civil war and periods of renewed assertion by the senate finally ended in 27 BCE, when Octavian was granted the title of Augustus. Although the senate continued to exist, as did many of the constitutional forms, Augustus had immense political power as a result of his wealth, his control of armies, and his popularity. Over time, he and his successors would receive de jure recognition of their imperial authority.

Many of the ancients blamed the collapse of the Roman Republic on decadence and the corruption of public morals that resulted from the vast wealth that flowed into Rome from its conquests.[7] Sallust and

[7] Modern historians note that this view served Augustus' interests and for that reason may not be trustworthy. One might also note that every age seems to think it is decadent.

some modern historians point to changes in military organization. In the earlier Republic, soldiers were recruited from among propertied farmers; in the later Republic, commanders (beginning with Marius) recruited them from the proletariat (Sallust, *Jug.* 86.2, with de Ligt 2012: 183–4). Thanks to the immense rewards from a successful military campaign, soldiers transferred their loyalty from the Republic to particular military commanders such as Marius, Sulla, Pompey, and Caesar. Polybius and Machiavelli believed that the Roman constitution had lost its "balance" between monarchical, aristocratic, and popular elements as a result of the expansion of the power of the plebeians (Polybius 2009; Machiavelli 2009). In the same spirit, Montesquieu (1965: 91–5) argued that Roman conquests resulted in an influx of defeated populations, who did not share the interests of the Romans. Modern historians concur that Rome's conquest of foreign countries enriched the wealthy while generating a larger class of poor people who were absorbed into the state; the tensions between these classes eventually could not be contained in a republican system.

The historical debate was dominated by the image of the balanced constitution introduced by Polybius, who himself drew on themes in Plato, Aristotle, and other philosophers. But there are two problems with the idea of the balanced constitution. First, it draws on an old notion that society is divided into classes that pursue their class interests rather than the modern notion that society simply consists of individuals who pursue their self-interest (Ferejohn 2013). Polybius imagined an aristocracy ("the few") and the common people ("the many"), and an inherent struggle between them over social resources. This is certainly not an accurate picture of society today; it is not a good starting point for political analysis even for the ancient world. People then as now had individual projects and ambitions. They lived in a class system but there is no evidence that the classes acted as unified agents. The classes were relatively fluid. Many plebeians joined the ruling class, becoming "nobles," a more comprehensive group of wealthy and influential people than the "patricians." Many patricians sought political power by offering leadership to the plebes.

Second, the idea of balance is ambiguous. Putting aside the extreme cases of absolute monarchy and mob rule, one cannot evaluate the "balance" of a constitution because the different elements do not have "weights" that can be compared along a common metric. When the U.S. Senate became popularly elected, the many gained at the expense of the few, but did the constitution become unbalanced as a result or just more perfectly balanced? Such a question is impossible to answer. Polybius believed that the Roman constitution became "unbalanced," as the senate lost power to popular assemblies, but one could just as easily argue that the constitution became more balanced as otherwise the senate was not adequately checked.

The better approach is to think about constitutions in terms of whether they generate good political outcomes—order, security, prosperity, and the like. The U.S. founders, although captivated by the ancient notion of balance, did make arguments along these lines. They rejected the Roman elements of direct democracy, which resulted in sometimes hysterical and inconsistent political outcomes, and favored the senate, which is portrayed as a sober deliberative body (Sellers 2004: 350–2). Hamilton (Wills, ed. 1982: 321) criticized the division of the executive between two consuls because it led to conflict. Madison criticized the concentration of separate legislative, executive, and judicial powers in individual magistrates because it led to "tyranny" (Wills, ed. 1982: 356–7).

The conventional wisdom beginning with Polybius is that the Roman constitution failed because the public obtained too much power. It foolishly marginalized the senate—the only continuous deliberative body—and put its faith in demagogues and tyrants. However, the opposite view seems more plausible. The senate refused to acknowledge that a de facto shift in political power had occurred as a result of the expansion of the population, and insisted on maintaining its de jure privileges rather than yielding constitutional power to the people, except in small grudging squibs. The elites became vastly wealthier during the time period as a result of conquest, which produced an influx of valuable goods including slaves that accrued mostly to the upper class. The increase in the number of slaves both increased the value of farmland, which was mostly held by the elites, and reduced the value of free labor, resulting in the reduction of wages and employment. Meanwhile, many Roman soldiers lost their farms as a result of war, political disruption, and their long tenure in the field (see de Ligt 2012: 135–92). All this exacerbated the conflict between the lower and upper classes. In addition, the senate kept the magistrates weak because it feared that powerful magistrates would redistribute wealth to the people; but in the process it also failed to give magistrates the power to keep order and prosecute wars in an efficient manner. All of this gave rise to a demand for powerful figures who would serve the interests of the masses and engage in efficient governance. A number of individuals saw the opportunity to obtain power by appealing to the masses and adopting redistributive programs. These included Tiberius and Gaius Gracchus from roughly 133 to 121 BCE; Gaius Marius, who was consul seven times between 107 and 86 BCE; Lucius Sergius Catilina and Publius Clodius Pulcher in succeeding years; Pompey; and finally Julius Caesar, who was consul in 59 and then dictator from 49 to his assassination in 44 BCE. It seems apparent that, backed by soldiers and common people, these individuals had political power that greatly exceeded the constitutional authority that they could obtain. Because the senate and other vested interests blocked peaceful constitutional change, constitutional change occurred through violence.

The transition to absolute monarchy is treated as a tragic failure of self-government, but it should also be kept in mind that the monarchy ended the civil wars, kept the peace, and initiated a new era of conquest and prosperity for the Romans. It may well be the case that monarchy was the better constitutional form for the times—for a much larger and more diverse Rome than existed in the first few centuries of the Republic. After all, monarchy would be the dominant constitutional form for large states for the next two millennia, so it is likely that it had significant advantages over the republican form of government in that era. It seems likely that as Rome became more populous and heterogeneous, the cumbersome republican system could not arrange transfers from policy winners to policy losers whenever the government created a new public good. Too many veto points blocked the way. A dictator can more easily arrange for transfers, and can stay in power as long as he makes sufficient transfers to the policy losers (Alesina and Spolaore 2003; Acemoglu and Robinson 2003; Wintrobe 1998). The major cost of dictatorship—that the dictator favors a clique of supporters—may have been tolerable when the alternative was either gridlock or anarchy and civil war. Maintaining order requires constant vigilance, and flexibility that allows one to redeploy resources whenever a new threat arises. The Republic did not have a powerful enough executive once it exceeded a certain size; by dividing executive power among multiple offices and institutions, it created a system that was too cumbersome to react to new threats as they arose.

3.3. CONCLUSION: LESSONS FOR THE U.S. CONSTITUTION

The founders of the U.S. constitution were deeply knowledgeable about the constitution of the Roman Republic and heavily influenced by it (Richard 1994). They accepted Polybius' view that if a constitution is not balanced, the political system will degenerate into tyranny or mob rule, but they rejected the particular checks and balances of the Roman constitution (Gummere 1963: 176). Instead, they were persuaded by Montesquieu, and their own experiences with the state governments, that the better approach was to divide the government into legislative, executive, and judicial branches that had the power to check each other and the institutional motivation to maintain their authority.

With the benefit of centuries of research not available to the founders, one might worry that the founders took the checks and balances of the Roman constitution too literally. Many historians attribute the success of the Romans to the relatively coherent class of elites, who had a common worldview (emphasizing conquest and imperial expansion) and could buy off the masses through patron-client relationships and occasional redistributive laws and political institutions. The key to success, then, was a small, homogenous population—where everyone in the political class knew each other, and everyone could observe what everyone else was doing as they were doing it, at least within the confines of Rome. It was the expansion of the population after the Social Wars that finally destroyed Republican Rome and necessitated the replacement of Republican institutions with the dictatorship.

Madison, influenced by Montesquieu's skepticism about large republics, worried about this problem; federalism was supposed to be the solution. And indeed state constitutions did not fetishize the separation of powers as the national constitution did. Over time, the independence of the judiciary diminished in the states—judicial terms in nearly all states have been relatively short, and electoral systems in most states kept judges in check—and party politics overcame institutional checks and balances. So an institutionally weak national government sat atop institutionally powerful state governments.

But in the twentieth century federalism eroded in the United States under the pressure of scale economies that favor a national market and national security. Separation of powers at the national level also yielded to a system dominated by the executive who controls a vast bureaucracy, and is weakly checked by a largely reactive Congress, and a deferential judiciary (Schlesinger 2004). So one might see a parallel development in Rome and the United States: a formal system of checks and balances that may have worked adequately early on, but that produced gridlock as the population expanded, with the result that political agents worked around and undermined the original constitutional structure. In Rome, this process occurred through a series of constitutional crises that culminated in the establishment of a permanent monarchy. In the United States, however, the process was more gradual, and dictatorship seems no more likely today that an at any time in the past. Fortunately, we have advantages that the Romans lacked—notably, a free press; a wealthy, literate, and educated citizenry; a robust party system; and a widely respected norm of political equality that extends throughout the entire population. These hard-won cultural endowments have taken up the slack left by the relaxation of the archaic system of checks and balances we inherited from the Romans.[8]

REFERENCES

Abbott, Frank Frost. 1901. *A History and Description of Roman Political Institutions*. Boston: Ginn & Company.

Acemoglu, Daron, and James A. Robinson. 2003. *Economic Origins of Dictatorship and Democracy*. Cambridge: Cambridge University Press.

Alesina, Alberto, and Enrico Spolaore. 2003. *The Size of Nations*. Boston: The MIT Press.

Banergee, Abhijit V. 1992. "A Simple Model of Herd Behavior." 108 *Quarterly Journal of Economics* 797–817.

[8] Thanks to Jacob Gersen, Martha Nussbaum, Josh Ober, Richard Posner, Matthew Stephenson, Adrian Vermeule, David Zaring, and participants at a conference at the University of Chicago Law School, for helpful comments, and to Greg Pesce for research assistance. Special thanks to John Ferejohn who delivered very helpful formal comments at that conference. The classicist Dennis Kehoe corrected numerous errors in a previous draft and greatly improved my account of the Roman constitution. I am very grateful for his help and patience.

Beard, Mary. 2007. *The Roman Triumph*. Boston: Belknap Press of Harvard University Press.

Beck, Hans, Antonio Duplá, Martin Jehne, and Francisco Pina Polo. 2011. *Consuls and* Res Publica: *Holding High Office in the Roman Republic*. Cambridge: Cambridge University Press.

Berry, Christopher R., and Jacob E. Gersen. 2008. "The Unbundled Executive." 75 *University of Chicago Law Review* 1385–1434.

Besley, Timothy, and Anne Case. 1995. "Does Electoral Accountability Affect Economic Policy Choices? Evidence from Gubernatorial Term Limits." 110 *Quarterly Journal of Economics* 769–98.

Boatwright, Mary T. et al. 2004. *The Romans: From Village to Empire*. New York: Oxford University Press.

Brennan, Geoffrey, and Alan Hamlin. 1994. "A Revisionist View of the Separation of Powers." 6 *Journal of Theoretical Politics* 345–68.

Brennan, T. Corey. 2004. "Power and Process under the Republican 'Constitution,'" in Harriet I. Flower, ed., *The Cambridge Companion to the Roman Republic*. Cambridge: Cambridge University Press, 31–65.

Buchanan, James M., and Gordon Tullock. 1962. *The Calculus of Consent: Logical Foundations of Constitutional Democracy*. Ann Arbor: University of Michigan Press.

Bueno de Mesquita, Ethan, and Dimitra Landa. 2007. "An Equilibrium Theory of Clarity of Responsibility," unpublished manuscript available at http://home.uchicago.edu/~bdm/PDF/clarity.pdf.

Capogrossi Colognesi, Luigi. 2014. *Law and Power in the Making of the Roman Commonwealth*. Trans. Laura Kopp. Cambridge: Cambridge University Press.

de Ligt, Luuk. 2012. *Peasants, Citizens and Soldiers: Studies in the Demographic History of Roman Italy 225 BC—AD 100*. Cambridge: Cambridge University Press.

de Ste. Croix, Geoffrey E. M. 1981. *The Class Struggle in the Ancient Greek World: From the Archaic Age to the Arab Conquests*. Ithaca: Cornell University Press.

Elkins, Zachary, Tom Ginsburg, and James Melton. 2009. *The Endurance of National Constitutions*. Cambridge: Cambridge University Press.

Ferejohn, John A. 2013. "Two Views of the City: Republicanism and the Law," in Andreas Niederberger and Philipp Schink, eds, *Republican Democracy: Liberty, Law and Politics*. Edinburgh: Edinburgh University Press, 128–53.

Finer, Samuel E. 1997. *The History of Government*. New York: Oxford University Press.

Flower, Harriet. 2010. *Roman Republics*. Princeton: Princeton University Press.

Gersen, Jacob E. 2010. "Unbundled Powers." 96 *Virginia Law Review* 301–58.

Gummere, Richard M. 1963. *The American Colonial Mind and the Classical Tradition*. Cambridge: Harvard University Press.

Jackson, Vicki C., and Mark Tushnet. 1999. *Comparative Constitutional Law.* New York: Foundation Press.

Law, David S., and Mila Versteeg. 2011. "The Evolution and Ideology of Global Constitutionalism." 99 *California Law Review* 1163–1258.

Lintott, Andrew. 1999. *The Constitution of the Roman Republic.* Oxford: Clarendon Press.

Machiavelli, Niccolo. 2009. *The Discourses on Livy.* Trans. Julia Conaway Bondanella and Peter Bondanella. New York: Oxford World's Classics.

Millar, Fergus. 2002. *The Roman Republic and the Augustan Revolution.* Chapel Hill: University of North Carolina Press.

Mittal, Sonia, and Barry R. Weingast. 2013 "Self-Enforcing Constitutions: With an Application to Democratic Stability in America's First Century." 29 *Journal of Law, Economics, and Organizations* 278–302.

Montesquieu. 1965. *Considerations on the Causes of the Greatness of the Romans and Their Decline.* Trans. David Lowenthal. New York: Free Press.

Mousourakis, George. 2003. *The Historical and Institutional Context of Roman Law.* Hampshire: Ashgate.

Mueller, Dennis C. 2003. *Public Choice III.* Cambridge: Cambridge University Press.

Nicolet, Claude. 1980. *The World of the Citizen in Republican Rome.* Berkeley: University of California Press.

Persson, Torsten, Gerard Roland, and Guido Tabellini. 1997. "Separation of Powers and Political Accountability." 112 *Quarterly Journal of Economics* 1163–1202.

Posner, Eric A., and Adrian Vermeule. 2011. *The Executive Unbound: After the Madisonian Republic.* New York: Oxford University Press.

Richard, Carl J. 1994. *The Founders and the Classics: Greece, Rome, and the American Enlightenment.* Cambridge: Harvard University Press.

Schlesinger, Arthur M., Jr. 2004. *The Imperial Presidency.* New York: Houghton Mifflin.

Sellers, Mortimer N. S. 2004. "The Roman Republic and the French and American Revolutions," in Harriet I. Flower, ed., *The Cambridge Companion to the Roman Republic.* Cambridge: Cambridge University Press, 347–65.

Stewart, Roberta. 2010. *Public Office in Early Rome: Ritual Procedure and Political Practice.* Ann Arbor: The University of Michigan Press.

Syme, Ronald. 1952. *The Roman Revolution,* rev. edn. Oxford: Clarendon Press.

Taylor, Lily Ross. 1966. *Roman Voting Assemblies.* Ann Arbor: University of Michigan Press.

Voigt, Stefan, ed. 2005. *Constitutional Political Economy.* Northampton: Edward Elgar Publishing.

Wills, Gary, ed. 1982. *The Federalist Papers.* New York: Bantam Books.

Williamson, Callie. 2005. *The Laws of the Roman People: Public Law in the Expansion and Decline of the Roman Republic.* Ann Arbor: University of Michigan Press.

Wintrobe, Ronald. 1998. *The Political Economy of Dictatorship.* Cambridge: Cambridge University Press.

Primary Sources

Cicero. 1998. "Of the Laws," in Niall Rudd, trans., *The Republic and the Laws.* Oxford: Oxford University Press.

Polybius. 2009. *The Complete Histories of Polybius.* Trans. W. R. Paton. Lawrence: Neeland Media LLC.

Sallust. 2008. *Catiline's War, The Jugurthine War, Histories.* Trans. A. J. Woodman. New York: Penguin Classics.

4

Law-Making and Economic Change during the Republic and Early Empire

Luuk de Ligt

4.1. INTRODUCTION

During the past decade approaches based on new institutional economics or on the closely related law and economics school of thought have gained popularity among ancient historians. The basic idea behind these approaches is that the performance of all historical and existing economies has been, and is being, determined not only by technology and population but also by the institutional environment in which productive, commercial, and financial activities are carried out. Institutions that co-determine levels of economic efficiency and performance include firms, concrete and abstract markets, as well as formal rules and social conventions influencing the behavior of producers, investors, and traders.[1]

The focus of this chapter will be on formal rules or, to use a more accurate formulation, on the historical development of legal rules that were part of the institutional context in which economic activities were carried out in the Roman world. My principal aim will be to examine the relationships between economic and legal developments. As we shall see, the third to first centuries BC witnessed the creation of a wide range of new legal remedies. Can we say anything about the

[1] For convenient introductions, see Furubotn and Richter (2005) and the valuable collection of essays in Ménard and Shirley (2005). Frier and Kehoe (2007) attempt an analysis of Roman law from a law and economics perspective. See also Kehoe (2007).

Luuk de Ligt, *Law-Making and Economic Change during the Republic and Early Empire* In: *Roman Law and Economics: Institutions and Organizations, Volume I.* Edited by: Giuseppe Dari-Mattiacci and Dennis P. Kehoe, Oxford University Press (2020).
DOI: 10.1093/oso/9780198787204.003.0004

aims pursued by the law-making magistrates who were responsible for this remarkable development? And exactly how did legal developments intertwine with processes of economic change? Are there any indications that legal change lagged behind economic developments during this period, or were law-making magistrates quick to respond to challenges resulting from the emergence of an increasingly complex economy? Can Roman law perhaps even be regarded as a major determinant of economic change during the final centuries of the Republic?

Another important topic is the contribution to the further development of Roman law made by the late republican and early imperial jurists. It is generally agreed that the classical jurists were reluctant to give up certain basic rules and principles. Are there any signs that this attitude created obstacles for economic development, or could seemingly inconvenient rules and principles be applied or re-interpreted in such a way that there was no discernible negative impact on economic development or growth?

4.2. LAWMAKING BY MAGISTRATES

In order to get an idea of the manifold ways in which Roman law developed between the beginning the Republic and the start of the Principate it is enough to compare the surviving fragments of the Law of the Twelve Tables with Lenel's reconstruction of the final version of the praetorian edict and with the sophisticated comments and solutions referred to in various fragments of the late republican jurists.[2] To judge by the contents of the Twelve Tables, early republican Rome was a thoroughly agrarian society (Watson 1975: 157–65). The seventh and eighth tables contained provisions concerning the boundaries between farms, overhanging trees, quadrupeds causing damage to other people's property, animals pasturing on fruit on other people's land, and people casting spells on fruits or harvests belonging to other people (Crawford 1996: 580–1).[3]

[2] Law of the Twelve Tables: Crawford (1996: 555–721); praetorian edict: Lenel (1927).

[3] Crawford's reconstruction of the Law of the Twelve Tables differs substantially from any others. The edition in *FIRA* also assigns the fragments referred to in the main text to the seventh and eighth tables but presents them in a somewhat different order.

Two provisions contained in table ten refer to flute-players and goldwork (X, 3 and X, 8), and there can be no doubt that the population of early republican Rome included a significant number of craftsmen. There is, however, not a single provision dealing with manufacturing or trade. The only types of "sale" referred to in the Law of the Twelve Tables are transfer of ownership through formal conveyance (*mancipatio*) and conveyance before a magistrate (*in iure cessio*).[4]

Four centuries later the edicts of the praetors contained a long list of remedies relating to contractual relationships or to various types of liability arising from the use of "agents" in economic transactions. In the law of property we now encounter a sophisticated distinction between ownership according to *ius civile* (law reserved for Roman citizens) and ownership according to praetorian law, both of which are distinguished from "possession". The praetorian edicts of the mid-first century BC listed three different legal remedies reflecting these distinctions.

Very little can be said about developments during the period 450–250 BC. The surviving sources, all of them late republican or early imperial, are unanimous that "law-based procedures" (*legis actiones*) were the most important type of lawsuit during this period. There were fixed templates for each type of *legis actio* that litigants had to recite when presenting their claim in court. Any mistake in pronouncing the prescribed words meant that the litigant lost his case.[5]

At first sight a legal system characterized by such formal rigidity might seem to offer little scope for creative reinterpretation. There are, however, some indications to suggest that some important legal changes did occur. An obvious example concerns the creation of the legal device of *emancipatio*, an act by which a *pater familias* could release a son from his paternal power. The fourth table of the Law of the Twelve Tables contained the following provision: "If a father sells his son three times, the son is to be free from the father" (IV.2). At some point during the fifth or fourth century, this rule, which must originally have referred to fathers hiring out their sons for a certain period of time, began to be used to release a dependent son from paternal power by means of an imaginary sale (Kaser 1971: 70). As Jhering observed long ago (1898: 528–59), the capacity of archaic

[4] For the latter type, see Paul., *Frag. Vat.* 50.

[5] See, for instance, Gai., *Inst.* 4.11. Cf. Schiavone (2012: 100–2).

legal systems based on formal rigidity to reach satisfactory solutions to a wide range of juridical problems should not be underestimated.

A major limitation of the system of *legis actiones* was that Roman laws applied to citizens only. For this reason foreigners could not use any of the "law-based" procedures created or confirmed by the Law of the Twelve Tables or subsequent laws. One way of circumventing the practical problems arising from this limitation was to grant various groups of non-Romans the right of *commercium*. Those foreigners who had been given *commercium* could take part in formal conveyances (*mancipationes*) and enforce any claims arising from such transactions in a Roman court.[6] In his *Institutes* Gaius also refers to another technique used to make it possible for non-citizens to avail themselves of a *legis actio*. In those cases in which it was considered just (*iustum*) that a *legis actio* be extended to a non-citizen, citizenship could be attributed fictively by granting a formula containing the phrase *si civis Romanus esset*, "as if he were a Roman citizen" (Gai., *Inst.* 4.37; Ando 2015: 300). According to Gaius this technique was used if a Roman citizen wanted to use an *actio furti* (action of theft) or an *actio legis Aquiliae* (action arising from damage to property) against a non-citizen, or the other way around.

In the end most of the practical problems arising from the rigidity of the system of *legis actiones* and from its non-accessibility to non-Romans were resolved not by a gradual adaptation of the early republican procedures but by the emergence of an entirely new system of litigation. Instead of being based on laws passed by the *comitia centuriata* or by the *comitia tributa*, the lawsuits available under this new system were creations of magistrates with jurisdictional powers. The most important of these were the praetors, although some new remedies were also created by the *aediles curules*. Collectively, the remedies created by these magistrates are known as the *ius honorarium*.

In the absence of any reliable evidence relating to developments during the fourth and early third centuries BC, it cannot be determined when this new body of law started to develop. According to a widely held theory, the creation of the first *praetor peregrinus* (in around 242 BC) was a key factor in this process. The underlying idea is that any lawsuits belonging to the *ius honorarium* could be used by foreigners. The creation of a separate praetor responsible for the first

[6] Recent discussions of *commercium* include Coşkun (2009) and Roselaar (2012).

stage of litigation between citizens and foreigners, and for that of lawsuits between foreigners, suggests that access of non-citizens to Roman courts had become an important issue by the mid-third century BC. On closer inspection, this line of argumentation appears fragile. Before 242 BC there was only one praetor, and this magistrate must have dealt with Roman and non-Roman litigants. So the new system might well have started to develop at a much earlier date than is often assumed, perhaps as early as the second half of the fourth century BC (Kaser 1966: 109–14). Conceding this possibility, some legal historians have argued that the praetors of the late fourth and early third centuries BC must have concentrated on the rules of litigation rather than on the creation of new remedies relating to contractual or other relationships between parties (Kelly 1966b). Again there is not a shred of positive evidence to support this theory. As we shall see, at least some areas of the *ius honorarium* appear to have been well developed by the end of the third century BC.

The edict issued by the republican praetors at the beginning of their office was basically a list of procedural forms (*formulae*) describing the legal issue at hand. Many *formulae* dealing with contractual relationships also specified that the obligations created by the contract were based on "good faith" (*bona fides*). The introduction of procedural forms containing this phrase must be understood as a way of providing obligations not based on any law with a solid foundation.[7] From a jurisdictional point of view the use of *formulae* meant that cases were assigned to particular categories before they reached the courts. An important difference with the earlier system of *legis actiones* was that the *formulae* of the new system, instead of being quasi-ritual formulations that litigating parties had to pronounce in court, took the form of an instruction issued by the praetor to the judge presiding over the actual lawsuit, which was the second stage of the procedure. As a result of this important change, litigants no longer ran the risk of losing their case by making a mistake in quoting or reading out the prescribed forms.

From the point of view of economic history, it is of great interest to see that many of the new types of lawsuits introduced by the praetors of the third and second centuries BC concerned contractual relationships

[7] The reinterpretation of *bona fides* as a criterion for establishing the obligations and claims arising from contractual and other relationships clearly is a later development.

that must have accounted for a large proportion of economic transactions.[8] Obvious examples include the contracts of sale (*emptio-venditio*) and lease (*locatio-conductio*). According to the rules of *ius honorarium*, consent between the seller and the buyer about the essentials of the contract was enough to create the contractual relationship, without any specific form being prescribed for the oral or written contract. Roman citizens might still use *mancipatio* to convey the ownership of certain types of goods (*res mancipi*) after concluding a contract of *emptio venditio*, but carrying out such a transfer now meant fulfilling a contractual obligation rather than creating it. Gradually, it became more common to transfer *res mancipi*, such as slaves or Italian land, informally, and starting with the praetorian edict of 67 BC any Roman citizen who had bought a *res mancipi* from the owner and had received it from him informally was given an unassailable position.[9]

Other important contracts belonging to the *ius honorarium* were *fideipromissio* (suretyship), *pignus* (pledge), *depositum* (deposit), and *mutuum* (informal lending of money and other generic objects).

In some cases the historical evolution of a particular contract can be reconstructed with a reasonable degree of confidence. One of the best examples is the contract of partnership (*societas*).[10] According to early republican law, if a *pater familias* died without a will, his property passed to the so-called *sui heredes*, made up of all freeborn members of the *familia* who had been directly subject to the father's authority and became independent as a result of his death. After the death of the *pater* these coheirs continued to own and administer the

[8] For a thorough discussion of the introduction of these contracts, see Watson 1965.

[9] See, for instance, Kaser (1971: 438–9). In the scholarly literature this unassailable position is often referred to as 'bonitary ownership' because the person who had acquired the thing held it *in bonis*, 'among his goods'. According to the *ius civile* the ownership of a *res mancipi* which the owner had conveyed informally remained with that owner (for a period of one or two years, depending on whether the thing transferred was a movable piece of property or real estate), but if the *dominus* attempted to recover the thing, the praetor would insert the *exceptio rei venditae et traditae* in the *formula* for the lawsuit. Since this clause specified that the lawsuit started by the *dominus* could only be successful 'if he had not sold and informally conveyed the thing in question to the defendant', it gave the buyer holding it *in bonis* full protection. For details see Buckland (1921: 193–4). For the development of 'bonitary ownership' in Roman law, see also Ankum and Pool (1989), with Crook (1990).

[10] On the historical development of the Roman *societas*, see Arangio-Ruiz (1950); Guarino (1988); Zimmermann (1996: 451–66); and Johnston (1999: 106–7).

family estate without partitioning it, unless and until one of them died or decided to end this arrangement. The technical term for such a grouping was *consortium* or *societas ercto non cito*.

Taking this old arrangement as a model, an unknown praetor of the fourth or third century BC introduced a new type of lawsuit that could be used by any citizens or non-citizens who had pooled all of their assets on a voluntary basis. Unlike the relationship that had existed between the members of a *consortium*, that between partners participating in a *societas* of this type had a contractual basis.[11] If a conflict arose that could not be resolved through mutual agreement, any *socius* who wished to do so could sue his partner, or partners, with a praetorian *actio pro socio* ("lawsuit concerning partnership") in order to claim what he thought he was entitled to. Since the emergence of a legal conflict between *socii* signaled the end of the relationship of trust (*fides*) upon which their contractual relationship had rested, the republican and early imperial jurists regarded the decision to start an *actio pro socio* as terminating the *societas*. Partnerships of this type might have been used by close friends or relatives, or by farmers, but did not suit the needs of businessmen wishing to operate a joint enterprise.

By the late third century BC an important new form of partnership had been recognized as creating the possibility of bringing an *actio pro socio*. Whereas the earliest contractual *societates* involved a pooling of all assets owned by the partners, it now became possible to pool *some* resources for the purpose of a single business enterprise. Some of the classical jurists refer to this type of partnership as a *societas negotiationis* or as a *societas unius rei*. The earliest historical example is the three *societates* that undertook to supply the Roman army in Spain with grain and clothing in 215 BC (Livy 23.48.4–49.4; 25.3.8–5.1). A couple of decades later Cato the Elder encouraged his debtors to form a *societas* operating fifty seagoing ships, in which Cato himself took a single share in the name of his freedman Quintio (Plut., *Cat. Mai.* 21).

During approximately the same period the praetors started to create a series of legal remedies relating to the use of "agents" in economic life. Everything suggests that the first three remedies belonging to this category concerned the effects of transactions performed by slaves and dependent sons, that is to say, by members of

[11] Guarino (1988: 13–19) argues that the *societas omnium bonorum* was a creation of the second or third centuries AD, but see Zimmermann (1996: 452–3).

the *familia*. As early as the second half of the third century BC a *pater familias* who had assigned a fund of property (*peculium*) to a slave or to a dependent son could be held liable for any transaction carried out by that slave or son, but only up to the amount of the *peculium* (*dumtaxat de peculio*). Not much later the *pater familias* could also be sued with an *actio de in rem verso* ("action concerning enrichment of property") if his property had been enriched as a result of a transaction concluded by a slave or dependent son. In this case his liability was limited to the amount with which he had been enriched (de Ligt 1999).

Taking yet one step further, a praetor of the late third or early second century BC made it possible to sue the *pater familias* for the full amount if he had specifically authorized a transaction concluded between a slave or son and a third party. The *actio de peculio* certainly existed during Plautus' lifetime, and a passage from Terence's *Heauton Timorumenos* has been interpreted as referring to the *actio de in rem verso* and to the *actio quod iussu*.[12]

Building on these early developments, unknown praetors of the second century BC introduced actions with which someone could be held liable for the full amount if he had appointed another person as a ship's captain (*magister navis*) or as a business manager (*institor*). These types of lawsuits were available even if the captain or business manager did not belong to the principal's *familia*.[13]

While the praetors of the middle and late Republic were responsible for the vast majority of legal innovations, one important novelty is associated with the curule aediles, whose responsibilities included supervision of the markets of Rome. According to the classical jurists the aedilician edict offered the possibility of suing the seller of a defective slave or draft animal if the seller had failed to mention certain defects that he was obliged to reveal, regardless of whether he actually knew about these defects, or if he had explicitly declared that the slave or animal did not have certain defects, and also if he had behaved fraudulently in making the sale. After discovering the presence of undeclared defects, or of defects that the seller had declared to

[12] Aubert (1994: 78–82) sees the *actio quod iussu* as the oldest *actio adiecticiae qualitatis* and assigns all the 'added actions' to the second and first centuries BC, but see de Ligt (1999 and 2002), identifying the *actio de peculio* as the oldest *actio adiecticiae qualitatis*. Cf. also Bürge (1999: 192–4), referring to Ter. *Heaut*. 790–5.

[13] For good discussions of these actions, see Aubert 1994: 52–64; Johnston 1999: 102–3.

be absent, the buyer had two options: he could either bring an *actio redhibitoria* and demand restitution of the purchase price, in which case he had to give up the slave or animal, or he could keep the slave or animal and demand financial compensation for the fact that the object of the sale was worth less than the purchase price. We do not know exactly when these aedilician remedies were created, but the majority view is that they existed as early as the second quarter of the second century BC.[14]

4.3. PRINCIPLES GUIDING LAWMAKING BY MAGISTRATES

Which considerations might have prompted the praetors and aediles of the third and second centuries BC to introduce these spectacular innovations?

On one level the jurisdictional magistrates of the Roman Republic can be seen as responding to some of the dramatic economic changes that took place between the late fourth and early first centuries BC. Already during the first half of the third century BC Rome had become one the largest cities of the Mediterranean world. Even if almost nothing is known about the workings of the urban economy at this early date, we can be certain that arrangements for craft production and trade were becoming far more sophisticated than they had been during the early Republic. These new circumstances called for more flexible ways of concluding contracts not only between Romans and non-Romans but also between people of citizen status. Simultaneously, the more complex economic structures of the third century BC called for new arrangements making it easier for slaves and dependent sons to make independent economic decisions. More than twenty years ago Cornell (1995: 385–9) argued that as early as the mid-third century BC the city of Rome must have possessed a sophisticated economy in which many people were engaged in manufacturing and commerce. Slaves and freeborn dependants are likely to have made up a considerable proportion of skilled craftsmen and

[14] Impallomeni (1955: 90–1), followed by Serrao (2000: 52). Watson (1971: 82–3) and Jakab (1997: 128–9) argue that any date between the early second and the early first century BC can be defended.

traders. It is difficult to envisage how such an economy could have operated if each and every transaction had occurred without agents. In the rural economy we have to reckon with increasingly complex patterns of landholding, which must have made it increasingly difficult for landowners to keep a close eye on the activities of those slaves or ex-slaves to whom they had entrusted the management of their rural estates. Here too a pressing demand for new legal devices making it possible for such people to make independent decisions must have arisen at an early stage.

While the parallelism between legal and economic developments cannot be denied, the surviving sources have almost nothing to say on how the praetors and aediles of this period perceived their role as initiators of legal change. The only clear statement regarding this topic is to be found in a famous passage from a treatise written by the Severan jurist Papinian. In this passage Papinian explains that praetorian law is the law that the praetors introduced with the aim of assisting, supplementing, or correcting the *ius civile* with a view to "the public interest" (*propter utilitatem publicam*) (D. 1.1.7.1; Pap. 2 *def.*). Extensive discussions of the tripartite phrase "assisting, supplementing, or correcting" are to be found in almost every handbook on Roman legal history (Kaser 1971: 206; Jolowicz and Nicholas 1972: 100). Somewhat surprisingly, less attention has been paid to the consideration of *utilitas publica*, which Papinian identified as the driving force behind the innovative jurisdictional policies of the praetors.

According to Heumann-Seckel's *Handlexikon*, the phrase *utilitas publica* means something like "the best interests of the community" or "the general interest" in this passage.[15] There are, however, reasons to think that the intended meaning is more specific than this. In the *Digest* we find about thirty passages in which one of the classical jurists explains that a certain solution to a juridical problem has found acceptance *propter utilitatem* or *utilitatis causa*, "because of *utilitas*". For most of these passages Heumann-Seckel suggest "expediency" (Zweckmässigkeit) or "consideration of practical needs" (Rücksicht auf praktische Bedürfnisse) as appropriate or possible translations. In an article that appeared more than fifty years ago Ankum carried out an exhaustive investigation into the meaning of the phrase

[15] Heumann and Seckel (1926: 610). Their interpretation is correct to the extent that the phrase *utilitas publica* must be understood as referring to the interest of the *populus* rather than to the interest of the *res publica*.

utilitatis causa receptum. He observed that most of the classical jurists preferred to justify their decisions and recommendations with arguments based on purely juridical reasoning. Only when such reasoning did not result in solutions that were deemed satisfactory from a practical point of view do we find them invoking the criterion of *utilitas*. As Ankum points out, however, the "practical" considerations that appear to have guided the decisions of the classical jurists in these cases are still "juridical" in the sense that the concept of *utilitas* clearly refers to the desirability of finding a solution that is satisfactory from the point of view of practical juridical life (Ankum 1968).[16] Similarly, when Papinian refers to praetorian actions having been introduced *propter utilitatem publicam*, he must mean that the praetors responded to the needs of practical juridical life experienced by many people living in Roman Italy.

Of course, we cannot be certain that the republican praetors were guided by the considerations ascribed to them by Papinian. What can be said is that his conception of the driving forces behind the development of the *ius praetorium* provides us with a good explanation for the rapidity with which the praetors of the third and second centuries BC responded to the juridical challenges created by the fast unfolding of the urban and rural economy. If Papinian was right, the praetors of this period did not regard it as part of their responsibilities to facilitate economic development or growth. A more likely explanation for the remarkable willingness of law-making magistrates to create new legal remedies is that they were structurally disposed to find new solutions to juridical problems *resulting* from the emergence of an increasingly complex economy.

The creation of the aedilician edict concerning sales of slaves and draft animals should be seen in the same light. In a recent publication

[16] Examples include Ulpian's endorsement of Labeo's view that the praetor may assign the *administratio tutelae* to one of the *tutores legitimi* if others among them are mentally deranged or absent (D. 26.4.5.2; Ulp. 35 *ad ed.*), the recognition by the early imperial jurists that an *impubes infanti proximus* who can speak but does not understand what he is doing can carry out a valid stipulation (D. 46.6.6; Gai. 27 *ad ed. prov.*), and Papinian's endorsement of the prevailing view that a master can acquire possession of a thing when a slave acquires it *ex peculiari causa*, even if the former is unaware of the acquisition (D. 41.2.44.1; Pap. 23 *quaest.*). For some cautious criticisms of Ankum's interpretation of particular passages of the *Digest*, see Kruse (2006: 36); Stagl (2009: 309 n. 47). Navarra (2002) argues that the classical jurists did not use *utilitas* as an argument to endorse an existing opinion or to buttress a new solution; but see Ankum (2016: 1130–1).

that draws heavily on insights derived from new institutional economics, Frier and Kehoe analyse the aims and effects of this edict from the perspective of economic efficiency (Frier and Kehoe 2007: 120–1). Their starting observation is that "one-off" transactions involving valuable objects of sale have a special attraction to unscrupulous sellers because no long-term relationship of trust is involved. This problem is particularly acute where the object of sale is complex, making it possible for sellers to hide essential information. Applying this idea to the Roman slave trade, Frier and Kehoe point out that the deceptive practices of sellers trying to sell defective slaves were bound to result in an inefficient "lemon market" in which potential buyers demanded large discounts, thereby discouraging sellers of sound slaves from entering the market. Building on this analysis, they argue that the edict must have been issued with the aim of restoring confidence in the market by giving buyers an opportunity to undo the sale when the slave turned out to be defective.

This is certainly a highly original way of looking at the aedilician edict. We must, however, be careful not to confuse the probable economic effects of the edict with the perceptions and aims of the aediles who created it. In this context it seems significant that the comments of the classical jurists do not refer to the problem of honest sellers being deterred by low market prices or to any other form of "market failure". The only text alluding to the considerations that prompted the aediles to issue their edict, a fragment from Ulpian's commentary on the aedilician edict, states that "the reason for the promulgation of this edict is to take measures against the deceptive practices of sellers and to offer help to any buyers who have been deceived by sellers" (D. 21.1.1.2; Ulp. 1 *ad ed. aed. cur.*). We should therefore consider the possibility that the aediles might have perceived the problems caused by unscrupulous sellers or by the difficulty of obtaining full information on the defects present in slaves or draft animals in purely juridical terms.

4.4. LATE REPUBLICAN DEVELOPMENTS AND INTERPRETATION BY JURISTS

So far I have argued that many legal remedies belonging to the *ius honorarium* were introduced during the third and second centuries

BC, and indeed there are indications to suggest that the pace of legal innovation slowed down during the first century BC.[17] It is true that there are a number of important exceptions. One of these is the *interdictum Salvianum*, a new legal remedy which made it possible for lessors of agricultural land to obtain possession of any draft animals or equipment that a tenant had brought with him to the farm after concluding a contract of *locatio conductio* (Kaser 1982: 140–4; de Neeve 1984: 47–53). Another is the *actio Serviana*, which could be used to obtain possession of pieces of property that had been pledged. The latter remedy is thought to have been introduced by the jurist Servius Sulpicius Rufus, who was elected praetor in 65 BC (Kaser 1982: 8).[18] The *actio Publiciana*, available to those possessors who would become owners after one or two years, depending on whether the thing in their possession was a piece of movable property or a piece of real estate, seems to have been introduced by Q. Publicius, one of the praetors of 67 BC (Schulz 1951: 375; Kaser 1971: 438; Frier 1985: 51).[19]

Despite the introduction of these important innovations, there are clear signs that the praetorian edict was beginning to acquire a more or less stable form (Schiavone 2012: 358). Although some degree of fluidity persisted until the drafting of the Perpetual Edict under Hadrian, there is no secure evidence for new praetorian or aedilician remedies being created after the end of the Republic.[20]

[17] I am not suggesting that the *formulae* of those actions which were introduced during the third or second centuries remained unaltered during the second and first centuries BC. See Watson (1965) and Fiori (2012: 64). As Capogrossi Colognesi (2012: 170–1) points out, the contracts referred to in Cato the Elder's *De agri cultura*, written in around 160 BC, display various peculiarities not found in classical Roman law. This strongly suggests that the process of developing a neat contractual typology into which most contractual obligations could be fitted was still underway in the mid-second century BC.

[18] As Kaser points out, there is nothing to support the much earlier date suggested by Watson (1974: 32 and 41). Cf. also Frier (1985: 262).

[19] Watson (1968: 104–7) points out that the earliest surviving text referring to the *actio Publiciana* is from Neratius, who lived around AD 100, and that there may have been many other *Publicii* who held the praetorship, but the relative dearth of fragments from jurists living in the first century AD makes it impossible to use the silence of the surviving texts as an argument for a late date, and no other convincing candidate after whom the *actio Publiciana* might have been named has been identified. Cf. previous footnote for the insoluble controversy concerning the dating of the *actio Serviana*.

[20] The late republican and early imperial jurist Labeo widened the scope for using a *formula* starting with a description (*praescriptio*) of the specific circumstances for which the praetor was asked to intervene in certain cases not covered by any of the *actiones* listed in the edict, but the result was not the creation of a new action. See the illuminating discussion by Schiavone (2012: 334–5 and 413).

As the example of Servius Sulpicius Rufus shows, certain members of the senatorial elite who had received juridical training were beginning to play a prominent part in the development of Roman law during the last century of the Republic.[21] During the Principate jurists completely replaced law-making magistrates as custodians and developers of Roman civil law. As we have just seen, this change coincided with the gradual freezing of the praetorian edict. Taken in conjunction, these changes signify an important shift in the nature of Roman law-making. While the praetors of the final centuries of the Republic used their edictal powers to introduce large numbers of new legal remedies, the classical jurists devoted their efforts to adapting and extending the law through creative interpretation. It has been plausibly suggested that the need for drastic legal change diminished during the early empire because the most important economic changes had already taken place during the last three centuries BC (Garnsey and Saller 2014: 82). Some further changes undoubtedly occured and more satisfactory solutions were found for juridical problems arising from existing economic structures, but this could be done by developing and cautiously extending existing legal principles.[22]

These observations imply that the question as to whether Roman law furthered or impeded economic development acquires a new meaning with the start of the Principate. Since no completely new legal remedies were created, we can only ask how the jurists of the period 31 BC–AD 235 dealt with juridical problems arising from relationships between landowners, tenants, craftsmen, merchants, or bankers. Did the jurists invariably adopt a flexible approach in dealing with such issues or were they inclined to hang on to certain legal rules or principles that are likely to have impeded economic development or growth?

From the point of view of economic history, the topic of "agency" is of particular interest. According to modern definitions, the concept of "agency" refers to a situation in which an agent A, when concluding a transaction with a third party C on behalf of a principal B, creates a binding relationship between B and C without binding himself. In

[21] The best discussion of this topic is Frier (1985), although this monograph focuses too much on the age of Cicero as the crucial turning point.

[22] Of course it would be absurd to claim that the law remained utterly static, but it remains significant that few entirely new legal remedies seem to have been created during the Principate.

the modern world this legal device is seen as an essential requirement for the effective use of division of labour in processes of production and distribution.

It is a well-known fact that the classical jurists hang on to the principle that those "agents" capable of binding their fathers, masters, or principals could not do so without also binding themselves. From a strictly modern point of view this stance might look unsophisticated and ill-suited to the needs of a well-developed economy. However, as many scholars have pointed out, the "failure" of Roman law to develop the modern concept of agency may plausibly be interpreted as reflecting the importance of the *familia* in social and economic life. Given the centrality of this social institution, it is only to be expected that dependent members of the *familia*, such as slaves and sons subject to paternal authority, were extensively used as "agents" (e.g. Gordon 1983; Kirschenbaum 1987; Johnston 1999: 99–100).

In the case of slaves the basic rule that "agents" could not avoid binding themselves had no practical significance, since slaves could not be sued. It was possible to bring a lawsuit against a dependent son, but in this case the judgment could only be executed after the son in question had become *sui iuris* (Kaser 1966: 148–9). So here too the obligation incurred by the "agent" had little practical meaning.

If an entrepreneur had appointed a person *sui iuris* as a ship's captain or as a business manager, those who had done business with the captain or business manager had two options: they could sue either the "agent" or his principal. Under normal circumstances the third party must have preferred the second option, for the simple reason that most agents were poorer than their principals.

Since the rules governing "agency" are likely to have produced results that were entirely satisfactory from a practical point of view, it is hardly surprising that the classical jurists saw no need for any far-reaching innovations. In around AD 200 Papinian widened the scope for the use of "agents" by making it possible to sue the principals of administrators (*procuratores*) of private property with a lawsuit based on the *actio institoria*. This development might have been prompted by the fact that ex-slaves and freeborn individuals were more frequently used as administrators during the Principate than had been the case during the Republic (Kaser 1971: 608–9).[23]

[23] Between the early second and early third centuries AD the jurists also came round to the view that a person could acquire rights through an independent

Another topic that has attracted a considerable amount of attention from legal and economic historians is the Roman law of partnership. From a modern point of view the Roman *societas* displays two peculiarities that might be seen as impediments to commercial development. One of these is that, with two or three exceptions, a *socius* could not be held liable for any transactions concluded between one of his partners and a third party (Kaser 1971: 574; Johnston 1999: 107). The other peculiarity is that the *societas* ceased to exist as soon as one of the partners died or if one of the *socii* decided to sue his partner or partners with the *actio pro socio* (cf. §4.2 above).

The main question is whether these peculiarities are likely to have had any negative impact on economic activities. In all likelihood, the reason why the Roman *societas* did not have any external effects was simply that the principal aim of the contract of partnership was to pool resources and to share costs (Johnston 1999: 107). Third parties doing business with a member of a modern partnership have the possibility of holding the other partner or partners liable. This affords them with more security than they would otherwise have had. In Roman law, however, additional security could easily be obtained by demanding personal or real security (de Ligt 2007). In many cases the person providing security would not have been one of the other *socii*, but in the case of the *societates vectigalium* (tax-farming companies) the Roman state appears to have forced the partners of the *manceps* who had "bought" or "leased" the right to collect certain state taxes to provide security by prescribing that only those *socii* who had done so would be entitled to a share in the profits (van Gessel 2003; *SEG* 39, 1180, ll.105–9).

The seemingly inconvenient rule that the death of one of the *socii* had the effect of terminating the partnership might signify no more than that the Roman *familia* was seen as a more appropriate vehicle for long-term economic cooperation (see Hansmann, Kraakman, and Squire in this volume). The main strength of the Roman *societas* might have been precisely that it was a flexible instrument for short-term cooperation, allowing economic actors to adjust quickly to the opportunities offered by a shifting market (Bang 2008: 275). Viewed in this light it is all the more significant that in the late Republic the *societates vectigalium* were already given "the right to

procurator. See Johnston (1999: 106). For the increasing use of freedmen as *procuratores*, see Schäfer (1998: 198–200).

have a corporate body" (*ius corporis habendi*). Partnerships enjoying this privileged status were not dissolved by the death of a single *socius*, and a partner belonging to a *societas vectigalium* was allowed to sue his *socius* with an *actio pro socio* without bringing about the end of the partnership.[24] The main reason for creating these anomalies must have been that the Roman state wanted to be sure that the *societas* responsible for the collection of certain public revenues would have a stable existence during the whole period of the contract. It does not seem far-fetched to suppose that Roman legislators or the Roman jurists would have taken similar steps to ensure the durability of other types of *societas* had there been an urgent need for greater permanency.

In the context of a discussion focusing on the degree of flexibility displayed by the classical jurists, a brief examination of the rules governing the contract of *depositum* cannot be avoided. It is generally agreed that the legal concept of *depositum* originally referred to a contract obliging the depositary to give back the object or objects he had received. Accepting the obligation to look after a *res deposita* was traditionally seen as a favor, and this explains why initially no payments were involved.

As early as the third quarter of the first century BC the republican jurist Alfenus Varus appears to have recognized the possibility of depositing money while putting the depositary under the obligation to return the same amount of money rather than the same coins (D. 19.2.31; Alf. 5 *dig. a Paulo epit.*). The later classical jurists appear to have been divided over the question as to whether such "irregular" deposits should not be regarded rather as loans (*mutua*) (Klami 1969). Another controversial point was whether and under what circumstances someone who had deposited money "irregularly", or had given the depositary permission to use a deposited sum, could claim interest. Although the surviving texts are contradictory, it looks as if Cervidius Scaevola (active during the reign of Marcus Aurelius) was the only classical jurist to maintain that interest could be claimed if the depository had undertaken that the money received by him would yield a profit, and not simply if he used the money for his own

[24] *Ius corporis habendi*: Cimma (1981: 239); Malmendier (2002: 241–59). Possibility of bringing an action on partnership *manente societate* (with the partnership continuing to exist): D. 17.2.65.15 (Paul. 32 *ad ed.*).

purposes, but also after he lent it out to a third party (D. 16.3.28; Scaev. 1 *resp.*).[25]

The reluctance of the classical jurists to shift their position regarding the rules governing *depositum* has been interpreted as an indication that they were slow to take account of commercial realities (Garnsey and Saller 2014: 82). It is, however, possible to defend a more optimistic view. While there is clear evidence of financial entrepreneurs accepting loans, acting as paying agents and lending out money, most credit and lending appears to have taken place outside a strictly commercial context, on the basis of personal relationships (Johnston 1999: 86). It must also be emphasized that all of the classical jurists recognized the possibility of entrusting money to other people, including bankers, in such a way that it could be lent out. The only disputed issues were whether or not such transactions should be regarded as deposits or as loans, and exactly which legal arrangement had to be made by lenders or depositors wanting to receive interest. While these controversies are of great interest from a juridical point of view, their impact on the realities of financial and commercial life are likely to have been minimal.

My final example concerns the law of servitudes. From a fragment of Ulpian's commentary on the praetorian edict (D. 8.3.5; Ulp. 17 *ad ed.*), it appears that Neratius Priscus, a jurist of the late first and early second centuries AD, held the opinion that a person who did not own a nearby estate could not create a servitude to dig for clay or to burn lime on another person's land. According to Neratius, even the owner of a nearby estate could create such a servitude only in so far as it was required by the needs of his own estate. Elaborating on these observations, the Severan jurist Paul observes that it is not possible to create a servitude giving the owner of a nearby estate the right to dig up more clay than is required to produce the vessels needed to transport the crops harvested from that particular estate or to make roof tiles for the farm building (D. 8.3.6 pr.; Paul. 15 *ad Plaut.*). As he

[25] A fragment from a treatise written by Paul, a pupil of Scaevola, states that if a depositor gives the depositary permission to use a deposited sum of money, the latter starts to shoulder the risk because the money begins to behave as a loan rather than as a deposited sum (Paul., *Sent.* 2.12.9). In another fragment from the same treatise (D. 16.3.29.1; Paul. 2 *Sent.*) Paul recognizes the availability of the *actio depositi* in the case of 'irregular' deposits. One way of reconciling these seemingly contradictory positions is to interpret the first fragment restrictively as dealing exclusively with the issue of risk rather than as referring to a change in the nature of the contract.

explains, these restrictions imply that a servitude of digging for clay cannot be created with the aim of setting up a pottery producing vessels for the market.[26]

The rationale behind the views of Neratius and Paul is the purely juridical consideration that no servitude can be created unless the two requirements of *vicinitas* (ownership of a nearby estate) and *utilitas fundi* (usefulness for the estate) are met (Kaser 1971: 442). At first sight the consistent application of these criteria might seem to have restricted the scope for at least some types of rural craft production. However, as Paul explains in the final sentence of his comment, anyone wanting to dig up more clay than is required by the needs of a rural estate has the option of creating a right of usufruct (*ususfructus*) that will end with the death of the person who has acquired it. Leasing the clay pits must have been an alternative option. Presumably this option does not appear in Paul's comment because his discussion focuses on absolute rights.

The lesson to be learned from these texts is therefore that the understandable reluctance on the part of the classical jurists to allow too much scope for the creation of permanent servitudes did not keep them from finding alternative solutions that were fully compatible with the needs and ambitions of enterprising landowners or artisans keen to gain access to other people's resources.

4.5. CONCLUSIONS

Let us now return to the questions with which we started this chapter. Should we think of Roman law as flexibly adapting itself to the needs of an increasingly sophisticated economy, or did the praetors and jurists of the republican and imperial periods hang on to certain principles that can be said to have impeded economic development or growth?

Although my survey of more than five hundred years of legal history has been deliberately superficial, everything suggests that the former view is correct. It is unquestionably true that the praetors and jurists were reluctant to sacrifice certain basic ideas and assumptions,

[26] For a good discussion of these texts, see Capogrossi Colognesi (2012: 189–90).

but in almost every case they managed to find solutions that were completely satisfactory from a practical point of view.

At the same time there is nothing to suggest that praetors or jurists perceived economic development or growth as an important goal of those responsible for introducing new legal remedies or for the creative reinterpretation of existing ones. Instead, we find clear indications that law-making magistrates and jurists were intellectually disposed to perceive any challenges created by new economic developments from a strictly juridical angle. Papinian thought that *utilitas publica* had been an important aim of the republican praetors, and some thirty fragments of the classical jurists refer to *utilitas* as a decisive consideration, but as we have seen these concepts should be interpreted as referring to the desirability of finding solutions that were satisfactory from the point of view of practical juridical life rather than to any form of economic expediency or efficiency.

If we abstract from the goals pursued by law-making magistrates and jurists and from those considerations that appear to have guided their policies and decisions, we can still say that during a period spanning more than five centuries Roman law-makers created a clear system of property rights as well as an impressive range of contracts based on sophisticated and flexible legal concepts. In assessing the economic implications of the existence of this highly developed body of law, we must bear in mind that Roman society was characterized by enormous discrepancies in wealth and power, making it difficult for people of modest means to sue more powerful opponents or at least to bring any lawsuits involving such people to a successful conclusion.[27] In other words, even in situations in which property rights were crystal-clear, many litigants of humble status are likely to have encountered great difficulties when trying to enforce well-founded claims, and many powerful adversaries may have been disinclined to aim for the economically most efficient outcomes through cooperative bargaining. Still it seems a safe supposition that the existence of a large body of law assigning well-specified property rights and clear contractual claims and obligations created a favourable context for all kinds of economic activities.[28]

[27] This is the central point of Kelly (1966a). For a somewhat more optimistic view, see Johnston (1999: 123–4).

[28] A large proportion of litigation must have taken place between parties of approximately equal social standing.

A question that is more difficult to answer is whether Roman law can also be seen as an independent force that promoted the expansion of the Roman economy. The pattern of development followed by Roman law between the middle Republic and the early third century AD suggests that law-making magistrates and jurists were fundamentally pragmatic, and that Roman law developed *pari passu* with the economy. It would, however, be going too far to characterize the impressive body of remedies, concepts, rules, and interpretations created by Roman law-makers as a prime mover of economic change.[29]

REFERENCES

Ando, Clifford. 2015. "Fact, Fiction, and Social Reality in Roman Law," in M. del Mar and W. Twining, eds, *Legal Fictions in Theory and Practice*. Heidelberg: Springer, 295–323.

Ankum, Johan A. 1968. "*Utilitatis causa receptum*: On the Pragmatical Methods of the Roman Jurists," in Johan A. Ankum, Robert Feenstra, and Wilhelmus F. Leemans, eds, *Symbolae Iuridicae et Historicae Martino David Dedicatae*, vol. 1. Leiden: Brill, 1–31.

Ankum, Hans. 2016. "*Utilitatis causa* en los trabajos de los juristas clásicos romanos." 43 *Revista Chilena de Derecho* 1121–32.

Ankum, Hans, and Eric Pool. 1989. "Rem in bonis meis esse and rem in bonis meam esse: Traces of the Development of Roman Double Ownership," in Peter Birks, ed., *New Perspectives in the Roman Law of Property: Essays for Barry Nicholas*. Oxford: Oxford University Press, 5–41.

Arangio-Ruiz, Vincenzo. 1950. *La società in diritto romano*. Naples: Jovene.

Aubert, Jean-Jacques. 1994. *Business Managers in Ancient Rome: A Social and Economic History, 200 BC–AD 250*. Leiden: Brill.

Bang, Peter. 2008. *The Roman Bazaar: A Comparative Study of Trade and Markets in a Tributary Empire*. Cambridge: Cambridge University Press.

Buckland, William Warwick. 1921. *A Textbook of Roman Law from Augustus to Justinian*. Cambridge: Cambridge University Press.

Bürge, Alfons. 1999. *Römisches Privatrecht. Rechtsdenken und gesellschaftliche Verankerung. Eine Einführung*. Darmstadt: Wissenschafliche Buchgesellschaft.

[29] The author would like to thank Paul du Plessis and Dennis Kehoe for helpful comments on an earlier version of this chapter.

Capogrossi Colognesi, Luigi. 2012. *Padroni e contadini nell'Italia reppublicana*. Rome: L'Erma di Bretschneider.

Cimma, Maria Rosa. 1981. *Ricerche sulle società di publicani*. Milan: Giuffrè.

Cornell, Tim J. 1995. *The Beginnings of Rome: Italy and Rome from the Bronze Age to the Punic Wars (c.1000–264 BC)*. London and New York: Routledge.

Coşkun, Altay. 2009. *Bürgerrechtsentzug oder Fremdenausweisung? Studien zu den Rechten von Latinern und weiteren Fremden sowie zum Bürgerrechtswechsel in der römischen Republik (5. bis frühes 1. Jh. v. Chr.)*. Stuttgart: Steiner.

Crawford, Michael H., ed. 1996. *Roman Statutes*. 2 vols. Institute of Classical Studies. London: University of London.

Crook, John. 1990. Review of Peter Birks, ed., *New Perspectives in the Roman Law of Property* (1989). *Classical Review* 40.2 (1990): 331–3.

de Ligt, Luuk. 1999. "Legal History and Economic History: The Case of the *actiones adiecticiae qualitatis*." 67 *Tijdschrift voor Rechtsgeschiedenis* 205–26.

de Ligt, Luuk. 2002. "D. 15,1,1,1 and the Early History of the *actio quod iussu*," in Luuk de Ligt et al., eds, *Viva vox iuris Romani: Essays in Honour of Johannes Emil Spruit*. Amsterdam: Gieben, 197–204.

de Ligt, Luuk. 2007. "Roman Law and the Roman Economy: Three Case Studies." 66 *Latomus* 10–25.

de Neeve, Pieter W. 1984. *Colonus: Private Farm-Tenancy in Roman Italy during the Republic and the Early Principate*. Amsterdam: Gieben.

Fiori, Roberto. 2012. "The Roman Conception of Contract," in Thomas A. J. McGinn, ed., *Obligations in Roman Law: Past, Present, and Future*. Ann Arbor: University of Michigan Press, 40–75.

Frier, Bruce W. 1985. *The Rise of the Roman Jurists: Studies in Cicero's* Pro Caecina. Princeton: Princeton University Press.

Frier, Bruce W., and Dennis P. Kehoe. 2007. "Law and Economic Institutions," in Walter Scheidel, Ian Morris, and Richard Saller, eds, *The Cambridge Economic History of the Greco-Roman World*. Cambridge: Cambridge University Press, 113–43.

Furubotn, Eirik G., and Richter, Rudolf. 2005. *Institutions and Economic Theory: The Contribution of New Institutional Economics*. 2nd edn. Ann Arbor: University of Michigan Press.

Garnsey, Peter, and Richard Saller. 2014. *The Roman Empire: Economy, Society and Culture*. 2nd edn. London: Duckworth.

Gordon, William M. 1983. "Agency and Roman Law," in *Studi in onore di Cesare Sanfilippo*, vol. 2. Milan: Giuffrè, 339–49.

Guarino, Antonio. 1988. *La società in diritto romano*. Naples: Jovene.

Heumann, Hermann G., and Emil Seckel. 1926. *Handlexikon zu den Quellen des römischen Rechtes*. 9th edn. Jena: Auflage, Verlag von Gustav Fischer.

Impallomeni, Giambattista. 1955. *L'editto degli edili curuli.* Padua: Cedam.

Jakab, Eva. 1997. *Praedicere und cavere beim Marktkauf: Sachmängel im griechischen und römischen Recht.* Munich: Beck.

Jhering, Rudolf von. 1898. *Geist des römischen Rechtes auf den verschiedenen Stufen seiner Entwicklung.* 2. Teil, 2. Abt., 5th edn. Leipzig: Breitkopf und Härtel.

Johnston, David. 1999. *Roman Law in Context.* Cambridge: Cambridge University Press.

Jolowicz, Herbert F., and Barry Nicholas. 1972. *Historical Introduction to the Study of Roman Law*, 3rd edn. Cambridge: Cambridge University Press.

Kaser, Max. 1966. *Das römische Zivilprozessrecht.* Munich: Beck. Kaser/ Hackl 1996.

Kaser, Max. 1971. *Das römische Privatrecht, I. Das altrömische, das vorklassische und klassische Recht*, 2nd edn. Munich: Beck.

Kaser, Max. 1982. *Studien zum römischen Pfandrecht.* Naples: Jovene.

Kehoe, Dennis. 2007. *Law and the Rural Economy in the Roman Empire.* Ann Arbor: University of Michigan Press.

Kelly, John Maurice. 1966a. *Roman Litigation.* Oxford: Clarendon Press.

Kelly, John Maurice. 1966b. "The Growth-Pattern of the Praetor's Edict." 1 *The Irish Jurist* 341–55.

Kirschenbaum, Aaron. 1987. *Sons, Slaves and Freedmen in Roman Commerce.* Jerusalem and Washington, DC: The Magnes Press and The Catholic University of America Press.

Klami, Hannu T. 1969. *"Mutua magis videtur quam deposita": Über die Geldverwahrung im Denken der römischen Juristen.* Helsinki: Societas Scientiarum Fennica.

Kruse, Constantin. 2006. *Alternative Kausalität im Deliktsrecht: Eine historische und vergleichende Untersuchung.* Berlin: Lit Verlag.

Lenel, Otto. 1927. *Das Edictum Perpetuum: Ein Versuch zu seiner Wiederherstellung.* Leipzig: Tauchnitz.

Malmendier, Ulrike. 2002. *Societas publicanorum: Staatliche Wirtschaftsaktivitäten in den Händen privater Unternehmer.* Vienna and Cologne: Böhlau.

Ménard, Claude, and Mary M. Shirley, eds. 2005. *Handbook of New Institutional Economics.* Berlin-Heidelberg: Springer Verlag.

Navarra, Marialuisa. 2002. *Ricerche sulla utilitas nel pensiero dei giuristi romani.* Turin: Guappichelli.

Roselaar, Saskia. 2012. "The Concept of *commercium* in the Roman Republic." 66 *Phoenix* 381–413.

Schäfer, Christoph. 1998. *Spitzenmanagement in Republik und Kaiserzeit: Die Prokuratoren von Privatpersonen im Imperium Romanum vom 2. Jh. v. Chr. bis zum 3. Jh. n. Chr.* St. Katharinen: Scripta Mercaturae Verlag.

Schiavone, Aldo. 2012. *The Invention of Law in the West*. Trans. Jeremy Carden and Antony Shugaar. Cambridge: The Belknap Press of Harvard University Press.

Schulz, Fritz. 1951. *Classical Roman Law*. Oxford: Clarendon Press.

Serrao, Feliciano. 2000. "Impresa, mercato, diritto: riflessioni minime," in Elio Lo Cascio, ed., *Mercati permanenti e mercati periodici nel mondo romano*. Bari: Edipuglia, 31–67.

Stagl, Jakob F. 2009. *Favor dotis: Die Privilegierung der Mitgift im System des römischen Rechts*. Vienna and Cologne: Böhlau.

van Gessel, Christian. 2003. "Praedes, praedia, cognitores: les sûretés réelles et personnelles de l'adjudicataire du contrat public en droit romain (textes et réflexions)," in Jean-Jacques Aubert, ed., *Tâches publiques et entreprise privée dans le monde romain*. Geneva: Librairie Droz, 95–122.

Watson, Alan. 1965. *The Law of Obligations in the Later Roman Republic*. Oxford: Oxford University Press.

Watson, Alan. 1968. *The Law of Property in the Later Roman Republic*. Oxford: Clarendon Press.

Watson, Alan. 1971. "The Imperatives of the Aedilician Edict." 39 *Tijdschrift voor Rechtsgeschiedenis* 73–84.

Watson, Alan. 1974. *Lawmaking in the Later Roman Republic*. Oxford: Clarendon Press.

Watson, Alan. 1975. *Rome of the XII Tables: Persons and Property*. Princeton and London: Princeton University Press.

Zimmermann, Reinhard. 1996. *The Law of Obligations: Roman Foundations of the Civilian Tradition*. Oxford: Clarendon Press.

Part II

Markets and Trade

5

Setting the Rules of the Game

The Market and Its Working in the Roman Empire

Elio Lo Cascio

5.1. INTRODUCTION

The study of the economies of the ancient world, in particular of the Roman Empire, has been heavily influenced in recent years by the theoretical approach of the new institutional economics (henceforth NIE). The NIE's impact has been felt both on the overall reconstruction of structure and performance of these economies, and on the detailed analysis of specific issues: labor relations, credit, business transactions, the role played by so-called "trading communities," and so on.[1] In addition, the economic analysis of law, or law and economics, has suggested new and powerful, but admittedly controversial perspectives in the interpretation of the incomparably rich evidence of the Roman jurists.[2] The impact of the theoretical framework of the NIE is especially visible in the crucial role attributed to institutions in shaping the evolution of the Roman economy, and therefore in determining its performance: its growth—uncontroversial

[1] e.g. Kehoe (2007a, 2007b); Lo Cascio (2006, 2007); Terpstra (2008, 2013); Verboven (2015); for the impact of NIE also on the interpretation of the structure and performance of the Babylonian economy in the "long sixth century" BCE, see also Jursa (2010, 2013).

[2] e.g. Malmendier (2002), with the discussion of Maganzani (2004); see also Malmendier (2005).

Elio Lo Cascio, *Setting the Rules of the Game: The Market and Its Working in the Roman Empire* In: *Roman Law and Economics: Institutions and Organizations, Volume I*. Edited by: Giuseppe Dari-Mattiacci and Dennis P. Kehoe, Oxford University Press (2020).
DOI: 10.1093/oso/9780198787204.003.0005

as global growth, even if it is hotly debated whether it was also an intensive (i.e. per capita) growth—and its decline. The latter development is much more controversial, since it is either altogether denied, or postponed to the sixth or seventh centuries or even later.

The fundamental questions that arise are, first, whether the political and institutional developments that led to the conquest and the unification of the Mediterranean under the aegis of Rome caused market integration and a reduction of transaction costs, and if so, whether this reduction can explain the economic expansion, in the Italian peninsula of the conquerors and then in the provinces, better than other possible factors, such as the innovation and dissemination of technologies, especially in agriculture. The second question concerns the extent to which the threat of dissolution of a unitary political organization in the third century and then the actual dissolution in the fifth determined what I would define as economic decline.

5.2. CONTRASTING VIEWS ON THE ROLE OF INSTITUTIONS IN PROVOKING GROWTH AND ECONOMIC DECLINE

Nobody disputes the growth of real income experienced by Rome and Italy in the last two centuries of the Republic, and nobody doubts that this growth was the consequence of the conquest and therefore of the unification of the Mediterranean under Roman rule. But there is a lively debate over the factors producing this growth and its limits. Was the increase in total income just the effect of war plunder, of a brutal removal of resources from the progressively conquered regions, the substance of what Max Weber characterized as a "predatory capitalism", in a zero-sum game, or was it instead the result of genuine growth, the effect of the dissemination of more efficient productive processes and an enhanced market exchange? That is to say, what was the crucial factor in spurring this growth, the conquest itself or the political unification of the Mediterranean, which translated into a process of economic integration? Two opposing views of the general development of the Roman economy and of the role of the state in it have recently been proposed, one that can be labeled pessimistic, the other optimistic.

According to the former perspective, defended most recently by Peter Bang (2008), the formation of a tributary empire is the key. Predation went on after the conquest in the form of a regular levy of tribute from the conquered regions by the state and the collection of rents by the imperial elite. The emperors were "stationary bandits," to use the conceptualizations and the terminology of Mancur Olson (Olson 2000). The increase in total income, which had been initially achieved at the expense of the conquered territories, later widened to the subject regions themselves: the imposition of tax had paradoxically positive effects on the economic growth of the provinces, thanks to the triggering of the mechanism of "taxes and trade," according to a model that Walter Scheidel has recently labeled as "Keynesian" (Scheidel 2012: 9).

According to the latter perspective, the changes set in motion by the unification of the Mediterranean space were ultimately responsible for a growth that also affected, from the very beginning, the provincial areas: a process of rationalization in production, with a regional and local specialization, with the enlargement of the cultivated area, and with the increase in the variety and quantity of manufactured goods. The integration of the local economies within the Mediterranean space produced a "Smithian growth" (e.g. Wilson 2009). On the other hand, the political unification of the Mediterranean world under Roman rule and, even more, the establishment of lasting peaceful conditions with the advent of the Principate, in so far as they produced a drastic reduction of transaction costs, are deemed to have been at the root of the various developments that brought about both economic growth and intensification of trade: these were the suppression of piracy and the resulting increased safety of the seaborne commerce, a better circulation of information, which could mitigate the asymmetric positions of the individual economic actors, the spread of common metrological systems, the creation of a single monetary area, and the diffusion of common legal rules in what we can call commercial law (e.g. Lo Cascio 2000, 2007). All this certainly made the definition, protection, and exchange of property rights within the Empire much more secure and therefore less expensive than in the fragmented Mediterranean world of the previous centuries. The ways in which the Roman imperial state was able to secure its survival, drawing as tax a rather small proportion of the surplus and spending it chiefly on providing law and order, and on defense against external threats, were in fact conducive to growth.

The existence of a single political entity embracing the whole of Mediterranean promoted the integration of the economy, through the establishment of long-distance trading webs for the exchange of staples: this network was not simply a thin veneer which covered an economy still overwhelmingly based on subsistence. Moreover, urban centers, especially the larger ones, played a major role in promoting trade within the Mediterranean and the integration of the economy.

To this undeniably consistent general picture of the developments of the Mediterranean world under Roman rule several objections have been addressed on different levels. First of all, the periodization of growth and decline has been questioned. On the one hand, the general re-evaluation of late antiquity, which has characterized scholarship in recent decades, has extended itself also to the economy of the later Empire, especially of its eastern regions. In addition, it has been noted that the expansion of trade relations within the Mediterranean comes before the political unification, and is not the result of it (Bang 2012).

Secondly, the legitimacy of the comparison, often proposed by the so-called "optimists," with the more advanced economies of early modern Europe, is questioned: these economies, it is claimed, developed the institutional innovations in trading activities leading to the emergence of capitalism precisely because they were unable to create an imperial hegemony that extended to the whole of Europe (Bang 2012). The comparison would be more relevant and compelling with the great tributary empires like the Ottoman or the Mughal empire, in which the market would take the form of the bazaar: admittedly a complex market, but irregular in its working and fragmented, characterized by strong imbalances and asymmetries in information and high transaction costs. In such markets the merchants must adopt specific strategies and rely on family connections and personal relations, rather than on impersonal exchange. Prices would be volatile and they would not be formed in the way they are formed in a truly competitive market.

Finally, the vitality and the sheer size of the seaborne trade indicated by the material evidence would be ultimately the product of a huge redistributive activity by the state (e.g. Tchernia 2011), with the *annona civica* and *militaris*—the complex organization for supplying the basic foodstuffs to Rome and the army—and not an indication of an integrated market economy.

5.3. TRIBUTARY EMPIRES, MARKETS, AND REDISTRIBUTION

It seems to me that a careful consideration of the available evidence allows us, first, to question the proposition that the size of the seaborne commerce may be explained exclusively as a product of redistribution by the state: it must be doubted that tax and public spending were so high as to account for such a level of redistribution. The share of the state in the GDP was on the contrary comparatively low, as shown by the estimates that have been proposed recently both of the GDP and of the budget of the state.[3] Moreover, it must be underlined that the redistributive mechanisms still operated in a market scenario (Lo Cascio 2006). Indeed the state aimed to control the working of the market, as shown by the texts I am going to analyze. And the control of the market, which did not translate into a fixing of prices, but into the implementation of mechanisms for ensuring competitiveness, makes Roman markets very different from the model of the bazaar.

If tax and public spending were low in relation with GDP, the legitimacy of adopting Olson's conceptualizations and the characterization of the *princeps* as a "stationary bandit" can be called into question. We have to stress the different role of the new administrative structure that was built around the emperor compared to the republican magistrates, for instance in the realm of taxation. The disappearance of what Weber labeled "predatory capitalism" must be taken into account. This can be seen most clearly in the sharp discontinuity between the late Republic and the Augustan age from this specific point of view: the primacy of Italy in the new Augustan fabric is undeniable, but the most extreme forms of predation disappear. The one who sets the rules of the game now is the emperor, but the nature of the new order and the ambivalent role of the *princeps* make him a player as well, and this obviously affects the way in which the rules of the game are set. The emperor is a player among the other players, since he acts with his patrimony like the other private players. His position is different not because he behaves in a different way, but because he is the most prominent player

[3] Goldsmith (1984); Hopkins (1995/6); Temin (2006); Maddison (2007); Bang (2008); Scheidel-Friesen (2009); Lo Cascio and Malanima (2009, 2014).

(Lo Cascio 2015). And that means that the free market scenario that characterizes late republican Rome is still typical of the imperial age and even, as we will see, of the late Empire.

It is then perfectly understandable why the market, and not reciprocity or redistribution, goes on to be the transactional mode: given this scenario, the defense of a competitive market by the imperial authority seems to be a conscious choice, and a successful one, that fosters growth. In other words, one can say that growth and integration were not merely the unintended and unexpected result of the unification of the Mediterranean under Roman rule, but also the product of the role that the political organization of Rome purposely undertook in regulating market transactions, by guaranteeing the rights of all parties involved—producers, merchants, and consumers—and by curtailing opportunistic behavior, which could alter the working of the market and the formation of prices in it.[4]

5.4. SETTING THE RULES OF THE GAME

What seems to me undeniable in any case is that the rules directed to restrain or to punish speculative behavior would produce the effect of "lubricating" exchanges and of drastically reducing transaction costs, thus allowing the working of a free and competitive market. Boudewijn Sirks, who has defended the thesis of an active and considered promotion of market exchange as early as the late Republic, has appropriately pointed out, in reference to the control of markets at Rome, that "the overseeing magistrates, the aediles, did not regulate prices" (Sirks 2002: 135). It seems to me that the evidence I am going to analyze in detail shows two things: that there was a strict regulation of the market and that this regulation did not normally result in regulating or even fixing prices, but rather aimed at guaranteeing that the price in the *forum rerum venalium* (the "market" in the physical and concrete sense, but also, as we will see, the market in the abstract meaning of economics) would always be the market price, formed through the encounter between supply and demand: a market price conceived as a "fair price."

[4] For what follows in the next two paragraphs, see in more detail Lo Cascio (2018).

Moreover, the imperial state could define and enforce the fundamental "rules of the game," in particular, exclusive property rights, not only in that extension of Rome that was Italy, but also in the provinces, thanks to the spread of the Roman notion (and practice) of private property, fostered by the increase in the number of urban communities with Roman or Latin status. During the Empire, therefore, the *princeps* set the rules of the game first of all at the level of the central and provincial administration, but his actions extended, in various ways, to the level of the thousands of towns. Provincial governors and city governments were both called upon to oversee the enforcement of these rules.

I leave aside most of the manifold imperial interventions that had an impact on the economic relations between private people to focus on what seems to have been a constant policy of the imperial authority: precisely the control of the market in order to avoid opportunistic and speculative behavior. This control was implemented at the town's level by local authorities and sometimes with the intervention of the representative of the center, the governor.

5.4.1. *Pretium iustum, pretium aequum*

Perhaps the first explicit evidence for control of the market with the aim of curtailing speculative behavior is to be found in the *lex Flavia*, the municipal charter issued by Domitian for the communities of Spain on which Vespasian had bestowed the *ius Latii* (a sort of halfway status between the full Roman citizenship and the condition of *peregrini*, foreigners).[5] In ch. 75 there is a rule that sanctions speculative hoarding of goods and cartel agreements to raise the prices: "no one is to buy [*coemito*] or hoard [*supprimito*] anything or join with another or agree or enter into a partnership in order that something may be sold too dearly [*carius*] or not be sold or not be sold in sufficient quantity" (*Ne quis in eo municipio quid coemito supprimito neve coito con|uenito societatemue facito quo quit carius ueneat quoue|quit ne ueneat setiusue ueneat*).[6] The rule aims to safeguard the interests of consumers, by forbidding agreements to distort the correct working of the market. The chapter must be considered in

[5] González and Crawford (1986); Lamberti (1993).

[6] Trans. Harris (2003: 292); see also Harris (2011: 210, cf. 219).

connection with the preceding one, ch. 74, which forbids illegal meetings and associations.[7] Obviously, the rule would have primarily affected the essential foodstuffs, but apparently not just them: such a limitation seems to be excluded by the *quit* ("anything") in the text. It is certainly possible that the fundamental aim of the provision was to guarantee the food supply of the town and no more than that. But even accepting such a conclusion, the point about the rule remains completely valid, mainly because the instrument through which it was expected to attain this result consisted precisely in the safeguarding of the unimpeded working of the market. In fact, the "fair price" appears already in the *lex Flavia* as the market price. The prohibition is to sell *carius* than a price that cannot be other than the price which is formed in the market: this is the only possible explanation. There is no interference of the political organization (the Empire or the individual community) in the functioning of the market, but on the contrary there is an intervention that guarantees the correct working of the market: as Crawford and González have put it, "the chapter merely bans speculation and does not underwrite price control in general."[8]

That the provincial governors were also involved in the suppression of speculative behavior is shown by a well-known fragment of the eighth book of the *De officio proconsulis* (Duties of Proconsul) of Ulpian, included in the title *de extraordinariis criminibus* (extraordinary crimes) of the *Digest* (D. 47.11.6 pr.–1). This is the fragment in which the criminal behavior of the so-called *dardanarii* is discussed:

> *Annonam adtemptare et vexare vel maxime dardanarii solent: quorum avaritiae obviam itum est tam mandatis quam constitutionibus. mandatis denique ita cavetur: "Praeterea debebis custodire, ne dardanarii ullius mercis sint, ne aut ab his, qui coemptas merces supprimunt, aut a locupletioribus, qui fructus suos aequis pretiis vendere nollent, dum minus uberes proventus exspectant, annona oneretur." poena autem in hos varie statuitur: nam plerumque, si negotiantes sunt, negotiatione eis tantum interdicitur, interdum et relegari solent, humiliores ad opus publicum dari.* [1.] *Onerant annonam etiam staterae adulterinae, de quibus divus Traianus edictum proposuit, quo edicto poenam legis Corneliae in eos statuit, perinde ac si lege testamentaria, quod testamentum falsum scripsisset signasset recitasset, damnatus esset.*

[7] Höbenreich (1997: 166ff.). [8] González and Crawford (1986: 224).

> "In particular, forestallers and regraters, speculators generally, interfere with and disturb the corn supply, and a check is put upon their avarice both by imperial instructions and by enactments. By imperial instruction it is provided: 'You must further ensure that forestallers and regraters, speculators generally, indulge in no commerce and that the corn supply is not incommoded either by those who hold back what they have bought or by the more affluent who do not wish to sell their wares at a fair price because they anticipate that the next harvest will be less fruitful.' The penalties for such persons are varied; for, generally, if they be merchants, they are only banned from trading or, in some cases, relegated to an island, while those of the lower orders are condemned to forced labor. 1. The price of corn is also affected by false measures, concerning which the deified Trajan issued an edict whereby he imposed upon those who used them the penalty of the *lex Cornelia*, just as if, under the statute on wills, a person were condemned because he wrote, sealed or read aloud a will which was false." (trans. Watson)

The meaning of the term *dardanarii* is unknown and therefore several hypotheses have been put forward on its origin. I do not think that we have compelling reasons for deciding whether the term derives from the mythological figure of Dardanus, or from the Dardanii, a people of the Balkans area allegedly prone, in the aftermath of Trajan's conquest of Dacia, to the abusive behavior later punished, or whether the term has to be connected with the Greek word *danos*, in the sense of "loan" or "interest," and with the verb *daneizein* (an interpretation which does not seem very convincing, however). I just want to point out that the term *dardanarii* apparently refers to people engaging in abusive actions that were quite varied in scope: on the one hand, speculation consisting in *adtemptare* and *vexare* the *annona* ("interfere with and disturb the corn supply"), by suppressing the *coemptas merces* (by holding back what they have bought, or by refusing to sell the *fructus* of one's property); on the other hand, speculation consisting in counterfeiting the *mensurae* and more specifically the *staterae* (scales), as emerges from the other fragment of the *Digest* (a fragment of Paul) in which the obscure *dardanarii* are mentioned (D. 48.19.37; 1 sent.): "It is agreed that commodity hoarders may be punished *extra ordinem* according to the degree of their crime because of the false size of their measures; this is for the benefit of the people's corn dole" (trans. Watson, *In dardanarios propter falsum mensurarum modum ob utilitatem popularis annonae pro modo admissi extra ordinem vindicari placuit*).

This recalls Trajan's edict cited in Ulpian's *De officio proconsulis*, which extended the penalty established by the *lex Cornelia testamentaria* against those who used *staterae adulterinae* (counterfeit scales).

It seems interesting to me that the crimes of *dardanarii* (translated as "forestallers" and "regraters" in Watson's edition, evidently referring to the definition of prohibited behavior that appears in "Common Law") do not seem to encompass only the crimes of the *negotiatores* and the *mercatores*, but also of the richest landowners, who do not sell the *fructus* "*aequis pretiis*" and instead hoard them because they expect that the future harvest will be less abundant and therefore that prices will rise. I think it significant that the name or at least the identification of a similar criminal behavior brings together landowners and merchants, as the state seeks once again to defend consumers, and, in so doing, singles out, quite explicitly this time, the notion of the *aequum pretium*, the "fair price", as the price that is formed on the market, when speculative behavior is absent.

Another important and much studied text is the very famous edict of Antistius Rusticus, *legatus* of Cappadocia Galatia in the years of Domitian, directed to the citizen colony of Pisidian Antioch.[9] The intervention of the governor was requested by the *duoviri* (the higher magistrates) and the *decuriones* (the members of the council) of the colony: they were lamenting that, because of a harsh winter, the price of grain had shot up and so they asked that the populace might have an adequate amount of grain to buy (*pleps copiam emendi haberet*). Accordingly, the governor establishes that every *colonus* and every *incola* (resident foreigner) of the town must declare before the *duoviri* within thirty days how much grain he has and in what place and how much he needs for *semen* (the seed) and for the *cibaria annua familiae suae* (the foodstuffs of a year for his family): this part must be subtracted, but all the rest must be made available to the *emptores coloniae Antiochensis* (the buyers of the colony: and it is debated whether they are some sort of magistrates, like the *sitonai*, or, as seems more probable, the *Antiochenses* themselves). The time in which or (perhaps better) before which the grain must be sold is set at August 1 (evidently when the produce of the new harvest would have been available: it seems probable that that means that from the time in which the edict was delivered until August 1, the grain was

[9] *AÉ* 1925, 126; see most recently Baroni (2004); Erdkamp (2005: 286–8), and references there.

available to the *emptores*). But the governor also forbids that the grain be sold at more than 1 *denarius* per *modius*, the basis for this maximum price being the fact that the normal market price at Antioch before the dearth was 8 or 9 *asses* a *modius* (that is half or a bit more than a half of one *denarius*). Again what is significant is, first, that the governor intervenes by obliging people hoarding their grain to make it available for selling, and second, that the maximum price is conceived as being twice the normal market price, an oscillation which is deemed to be acceptable, provided that it does not depend on speculation.

The texts examined so far show a specific interest by the authorities for consumers. But there are other texts that show, first, that merchants and producers were also protected, and second, that the "fair price," conceived as the market price, was thought not only to benefit consumers. A fragment of the third book of *De cognitionibus* of Callistratus, included in the title *de nundinis* of the *Digest* (D. 50.11.2), refers to a case in which *cultores agrorum* and *piscatores* have been encouraged (presumably by civic magistrates, such as *agoranomoi* and *aediles*) to bring the *utensilia*, that is the products of land and sea, to the town, in order to sell them themselves. Such an action may prove detrimental to the supply of the town *cum avocentur ab opere rustici*, if the peasants are distracted from their usual occupations. Thus they must hand over (*tradere*)—that is they have to sell to merchants—their produce, or *merx*, immediately where they have brought it and return to their place and resume their activity. Callistratus quotes the passage of Plato's *Republic* in which the social, and even economic, function of the *kapeloi*, the retailers, is underlined. The fragment shows the will to guarantee the defense of the interests of *negotiatores* and *mercatores*, and specifically of the retailers, who are envisioned as fulfilling an important social and economic function. This view can be considered a significant departure from the traditional contempt towards them expressed, most clearly, in the famous passage in Cicero's *De officiis* (1.42.150–1).

The idea that a fair price is fair precisely because it is the market one, and that only speculative behavior can alter it, is found in a series of fragments of the *Digest* that refer to the role that the decurions (the members of the local senate) must play in order to ensure the regular supply of foodstuffs to their city. What is interesting in these fragments is that they seem to aim at defending the interests not only of the consumers and the traders, but also, in a sense, of the producers.

One of these fragments (D. 48.12.3 pr.–1; Papirius Iustus 1 *de const.*) refers to a rescript by Marcus and Verus, in which it is affirmed that "it is grossly unjust for the decurions to sell grain to their citizens more cheaply than the corn supply requires" (trans. Watson, *Minime aequum est decuriones civibus suis frumentum vilius quam annona exigit vendere*). The jurist adds that the same emperors wrote that "it is not lawful for the *ordo* [of decurions] of any *civitas* to lay down the price of any grain which is found" (*ius non esse ordini cuiusque civitatis pretium grani quod invenitur statuere*). A text of the Severan-age jurist Marcian (D. 50.1.8; 1 *de iudic. publ.*) also refers to a rescript of these same emperors, whose content would have been present in other imperial enactments, and on whose basis "decurions were not to be forced to provide corn to their fellow citizens at less than the market price" (*Non debere cogi decuriones vilius praestare frumentum civibus suis, quam annona exigit*). In still another fragment (D. 50.8.7 [5]; Paul. 1 sent.) it is stated that "decurions may not be forced to provide corn at a price cheaper than the price of corn at the time in their *patria*" (*Decuriones pretio viliori frumentum, quod annona temporalis est patriae suae, praestare non sunt cogendi*). Finally a fragment of Ulpian (D. 7.1.27.3; 18 *ad Sab.*) can be compared with these passages. In this fragment the jurist says quite explicitly, in the context of a discussion of the *onera* of the *fructuarii*, that "as a matter of fact, occupiers of land generally sell a fixed portion of the fruits of their land to the municipal authorities at a lower price" (*nam solent possessores certam partem fructuum municipio viliori pretio addicere*)—but it is not said explicitly in comparison with what price this price is lower. Various interpretations have been offered recently of these passages, on which I do not dwell.[10] It seems to me that Jean-Michel Carrié has advanced the most convincing explanation when he has seen in the first fragment "la défense d'une sorte de libéralisme économique déliberé, exprimant un choix social et impliquant une réflexion élémentaire sur la formation du prix et sur son rôle économique: il est un niveau minimum au dessus duquel les prix doivent se tenir pour stimuler la production agricole."[11] The constitution of Marcus and Verus quoted in the fragment of Papirius Iustus aims at defending the interests of the decurions, who could be obliged by popular pressure to sell

[10] See Lo Cascio (2018) and references there.

[11] Carrié (1975: 1096–7).

below the market price.[12] In a period of crisis the emperors felt themselves obliged to defend the local senates from intolerable pressures. (I would add that the ruling of Marcus and Verus would be perfectly understandable in a phase of probable general disruption of the urban supplies, following the spread of the Antonine plague, in the sixties of the second century CE.)

However these texts are interpreted, a conclusion seems to emerge: that imperial intervention was certainly aimed at "regulating" the market, in order to avoid speculative behavior, but that an additional preoccupation, and one which was suggested by a feeling of equity, was to avoid an artificial lowering of prices. The "comparative advantage in violence,"[13] which gives the state the authority to set and the concrete possibility to enforce the "rules of the game" in market transactions between private economic actors, could therefore add considerably to the efficiency of contracting, by protecting the interests of all the parties involved.

It might be significant that the imperial interventions quoted in the various texts that have been examined in detail—both those that reveal the attention of the imperial power towards the interests of consumers and those which witness a similar attention towards *negotiatores* and *locupletes*—all fall within the decades ranging from the *divi fratres* (Marcus and Verus) to the Severans. These are the decades in which, in consequence of the wars and above all of the plague spreading all over the regions under Roman rule since the mid-160s, the Empire was entering a phase of crisis. This crisis had its obvious outcome in the financial crisis of the state and of the towns.

5.5. A DIFFERENT SCENARIO IN LATE ANTIQUITY?

I think in any case that a result of the crisis cannot have been a shift towards a "dirigiste" policy, which would anticipate the economic scenario of late antiquity: a more decided tendency towards the pervasiveness of the so-called "administered trade."[14] In recent

[12] Durliat (1990: 295ff.); Höbenreich (1997: 178ff.).

[13] North (1979: 250).

[14] Lo Cascio (2009a: 273–85).

decades, the traditional view of a strong opposition between an economy based on free markets of the high Empire and the economy of late antiquity, which Rostovtzeff once defined as "a blend of oriental *étatisme* and city-state socialism" (in the essay on "The Decay of the Ancient World and Its Economic Explanations," published in *The Economic History Review* of 1930),[15] has proven to be untenable on several grounds as a result of a thorough analysis of all the evidence, especially the juridical sources. The free market scenario still seems to be prevailing or to be even more pervasive than before. Thus it is debatable whether it is legitimate to speak of an increasing importance of redistributive mechanisms different from the market, that is, of "administered trade" put into effect by a "dirigiste" policy of the "state," or, according to another view, influential in the past, of an opposition between the natural economy of the "state" and the monetary economy of the private sector. The complex rules regulating the *annona civica* and *militaris* (the collection of goods to be distributed to the populace at Rome and to the soldiers), with the procedures of *adaeratio* (the commutation of the levy in kind from the tax-payers into a monetary contribution) and *coemptio* (the compulsory purchase of the goods), presuppose, as I have argued elsewhere,[16] the working of the market and price formation in it. What changed was perhaps the degree of market integration across the Mediterranean area, with a decrease in long-distance seaborne commerce, apparently attested by the decreasing number of shipwrecks from the second half of the second century CE onwards (e.g. Wilson 2009). But even this conclusion has to be nuanced. On the one hand, the markets of the first two centuries are thought to have been certainly less "integrated" or less "interdependent" than Peter Temin would suggest (Temin 2013), as is shown, if anywhere, by certain very clear passages in the Elder Pliny (*HN* 23.164) and in Gaius (D. 13.4.3; 9 *ad ed. prov.*), both stressing the variety of prices of different things in different places. On the other hand, the economic fragmentation of the Mediterranean empire from the third century CE onwards was certainly less pronounced than commonly believed, as is shown *inter alia* by the evidence of the maritime routes for which the maximum freights were established by Diocletian's price edict. It goes without saying that to recognize the continuing working and even the vitality

[15] Reprinted in Rostovtzeff (1995: 215–30).
[16] Lo Cascio (2009a: 273–85); Lo Cascio (2007).

of free market mechanisms does not necessarily amount to giving a positive evaluation of the performance of the economy in the fourth century, let alone in the fifth, especially in the western half of the Empire. It is the contention of this chapter that the preservation of a free market scenario was the result of a recognizable and to some extent conscious choice of the "state." As we have seen, the role that the imperial administration already undertook purposefully during the Principate was in fact to regulate market transactions, by guaranteeing the rights of all involved parties—producers, merchants, and consumers—and by preventing opportunistic or speculative behavior, which could alter the working of the market and the formation of prices in it. And one can conclude that, by regulating the market in this way, the authorities (at the local, provincial, and central level) contributed to the drastic reduction of transaction costs brought about by the unification of the Mediterranean under Roman rule.

Several passages in the *Digest*, as we have seen, show this concern. But this role of the imperial administration is still or even more visible in the evidence offered, on the one hand, by some laws of the Codes of Theodosius and of Justinian and, on the other hand, for Ostrogothic Italy, by some of Cassiodorus' *Variae* (which, given the substantial continuity of the economic, social, and administrative structures between the late Western Empire and the kingdom of Theoderic and his successors, can be taken to reflect to a large extent late Roman conditions). I will analyze in detail this evidence in what follows.

Some of these texts show, first of all, that public authority sought to ensure the working of a competitive market by preventing a too dominant position of any of the actors involved. Thus a specific concern on the part of the imperial authorities to defend the interests of merchants (and also of consumers) against the power of the big landowners is revealed by a law of Honorius and Theodosius II of 408 or 409 (C. 4.63.3): the emperors forbid the noblest and richest (*Nobiliores natalibus et honorum luce conspicuos et patrimonio ditiores*) from exercising trade (*mercimonium*) which can be harmful (*perniciosum*) to towns, and they do so with a clear intention "so that between the commoner and the merchant the exchange could be easier" (*ut inter plebeium et negotiatorem facilius sit emendi vendendique commercium*). The aim is to curb speculation, which prevents the formation of a market price.

5.6. *PRETIA IUSTA, AEQUA ET LEGITIMA* IN LATE ANTIQUITY

Other texts show that the prices which were formed by the meeting of demand and supply were thought to be *aequa* or *iusta*, and *legitima*. They seem to give, therefore, a positive evaluation, in moral terms, of the working of the market as a market and even a justification of the volatility of prices, if that was not the result of speculative practices. The expression of *aequum pretium* was already present in the famous passage of Ulpian we analyzed above on the so-called *dardanarii*, with reference to the richest landowners, who did not sell their *fructus* "aequis pretiis" and instead hoarded them because they expected the next harvest to be less abundant and therefore prices to rise. The expression *iustum pretium*, on the other hand, is used by the same Ulpian in a fragment taken from his *De officio praefecti urbi* referring to the sale of *caro porcina* (pork) in the *forum suarium*: the *praefectus urbi* has to see to it that the meat is sold *iusto pretio*, that is without speculation (D. 1.12.1.11: *Cura carnis omnis ut iusto pretio praebeatur ad curam praefecturae pertinet, et ideo et forum suarium sub ipsius cura est*). Now one of the dispositions about the supply of pigs for Roman consumption that we read in the title *De suariis, pecuariis et susceptoribus vini ceterisque corporatis* of the Theodosian Code (14.4.4) says explicitly that the *pretium* on which the complex procedure of *adaeratio* ought to be based must be the *legitimum* one, that is, the *pretium* of the *Romanum forum*. The law seems to convey not only the idea that the price to be considered, in order to calculate the rate of *adaeratio*, must be the prescribed price, *legitimum* in this sense, but also that this is the prescribed price in so far as it is the market price current in the place where the contribution has to be delivered.

The expression *pretia iusta* appears in a letter written by Cassiodorus as the praetorian prefect of King Witiges in 536–7 (*Var.* 12.26): because of a crop failure, the requisitioning of wine, grain, and millet "for the supply of the army" (*in apparatum exercitus*) had to be condoned in some districts of northeastern Italy (Concordia, Aquileia, and Forum Iulii). However, since there was an abundant production of wine in Istria, wine could be collected there: but *pretia iusta* must be paid for it, so that the people of this region would not suffer harm. The *pretia iusta* are clearly the *pretia* of the *forum rerum venalium*, that is, the free-market prices: "and since I have learnt that much wine has been produced in Istria, you are to demand from there an amount equal to what had been requested from the above mentioned cities—at market rates, so that the Istrians themselves may suffer no injury, when just prices are preserved for their benefit" (trans. Barnish; *Et quoniam in Histria vinum abunde natum esse comperimus, exinde, quantum de supra dictis civitatibus speratum est, postulate, sicut in foro rerum venalium reperitur, quatenus nec ipsi laedi possint, cum eis pretia iusta servantur*).

Another of the *Variae* of Cassiodorus, which contains the *Edictum pretiorum per Flaminiam*, speaks of, the "justness of prices," *pretiorum iustitia* (11.12): the reference is, in this case, to the prices current in the towns, which seem to have been controlled, if not fixed. I return to this passage below.

Some other texts show that price fluctuations as a consequence of the changing relationship between demand and supply were justified to a certain extent, when they were not the result of speculation. This is shown by another of the *Variae* of Cassiodorus, written for Theoderic in 508/511. There was a dearth of foodstuffs (*victualia*) in the Gallic provinces of the kingdom (*Var.* 4.5). Theoderic writes to the *comes* Amabilis in order to solve this situation: the shipowners (*navicularii*) of Campania, Lucania, and Tuscia (that is, the Tyrrhenian regions) have to employ their ships to convoy the food supplies (*victuales species*) only as far as the Gallic provinces and not elsewhere. It is interesting that the king's intervention does not affect the prices at which they have to sell these *victuales species*: it is even conceded that the *negotiatores* have the liberty to sell them at market prices: "with licence to dispose of them [the food-stuffs] as may be agreed between buyer and seller" (trans. Barnish; *habituri licentiam distrahendi sic ut inter emptorem venditoremque convenerit*), namely at market prices which were higher than before because of the shortage, and this behavior is accepted and, one may say, even justified, because that will be an incentive for the *negotiatores* to carry and market the *victualia*: "It is a great convenience to deal with the needy, since famine gives no heed to anything, in order to make good its wants. For he who sells when solicited seems almost to make a gift, even when he serves his own profit. To go with merchandise to the well supplied means a struggle; but he who can bring food-stuffs to the hungry, prices them at his own judgement" (trans. Barnish; *Grande commodum est cum indigentibus pacisci: quando fames totum solet contemnere, ut suam necessitatem potest explere.*

Nam cum ambitioni suae serviat, prope modum donare videtur, qui vendit rogatus. Ad saturatos cum mercibus ire certamen est: suo autem pretium poscit arbitrio, qui victualia potest ferre ieiunis). Even more interesting is the way in which Cassiodorus, writing on behalf of Theoderic, describes in general terms the function of *negotiatio* where and when there is a scarcity (*caritas*): "Now, in the region of Gaul, I am aware that there is a dearth of food-stuffs, something to which commerce makes haste in its constant alertness, so that it may sell for a higher price what was bought for a lower" (trans. Barnish; *In Gallicana igitur regione victualium cognovimus caritatem, ad quam negotiatio semper prompta festinat, ut empta largius angustiore pretio distrahantur*).

Mommsen has, without justification, in my view, against the unanimous reading of the MSS, inverted the order of the words: *ut empta angustiore pretio largius distrahantur*; and Traube has interpreted *angustiore pretio* in a very peculiar way, as the "pretium quod pauci persolvere possunt" ("a price that few people can pay"). The TLL has followed Traube and has proposed to understand *angustiore pretio* as the *pretium* "quod caritate angustum emptorum numerum admittit" ("that, being so dear, can be paid just by a small number of buyers"), an even more vulnerable solution, since it transfers illegitimately the attribution of *angustus* from the price to a not-mentioned *emptorum numerus*.[17] The translation of Barnish seems to accept the inversion proposed by Mommsen, but seems to interpret rightly *angustiore pretio* as the lower price at which the *victualia* are bought and the subordinate as a consecutive clause; he understands, however, *largius* as referring to the higher price at which the *victualia* are sold.[18] Recently, in his dissertation on *Theoderic, the Goths, and the Restoration of the Roman Empire*,[19] Jonathan J. Arnold, without properly translating the passage, but tacitly accepting the inversion proposed by Mommsen, has interpreted the situation in the following way: "Here a general scarcity of subsistence goods in Gaul had led to rampant inflation and profiteering, and as a result Gallic consumers had suffered further impoverishment, unjustly denuded of their resources through provisions being 'sold at a price more lavish than their meager value (should permit).'" As I said, however, the inversion proposed by Mommsen is wholly unjustified given the

[17] Traube (1894: 572), s.v. *pretium*. [18] Barnish (1992: 75).
[19] University of Michigan (2008: 265 n. 293); see now Arnold (2016: 285 n. 125).

unanimous reading of the MSS. And secondly it is very hard to interpret *largius* as referring to a higher price. It seems to me that what Cassiodorus means is that *negotiatio* can better deal with *caritas* since what has been bought *in greater quantity* (*largius*) is inevitably sold at a *lower* price (*angustiore pretio*). I would translate: "the commerce makes haste in its constant alertness to a dearth, so that what has been bought in a greater quantity is sold at a lower price." One can better understand, then, what follows: "It so happens that my forethought will both satisfy the sellers and rescue those in need" (trans. Barnish, *sic evenit ut et venditoribus satisfiat et illis provisio nostra subveniat*); the "forethought" (*provisio*) being to reserve all the foodstuffs that the *navicularii* can take from the Tyrrhenian regions exclusively to the Gallic provinces. In the general observation according to which, thanks to *negotiatio*, "what has been bought in a greater quantity can be sold at a lower price," one can recognize the awareness of the economic, and social, function of *negotiatio*. In another of the *Variae*, to which we will come back shortly (*Var.* 11.11), it is clearly stated that *venalitas victualium rerum temporis debet subiacere rationi*, so that one cannot look for *caritas* (that is, high prices) when there is *vilitas*, or for *vilitas* (low prices) when there is *caritas* (dearth), and Cassiodorus goes on to say that *aequalitate perpensa* it is possible to take away from the consumers their "grumbling" (*murmur*) and from the traders, who always complain, a "burden" (*gravamen*). Again, there is an obvious justification of the variability of prices and the awareness of the role that market regulation can have in balancing the needs of consumers and traders.

5.7. THE *FORUM RERUM VENALIUM*

Several other texts seem to suggest that the abstract conception of the market, as opposed to physical markets, was beginning to be present and that the expression *forum rerum venalium* could designate not only the specific market of the individual town, but also the abstract market. Most of these texts relate to the procedures for commutating taxes in kind and for making payments in kind to officers and soldiers (the "Erhebungsadäration" and the "Verausgabungsadäration" of Persson, or the "Steueradäration" and the "Verteilungsadäration" of Kolb). In certain of these texts the *forum rerum venalium* is a specific market—of

Rome or of Campania. Thus, a constitution of Valentinian and Valens of 364 (C.Th. 7.4.10), addressed to Symmachus as the Prefect of the city of Rome (*praefectus urbi*), states that the *protectores* must obtain, "for the benefit of their food supply" (*in annonarum suarum conmoda*), according to the "ancient custom" (*vetus mos*), the prices (*pretia*) of the *forum rerum venalium*, and in this case the reference seems to be to the prices current in Rome. Likewise, the same emperors state, in a law addressed to the same Symmachus as City Prefect (C.Th. 11.2.2, 365 CE), that the different qualities of wine must be sold, as a particular provision in favor of the population of Rome, with an abatement of a quarter compared to the prices current in the *forum rerum venalium* of Rome. Again, in a Constantinian law on the supply of pigs for consumption at Rome effected through the corporation of the pork suppliers (*corpus suariorum*; C.Th. 14.4.2, 326 CE?), which gives to the taxpayers the possibility of choosing whether to give pigs or money, it is stated that the commutation price, the price of *adaeratio*, must be the price of the *publica conversatio*, that is, the market price, but that it must be different according to the various places and times. A law of Julian (C.Th. 14.4.3, 363 CE) establishes that the *suarii* of Rome must be paid at the prices which are found (*repperiuntur*: note the verb) year by year in Campania and not at the prices prevailing in Rome, which were evidently higher.

In other texts, however, it seems incontrovertible that the expression *forum rerum venalium* does not apply to a specific and localized market, but to *the* market. Thus a law of Gratian, Valentinian, and Theodosius (C.Th. 11.15.2, 384 CE) is a piece of legislation of general validity addressed to all taxpayers. It states that the procedure of public purchase (*publica comparatio*) must be effected without any kind of compulsion (*necessitas indictionis*), except in the case of the "more capable" (*potiores*), and at market prices: "each of Our provincials, at his own discretion and with loyal spirit, shall gladly furnish and sell the requested supplies at the same prices as those current in the public market" (trans. Pharr; *unusquisque provincialium nostrorum arbitratu proprio et mente devota species petitas isdem pretiis, quae in foro rerum venalium habebuntur, libens praestet ac distrahat*). In this case the expression *forum rerum venalium* can only refer to *the* market and not to any particular market. And the same is true of other constitutions of Arcadius, Honorius, and Theodosius (C.Th. 7.4.28, 406 CE), and of Honorius and Theodosius (C.Th. 7.4.32 and C.Th. 7.4.36, 412 CE and 424 CE), whereas another law of the same emperors (C.Th. 11.1.37, 436 CE) establishes a more complex and elaborate system for stating the rate of *adaeratio* for taxpayers, which involves a balancing of the accounts for a five-year period "with the reckoning of barrenness and productivity made in accordance with the current market prices and of such sum which is computed by carefully considering the fruits of the five-year period" (trans. Pharr; *communicata aestimatione quinquennii, sterilitatis ac fecunditatis pro foro rerum venalium habita ratione, ex eadem summa, quae eiusdem quinquennii perpensis frugibus colligitur*).

As we have seen, one of the *Variae* of Cassiodorus, which contains the "Edict of prices for Flaminia" (*Edictum pretiorum per Flaminiam*), speaks of the "justness of the prices" (*pretiorum iustitia*, 11.12) an expression that apparently refers to an effective price regulation in favor of consumers. And the same can be said of the "Edict on maintaining prices at Ravenna" (*Edictum de pretiis custodiendis Ravenna*, Cassiod. *Var.* 11.11). This poses a more general question. If the prices formed in a competitive market were considered *aequa* or *iusta* or *legitima*, how can we explain the attempts to fix prices, instead of simply regulating the market, starting with the most ambitious of these attempts by the Tetrarchic government in the early fourth century? These were conceived as attempts to curb speculative behavior, as is explained in the preamble of Diocletian's edict on prices itself (*edictum de pretiis rerum venalium*). In this sense they do not contradict the notion of a positive evaluation of the working of a competitive market and of the activity of traders in it. That the traders get profits (*lucra*) is perfectly acceptable, but the *lucra* must be *honesta* (*Var.* 11.12.3). Moreover, the attempts to control prices in any case presuppose the working of a *forum rerum venalium* and the registration of the prices prevailing in it: otherwise the fixing of prices would be wholly unrealistic and unreasonable. We must assume that even Diocletian's *edictum* must have been based on a general investigation or survey of what the market prices were.

But there were certainly other possible reasons for surveying and registering prices, even without fixing them. As I have pointed out elsewhere, the laws of the Theodosian Code referring to the supply of pork (*caro porcina*) to Rome can be explained only if the complex mechanisms of *adaeratio* and *coemptio* (that is, the purchasing of the pigs to be brought to Rome) were based on the continuous gathering of the data on the prices prevailing in the regions of Italy where the *canon suarius*, the contribution in pigs, was exacted. And an explicit reference to this activity of periodical registration of prices is in the Constantinian law referred to above (C.Th. 14.4.2).[20]

The same story is told, for the fourth century, by the declarations delivered every month by the heads of the *koina*, the professional associations of craftsmen and merchants, which were active in the Egyptian *poleis*.[21] These declarations concern the current price of the goods, handled by them, and were made at the office of the *logistes* (the *curator civitatis*), the highest officer of the city. They have a standard format and it is demonstrable that some indications were added at a later time, along with the signature of the subscriber: that means that they were produced using a form already written in the office of the *logistes* and then filled in by the subscriber or the subscribers, the *meniarches* or the *meniarchai* of the *koinon* (the head of the association for the specific month). The standard formula, for the earliest declarations, says "I declare the price below for the goods which I handle, and I swear the divine oath that I have not been deceitful." Next there is the mention of the commodity or the commodities, then the price or the prices, and finally the date, which is always the last day of the month. The format changes a bit starting from the declarations of the late twenties of the fourth century. From that time on it is made clearer that the declared price is the price of the month just elapsed. The aim of these declarations is debated: some scholars have thought that, following Diocletian's edict, and in the face of the monetary difficulties of the period, the imperial authority would have given the guilds the duty of fixing the prices. But it seems clear that the price, at least in the documents of the second period, is not the price which will be in force in the following month, but the price which has been in force in the month just elapsed. One has to conclude that this declared price, at least in the documents of the second phase, is not an imposed price, but is the market price, and that it was thought to be useful to collect and register these data. What for? Because, as with the price of *caro porcina* in the regions of southern Italy which paid the contribution, it was necessary to collect this information to guarantee the working

[20] C.Th. 14.4.2: *iudices autem regionum monendi sunt, ut per singulos annos ad scientiam tuam referant, quae in quibus locis sunt pretia porcinae, ut instructione hac a tua gravitate perpensa tunc demum suarii per diversa proficiscantur et pretia suscipiant, quae in his regionibus versari cognoveris.*

[21] Lo Cascio (2009: 259–72).

of the system of *adaeratio* and *coemptio*. The declarations of the first period could be connected with an attempt to fix the prices, but certainly the fact that the practice of collecting and registering prices was not discontinued shows that it was thought to be useful for the fiscal administration. An analogous practice of registering prices is, on the other hand, attested in Ostrogothic Italy, where tax adjusters (*peraequatores*) subordinate to the Master of Offices (*magister officiorum*) were in charge of establishing in Ravenna the prices of *victualia* (Var. 6.6.6).

No wonder, then, that the large majority of texts from which one can deduce the continuing importance of the free market were inserted in dispositions referring to the complex financial mechanisms of the imperial "state" and afterwards of some of the barbarian kingdoms. One can confidently conclude that the notion of a dirigiste state or of a command economy or of prevailing redistributive mechanisms in late antiquity must be abandoned. The unimpeded working of the *forum rerum venalium* was of paramount importance for the financial management and therefore for the survival of the political organization. Other types of sources attest the vitality of the market, in the relations of private actors between themselves. But to analyze them even summarily would require at least another paper.

REFERENCES

Arnold, Jonathan J. 2008. *Theoderic, the Goths, and the Restoration of the Roman Empire*. Diss. University of Michigan.

Arnold, Jonathan J. 2016. *Theoderic and the Roman Imperial Restoration*. Cambridge: Cambridge University Press.

Bang, Peter. 2008. *The Roman Bazaar*. Cambridge: Cambridge University Press.

Bang, Peter. 2012. "A Forum on Trade," in Walter Scheidel, ed., *The Cambridge Companion to the Roman Economy*. Cambridge: Cambridge University Press, 296–303.

Barnish, Sam J. B. 1992. *The Variae of Magnus Aurelius Cassiodorus Senator, Translated with Notes and Introduction*. Liverpool: Liverpool University Press.

Baroni, Anselmo. 2004. "La colonia e il governatore," in Giovanni Salmeri, Andrea Raggi, and Anselmo Baroni, eds, *Colonie romane nel mondo greco*. Rome: L'Erma di Bretschneider, 8–54.

Carrié, Jean-Michel. 1975. "Les distributions alimentaires dans les cités de l'Empire romain tardif." *Mélanges de l'École française de Rome. 87 Antiquité* 995–1101.

Durliat, Jean. 1990. *De la ville antique à la ville byzantine: Le problème des subsistances*. Rome: École française de Rome.

Erdkamp, Paul. 2005. *The Grain Market in the Roman Empire: A Social, Political and Economic Study*. Cambridge: Cambridge University Press.

Goldsmith, Raymond W. 1984. "An Estimate of the Size and Structure of the National Product of the Early Roman Empire." 30 *Review of Income and Wealth* 263–88.

González, Julián, and Michael H. Crawford. 1986. "The *Lex Irnitana*: A New Copy of the Flavian Municipal Law." 76 *Journal of Roman Studies* 147–243.

Harris, William V. 2003. "Roman Government and Commerce, 300 B.C.–A.D. 300," in Carlo Zaccagnini, ed., *Mercanti e politica nel mondo antico*. Rome: L'Erma di Bretschneider, 275–305 (repr. with an *addendum* in Harris 2011: 198–219).

Harris, William V. 2011. *Rome's Imperial Economy: Twelve Essays*. Oxford: Oxford University Press.

Höbenreich, Evelyn. 1997. *Annona: Juristische Aspekte der stadtrömischen Lebensmittelversorgung im Prinzipat*. Graz: Leykam.

Hopkins, M. Keith. 1995/6. "Rome, Taxes, Rents and Trade," 6/7 *Kodai* 41–75. Repr. in Walter Scheidel and Sitta von Reden, eds, *The Ancient Economy*. New York: Routledge, 190–230.

Jursa, Michael 2010. *Aspects of the Economic History of Babylonia in the First Millennium* BC. Münster: Ugarit-Verlag.

Jursa, Michael. 2013, "L'economia babilonese nel sesto secolo a.C.: crescita economica in contesto imperiale." 54 *Studi storici* 247–66.

Kehoe, Dennis P. 2007a. *Law and the Rural Economy in the Roman Empire*. Ann Arbor: University of Michigan Press.

Kehoe, Dennis P. 2007b. "The Early Roman Empire: Production," in Walter Scheidel, Ian Morris, and Richard Saller, eds, *The Cambridge Economic History of the Greco-Roman World*. Cambridge: Cambridge University Press, 543–69.

Lamberti, Francesca. 1993. *«Tabulae Irnitanae». Municipalità e «Ius Romanorum»*. Naples: Jovene.

Lo Cascio, Elio. 2000. "The Roman Principate: The Impact of the Organization of the Empire on Production," in Elio Lo Cascio and Dominic Rathbone, eds, *Production and Public Powers in Classical Antiquity. Proceedings of the Cambridge Philological Society*. Suppl. Vol. 26. Cambridge: Cambridge University Press, 77–85.

Lo Cascio, Elio. 2006. "The Role of the State in the Roman Economy—Making Use of the New Institutional Economics," in Peter Fibiger Bang,

Mamoru Ikeguchi, and Harmut G. Ziche, eds, *Ancient Economies, Modern Methodologies: Archaeology, Comparative History, Models and Institutions*. Bari: Edipuglia, 215–34.

Lo Cascio, Elio. 2007. "The Early Roman Empire: The State and the Economy," in Walter Scheidel, Ian Morris, and Richard Saller, eds, *The Cambridge Economic History of the Greco-Roman World*. Cambridge: Cambridge University Press, 619–47.

Lo Cascio, Elio. 2015. "The Imperial Property and Its Development," in Paul Erdkamp, Koenraad Verboven, and Arjan Zuiderhoek, eds, *Ownership and Exploitation of Land and Natural Resources in the Roman World*. Oxford: Oxford University Press, 62–70.

Lo Cascio, Elio. 2018. "Market Regulation and Transaction Costs in the Roman Empire," in Alan Bowman and Andrew Wilson, eds, *Trade, Commerce, and the State in the Roman World*. Oxford: Oxford University Press, 117–32.

Lo Cascio, Elio, and Paolo Malanima. 2009. "GDP in Pre-Modern Agrarian Economies (1–1820 AD): A Revision of the Estimates." 25 *Rivista di Storia Economica* 391–419.

Lo Cascio, Elio, and Paolo Malanima. 2014. "Ancient and Pre-Modern Economies: GDP in the Roman Empire and Early Modern Europe," in Franćois de Callataÿ, ed., *Long-term Quantification in Ancient Mediterranean History*. Bari: Edipuglia, 211–19.

Maddison, Angus. 2007. *Contours of the World Economy, 1–2030 AD: Essays in Macro-Economic History*. Oxford: Oxford University Press.

Maganzani, Lauretta. 2004. "Analisi economica e studio storico del diritto: le societates publicanorum rivisitate con gli strumenti concettuali dell'economista." 55 *Iura* 216–36.

Malmendier, Ulrike. 2002. *Societas publicanorum*. Cologne/Weimer/Vienna: Böhlau.

Malmendier, Ulrike. 2005. "Roman Shares," in William N. Goetzmann and K. Geert Rouwenhorst, eds, *The Origins of Value: The Financial Innovations That Created Modern Capital Markets*. Oxford: Oxford University Press, 31–42.

North, Douglass C. 1979. "A Framework for Analysing the State in Economic History." 16 *Explorations in Economic History* 249–59.

Olson, Mancur. 2000. *Power and Prosperity: Outgrowing Communist and Capitalist Dictatorships*. Oxford: Oxford University Press.

Rostovtzeff, Michael I. 1995. "Scripta Varia," in Arnaldo Marcone, ed., *Ellenismo e impero romano*. Bari: Edipuglia.

Scheidel, Walter. 2012. "Approaching the Roman Economy," in Walter Scheidel, ed., *The Cambridge Companion to the Roman Economy*. Cambridge: Cambridge University Press, 1–21.

Scheidel, Walter, and Steven J. Friesen. 2009. "The Size of the Economy and the Distribution of Income in the Roman Empire." 99 *Journal of Roman Studies* 61–91.

Sirks, Boudewijn. 2002. "Sailing in the Off-season with Reduced Financial Risk," in Jean-Jacques Aubert and Boudewijn Sirks, eds, Speculum iuris*: Roman Law as a Reflection of Social and Economic Life in Antiquity*. Ann Arbor: University of Michigan Press, 134–50.

Tchernia, André. 2011. *Les Romains e le commerce*. Naples: Centre Jean Bérard-Centre Camille Jullian (Engl. transl. *The Romans and Trade*. Oxford: Oxford University Press. 2016).

Temin, Peter. 2006. "Estimating GDP in the Early Roman Empire," in Elio Lo Cascio, ed., *Innovazione tecnica e progresso economico nel mondo romano*. Bari: Edipuglia, 31–54.

Temin, Peter. 2013. *The Roman Market Economy*. Princeton: Princeton University Press.

Terpstra, Taco. 2008. "Roman Law, Transaction Costs and the Roman Economy: Evidence from the Sulpicii Archive," in Koenraad Verboven, Katelijn Vandorpe, and Véroniqe Chankowski, eds, *PISTOI DIA TÈN TECHNÈN: Bankers, Loans and Archives in the Ancient World. Studies in Honour of Raymond Bogaert*. Leuven: Peeters, 345–69.

Terpstra, Taco. 2013. *Trading Communities in the Roman World: A Micro-Economic and Institutional Perspective*. Leiden: Brill.

Verboven, Koenraad. 2015. "The Knights Who Say NIE: Can Neo-institutional Economics Live Up to Its Expectations in Ancient History Research?" in Paul Erdkamp and Koenraad Verboven, eds, *Structure and Performance in the Roman Economy: Models, Methods and Case Studies* (Coll. Latomus 350). Brussels: Éditions Latomus, 33–57.

Wilson, Andrew I. 2009. "Approaches to Quantifying Roman Trade," in Alan K. Bowman and Andrew I. Wilson, eds, *Quantifying the Roman Economy: Methods and Problems*. Oxford: Oxford University Press, 213–49.

6

Statistics in Ancient History

Prices and Trade in the Pax Romana

Peter Temin

6.1. INTRODUCTION

I assume we all believe in facts. Whether we study science or economics or history, we base our conclusions on facts or, as they are called frequently, observations. When we turn to ancient history, we quickly discover there is lots of information about the ancient economy, but little that economists would classify as data (Temin 2006). We therefore need to use the scraps of evidence that have survived for two thousand years to construct a view of ancient societies. The resulting intellectual edifice will be speculative and subject to revision as more data are found. I explore in this chapter how to extract the most information from the sparse data we have. This approach also suggests how to incorporate new data when they appear and update our views.

I argue that statistics provide an illuminating tool to aid understanding of the data we have about the Roman economy. This has the corollary that there is rather surprising information that a Mediterranean wheat market operated well during the early Roman Empire. For economists, I explore the advantages and limitations of a small-sample regression—topics interesting enough to econometricians that the first regressions in this chapter are taught annually to economics graduate students at MIT. For ancient historians, I examine how we extrapolate from occasional comments made in speeches and

Peter Temin, *Statistics in Ancient History: Prices and Trade in the* Pax Romana In: *Roman Law and Economics: Institutions and Organizations, Volume I.* Edited by: Giuseppe Dari-Mattiacci and Dennis P. Kehoe,
Oxford University Press (2020).
DOI: 10.1093/oso/9780198787204.003.0006

letters to Roman society as a whole. This chapter draws on research originally published in Kessler and Temin (2008) and extended further in my book (Temin 2013).

I use statistics here to test the hypothesis that the Romans had created the conditions for trade from one end to the other of the Mediterranean Sea by their *Pax Romana*. This may not be startling to ancient historians at this level. But if this market was dense enough to equalize prices around the Mediterranean, that would be remarkable. I show that is exactly what happened for the most widely traded good, wheat, in the late Roman Republic and early Roman Empire. Note that this is not gold or jewelry that is so high value that it can be transported easily; it is a bulk commodity for mass consumption.

Although this chapter focuses on prices, the prices existed in the context of the *Pax Romana* and the legal framework that organized it. Markets do not stand alone; they are parts of societies that organize economic activity according to some rules. Roman law provided rules for the areas around the Mediterranean Sea where Roman prices are observed (Kehoe 2007). Other chapters in these volumes focus on the rules; I argue that they enabled and supported a market for wheat that extended from one end of the Mediterranean to the other.

If there had been a unified wheat market, the main market would have been in the city of Rome, where the largest number of potential consumers lived and the center of imperial administration was located. In other words, Rome was where the largest supplies and demands for wheat would have come together and where the price of wheat consequently would have been set. The price would have varied over time as supplies fluctuated due to harvests across the Roman world, storms affected the cost of transportation, and government actions altered the value of the currency. Normal variations in supplies and demands elsewhere in the Empire would have affected the price, although most fluctuations would have been small relative to the total production and the consumption at Rome. Most places outside of Rome would have had an excess supply of wheat, and the price would have been set in Rome where the excess supplies and the largest excess demand came together. When local places were isolated, there could have been excess local demand as well as excess local supply, that is, local famines as well as local gluts.

Under these circumstances, wheat outside of Rome would be valued by what it was worth in Rome. Wheat at Palermo in Sicily, for example, normally would be worth less than wheat in Rome because it would have to be transported to Rome to be sold. The price of wheat in Sicily would be the price of wheat in Rome less the cost of getting wheat from Sicily to Rome. This would be true almost always, but there undoubtedly were circumstances when it was not. If storms prevented the shipment of grain to Rome, the Sicilian price might temporarily deviate from the level set by the price in Rome. If a harvest failure in Sicily created a local famine, the price of wheat in Sicily would rise above the level indicated by the Roman price until new wheat supplies could be brought in. In the absence of extreme events like these, a unified market would keep Sicilian prices near the Roman price less the transportation cost.

More concretely, competition would determine Sicilian prices if there was a unified market. If the Sicilian price of wheat rose above the Roman level minus transportation costs, it would not make sense for merchants to buy wheat in Sicily to sell in Rome. The amount of wheat demanded in Sicily would fall, and the price consequently would fall as well. If the Sicilian price of wheat fell below the Roman level minus transportation costs, merchants would increase the amount of wheat they would buy in Sicily, for they could make an unusually high profit by taking it to Rome and selling it there. Merchants would bid against each other, raising the Sicilian price.

Wheat at Lusitania in Spain would be worth less than wheat at Palermo because it was further from Rome. The cost of transporting wheat from Spain to Rome was larger than the cost of bringing it from Sicily, and the price of wheat in Spain correspondingly would be lower. The reasoning is exactly like that for Sicily, only the transport cost is different. But while each price is compared to that in Rome, the price in Spain would be lower than the price in Sicily if there were a unified market. In fact, wheat around the Mediterranean would be worth less than the price at Rome, with the amount less depending on the distance from Rome. We do not know the transport cost in any detail, but we are reasonably sure that it rose with distance. If there was a unified wheat market, therefore, the price of wheat would have decreased as one moved farther and farther from Rome. As Adam Smith (1776, Book 3, Chapter 1) stated it: "The corn which grows within a mile of the town, sells there for the same price with that which comes from twenty miles distance."

If there were not a unified market, if there were only independent local markets, then there would not be any relationship between local and Roman prices. There would be prices in local markets that would be determined by local conditions. The prices might move together at certain times, if storms across the Mediterranean caused simultaneous harvest failures everywhere or currency debasements caused prices to rise everywhere, but they would not in general be related one to another; any single identity of prices could be a coincidence. If we find several wheat prices in different places, however, we can test whether the pattern we find is due to coincidence or an underlying market process.

The question is not whether one or the other of these ideal types was observed, whether there was an efficient market, or whether there were any factors unifying separate local markets. It is rather whether the historical experience lies closer to one end of a continuum than the other. Many interventions into Roman markets and local actions elsewhere around the Mediterranean are well known. There must have been at least occasional local grain shortages and even famines. The question then is whether the normal state of affairs was one of interconnected markets, so that prices in different places typically were related, or one of separated and independent markets. In the latter case, we should not observe any systematic relationship between the location and the price of grain.

I approach this test in three steps, the first of which uses a small set of wheat prices from varied locations from Rickman (1980). This familiar sample provided a way to examine monetary integration at least provisionally. When dealing with fragmentary data it is necessary to collect a sample that is not determined by the desired outcome. Rickman was writing about the Roman wheat market, and he collected his sample to show habitual prices in different places. The sample, albeit small, therefore looks like a random sample. It is, in Rathbone's (2003: 201) felicitous phrase, "thin but nicely random." The second step is to check these results with a new data set in Rathbone (2011). These data were collected to exhibit the surviving prices from around the Mediterranean. They overlap Rickman's sample, but the two authors made different choices in collecting data that allow us to delimit more precisely the extent of the Roman Mediterranean wheat market. The third step is to consider an even newer data set from Bransbourg (2012) and the criticisms Bransbourg levels at the first step in this analysis. Scheidel (2014) reports Bransbourg's results and argues that they destroy my argument. He did not at that time present a new regression similar to those reported here; I hope the publication of these results will alter his negative views.

I use a simple model for two reasons. It supplies a clear representation of Roman trade around and across the Mediterranean world, where wheat prices in outlying provinces were related to those in the city of Rome. Given the extremely limited data on Roman prices, no more complex model could be tested. The simple model treated here also is compatible with a complex pattern of actual Roman trade. There must have been trades between provinces, local scarcities—labeled famines by ancient authors—where wheat was shipped to these localities rather than Rome, and times when storms or wars limited flows of wheat around the Mediterranean. Yet the extant Roman wheat prices suggest strongly that these special cases were unusual, that any historical diversity of trade was dominated by the pull of trade to the city of Rome in most times and places during the late Republic and early Empire.

The Rickman sample consists of price pairs in outlying locations and in Rome at roughly the same time, accumulating six price pairs in almost two centuries ranging from the late Republic to the early Empire. This is not an overwhelming amount of evidence, but it is enough to test whether the patterns in the data are random or not. In each case the Roman price was subtracted from the price at the distant location to give a price differential. Wheat prices at Rome were subject to slow inflation according to Rickman and Duncan-Jones (1982). I characterize this period as having stable prices elsewhere, with an allowance for slow and gradual price changes which will be described below (Temin 2013).

I describe the price observations in the order of their distance from Rome, calculated as straight-line distances on a map. This of course is only an approximation to the actual distance that wheat traveled, and this added randomness reduces the possibility of finding evidence of an integrated market. If observations are randomly drawn from a population, then even a few observations give information about the whole population. All of the statistical theory I draw on rests on the assumption of a random sample. How can we know whether the observations are random, as Rathbone's comment asserts? Two arguments are relevant here. First, the process of survival for two millennia is the product of many intervening events (Greenblatt 2011). Many independent actions add up to randomization. Second, the data used in a regression can be compared to regressions on other samples from the same population, indicating whether the initial results hold up. This is the subject of this chapter.

6.2. WHEAT PRICES IN THE ROMAN WORLD

The closest price was from Sicily and came from Cicero's *Verrine Orations*. One of his accusations was that Verres did not transact business at the market price, even though he acknowledged its level in a letter (Cicero, 2 *Verr.* 3. 189). This observation, like most of the others, reports the prevailing local price in round numbers. Since the observation is general rather than the record of any transaction, it is likely to be only approximate. This casual quality of the data also militates against finding any systematic relationship between prices. It introduces more noise into any relationship of the prices being paid because of the unknown difference between the reported averages and actual prices. These implications about the difficulty of drawing conclusions all depend on the randomness of the observations. If there are systematic biases in the observations, then something more than these general rules is needed.

The second price came from Polybius (34.8.7) in his discussion of conditions in Lusitania. As before, this is a general statement about the prevailing price. While it is good to have an average, the casual quality of the averaging process again adds noise into any comparison of prices in different places.

The third price comes from the Po Valley in Italy; it is another observation by Polybius (2.15.1). While this observation is closer to Rome than the first two prices, I made an exception to the general rule of measuring distance. The Po Valley was linked to Rome more by rivers rather than sea, although the transport of a bulk commodity like wheat may well have gone by sea (Harris 1989). I calculated the distance in two ways that fortunately give the same distance. Diocletian's *Price Edict* fixed river transport prices at five times the level of sea transport, and I first took the cost of river transport from the Po Valley to have been five times as expensive as by sea. This evidence dates from over a century later than any of the other prices, but I assumed the ratio of sea and river transport costs remained constant over time, as argued by Greene (1986: 40) and included the Po valley in the price data by multiplying the distance from Rome by five. In addition, the distance by sea from the Po Valley to Rome is the same as the distance I calculated from the Diocletian Edict. The sea distance is not a straight line, and this observation therefore is slightly different from the others even if measured by sea. Despite the small sample, there are enough data to test whether this unusual attention to distance for this observation affects the statistical result.

The fourth price comes from an official intervention in the local market. An inscription records that the wheat price in Pisidian Antioch was high in a time of scarcity. The normal price was eight or nine *asses* per *modius*; the acceptable limit price was one *denarius* per *modius* (*AÉ* 1925, no. 126b). This inscription reveals several important aspects of the Mediterranean wheat market in addition to reporting the normal price. The need to damp down famine prices indicates that local markets were subject to local scarcities; they were not so well linked that wheat from elsewhere would be brought in instantly in response to a local shortage. The apparent success of such interventions, in this case limiting the price to double its normal range, indicates that many famines were not severe.

For Egypt, I preserve the spirit of Rickman's data but improve on his data since Rathbone (1997) reworked the sale prices that Rickman took from Duncan-Jones. I averaged seven Egyptian prices from the "famine" of 45–7 CE to get a price for Egypt. Rathbone argued that these prices were unusual, but the previous discussion suggests that they may not be far from average. We of course cannot know how unusual these prices were, and any special conditions introduce noise into our data. The Egyptian prices also come from agricultural areas, not from a Mediterranean port. The purported famine would have raised the price, but using country prices would have depressed it compared to those at a port. These offsets introduce added uncertainty into the accuracy of this observation since there is no reason to expect them to be exact offsets. The average of Rathbone's seven prices was seven *drachmae* per *artaba*. These prices in Egyptian currency and units were converted to HS per *modius* by following Duncan-Jones (1990: 372) and dividing by 4.5.

The final observation, from distant Palestine, is taken from Tenney Frank's *Economic Survey*; it too is an average of a few actual transactions (Heichelheim 1938: 181–3).

6.3. STATISTICS AND ROMAN MARKETS

All of these prices were compared with roughly contemporaneous prices at Rome. Rickman argued that the price of wheat at Rome was between three and four HS per *modius* in the late Republic, rising to five to six HS in the early Empire. Duncan-Jones confirmed the general price level; Rathbone confirmed the inflation, at least for Egypt, where the data are more abundant. The order of observations turns out to be almost chronological even though the order of exposition was by distance. There are six prices in almost two centuries. This is not an overwhelming amount of evidence, but it is enough to test whether the patterns in the data are random or not. In each case the Roman price was subtracted from the price at the distant location to give a price differential. More prices come to light all the time, but this "thin but nicely random" sample provides a way to answer the question at least provisionally.

The prices and the differences between the prices at Rome and the local prices are listed in Table 6.1. The differences are all negative, consistent with the story of an integrated market and with general observations that agricultural prices were lower outside Rome (Garnsey 1998: 241). Wheat prices clearly were lower outside of Rome than in Rome itself. The straight-line distances from each location to Rome also are in Table 6.1. I test whether the differences between prices in these provincial locations and the price at Rome were proportional to their distance to Rome. The value of a statistical test is that one can say with some precision how unlikely it is that the observed result would be found if the data were generated by pure

Table 6.1. Distance and Prices for Grain.

(1) Region	Distance (km) from Rome	Rome Price (HS)	Province Price (HS)	Distance-from-Rome "Discount" (HS)	Year
Sicily (*Sicilia* province)	427	4.00 HS [a]	2.00–3.00 HS [c]	−1.50	77 BC
Spain (*Lusitania* province)	1363	3.00-4.00 HS [a]	1 HS [d]	−2.50	150 BC
Italy (*Italia* province), by River	1510	3.00–4.00 HS [a]	0.5 HS [b]	−3.00	150 BC
Asia Minor (city of Pisidian Antioch)	1724	5.00–6.00 HS [a]	2.00–2.25 HS [e]	−3.13	80s AD
Egypt (Region of the Fayum)	1953	5.00–6.00 HS [a]	1.5 HS [f]	−4.00	20 BC–AD 56
Palestine	2298	5.00–6.00 HS [a]	2.00–2.50 HS [g]	−3.25	15 AD

Sources: [a]Rickman, 1980, 153–4; [b]Polyb. 2.15; [c]Cicero, 2 Verr. 3.189; [d]Polyb. 34.8.7; [e]Æ. 1925.126b; [f]P. Mich. II 1271.1.8–38; [g]Frank, ESAR iv, 181 and 183.

chance. I described how the data are only approximate. Each approximation introduces an added element of randomness into the data, increasing the probability that any observed pattern is simply noise.

The price differentials are graphed against the distance to Rome in Figure 6.1. The results are quite striking; prices were lower in places further from Rome, and the price differentials appear almost proportional to the distance from Rome. These prices come from all over the Mediterranean and from various times in the late Republic and early Empire. If there were not a unified grain market, there would be no reason to expect a pattern in these prices. Even if there was a unified market, our inability to find more prices or more accurate transportation costs might have obscured any true relationship among the prices. Yet Figure 6.1 reveals a clear picture.

It may appear as if the picture in Figure 6.1 could only *suggest* such a story. It seems like a tiny bit of evidence on which to hang such a grand story of universal monetization and market integration. However, regression analysis can be used to evaluate how likely it is that a picture like Figure 6.1 could arise by chance. We can test the probability that the separate areas of the early Roman Empire were isolated and out of economic connection with Rome. Their prices would have been determined by local conditions, including perhaps the degree of monetization. There would have been no connection between the distance to Rome and the level of local prices.

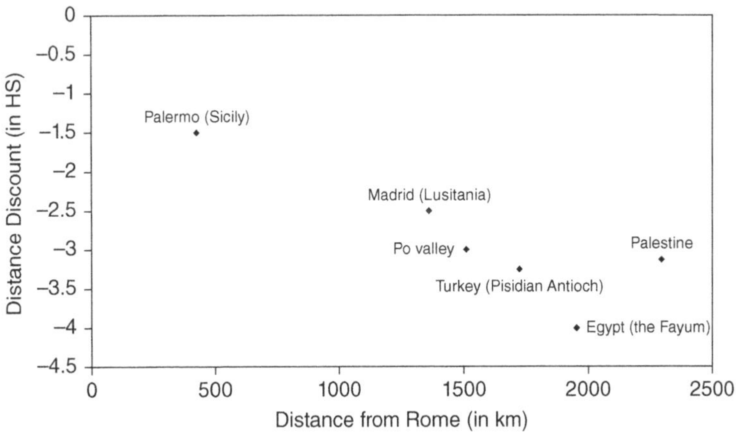

Figure 6.1. Plot of distance and Roman distance discount.

We start by trying to draw a line that relates the price difference between the local price and the Roman price to the distance from Rome. We then adjust the line to make it the best description of the data in the sense that it minimizes the squared distance of the individual observations from the line. (We use the square of the distance to minimize the distance from points both above and below the line and to simplify the mathematics.) This process of regression analysis also is known as the method of "least squares," and the resulting least-squares line is the regression line. It is shown in Figure 6.2.

One of the values of regression analysis is that it generates tests of the hypotheses being tested. We can ask if an apparent relationship between the price discount and the distance from Rome is illusory, a result of observing only a few prices, rather than the result of a systematic process. In order to draw this line, we assumed that there was a relationship between the distance from Rome and the price discount. Regression analysis provides a test whether there is such an association in the data. This test tells us how unlikely it is for us to find a line like the one shown in Figure 6.2 by chance. Assume that the prices we gathered from Rickman were randomly drawn from an underlying distribution of price observations. In another world, different prices could have survived from this same distribution.

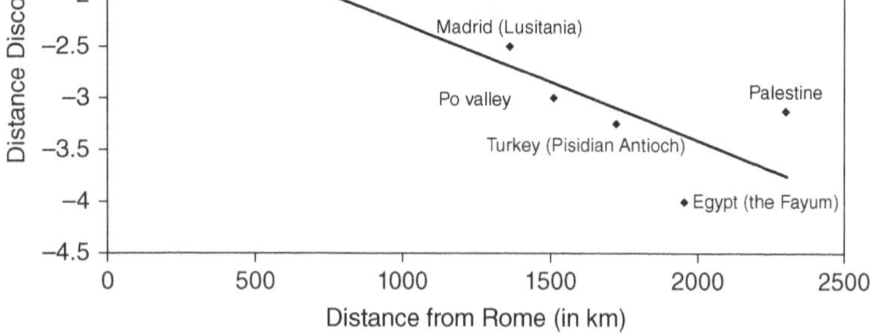

Figure 6.2. Relationship between distance and Roman distance discount.

Taking account of the random quality of the observations we actually have, how unlikely is it for us to find the line in Figure 6.2 by chance?

Regression analysis acknowledges that the slope of the line in Figure 6.2 is not known with certainty. It is the best line that can be drawn with the data at hand, but it is subject to errors deriving from the incomplete sampling of the underlying distribution. In the jargon of regression analysis, the slope of the line has a standard error. If all the points in Figures 6.1 and 6.2 lay in a straight line, then the slope of the regression line would be clear, and the standard error of the slope would be close to zero. If the points are spread out as they are in the figures here, then the line is not known as clearly, and there is a chance that the line has no slope at all, that is, that there is no relationship between the distance from Rome and the price difference.

The test is to compare the size of the slope, the coefficient in the regression, with the size of its standard error. If the coefficient is large relative to the standard error, then it is unlikely that the line was a random finding without support in the price data. On the other hand, if the coefficient is small relative to its standard error, then it is possible that even though the regression line has a slope, there is no underlying relationship between the price and distance. Statisticians call this ratio a t-statistic, and they have calculated tables that can translate t-statistics into probabilities that the line is observed by chance.

The tables take account of degrees of freedom, that is, the number of observations minus the number of coefficients. It takes two variables to define a line, its slope and its position (its height in the figures). With six observations and two variables, there are four degrees of freedom. Omitting the observation with river transport reduces the number of observations by one and the degrees of freedom to three. The t-statistic has to be larger with such few degrees of freedom than with more degrees of freedom to show that a given regression line is unlikely to be the result of chance.

One might think that the data—composed of only a few, badly observed values—are too poor for statistical analysis. Statistics, however, are the best way of distinguishing signal from noise; they are particularly useful when there is a lot of noise in the system. They give us a precise sense of how unlikely it is that any putative pattern we think we observe would have been generated by random processes, that is, how unlikely it is that what looks like a pattern actually is noise. The value of statistics is that we can test a formal hypothesis, namely that wheat prices around the Mediterranean Sea were related in a simple way to those at Rome. We also can derive an explicit probability that this hypothesis is true, given the observations we have.

The key, again, is randomness. If observations are randomly drawn from a population, then even a few observations give information about the whole population. There is a lot of theory that analyzes how difficult this is. In particular, errors in the transcription or treatment of data militate against finding stable results to be generalized because they increase the randomness of the observations. In other words, finding a pattern in these few data points is quite remarkable.

Errors in variables are a common problem in doing regressions. We often hypothesize a relationship between two variables—like the price in Rome and the price in Egypt—but cannot observe one or the other of them precisely. We then use a proxy such as the occasional price that happens to be mentioned in a surviving document. The errors introduced by such a procedure have been studied, and their effects are well known. The extra uncertainty introduced by using imperfect proxies reduces the explanatory power of regressions and tends to result in coefficients that are near zero; the addition of noise through imperfect observations makes the results look more like noise. The well-known scarcity of Roman prices therefore makes it very hard to find a pattern in them. When a pattern is found, however, it indicates both that there is a strong relationship between the prices and that the observations we have are reasonably representative.

Statistical tests are needed to tell if the observed pattern could be the result of chance. The results of four separate regressions of the price differential on the distance from Rome are shown in Table 6.2. Since the transportation from Bologna was by river rather than sea, I was not sure that the correction for the relative cost of transport was accurate and tried the regressions both with and without the Bologna data point. In addition, in the bottom two regressions the price differentials are expressed in logarithms to measure the proportional change in them. Since there are no logarithms of negative numbers, the signs in the bottom two regressions are changed. The dependent variable is the premium of the Roman price over the local price instead of the discount of the local price from the Roman price.

Several conclusions emerge from these results. The R^2 shown in the final column measures the share of the variance of the price differentials that is explained by these simple regressions. Using the price differentials themselves, the regression explains three-quarters of the variation. Using logarithms of the differentials, the regressions explain even more. This result confirms the impression in Table 6.2 and Figure 6.1 that distance from Rome was a powerful explanatory factor in determining wheat prices around the Roman Mediterranean.

T-statistics are shown in parentheses beneath the coefficients in Table 6.3, and they indicate whether the relationship between price differentials and distance was the result of chance. These statistics measure the probability that each coefficient is different from zero, taking account of the number of observations used to derive it as well as their variation. T-statistics above three indicate that there is less than one chance in twenty that the observed relationship between distance and price differentials was due to chance. In the more precise language normally used for regressions, the probability of observing the coefficients in the table if there were no relationship between the price of wheat and the distance from Rome is less than 5 percent in

Table 6.2. Rickman regression results.

	N	Constant	Distance	R^2
Distance Discount	6	1.150	−0.001	0.74
		(−2.10)	(−3.41)	
Distance Discount (No Po Valley)	5	−1.116	−0.001	0.75
		(1.76)	(3.01)	
Log Distance Discount	6	0.125	0.002	0.81
		(1.52)	(4.12)	
Log Distance Discount (No Po Valley)	5	0.116	0.002	0.83
		(1.26)	(3.78)	

Source: Rickman (1980) table 1.

Table 6.3. Rathbone regression results.

	N	Constant	Distance	Time	R^2
Distance	8	34.8	−.009	.058	.42
		(5.77)	(2.13)	(2.15)	
Distance (No Po Valley or III)	6	46.6	−.016	.088	.46
		(4.60)	(2.30)	(2.09)	

Source: Rathbone (2011).

three out of four regressions and close to that probability in the fourth. The 5 percent value of the t-statistic for four degrees of freedom (six observations) is 2.8; for three degrees of freedom (five observations), 3.2. Higher t-statistics indicate lower probabilities that the observed relationship is the result of chance.

In other words, the regressions confirm with very high probability that there was a unified wheat market that extended from one end to the other of the Mediterranean Sea. Transport costs were roughly proportional to distance, and the effects of distance were larger than the idiosyncratic influences of particular markets and places.

The constant terms in these regressions were negative in the regressions for price discounts and positive in the regressions for the logarithms. They were not estimated as precisely as the relationship between distance and the price differentials, and they consequently could be the result of chance (as indicated by smaller t-statistics). The constant terms, however, are historically reasonable and indicate that not all costs were proportional to distance. There appear to have been other costs as well, albeit smaller and less well observed. These other costs were partly physical—the costs of transshipping wheat to and from sea-going ships—and partly administrative—port charges and taxes. Their presence does not detract from the effect of distance or the evidence in favor of a unified wheat market.

Finally, it does not make a difference whether Bologna is included or not. Removing this observation reduced our comparisons to five, but it did not affect the proportion of the variance explained or the evidence that the relationship of distance to price differentials was not random. The t-statistics take account of the reduction in the number of observations to calculate the probability that the observed correlation was due to chance. The logic behind this finding can be seen in Figure 6.2. The observation for Bologna lies close to the regression line. Removing it therefore does not change the line.

6.4. COMPARISON WITH OTHER DATA

The second step in this exploration is to compare these data with a newer data set from Rathbone (2011), an expanded version of the data in Rathbone (2009). They are repeated and expanded to a longer period in time in Rathbone and von Reden (2015). At first glance, this looks like a larger data set, with twenty-three observations and more power to test hypotheses. It turns out, however, that the added data give us a way to clarify the previous results rather than to make a new start. We need first to consider how this sample was constructed. In Rathbone's words, the data consist of the extant prices "which are significant for market behavior." In other words, they were not picked to prove a hypothesis, but rather to show what we know about Roman wheat markets. Again, thin but nicely random.

Eight of these observations are for prices at Rome. Rathbone recognized that the *annona* distorted the market at Rome, and he did not attempt to find a market price that prevailed in normal times. He presented high prices in severe shortages, although one of them is close to Rickman's Rome price, and state subsidized prices. He did not follow Rickman and try to estimate an average from these very diverse prices. I decided to ignore these Roman prices as being for unusual dire circumstances and irrelevant to the question of provincial prices. Without a set of prices at Rome, I used the prices elsewhere instead of discounting them from the Roman price and added a time variable to account for the slight inflation visible in Rickman's data. The result is to lose eight observations and add a variable, decreasing the degrees of freedom by nine.

For other observations, I used the average where Rathbone provided ranges. I disregarded the few prices where Rathbone—ever cautious about data—added question marks to the prices or dates and a few prices from "extreme shortages." I also discarded the observation for Judaea as being too imprecise and probably irrelevant. The timing was given only as the long second century, which is after the Judaean revolt. It is likely that the turmoil after the destruction of the Judean temple caused trade to be disrupted. In fact, the Talmud prohibited wheat exports (Heichelheim 1938: 182). The date and effectiveness of this prohibition are not known, but it suggests that the kind of price arbitrage discussed earlier in setting up the regressions was not operative after the revolt. (I did not inquire into the timing of my Judaean observation in using the Rickman data, but removing the Judaean price does not affect the results in Table 6.3, although of course it decreases the degrees of freedom.)

I ended up with eight observations. I used them all and also tried omitting the observations on the Po Valley since the distance measure is problematical as noted already, as well as an Egyptian price from the third century after inflation had picked up. The results are shown in Table 6.3, where it can be seen that these regressions reproduce the coefficients on distance in Table 6.2. The coefficients are the same size and known with the same precision. The regressions as a whole, however, do not have the same explanatory power as those from Rickman's data. Despite the overlap between the two data sets, there is more unexplained variation in this data set. In addition, when the two problematical observations are dropped, there are no more observations than in Table 6.1. Since there is an additional variable, the degrees of freedom are like the second and fourth regressions in Table 6.2 with only three degrees of freedom. As before, it is good that omitting these observations does not affect the results. The constant is larger than before because it includes an implied price at Rome in addition to any costs of taxes or transport to the city. The estimated inflation rate mysteriously is very large.

It is good that Rathbone's data confirm the effect of distance on price that I found in Rickman's data. There are some problems that should be acknowledged. Differing from my earlier regressions, I did not use all of Rathbone's data. I had good reasons for my selections, but I cannot be sure that the resulting data constitute another random sample. The reason is that I already knew what I wanted the regression to look like, and I may have selected data to show the pattern I desired. Even if I did not explicitly set out to reproduce my results, I may have done so unconsciously. To test the randomness of the Rickman sample, it would be better to have a data set constructed by someone not invested in the results in Table 6.2.

The third step in this argument uses such data. Bransbourg (2012) did not start out as supportive of my results. The first graph in his chapter shows the effect of moving the measured distance for one of my observations, a move that he claims makes my regression "very weak to a point of near irrelevance." This claim of course is unfounded. It is clear that you get different answers with different data. To change the data after the results appear in order to change the results does not allow you to test hypotheses. If you do not believe in data, then you can reach any conclusion you desire. If you feel free to change the facts, then you leave the domains of history and economics.

Bransbourg also said that "statisticians try to avoid situations where they have to rely on a dozen or fewer observations." This is correct but irrelevant. If we had more Roman price data, we would use it. When I found more data for prices in Hellenistic Babylon,

I used all the econometric tools I could to ask if these were market prices, if they moved in response to historical events, and other related questions (Temin 2002). But we lack more prices for Rome in the late Republic and early Empire. If we had more data, we would use it. Given the limited number of observations, we console ourselves with calculations that require higher t-statistics for any level of significance with fewer observations. These higher levels keep us from making excessive claims for estimated coefficients when we have only six observations rather than six hundred.

After additional criticism of my methodology—"the equation as formulated [Table 6.2] cannot be statistically upheld"—Bransbourg set about collecting a new set of prices. He added more prices to those reported in Rickman, and he recalculated Rickman's data to provide what he considered more accurate distances and sometimes new values. Despite the overlap with Rickman's sample, the new data set provides a new sample from this ancient price distribution that can be used to see if another sample yields the same result as the first sample.

And the answer is . . . the new sample replicates the results of the original one. Despite Bransbourg's effort to discredit my results, he obtained the same results even as he stacked the deck against them. The results shown in Table 6.4 reveal that even with Bransbourg's data, the negative association between price and distance is clear. The first two regressions appear in Bransbourg's chapter as reported here. I replicated the regressions, but I use his results here to make my emendations consistent with his work.

With his full data set of a dozen observations, he reproduced the significant effect of distance on price, but with a lower R^2. He concluded that the effect of distance explained far less of the variation of Roman prices than I claimed. Bransbourg suggested that the market may have worked better for coastal cities than inland ones, and tested this proposition in the second regression. Using only coastal cities,

Table 6.4. Bransbourg regression results

	N	Constant	Distance	Inland	R^2
Distance	12	−2.43 (−7.57)	−.00041 (−3.56)		.56
Distance	6	−0.93 (−8.65)	−00072 (−4.96)		.86
Distance **(with a dummy for inland cities)**	12	−2.78 (−10.16)	−.00050 (−5.37)	0.95 (−2.87)	.77
Distance **(No Antioch in Pisidia)**	11	−2.65 (−8.25)	−.00059 (−4.12)	0.95 (−2.84)	.72

Source: Bransbourg (2012).

and reducing his sample size to the familiar half-dozen, he found that not only was the effect of distance clearer, but that distance from Rome explained 86 percent of the variation of prices around the Mediterranean.

If Bransbourg's reasoning is correct, then a regression of the other six observations—the ones from inland cities—should not show much effect of the distance from Rome. I did that regression and found exactly the opposite. The coefficient of distance was estimated precisely, and the regression line explained 87 percent of the price variation. This result (not shown in Table 6.4) suggested that distance was important, but it was slightly different for coastal and inland cities. I therefore did a regression with all twelve of Bransbourg's observations and an additional variable, a dummy for inland cities.

The results are shown in the third equation of Table 6.4. There the results of my original regressions clearly are reproduced. The effect of distance on wheat prices is clearly estimated and the regression explains three-quarters of the variation of Roman wheat prices around the Mediterranean once one makes an allowance for the difference between coastal and inland cities. The effect of the extra cost of transportation is not clearly estimated, but it appears that the price discounts from the price in Rome in coastal cities were about one *sestertius* per *modius* smaller than inland cities at the same distance from Rome.

This is perplexing. The effect of distance shows up well in the combined regression with twelve observations, but it puts the constant term higher for inland cities. In other words, inland cities at the same distance from Rome as coastal cities had *higher* wheat prices. I tried to see if this was due to an outlying observation. Bransbourg placed Antioch in Pisidia much farther from Rome by adding many sea-mile equivalents for overland transportation to the coast. I omitted this observation—as I did in Table 6.2 for the Po Valley—and obtained the final regression in Table 6.4. This regression, with eleven observations is almost exactly like the one above it with twe observations; the extreme observation did not dictate the rise in the inland price. And the R^2 is as high as in the original regressions in Table 6.2.

I cannot resolve the issue of inland prices at this time. Perhaps all the inland cities have their distances in equivalent sea miles inflated in this data set. Perhaps there is another explanation. Nevertheless, the equations are stable and the coefficient on distance clear in all regressions. It appears that the influence of the Mediterranean market was as strong for inland cities as for coastal. While not totally distinct from the original Rickman sample, this sample shows similar patterns, reinforcing the randomness of the original sample.

6.5. ANALYSIS OF PRICES

Having justified the assumption of randomness to enable statistical distributions to be used, I turn to several more general objections that have been raised to this kind of test and its conclusion. The first objection is that prices were low outside Rome because coined money was scarce, not because transport to Rome was costly. This alternative cannot explain the prices in Table 6.1. Coins may have been scarce in Lusitania at the time of Polybius, but coins were abundant in the eastern Mediterranean where the monetized Greek economy preceded the Roman one. Wheat prices there were lower than in Lusitania, as can be seen from the figures. Distance from Rome is a much better predictor of prices than coin scarcity.

A second objection is that the prices are unrepresentative because they are notional, biased because the observers had political motives, or unrepresentative due to price fluctuations. Such errors in the price observations may have been present, although Polybius was a very careful historian, not liable to falsify his evidence to make a rhetorical point. As noted already, such errors in recording the "true" prices introduce noise into the relationship between the price differential and distance from Rome. If there was a great deal of this distortion, any existing relationship might be obscured. Since the regressions show such a relation, it means that the relationship between distance and price was a strong one, visible even through the noise introduced by casual or distorted price observations.

More formally, we can think of the observed prices being determined by the true prevailing prices, which we observe with an error due to our approximation. Then the dependent variable we used in the regression is the true price differential plus an error. That error would add onto the error of the regression and result in a lower t-statistic and R^2. Given that they both are large, the data show that this rough assumption in fact is quite good, that the observed prices appear to represent prevailing prices in a reasonable fashion.

Another related objection is that prices fluctuated during the year and observations may have come from different seasons. Again, this source of noise strengthens the results because the seasonal price variation introduces another source of noise into the hypothesized relationship. I suspect that the casual nature of the price observations has helped here. Travelers were told of the prevailing price, not sometimes the high price that obtains just before the harvest comes in and sometimes the low price following the harvest. The result appears to be a consistent set of prices. Phrased differently, while the few prices that have survived for two millennia are quite random, it is perverse to insist that any observed pattern has to be spurious. There does not seem to be a reason to throw out evidence from the ancient world on the grounds that the pattern must be as random as the observations.

Yet another objection to the use of these prices is that the argument is circular: I assume the data are sound because they support the hypothesis, but the test of the hypothesis requires the data to be sound. On the contrary, I assume that the observed prices are drawn randomly from a distribution of prices in the late Republic and early Roman Empire. I do not assume they are accurate or come from a particular kind of investigation or a particular time of year (as in the previous paragraph), and I compared my results with those from other data sets. Given that I am sampling from the population of wheat prices, the t-statistic tells us whether there is a relationship between price and distance. There is no more circularity here than in any statistical test of a hypothesis.

The tiny size of the samples, often only six price pairs or eight prices, may also raise objections. The small samples are unfortunate, but no barrier to the test of this hypothesis. As noted above, the standard errors and t-statistics are corrected for degrees of freedom. Having few observations makes it easier to reject hypotheses, but it does not affect the validity of the test. We would of course like to have many more prices, but there are no more to be found at this time. The new Rathbone sample has hardly more useable prices, and it confirms the main outlines of the test. Bransbourg's additional observations again confirm the importance of distance from Rome in determining provincial wheat prices.

Rathbone's data set includes observations from periods of severe shortages. The few added observations do not give us information on the frequency of these shortages, but they remind us that the

Mediterranean wheat market was subject to events that increased the difficulty and cost of shipping wheat across the sea. The market worked in general, but there was not enough storage to smooth out the difficulties that arose from time to time.

Some objections are imprecisely formulated. Erdkamp (2005: 256) talks of "the weaknesses of the grain market." This is not an economic term; perhaps it refers to the occasional shortages. Seminar participants have said that if one data point of this small data set was moved, then the result would disappear. But choosing data points to make a result come out the way you want it makes the process circular; a statistical test only is possible when the data are chosen for reasons other than influencing the result of a test.

Bang (2008: 31) stated dramatically:

> Peter Temin argued that Finley was quite simply wrong; the economy of the Roman Empire represented just such a conglomeration ["an enormous conglomeration of interdependent markets"]. This is an extraordinary claim. One might conceivably imagine that some markets had begun to be linked by middle- and long-distance trade. But to see the entire economy, spanning several continents, as organized by a set of interlinked markets is quite another matter. It is doubtful whether the mature eighteenth-century European economy, outside some restricted pockets, could be described in such terms.

The last sentence reveals a difficulty with references to early modern European economic history that is all too common among ancient historians. Bang reported staples of early modern trade practices—reports from agents, family networks, need for supercargoes, etc.—as if they precluded long-distance trade. He quoted the boilerplate at the end of a typical agent letter saying that prices vary over time as evidence that planning is impossible, and he decried the Roman failure to develop bills of exchange without understanding that the Roman universal currency area obviated the need for such bills. In fact, eighteenth-century international trade stimulated the Industrial Revolution (Allen 2009).

An additional point is that the existence of an integrated wheat market in the Mediterranean is not ruled out by the lack of complete specialization in any provinces, as Bang also suggests in denying the presence of "Ricardian trade" in the Roman Empire (Bang 2008: 73–6). Over the course of two centuries since Ricardo's original formulation, however, scholars have elaborated his theory of comparative advantage. Thus Ricardo's model still illuminates the principle of comparative advantage when we acknowledge there are two factors of production and prices change when countries approach specialization. The only difference is that the model used today allows for partial specialization if countries or regions are not too different. No ancient historian denies that Roman Egypt had a comparative advantage in wheat production.

All these objections come, I think, from two causes. First, the regressions challenge long-held beliefs about the primitivism of ancient societies. Second, we must avoid the hazards of thinking identified by Daniel Kahneman. He argues that many people are prone to assuming that what you see is all there is instead of extrapolating from what they see. And he says that "people are prone to apply causal thinking inappropriately, to situations that require statistical reasoning" (Kahneman 2011: 77).

This chapter has explored the usefulness of small-sample regressions when more observations are not available. As I said earlier, my econometric colleagues like to use these regressions to illustrate the usefulness of econometric theory because the students can calculate directly the significance of their results. They are taught regularly to graduate students at MIT. Economics increasingly is using larger and larger data sets, but every once and a while a small data set is all that is available. It is important to understand how useful such a small data set can be.

This chapter presents evidence for the presence of a series of unified grain markets that stretched from one end of the Mediterranean to the other in the late Roman Republic and early Empire. The extent of the Roman market has been debated exhaustively, but evidence to date has been restricted to local markets. The presence of localized market activity has ceased to be controversial, but the question of market integration is still alive. The evidence produced here demonstrates that there was something approaching a unified grain market in the Roman Mediterranean.

Government interventions in wheat markets make it clear that the market could not prevent shortages even in Rome (Garnsey 1999). The government intervened in the wheat market from time to time to lower prices and alleviate shortages, particularly under Augustus. It also is clear, even from what must be a partial list, that the known interventions were intermittent. The market for wheat was allowed to work on its own in other years. In addition, if traders expected the government to interfere when famine loomed, they might have been discouraged from trying to corner the market in adversity. Government intervention therefore may have dampened speculation and made the underlying pattern of prices easier to see.

Of course, there also were local shortages and famines, and local areas were not always connected to the market in Rome. Rathbone records examples of isolated markets—with prices that do not fit this regression line—showing examples of prices not connected to the regular market. The regressions demonstrate that there were many connections between far-flung Roman grain markets; only with more data will we be able to get a better idea how often outlying markets were connected to the major consuming market in Rome.

This question parallels questions about the reach of Roman law into the provinces. Laws do not appear directly in the statistics, but they provided the context in which observed behavior took place. Explicit government interventions were recorded by contemporary observers; underlying legal frameworks need to be extrapolated from the various actions that have left records for us to find.

This chapter illustrates the usefulness of regression analysis in ancient history. My approach has compiled existing information into a format that suggested the existence of a unified market, as in Figure 6.1. It also provides a test whether the observed pattern could have arisen by chance. Given the small number of observations, it always is possible that the pattern was simply a coincidence. Regression analysis allows us to quantify that possibility. The probability that the line in Figure 6.2 was due to chance is about 5 percent, that is, one in twenty. This is a far more precise estimate of the probability that we are observing an actual relationship than has been available previously. Given the scarcity of data and the prevalence of shortages, it is clear that regressions can only help interpret existing data, not provide additional information to provide definitive answers to all questions.

Finally, these regressions tested a very simple model of Roman trade, that there was a single wheat market across the whole Mediterranean. I tested this hypothesis with simple regressions with few degrees of freedom. Why should any ancient historian believe such a simple model and test? The purpose of a model is to provide an overall view of trade in Rome; it cannot explain every detail. Instead it provides an overview that helps our thinking. In this case, the regressions show that there were interconnected markets in the

Mediterranean, but we also saw in the data that these markets did not work all the time or in all places. As expressed by Rathbone (2011):

> Unsatisfactorily thin as the Roman wheat price data are, they seem to suggest a partially integrated market, determined primarily by regional productivity and demand on the one hand, and on the other by the ease or difficulty of transport. Basically the major coastal zones of the empire were linked into a hierarchical structure with the highest price band in Rome and Campania, where demand most exceeded production, a middle band in Sicily, the Greek cities and, to some extent, Judaea, and the lowest band in Egypt, which though not coastal was linked to the Mediterranean by the Nile, and where production most exceeded demand.

And as reiterated more closely in the spirit of this chapter in Rathbone and von Reden (2015: 189):

> In conclusion, various factors made the Roman world and economy of the first to third centuries AD different from ancient Babylonia on the one hand and early modern Europe on the other. The market for wheat in the Roman world was essentially a free market, which in the imperial period comprised and was influenced by the administered market of the imperial Annona and civic intervention.

Rathbone sees a hierarchy where I see continuity, but we describe much the same conditions. He notes that the excess of demand over the supply of wheat was greatest in and around Rome, and he says other regions were "linked into a hierarchical structure." This is the structure of an interconnected set of Mediterranean markets that extended—with occasional interruptions and the probable exception of turbulent Judaea—from Egypt to Lusitania in the late Roman Republic and early Roman Empire.

REFERENCES

Allen, Robert C. 2009. *The British Industrial Revolution in Global Perspective.* Cambridge: Cambridge University Press.

Bang, Peter F. 2008. *The Roman Bazaar: A Comparative Study of Trade and Markets in a Tributary Empire.* Cambridge: Cambridge University Press.

Bransbourg, Gilles. 2012. "Rome and the Economic Integration of Empire." Institute for the Study of the Ancient World Papers 3. Available at http:/dlib.nyu.edu/awdl/isaw/isaw-papers/3.

Duncan-Jones, Richard. 1982. *The Economy of the Roman Empire: Quantitative Studies*. 2nd edn. Cambridge: Cambridge University Press.
Duncan-Jones, Richard. 1990. *Structure and Scale in the Roman Economy*. Cambridge: Cambridge University Press.
Erdkamp, Paul. 2005. *The Grain Market in the Roman Empire*. Cambridge: Cambridge University Press.
Garnsey, Peter. 1998. *Cities, Peasants and Food in Classical Antiquity*. Cambridge: Cambridge University Press.
Garnsey, Peter. 1999. *Food and Society in Classical Antiquity*. Cambridge: Cambridge University Press.
Greenblatt, Stephen. 2011. *The Swerve: How the World Became Modern*. New York: Norton.
Greene, Kevin. 1986. *The Archeology of the Roman Economy*. London: Batsford.
Harris, William V. 1989. "Trade and the River Po: A Problem in the Economic History of the Roman Empire," in Jean-François Bergier, ed., *Montagnes, fleuves, forêts dans l'histoire*. St. Katharinen: Scripta Mercaturae Verlag, 123–34; reprinted in William V. Harris. 2011. *Rome's Imperial Economy: Twelve Essays*. New York: Oxford University Press.
Heichelheim, Fritz M. 1938. "Roman Syria," in Tenney Frank, ed., *Economic Survey of Ancient Rome*, vol. 4. Baltimore: Johns Hopkins Press, 121–57.
Kahneman, Daniel. 2011. *Thinking, Fast and Slow*. New York: Farrar, Straus, and Giroux.
Kehoe, Dennis P. 2007. *Law and the Rural Economy in the Roman Empire*. Ann Arbor: University of Michigan Press.
Kessler, David, and Peter Temin. 2008. "Money and Prices in the Early Roman Empire," in William V. Harris, ed., *The Monetary Systems of the Greeks and Romans*. Oxford: Oxford University Press, 137–59.
Rathbone, Dominic. 1997. "Prices and Price Formation in Roman Egypt," in Jean Andreau, ed., *Économie antique. Prix et formation des prix dans les économies antiques*. Saint-Bertrand-de-Comminges: Musée archéologique départemental, 183–244.
Rathbone, Dominic. 2003. "The Financing of Maritime Commerce in the Roman Empire, I–II AD", in Elio Lo Cascio, ed., *Credito e moneta nel mondo romano: atti degli Incontri capresi di storia dell'economia antica*: Capri, 12–14 ottobre 2000. Naples: Edipuglia, 197–229.
Rathbone, Dominic. 2009. "Earnings and Costs: Living Standards and the Roman Economy," in Alan Bowman and Andrew Wilson, eds, *Quantifying the Roman Economy*. Oxford: Oxford University Press, 299–326.
Rathbone, Dominic. 2011. "Grain Prices and Grain Markets in the Roman World," presented at the conference on the Efficiency of Markets in Preindustrial Societies, Amsterdam, May 19–21, 2011. Available at: http://www.cgeh.nl/efficiency-markets-preindustrial-societies.

Rathbone, Dominic, and Sitta von Reden. 2015. "Mediterranean Grain Prices in Classical Antiquity," in R. J. van der Spek, Jan Luiten van Zanden, and Bas van Leeuwen, eds, *A History of Market Performance: From Ancient Babylonia to the Modern World*. London: Routledge, 149–235.

Rickman, Geoffrey. 1980. *The Corn Supply of Ancient Rome*. Oxford: Clarendon Press.

Scheidel, Walter. 2014. "The Shape of the Roman World." 27 *Journal of Roman Archaeology* 7–32.

Smith, Adam. 1776. *The Wealth of Nations*. London: Strahan and Cadell.

Temin, Peter. 2002. "Price Behavior in Ancient Babylon." 39 *Explorations in Economic History* 46–60.

Temin, Peter. 2006. "The Economy of the Early Roman Empire." 20 *Journal of Economic Perspectives* 133–51.

Temin, Peter. 2013. *The Roman Market Economy*. Princeton: Princeton University Press.

7

The Organization of India-to-Rome Trade

Loans and Agents in the Muziris Papyrus

Ron Harris

7.1. ORGANIZING LONG-DISTANCE TRADE

In pre-modern times, long-distance trade was the most demanding business activity. Men and goods had to be sent on long oceanic or overland routes to unfamiliar lands whose market conditions were unknown and whose rulers' willingness to allow their entry and commitment not to expropriate them were unpredictable. Such trade involved considerable uncertainties, only partially converted into measurable risk. The risk included a relatively high probability of total loss, alongside, to be sure, a probability of exceptionally hefty gains. It involved significant informational asymmetry and high agency costs. Contracts with foreign counterparts were simply not enforceable, under either local or foreign rulers. Contracts with agents were subject to the problem of the limited ability of the principal who stayed behind to observe and verify any breach by the agent and to the possibility that the agent would defect and stay overseas with the goods or money. Capital investment was relatively high and the circulation time long. There were tantalizing hopes of enormous profits upon return of the ships or arrival of the caravans due to the huge arbitrage gaps between distant markets. But there was a real possibility of loss at sea, at the hands of pirates or bandits, or due to expropriation by a foreign ruler; and loss of goods, money,

Ron Harris, *The Organization of India-to-Rome Trade: Loans and Agents in the Muziris Papyrus* In: *Roman Law and Economics: Institutions and Organizations, Volume I.* Edited by: Giuseppe Dari-Mattiacci and Dennis P. Kehoe, Oxford University Press (2020).
DOI: 10.1093/oso/9780198787204.003.0007

ships, and lives.[1] Such challenges made this sector of business activity the frontier of organizational innovation. The organization of long-distance trade had to address the most severe agency problems, contract enforcement problems, expropriation concerns, managerial challenges, and complex financial investment tools.

Historians over the centuries have encountered difficulties in studying how merchants and rulers dealt with these organizational challenges. The main obstacle facing them was—and continues to be—the scarcity of surviving records that specify the detailed organization of trade, compared to the surviving material and textual evidence with respect to commodities, routes, and ports. Organizational snapshots of Eurasian trade exist for the period starting with the eleventh-century India trade-related correspondence and legal documents found in the Cairo Geniza. But until the discovery of the Muziris Papyrus in the 1980s, no records dealing directly with legal–economic praxis were known for the organization of Roman trade with India or, in fact, for any period that pre-dated the Geniza records.

For the last three decades, the Muziris Papyrus has been the subject of an intensive study by papyrologists and by historians of ancient Rome, the Greek Eastern Mediterranean, and India. The study began with philological analysis, textual reconstruction, glossing, and intertextuality, which gave rise to conflicting interpretations of the meaning of the text. The present chapter, which is written by an outsider to these fields, does not aim to add to this course of study. It will use organizational theory and the scholarship about medieval organizational forms (taking into account the known drawbacks and advantages of employing such approaches) to place the Muziris Papyrus and the organization of India-to-Egypt trade in the Roman era in a wider historical context. The aim is dual: to provide scholars of the organization of Roman-era trade with insights from these perspectives; and to introduce the Muziris Papyrus to scholars of the organization of medieval and early modern trade. This chapter will first provide some important background on Rome's trade with India, the Muziris papyrus itself, and law in Greco-Roman Egypt. It will then analyze the legal and economic significance of the papyrus in interaction with these backgrounds. It will lastly examine continuity and change in the organization of trade with India, from Roman times to the medieval period.

[1] For the unique organizational challenges involved in Eurasian trade, see Harris (2005, 2009, 2010).

7.2. ROME'S INDIA TRADE

The Roman Empire was vast and diverse enough to keep much of its trade within its own boundaries.[2] This provided numerous advantages, including a secure trade environment, an Empire-wide contract-enforcement system, political commitment not to arbitrarily expropriate, an information-flow infrastructure, and more. The Mediterranean, *Mare Nostrum*, was the cradle of Roman maritime trade, as it had been for Greek trade. This trade environment was very different from the environment of the era of the Cairo Geniza and beyond, in which Mediterranean trade was international—with all the resulting organizational challenges. Trading outside of the Empire was only worthwhile when merchants could obtain exceptional goods, say tropical products, which promised exceptionally high profits. The difference between the political environments in Mediterranean and Indian trade was much starker in antiquity than in the Middle Ages. This could potentially have organizational ramifications.

Rome's eastern trade was carried out along four major routes. The main overland route was from Palmyra (Tadmor) in Syria to Mesopotamia, the Parthian Empire, and beyond. A secondary, more northerly, overland route branched off from the first and connected Armenia to the western segment of the Silk Road leading to Central Asia. A southern overland route led from Gaza on the Mediterranean, through the Nabataean Kingdom, with Petra at its hub, into Arabia. It served the incense and aromatics trade, carrying products from the southern regions of Arabia into the Roman Empire (Young 2001). Figure 7.1 shows the main overland and maritime routes that connected the Eastern Mediterranean with Asia.

India was on the edge of civilization as it was known to the Romans. Its goods were exotic, rare, and of high value in the markets of the Roman Empire. Overland trade with India via Palmyra involved long and risky journeys and high transportation costs. Indian Ocean trade was sporadic and high-risk, and confined to short seasons. As Roman mariners, in or about the first century CE, learned how to cope with monsoons, more of the trade to India was diverted from overland caravan routes (originating in Palmyra) to the Red Sea and Indian Ocean route (Warmington 1974: 35–83; Casson 1980).

[2] For Rome's trade with India, see now Cobb (2018).

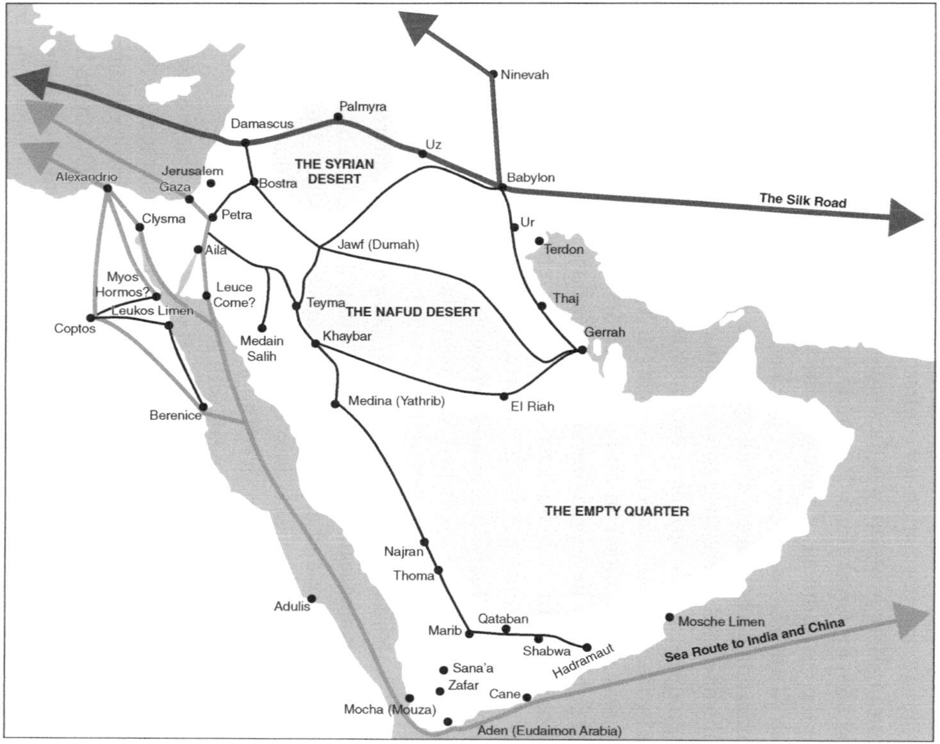

Figure 7.1. Rome's eastern trade routes.

Source: http://nabataea.net/trader.html.

Trade practices on the Indian Ocean routes are sporadically mentioned in surviving manuscripts (Casson 1980: 22–3; McLaughlin 2010: 7–23). The most notable of these is *Periplus Maris Erythraei*, a Greco-Roman voyage manual describing navigation and trading opportunities from Roman Egyptian Red Sea ports to destinations in India and East Africa. Written roughly around the time of the Muziris Papyrus, it provides much information about ports, routes, and goods, but not on how trade was organized, managed, or financed (Casson 1989).

The fourth route connecting Rome with the east is the one that is relevant for us. It was the main oceanic route from India to the Roman Empire that began in one of the ports of the Malabar Coast of southern India, famously Muziris, and infrequently in Sri Lanka or destinations further afield in the Indian Ocean. From any of these ports, the ships sailed the western Indian Ocean, usually along the coastline of India, Persia, and Southern Arabia, and entered the Bab el-Mandab Strait into the Red Sea. At this point, this route joined the East African trade route. The ships sailed northward across the Red Sea and anchored in one of the ports on the Egyptian side, notably Myos Hormos (identified by some scholars with Quseir al-Qadim) and Berenike. Goods next crossed the desert on camel caravans to Koptos (Coptos, Coptus) in Upper Egypt, the closest point on the Nile to the Red Sea. Koptos was located on the Nile banks as well as at the head of the cross-Eastern Desert routes to the Red Sea. Its unique location made it the hub of trade with Arabia, East Africa, and India. The desert roads between the Red Sea and the Nile, along Wadi Hammamat and Wadi Minayh, were well developed in the time of the Muziris Papyrus. They provided travelers with transportation facilities and protection posts. Much is known about the use of these roads from independent sources such as inscriptions and graffiti, archeological excavations, and other papyri, and this independent knowledge has ramifications for understanding the Muziris papyrus, as we shall see (Sidebotham 2011; Wilson 2015; Grønlund Evers 2017: 91–108, 117–24).

Once at the Nile, the goods were loaded on boats and shipped down the river on the well-traveled route to Alexandria. From Alexandria, the Indian goods were shipped to Rome, Antioch, Ephesus, or other Mediterranean ports, and distributed to markets throughout the Roman Empire (Warmington 1974: 1–18; Young 2001: 28–36; McLaughlin 2010: 23–33). We can observe from Figure 7.2 the routes that connected the Red Sea ports with the Nile via the Eastern Desert.

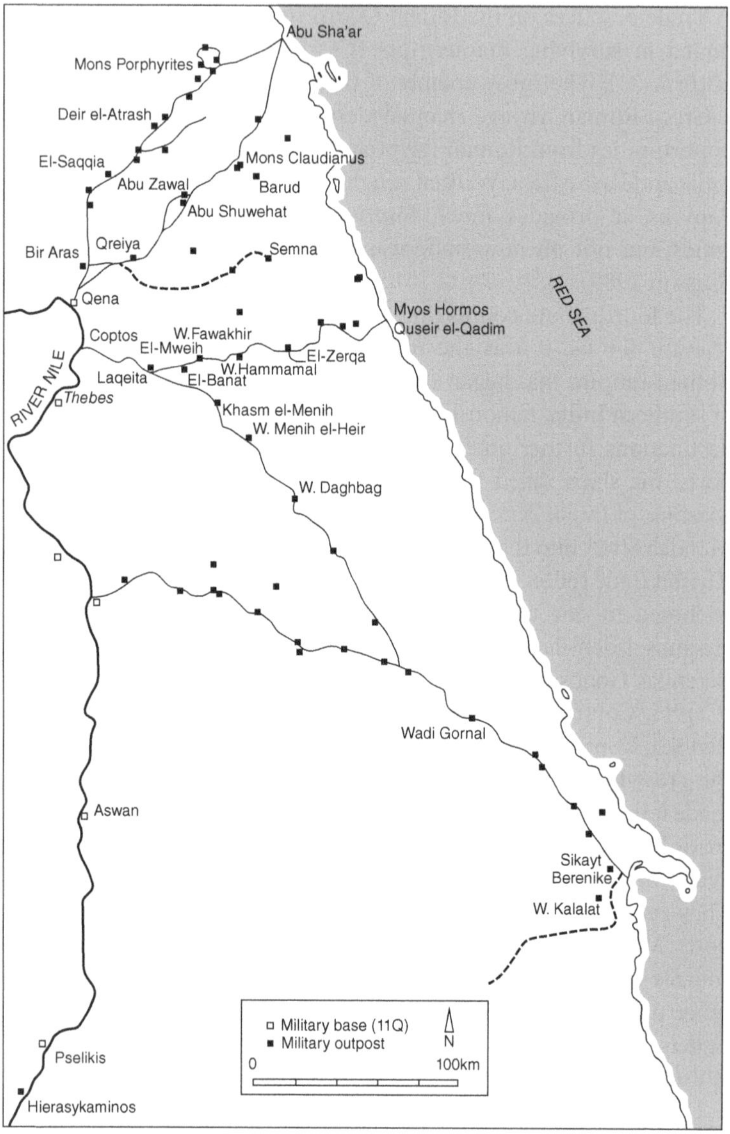

Figure 7.2. The Eastern Desert of Egypt.

Source: Maxfield, 2003.

Our knowledge of the goods traded is based on archeological evidence and tax collection records, and is thus quite solid. Black pepper was the most common good found in the Berenike and Quseir excavations (Tomber 2012). Other imports from India and the Indian Ocean that left traces in archeological sites along the way, in inscriptions and in preserved papyri and literary texts, include spices, coconut, glass, coins, and precious stones (Young 2001: 221–51; McLaughlin 2010: 179–81). Evidence from Indian archeological sites on imports from the Roman Empire is more incomplete, but it suggests that such goods included wine, olive oil, red corals, and Roman coins (Gurukkal 2013).

Not much is known about the organization of the trade between Egypt and India in Roman times. Actual organizational documents were practically unavailable until 1985, when the discovery and publication of the Muziris Papyrus provided a rare opportunity to study the organization of Rome's most challenging trade route. The analysis of this unique papyrus is at the core of the current chapter.

This chapter will proceed as follows: I will first present the Muziris Papyrus; then discuss the legal framework within which it was drafted; analyze it in light of its legal framework; and lastly explore it in light of the wider historical context.

7.3. THE MUZIRIS PAPYRUS

The Muziris Papyrus, named after the port on the Malabar coast of India, is also known as the Vienna Papyrus, because it was purchased in 1980 by the Austrian National Archive from an antiques merchant. Its exact place of origin in Egypt is unknown. It is written in Greek, the transcript of it first being published in 1985, and is dated by papyrology scholars to the mid-second century CE. Because it is unique in the papyrological corpus of Greco-Roman Egypt, in that it singularly mentions a port in India, it soon became the subject of great interest among papyrology scholars. It adds a new dimension to our knowledge of the organizational practices of Eurasia trade in antiquity and is, in fact, the best available source on the contractual arrangements of Middle Eastern India merchants in antiquity and in the early Middle Ages, up to the era of the Cairo Geniza, almost a millennium later.

The papyrus contains incomplete texts on both sides. Figure 7.3 shows the fragmented state of the front side of the Muziris Papyrus.

Its reverse side (verso) provides an account of goods shipped from India to Egypt on a single voyage of the *Hermapollon*. It calculates values and customs payments based on the weight and prices of the

Figure 7.3. Muziris Papyrus recto.

P.Vindob. G 40822. Austrian National Library. http://data.onb.ac.at/rec/RZ00001642.

goods listed. The goods that could be identified in the one column that was sufficiently preserved include sixty containers of Gangetic nard (a fragrance), ivory tusks, and ivory fragments. Much of the list was not preserved, and the exact status of the prices (pre-tax or after tax) is debated.[3] The total weight of the shipment is calculated at nearly 4,000 kg, and its value in Alexandrian prices after tax, according to one calculation, was nearly seven million drachmas, a huge amount equal to that needed to buy a luxury estate in Roman Italy of the time (Cobb 2018: 78–83, 90).

The front side (recto) of the papyrus looks like a contract. Due to its importance for the present study, which focuses on organizational–legal aspects of the trade, I will provide its text in full. I use Rathbone's 2000 transcription and English translation, with Morelli's 2011 amendments (marked with *), as published by Grønlund Evers in 2017 (99–100):

The Muziris Papyrus (SB XVIII, 13167)
Recto, column ii (column one being lost)

- - -] your other administrators or managers, and on agreement(?)
I will give(?)] to your trustworthy camel-driver [- - -] (?) for the conduct*
of the journey up] to Koptos; and I will convey (the goods) through the desert under guard and protection
up to the] public tax-receiving warehouses at Koptos, and
I will] place them under the [authority] and seal of yourself, or of your administrators or whichever
one of them is present, until their loading at the river; and I will load them
at the requi]red time onto a safe ship on the river; and I will convey them down
to the warehouse for receiving the quarter-tax [at Alex]andria, and
likewise] will place them under the authority and seal of yourself or your men.
All the payments out of my own pocket from now to collection of the quarter-tax, and of(?) the*
desert tran[sport] and the carrying-charges of the river-workers and the other incidental(?)
exp[ens]es [- - -] on occurrence of the date for repayment specified in

[3] For an analysis of this side in an attempt to reconstruct the cargo of the *Hermapollon*, see De Romanis (2012).

the contracts of lo[an] for (the trip to) Muziris, if I do not
then] duly discharge the aforesaid loan in my name, that then
you] and your administrators or managers are to have the option and
com[plete] authority, if you so choose, to carry out execution without
notifica]tion or summons to judgement, to possess and own the
afore[said] security and pay the quarter-tax, to convey the
three] parts which will be left where you choose and to sell or use them as security
and] to transfer them to another person, if you so choose, and to deal with the
items of the security in whatsoever way you choose, and to buy them for yourself at the
price current at the time, and to subtract and reckon in what falls due
on account of the aforesai]d loan, on terms that the responsibility for what falls due
lies] with you and your administrators or managers and we are free from
accus[at]ion in every respect, and that the surplus or shortfall from the capital
goes] to me the borrower and giver of sec[urity- - -

This is not the only translation of the papyrus. Since 1985 it has been transcribed in Greek and translated to English and other European languages and annotated several times. The document is fragmented, with the top and bottom both missing. There are some unintelligible words in the surviving text, and some of the readable sentences are ambiguous. All of these factors have given rise to a variety of annotations, glosses, gap-fillings, and interpretations (Casson 1986, 1990; Harrauer and Sijpesteijn 1986; Thür 1987; Rathbone 2000: 39–41; Morelli 2011; De Romanis 2012, 2014; Grønlund Evers 2017).

As I am trained in neither papyrology nor classics, the current chapter does not, and cannot, aim to provide a new translation, gloss, exegesis, or close annotation of the papyrus. It offers instead theoretically informed comparative understanding of the organization of Rome-to-India trade, using the papyrus as its starting point. For this purpose, I will mainly use Rathbone's translation of the text, and at some specific points will compare it to Casson's translation, to Morelli's suggested corrections, and to the relevant controversies about the meaning of the text in the literature.

The debates regarding the meaning of the contract on the recto have unfolded over the last three decades. The original 1985 editors,

Harrauer and Sijpesteijn, viewed it as a freight agreement and sea loan contract drafted in Muziris with respect to the trip back to Alexandria. Casson, in 1986, understood the agreement to be a regular loan contract produced in a Red Sea port to supplement a sea loan concluded on another document. Thür, in 1987, interpreted it as a document drafted in Alexandria as a contractual supplement to a sea loan—a document dealing with the security provided for that loan. Rathbone, in 2000, held the papyrus to be the preserved part of a sea loan agreement made in Alexandria for a return voyage to Muziris, in which details of the first leg of the voyage (from Muziris to the Red Sea port) were lost with the missing column. For Rathbone, the document was a generic master supplement rather than a specific agreement between named parties. Morelli, in 2011, understood the document to be an agreement made in a Red Sea port to replace an earlier loan made in Alexandria before the onward trip, with a second regular loan covering the last leg back. De Romanis, in 2012 and 2014, asserted that it is a complete agreement that has to be read together with common background practices and customs. Lastly, for now, Grønlund Evers concluded in 2017 that the agreement is not a sea loan agreement—on the basis that it does not use the relevant terminology—but rather a regular loan with a security pertaining to the well-serviced and monitored leg from the Red Sea to Alexandria (Grønlund Evers 2017).

The map of the debated issues is now apparent. Geographically, some argued that the contract covered the entire route from Muziris to Alexandria, and others that it dealt only with the overland route from the Red Sea port to Alexandria. Some argued that it was drafted in India, and some that it was drafted in Egypt. Some held that it was in the legal format of a sea loan, while others claimed it was an ordinary loan agreement. There were at least three distinct identifications of the identity of the parties involved: that one party was a financier and the other a merchant; that both parties were merchants; and that one party was a merchant and the other an agent of another merchant. There was also a debate as to who was the active—initiating—party. Further, there was disagreement as to which assets were used as security in this transaction. Lastly, there was a lack of consensus as to whether the text is of an individualized contract, whose parties' names are unknown due to the top and bottom sections being missing, or a master template in its original form that was never intended to bear the names of any parties.

7.4. THE LAW IN GRECO-ROMAN EGYPT

The Muziris Papyrus is universally viewed by researchers as a document that was meant to be a legally binding contract. The meaning of a legal document cannot be reconstructed in detachment from the applicable legal rules. The applicable rules can be inferred top-down through determination of the legal system that applied to the contract. The applicable law can be inferred bottom-up from the contract to the applicable legal system. In the case of the Muziris Papyrus, neither exercise is simple. As much as the law applied territorially, the location of the contract (its drafting, execution, or operation) has to be concluded from its text. As much as it applied personally, then the identity of the parties to the contract has to be determined based on its text. The text does not provide either explicitly. Another possibility is that it refers to legal terms from which we can conclude the particular law the drafters of the text envisioned applying to the contract. So it seems a pragmatic combination of top-down and bottom-up approaches will provide helpful insights.

There are good reasons to infer (based on its apparent place of discovery, on its Greek language, and on the place names mentioned in its text) that the Muziris Papyrus was drafted in Egypt, or that it was intended to apply to transactions that centered, or at least began and terminated, in Egypt. But which law might the drafters of the text have envisioned as being applicable to such an agreement in second-century CE Egypt?

The Roman legions moved forward much faster than Roman culture and law. The Romanization of the Empire was a slow and uneven process. Roman law expanded primarily by the granting of full or partial citizenship to additional groups (Latins, allies, soldiers, or manumitted slaves, for instance) within the Empire. Provincials were the last group to acquire Roman citizenship, in 212 CE. The Eastern Mediterranean, a central part of the Empire, had its own unique legal mix. The well-established and highly developed Hellenistic culture, language, and law did not easily yield to Romanization. Romanization in the Eastern Mediterranean often meant infusion of Greek and Roman law rather than transplantation of Roman law.

Greco-Roman Egypt, the pivotal part of the Empire for studying trade with India, was even more unique because it had an ancient Egyptian Pharaonic (pre-Greek) layer. The current understanding among historians is that the law in Egypt cannot be clearly divided chronologically, based on political domination, into distinct demotic, Greek, and Roman law eras. Rather, the law was formed layer upon layer, in a manner in which the newly arriving law gradually diffused into the existing law. The older layer of legal texts using demotic script is associated with earlier Egyptian legal traditions (Manning 2003: 819). Hellenization of Egypt began with the formation of the Hellenistic Ptolemaic kingdom in 305 BCE. In the next legal layer, older Egyptian law went through a long and impactful process of mixture with Greek law. Demotic and Greek laws co-existed for centuries, the latter gradually making more inroads, initially applying only to Greeks, but later also affecting demotic rules and institutions and applying to Egyptians. The Hellenization of law continued well into the Roman period. Contract law was particularly dominated by Greek formats and was written by Greek scribes, in Greek (Taubenschlag 1944–48: 607–9; Yiftach-Firanko 2009; Rowlandson 2010: 248).

Despite the fact that Egypt became part of the Roman Empire in 30 BCE, it did not experience swift Romanization of its law. Local Greek law at the time of the occupation was already well developed and resilient. Roman law applied to Roman citizens but not to locals. "The law of the Egyptians" was a fusion of demotic and Greek law that was, so to speak, "invented" by Roman provincial administrators to allow Roman judges and jurists to apply the local law in Roman tribunals to non-Roman litigants. This process of consolidation and codification of local law further strengthened and updated Greek law. The Antonine Constitution (*c.*212 CE) that granted Roman citizenship to all free men in the Empire, including Egyptians, post-dates the Muziris Papyrus.

The dating of the Muziris Papyrus—well into the Roman period, yet before the formal Romanization of provincial law—and its use of the Greek language suggest that it was drafted in the shadow of Greek law, not Roman (or demotic) law. Thus, trade between the Roman Empire and India, the most demanding commercial undertaking in the Roman Empire, was subject to Greek, and not to Roman, law. However, we do not know the identity of the parties to the agreement (or the intended parties, if the document was a template). Nor can we preclude the possibility that the segment visible in the papyrus was only part of a transaction or a network that went beyond Alexandria to Rome or another part of the Empire in which Roman law dominated, or that the parties to the agreement (or at least the financing party) were Roman citizens. Hence, we cannot rule out the possibility that the drafters envisioned Roman law to be the background law of the agreement.[4] That said, the question of which law applied to the Muziris Papyrus—Greek or Roman or a mixture of the two—is pertinent only in as much as the applicable rules in the two sets of laws were different.

7.5. LEGAL-ECONOMIC ANALYSIS OF THE AGREEMENT

7.5.1. Sea Loan

The legal-financial device mentioned explicitly on the recto of the Muziris Papyrus is a loan. The surviving sections of the text refer to "contracts of loan" and twice to "the aforesaid loan." The "I" party was the borrower. The "you" party was the lender. The Muziris Papyrus looks like a loan agreement.

The legal category that seems at first sight to be most relevant for reading the Muziris Papyrus is the sea loan. Both Athenian and Roman maritime law recognized a separate category of loan contract specifically applicable to the financing of sea voyages. In Athenian law, the category of sea loan was termed *nauticum* (Cohen 1992: 160–71; Millett 2002: 188–96).[5] In Roman law, the category of *faenus nauticum* was applicable to maritime loans (Hoover 1926: 475–500). The sea loan was distinct from other loans in two major respects. First, the rate of interest: unlike gratuitous loan contracts such as the *mutuum*, it allowed the charging of interest; and unlike other forms of non-gratuitous loans, such as the *stipulatio*, it was not subject to strict usury restrictions and permitted the charging of higher interest due to risk. Second, the ability to allocate different risks to the various parties separately: the sea risk was allocated to the lender, while the business risk was held by the borrower. More specifically, in the case of loss of the ship or goods at sea, either due to natural causes or to piracy, the borrower was discharged of the debt.

[4] For discussion of the Roman law governing contracts for transporting goods by sea, with particular focus on the allocation of risk, see Fiori (2018).

[5] The Athenian form may have been based on even earlier Phoenician merchant practices (Ziskind 1974).

When a separate legal category applied to maritime loans, it often involved not only distinct legal rules but also distinct courts. Athenian maritime courts differed from regular Athenian courts, and the two appeared as separate as early as the fourth century BCE. They used different procedures and applied distinct forms of customs, contracts, and rules (Cohen 1973: 3–10; Chowdharay-Best 1976; Lanni 2006: 149–74). The Athenian maritime courts also adjudicated non-Athenians.

According to the historians, sea loans were commonly used in fourth-century BCE Athens. Demosthenes' speeches include references to some twenty such loans. They were mostly used for financing voyages from Athens to various ports, some as far away as Sicily or the Black Sea. A traveling merchant with limited wealth, or wishing to spread risk or leverage, would borrow money from a wealthier person, an older person who did not wish to travel, a non-merchant, or a syndicate of several individuals to fund the purchase of a ship or goods, or both, for a single or return voyage. Legal scholars and classicists have long thought that Athenian sea loans were based on fixed formulae or templates. But, more recently, economic and business historians, notably Cohen, have identified a significant level of flexibility and modularity in the drafting of sea loans, so as to meet the conditions of diverse voyages and the risk-taking inclinations, wealth constraints, and business preferences of the parties. Among these more flexible elements: risk of sea loss could be allocated to either party; interest was set, based on the estimated level of sea risk, given the season and destination; and security could be created in either the goods, the ship itself, or real estate back home. The moral hazard created by the shift of the sea risk away from the borrower was dealt with in several ways: minimum equity investment by the borrowers was sometimes required; different monitoring devices could be agreed upon; and loans could be provided by individuals or syndicates (Cohen 1992: 134–48). While there is ample evidence of the use of sea loans in fourth-century BCE Athens, mainly in literary sources, the evidence for their use in either Greece or Egypt in later periods is more scant. A papyrus dated from the Ptolemaic period records a contract between a consortium of five merchants and a financier, in which the consortium borrowed money in the form of a sea loan to finance a voyage to "the spice-bearing lands" (Young 2001: 55; McLaughlin 2010: 157). In Rome itself, the main evidence is found in juristic sources, notably in the *Digest* of Justinian. Much of what we know about sea loans in second-century CE Greco-Roman Egypt is either a forward interpolation from fourth-century BCE Athens or a backward interpolation from sixth-century CE Constantinople. But there is no reason to believe that these interpolations are not valid or that the sea loan was not a well-recognized and enforceable form of organizing trade in second-century CE Egypt.

Let us turn now to interpreting the text of the contract itself and reconstructing what the underlying transaction was likely to have been, given the nature of Egypt–India trade in Roman times. The text mentions an agreement made in Muziris, and Muziris could practically only be reached from Egypt by sea. Thus, the core transaction recorded in the Muziris Papyrus—that of importing goods from India to Egypt—would have been a maritime transaction. It follows, then, that a loan connected to it can be understood to be a sea loan, *faenus nauticum*. Most scholars of the papyrus assert that the loan to which it refers was a sea loan, although Grønlund Evers, as we saw earlier, recently concluded that it was *not* a sea loan, because it does not use sea loan terminology.

But some of these scholars who hold the agreement to be a sea loan suggest the text could be a subsequent agreement to an original sea-loan arrangement concluded in Muziris. If this was the case and the text refers to a subsequent agreement that applied to the Red Sea–Alexandria section, an overland (and down-river) segment, was it nevertheless referring to a sea loan, as these scholars assume? Or was this a contract that converted a sea loan into a regular loan? The answer might be that the contract can nevertheless be classified as a sea loan, if the law viewed the different segments and agreements as part of the same maritime transaction. If such a legal doctrine existed, then the question of which precise segment was covered by the Muziris Papyrus is immaterial for identifying the legal nature of the transaction.

Did such a legal doctrine exist in that place and time? A doctrine that would classify a combined sea-cum-land trade was less likely to develop in the Mediterranean context, which involved mostly port-to-port trade. It was more likely to develop in the exceptionally long and combined Egypt-to-India trade. So it makes sense to search for it in Alexandria rather than in Athens or Rome. I leave this task to legal historians of Greco-Roman Egypt.

If the agreement did refer to the Red Sea–Alexandria segment and if there was no legal doctrine that applied sea loans to the overland segments of a longer maritime route, then the applicable loan could be a regular loan, and the agreement in the Papyrus could be viewed as converting a sea loan into a regular loan.

Regular financial loans could typically be made in the form of the *stipulatio* contract or the *mutuum* contract. The *stipulatio* was recognized by Greek and Roman law by the uttering of formal words (*verbis*), and this contractual form could apply to loans. In Roman law, there were two loan contracts created by the transfer of an object (a *res*, hence termed "re" or "real" contracts), the *mutuum* and *commodatum*. *Mutuum* refers to the loan of something whose use requires its consumption (e.g. money), and *commodatum* refers to the loan of an object that is not to be consumed (and is thus not relevant for our purpose here) (Schulz 1951: 400–1; Zimmermann 1996: 47–58; Knopf 2005: 138; Riggsby 2010: 121–34). The *mutuum* was traditionally a gratuitous loan that could not bear interest, and, as such, was not very useful for financing business activity. To charge interest and make the loan feasible, the parties had to resort to the more formal *stipulatio*. Thus, a regular loan, if not made with the formality required to establish a *stipulatio*, could not bear interest.

For the time being, we cannot definitely determine whether the agreement preserved in the Muziris Papyrus is that of a sea loan. Yet we do know that sea loans were recognized in both Greek and Roman law, and were most likely available for the use of financiers and merchants in Greco-Roman Egypt, whatever their civic status was. We can affirm that the Muziris Papyrus Egypt-to-India trade involved higher risks, particularly maritime risks, due to the longer voyages in the less familiar monsoon-ridden Indian Ocean, outside the protection of the Empire. Given the risky environment, there is good reason to hold that sea loans were suitable for that trade, at least as much as they were suited to Mediterranean trade. Sea loans were most likely a core organizational component of Egypt-to-India trade, be they reflected in the Papyrus itself or in the wider transaction of which it was only a segment.

7.5.2. Agency

The agreement does not declare itself to be an agency or an employment agreement. Yet one party, the "I," makes repeated references to instructions given to him by the other party, the "you." Note here the elements I have underlined:

> I will give(?)] to your trustworthy camel-driver [- - -] (?) for the conduct of the journey up] to Koptos; and I will convey (the goods) through the desert under guard and protection up to the] public tax-receiving warehouses at Koptos, and [I will] place them under the [authority] and seal of yourself, or of your administrators or whichever one of them is present, until their loading at the river; and I will load them [at the requi]red time onto a safe ship on the river; and I will convey them down to the warehouse for receiving the quarter-tax [at Alex]andria. . . .

The text is, in fact, saying that the "I" has been given instructions by the "you." It includes a set of five operational instructions, covering the entire span from the Red Sea port to Alexandria. Furthermore, the last paragraph of the surviving text lists expenses that had to be accounted for. Expenses are typically incurred by agents (or partners) and not by lenders, as the latter are responsible for their own expenses.

The basic contractual category in Roman law that could apply to the employment of agents in trade was the *mandatum* (Watson 1961). The *mandatum* was a gratuitous consensual contract between a mandator and mandatary according to which the later would act on behalf of the former. It was used for commercial transaction such as personal security, suretyship, or guarantee. It is regarded by scholars as the Roman equivalent of agency. The above-quoted parts of the agreement can be viewed as a mandate (*mandatum*) provided by the "you" party, the principal, to his agent, the "I" party, in an agency contract. Yet a *mandatum* was a gratuitous relationship formed among friends, not in return for payment. At most, an honorarium could be granted. One alternative is to view the legal arrangement as contract for the hiring of services, a *locatio conductio operarum* contract. If there was no need for the agent to perform legal actions that would be attributed to the principal, and if the discretion of the agent was confined, then a service contract was what was needed. A further alternative interpretation, applicable to the relationships between ship owners, ship captains, and third parties, is that the papyrus was an agency contract of the legal category known as *actio exercitoria*.

In addition, the text reflects the wide use of agents in the India trade. The phrase "your administrator" (or in Casson's translation, "your agent") appears four times in the short text; the phrase "your manager," three times; and "your camel-driver" and "your men" appear once each. One of the parties to the agreement, the stationed party, the "you," seems to have agents spread throughout the trade route, in the Red Sea port, in Koptos, and in Alexandria. But the text is not an agency contract with respect to those agents who are not parties to it. It only acknowledges, and preserves as historical evidence, their existence.

7.5.3. Partnership

The basic category that could apply to partnership in Roman law was the *societas* (Randazzo 2005). The partnership was based on ex-post splitting of profits (the upside) or losses (the downside). In this respect, it was different from the loan or the employment contracts in which pay (in the form of interest or wages) was set ex-ante. The partnership form of business organization is not referred to in the text. Yet one of only a handful of other records that refer to trade with "the spice-bearing lands," possibly India, mentions a consortium. That papyrus, dated to the Ptolemaic period, records a contract between a consortium of five merchants and a financier, in which the consortium borrowed money in the form of a sea loan to finance a voyage. This arrangement can, in fact, be understood as a partnership—a partnership of five that borrowed money (Young 2001: 55; McLaughlin 2010: 157).

7.5.4. Security

Much of the first part of the text deals with the passage and control of goods along the route from the Red Sea to Alexandria. The goods were placed under the supervision of the lender's agents in the Red Sea port, in Koptos, and in Alexandria. These agents could make sure the goods would not escape the lender's control. They could repossess the goods on behalf of the lender in the case of repayment default. This could be understood as a technical shipping method that offered the lender closer monitoring of the whereabouts of the goods and their upkeep. The second part of the text deals not with physical monitoring but with the use of the goods as security for the loan: "then [you] and your administrators or managers are to have the option and com[plete] authority, if you so choose, to carry out execution without [notifica]tion or summons to judgement, to possess and own the afore[said] security" (my emphasis). This looks like a legal act making the goods subject to *hypotheca* or pledge.[6] This part of the agreement repeatedly uses the term "security," and in Casson's translation also "pledge" and "rehypothecate," clearly indicative terminology. What was the meaning of the security in the goods held by the lender? Security provides the lender with recourse in the event that the borrowers default on repayment in full and on time. As far as securing the lender against sea risks was concerned, it did not provide much. Had the goods been lost, the security in them was worthless. The security was most relevant vis-à-vis other creditors of the borrower in Egypt. These could not take possession of the imported goods because the lender was the senior and secured creditor.

7.5.5. Option

The clauses preceding the security-forming clauses can be viewed as an optional feature built into a sea loan contract. Note the elements I underline here: ". . . on occurrence of the date for repayment specified in the contracts of lo[an] for (the trip to) Muziris, if I do not [then] duly discharge the aforesaid loan in my name, that then [you] and your administrators or managers are to have the option and com[plete] authority, if you so choose, to carry out execution without [notifica]tion or summons to judgement." It seems to be a call option for the lending financier to repossess the goods rather than await the money any longer. The "you" party could "buy them for yourself at the price current at the time." In fact, the borrowing party could also exercise a call option by failing to repay his debt promptly. Instead, he could hand over the goods rather than go through the effort of trying to sell them on the market.

Another conceptualization of the nature of the contract focuses on the phrase: "we are free from accus[at]ion in every respect, and that the surplus or shortfall from the capital [goes] to me the borrower and giver of sec[urity]." This can be viewed as amounting to a non-recourse loan. According to the terms of the loan agreement, the lender has recourse only to the assets, for whose purchase the loan

6 See Hendrik L. E. Verhagen in Volume II.

was used, but has no recourse to the borrower personally, his other business assets, his personal assets, or his body. Admittedly, non-recourse is viewed in the finance literature as an option contract.[7] But from an asset-partitioning perspective, the non-recourse clause has the effect of separating pools of assets rather than establishing a right to sell at will, at an agreed price (Hansmann, Kraakman, and Squire 2006).

This option hedges the downside risks of the borrowing traveling merchant, allowing him to hand over the goods when their Alexandria market price drops. The lender's option allows the lender to capture some of the upside, in the case of a rise in prices in Alexandria, and share the profits. These options do not turn the sea loan into a fully fledged profit-sharing contract—a precursor of the *commenda* contract—but make it into a sea loan with some profit-sharing option or market-fluctuation hedging of the loan repayment. If one views the option as one that is routinely exercised by the "you" party, or even as a nominal clause, an option that is always exercised by either party, then what we have here is, in fact, a service or agency contract. The "I" party provides the "you" party with the service of carrying goods from Muziris or from the Red Sea port to Alexandria, and handing them over to the "you" party. He receives money, buys goods, brings them back, and delivers. This is not a loan, with an option or security attached to it, but rather a labor or agency contract.

Let us now sum up the content of the agreement. It has a loan element, a service element, a security-forming element, an option, and possibly a non-recourse element. The main economic concern that the agreement had to address, given the risks involved in long-distance maritime trade with India, was risk allocation. The various elements of the agreement focus on this concern. The sea risk was apparently allocated to the lender. The risk of a drop in the price of the imported goods in the Alexandria market was also allocated to the lender. The risks with respect to price fluctuations in Muziris, with respect to the life and health of the merchant, the loss of investment in labor if there were no profit, and loss of goods due to negligence rather than sea risks were borne by the traveling merchant. The merchant was monitored by the financiers' agents from the moment of his arrival back in Egypt, so that he would not be able to steal and

7 For an analysis of the non-recourse loan as an option contract, see Harris and Meir (2013: 131–7; Pavlov and Wachter, 2014).

privately sell some of the goods imported from India. The incentives of the traveling merchant were quite sophisticatedly aligned with those of financier.

7.5.6. Boilerplate

Rathbone suggests that the Papyrus contains a master contract, a boilerplate, a template—not an agreement between named parties (Rathbone 2000: 40–3). What supports such a conclusion? There are no party names and no signatures or seals. There are no specified sums, interest rates, goods, or dates. There is not even any reference by name to the Red Sea port, only to Muziris, Koptos, and Alexandria: origin, destination, and unavoidable hub, respectively. It is possible, albeit not very likely, that all such mentions were lost due to the top and bottom parts being missing and the damage to the edges. It is possible that some of the missing specifications were assumed to be complete, according to well-known merchant practices. It is unlikely that the missing details result from neglect or unskilled drafting. The basic structure and drafting seem to be quite formal, legal, and detailed. This is not a hastily drafted text written at a brief meeting. But the scribing, on the other hand, is sloppy, including grammatical and syntax errors, and could possibly have been copied in haste from a master form.

These indications increase the likelihood that the recto side of the Muziris papyrus was not an individual contract but rather a template that could be filled in with different names, sums, and dates. Rathbone suggests that it should be understood as representing a system in which the financier is the repeat player and the initiating party, and the traveler—an agent or a service provider—was different in each use of the template (Rathbone 2000: 40–3).

The "you" party is the drafter. The contractual terms clearly favor him. It is likely that the "you" party was a financier in Alexandria and was, in fact, the first to take action, approaching traveling merchants on his own initiative and asking them to accept his boilerplate contract. These merchants could be viewed as his agents. They could be seen as counterparts to whom he granted sea loans. The financier selected experienced and reputable traveling merchants, provided them with funding and instructions, signed them up to the template contract that was preserved in the Muziris papyrus, and sent them to India. This view of the financier as the initiating party is supported by the fact, clearly stated in the papyrus, that he had agents and managers in the Red Sea port and in Koptos, and camel-drivers linking the two. A passive investor was unlikely to have such an infrastructure.

7.6. THE PAPYRUS IN A MERCHANT NETWORK CONTEXT

Understanding the Muziris Papyrus as a standard form contract used by an active financier fits other contemporary evidence about merchants and the trade infrastructure in Egypt and its Red Sea ports. The author of *Periplus Maris Erythraei* represents himself as a Greek-speaking merchant based in Egypt with firsthand experience in India and East Africa trade (Casson 1989: 7–10; Young 2001: 54). Inscriptions and archeological evidence from the upper Nile Valley, along the desert routes, and from the Red Sea ports, suggest the existence of wealthy merchants, bearing honorable Roman and Greek names, involved in trade coming from the Red Sea and the Indian Ocean. Notable evidence of such wealthy merchant families can be found in the Archive of Nicanor, which contains a group of *ostraca* found in Koptos dated between 6 CE and 62 CE. These are receipts for transport services provided by Nicanor and his family or partners by camel, between Koptos and Myos Hormos and Berenike, on the instruction of various people. The name of one of the recipients of the services mentioned in the archive also appears in an inscription dedicating a temple in Koptos to his honor. Another important figure mentioned in the archive is known to have been a member of a rich Jewish family in Alexandria. The multiple appearances of these names indicate that these were repeat merchants—most likely also professional and wealthy merchants like Nicanor. An inscription from a temple at Medamoud in the Nile Valley is dedicated to two female Red Sea merchants. An inscription in Latin found on the desert road between the Red Sea and the Nile alludes to a merchant, who is also mentioned by Pliny in his *Naturalis historia* as being connected with trade to Sri Lanka and elsewhere, as the Red Sea port's tax farmer. The accumulated evidence suggest that Nicanor and his partners were not unique, and that numerous merchants and agents were involved in the trade along the Red Sea to the Nile route (Young 2001: 54–60).

It is quite likely that on either side of the system—the financier or the traveling party—a consortium could be formed, though our specific papyrus does not provide evidence of this.

It is also likely that some of the capital invested in the India trade came from as far as Rome (Fitzpatrick 2011: 40). There is a growing sense among historians of the Roman economy that the expansion of the Roman Empire into the Greek Eastern Mediterranean after 30 BCE led to Roman investment in eastern trade. This provided Roman citizens who had accumulated capital the opportunity, not a particularly likely option though, to invest passively in that trade through financial intermediaries, such as banks, and institutional investors, such as a *societas publicanorum* (ibid.: 40–1). The trade in Asiatic goods combined with the trade in grains originating in Egypt, creating a combination of Greek and Roman merchant networks that traded between Alexandria and Rome. By the first and second centuries CE, Roman tax farmers and other contractors, Roman soldiers and veterans, the Imperial family, and Rome's wealthier elite began investing directly and actively in eastern trade (Rathbone 2007). Alongside investors, a pool of willing and able agents was formed. Some of them were freedmen, some were slaves; some had an Egyptian social and cultural background, and some Greek. The identity of the agents depended both on the background of the investors and on the tasks the former were expected to perform (Ruffing 2013).

This contextual evidence, though not directly engaging with the organization of India trade, fits an interpretation of the Muziris Papyrus as having a wealthy merchant for one of its parties. Such a merchant, one of a class of similarly situated merchants echoed in the inscriptions and the Nicanor Archive, had agents and service providers along the route between Alexandria and the Red Sea. He would have provided capital to traveling agents/merchants, either as sea loans or as money held by the agent on the principal's behalf.

7.7. CONTINUITY AND CHANGE IN THE ORGANIZATION OF ROMAN AND MEDIEVAL TRADE

Well-organized trade with India, based on sophisticated transactions and networks, declined with the decline and ultimate fall of the

Roman Empire and the weakening of the Byzantine Empire's hold on Egypt. Practically no shipwrecks from antiquity have been found to date in the western Indian Ocean, due to the oceanic conditions; hence one cannot count shipwrecks as a means of establishing this decline. But the ample evidence from the Mediterranean shows that the number of dateable shipwrecks plummeted in the second century CE and dropped even further in the fifth century CE. There is no reason to believe that Indian Ocean trade fared well, given the general decline of trade that accompanied the decay and ultimate collapse of the Roman Empire (Ray 2003; Nappo 2007; Jongman 2014).

There is evidence of the revival of trade between Islamic Egypt and India by the eleventh century, and it is presumed that the revival started a century or two earlier. While not enough is known about medieval trade, we nevertheless know much more about this period than about trade in the Roman period. Almost all the knowledge on medieval trade with India comes from the contracts and correspondence of Jewish merchants kept in the Cairo Geniza, a repository that was discovered in a Cairo synagogue. This source, which includes just a small subset of Islamic Egypt's trade as a whole, does not enable historians to estimate overall trade volume and compare it to Roman trade. But it does seem to indicate that trade routes and goods were similar in medieval and Roman periods. Historians believe that the Geniza represents the organizational forms used also by Muslim merchants.

The level of sophistication of the Geniza merchants' trade seems to have been much lower than that associated with the second century CE, as reflected in the Muziris Papyrus. There is no evidence of an extensive trade infrastructure along the Nile or across the desert; no evidence of the use of sophisticated contractual and financial instruments; no evidence of the use of boilerplates; and no evidence of drawing investments from further afield through intermediaries or consortia.

It is remarkable to note that the sea loan, which was renowned and legally enforceable in the Greco-Roman world and was apparently widely used in India trade, was not an available option for Geniza-era Jewish and Muslim merchants. The main explanation for its absence in the organizational menu of Islamic Egypt merchants is its prohibition by Islamic usury laws and by Jewish law in the Islamic world. The explanation for the difference between the acceptance of the sea loan in Christianity and its rejection in Islam, as I have elaborated elsewhere, is that Christianity in the East, in a continuation of the Greco-Roman tradition, did not view sea loans as usurious; and Christianity in the West began prohibiting commercial interest-bearing loans only late in the twelfth century. Islam, on the other hand, prohibited interest-bearing loans from its very beginning in the seventh century; and the sea loan, which bore a particularly high rate of interest because of the shift of the maritime risk to the lender, was considered particularly usurious (Harris 2020).[8]

The one notable contractual design that was used by the Geniza traders but not by their Greco-Roman predecessors was the *commenda*. The basic *commenda* was a bilateral contract involving only two parties, the sedentary investing party and the traveling agent who would follow the itinerary set by his principal. The *commenda* was an equity investment contract, specifying investments and payoffs. The investing party provided capital in the form of goods and cash (used for the purchase of the trade goods and for travel-related costs), and was entitled to a share of the profit. The traveling party typically did not invest capital. The *commenda* was also a labor contract, with the traveling party investing labor, expertise, information, contacts, and bodily risk. The profits of the *commenda* were split between the two parties (Lopez and Raymond 1955; Harris 2020).

The *commenda* is believed to have first been used in the long-distance trade of Arab merchants, either before or shortly after the beginning of Islam. The *qirad* or *mudaraba*, as this organizational form was termed in Islam, is discussed in detail in canonic Islamic legal treatises from the late eighth century to the eleventh century. Udovitch argues that the origins of the Islamic *commenda* can be found in earlier Middle Eastern organizational forms, the Jewish Talmud's *isqa*, and the Byzantine *chreokoinonia*, which were already known in late antiquity (Udovitch 1962). Most of what we know about medieval Egypt-to-India trade and the use of the *commenda* in that trade is thanks to the surviving records of the Cairo Geniza. The painstaking work of Goitein and Friedman on the Geniza corpus has identified some 460 India-trade-related documents in the collection, a strikingly different scale from the single document that survived from Roman times, the Muziris Papyrus (Goitein and Friedman 2007).

[8] For an investigation of the various organizational forms used in Eurasian trade by different civilizations in the early modern period, see Harris (2020).

These documents date from the eleventh to thirteenth centuries, primarily from the twelfth century. They comprise mainly merchants' letters and contracts that reflect the everyday use of *commenda* and allow historians to look beyond the legal treatises.

We know about the organization of Italian merchants' trade in Indian goods and their importation from places including Alexandria and Aleppo, thanks to notarial records that survived in Venice, Genoa, and other Italian towns. The Cairo merchants whose records were found in the Geniza often relied on the employment of paid-commission agents and *commenda* agents. The Italian merchants often used sea loans and *commenda* agents.

From a theoretical organizational perspective, the *commenda* could deal efficiently with the particular challenges faced by the longest-distance merchants of Roman times, such as attracting passive investors, incentivizing agents, and spreading and allocating risks. So, why was the *commenda* (or a functional equivalent of it) not designed by the legally and economically sophisticated lawyers, financiers, and merchants of the heyday of the Roman Empire's trade with India? Why did it develop in the context of post–Roman Empire long-distance trade? Why do we not observe in the surviving records other types of equity investment tools used by the Egypt-based India merchants? Is the explanation to be found in the non-preservation of records, in the supply side of Greco-Roman law, or in the demand side of the needs of Egypt-based merchants? These are questions worthy of future research.

The joint-stock business corporation, which came to dominate Europe's trade with India in the seventeenth century, is also conspicuously absent from the history of Roman India trade.[9] There were associations with some corporate features in the Roman Empire. But these were used for public or semi-public purposes, for example the *collegium*, and were not financed based on joint-stock. The corporation as a separate legal entity was significantly developed in late medieval Europe, when organizational and constitutional frameworks had to be

[9] Several scholars have identified additional organizational forms that have equity-investment features. Malmendier (2009) identified the Roman *societas publicanorum*, namely the "society of government leaseholders." Abatino, Dari-Mattiacci, and Perotti (2011) identified the *peculium* as the funds of a slave-run company. See also Fleckner in this volume.

provided to the Latin Church, the city, the university, and the guild. The early modern northwestern Europeans needed the joint-stock finance as a substitute for state- and taxation-based frameworks. They needed a more innovative and complex organizational form because they faced greater organizational challenges than the Greco-Roman merchants of Alexandria and the medieval merchants of Cairo. They had to sail all the way from London or Amsterdam to India and beyond, around the Cape of Good Hope. They needed their organizational forms to feature longevity, repeated voyages, hierarchical management, the ability to raise external equity finance, and enhanced information flows. They took a different institutional path from that of the Greco-Romans of Egypt because they used different building blocks and because they were trying to solve the new and more severe long-distance-trade-related problems that were created following the demise of Roman era infrastructure and networks. But the history of corporation-based India trade will also have to be told elsewhere (Harris 2009 and 2020).

The business organization model that was reconstructed in this chapter, based on the Muziris Papyrus, sea loans, agents, and networks, could possibly have been optimal for the heyday of the Roman Empire. There was ample wealth, markets within the Empire were well integrated, the legal system was effective and developed, and entrepreneurs were sophisticated. Large-scale trade was feasible and profitable. In later periods, the scarcity of capital, the disintegration of markets, the weakening of formal legal enforcement, the loss of institutional know-how, and the increased uncertainty drove merchants to use more risk-sharing and risk-spreading arrangements. Merchants in medieval Egypt sent agents to India using the commissioned agency and the *commenda* organizational forms. Early modern western European merchants, who had to travel larger distances around the Cape of Good Hope and were thus subject to greater uncertainties and risks, designed the joint-stock business corporation as an innovative solution to their graver problems. This is only an initial hypothesis. The question of why the *commenda* and the joint-stock business corporation were not designed in Roman times—and particularly the most complicated and risky trade of those times, with India—deserves more attention from legal and economic historians of the period.

Historians of both Greco-Roman Egypt and of Islamic Egypt can benefit from comparing the organizational forms used by Greek and

Roman merchants involved in India trade to those of medieval Islamic and Italian merchants. Can we learn from the Muziris Papyrus and its context anything about the origins of later organizational forms or the loss of organizational know-how? Was the *commenda* an option for the merchants of second-century CE Alexandria trading with India? Was the sea loan an option for the merchants of tenth-century CE Cairo trading with India? How did the Romans manage without the joint-stock corporation that became the cornerstone of European trade with India in the early modern period? The short discussion here is just a brief, initial demonstration of a worthwhile future research agenda.

7.8. CONCLUSION

The study of agreements conserved in papyri allows legal-economic historians to obtain a totally different perspective from the study of canonical juridical texts. It enables us to reconstruct the perspective of the contracts rather than contract legal doctrine. The methodology of interplaying between business practices and legal doctrine allows us to obtain a thicker, more realistic, and less abstract picture of the operation of commercial law in the Roman Empire.

The Muziris Papyrus captures only a glimpse: a single segment of a larger transaction conducted by an ongoing enterprise. It is not necessarily representative of Egypt-to-India trade. But it is all we have for now. And one can infer from it on related transactions and an established trade infrastructure. One can infer that merchants based in Egypt repeatedly transacted with India. They actively managed mercantile enterprises. They borrowed and lent capital and hired employees, agents, and itinerant merchants. They possibly used standard-form contractual templates in their trade. Their transactions were complex and included elements such as options, nonrecourse loans, and security in assets. One can conclude, based on the Muziris Papyrus and contextual evidence, that by the second century CE, a legally and financially sophisticated trade network connecting Egypt and Rome with India was in operation.

The legal categories found in canonic legal texts of the era were not used by merchants as trade manuals, and nor did they fully construct the transactions. Merchants did not necessarily make a selection between either one legal category (for contracting or employing agents or borrowing money) or another. Rather, to solve the very considerable challenges of long-distance trade, many interwove—in one single transaction—several organizational and contractual dimensions that did not fit neatly into a single legal category. It is not clear to me, given the scarcity of surviving records, whether the merchants were unaware of the legal doctrines and categories or, by contrast, if they deliberately decided to combine or override them, after seeking legal advice. Solutions to the challenges that arose extended not only beyond a single legal category but also beyond a single contract. They were knit together into trade networks, involving multiple investors, itinerant agents, and service providers, multiple transactions, numerous contracts, and a variety of legal tools. This complex organizational model is absent in the law books and could have escaped historians altogether, but for the accidental discovery of the Muziris papyrus. If and when any additional contractual evidence comes to light, we will be able to reconstruct more fully the business model used in Roman India trade and shorter-distance trade.[10]

REFERENCES

Abatino, Barbara, Giuseppe Dari-Mattiacci, and Enrico C. Perotti. 2011. "Depersonalization of Business in Ancient Rome." 31 *Oxford Journal of Legal Studies* 365–89.

Ashburner, Walter. 1909. *The Rhodian Sea-Law*. Oxford: Clarendon Press.

Casson, Lionel. 1980. "Rome's Trade with the East: The Sea Voyage to Africa and India." 110 *Transactions of the American Philological Association* 21–36.

Casson, Lionel. 1989. *The Periplus Maris Erythraei*. Princeton: Princeton University Press.

Casson, Lionel. 1986. "P. Vindob G 40822 and the Shipping of Goods from India." 23.3/4 *The Bulletin of the American Society of Papyrologists* 73–9.

Casson, Lionel. 1990. "New Light on Maritime Loans: P. Vindob G 40822." 84 *Zeitschrift für Papyrologie und Epigraphik* 195–206.

[10] The author would like to thank Giuseppe Dari-Mattiacci, Uri Yiftach-Firanko, Dennis Kehoe, and Merav Haklai Rotenberg for their invaluable advice and Mor Greif and Nathanel Habany for their excellent research assistance. The responsibility for any error is his alone.

Chowdharay-Best, Georg. 1976. "Ancient Maritime Law." 62 *The Marine's Mirror* 81–91.

Cobb, Matthew A. 2018. *Rome and the Indian Ocean Trade from Augustus to the Early Third Century* CE. Mnemosyne Supplements 418. Leiden: Brill.

Cohen, Edward E. 1973. *Ancient Athenian Maritime Courts.* Princeton: Princeton University Press.

Cohen, Edward E. 1992. *Athenian Economy and Society.* Princeton: Princeton University Press.

De Romanis, Federico. 2012. "Playing Sudoku on the Verso of the 'Muziris Papyrus': Pepper, Malabathron and Tortoise Shell in the Cargo of the Hermapollon." 27 *Journal of Ancient Indian History* 75–101.

De Romanis, Federico. 2014. "Ivory from Muziris." 8 *ISAW Papers.* Available at: http://dlib.nyu.edu/awdl/isaw/isaw-papers/8/.

Evers, Kasper Grønlund. 2017. *Worlds Apart Trading Together: The Organisation of Long-distance Trade between Rome and India in Antiquity.* Oxford: Archaeopress.

Fiori, Roberto. 2018. "L'allocazione del rischio nei contratti relativi al trasporto," in Elio Lo Cascio and Dario Mantovani, eds, *Diritto romano e economia: due modi di pensare e organizzare il mondo (nei primi tre secoli dell'Impero).* Padua: Padua University Press, 507–67.

Fitzpatrick, Matthew P. 2011. "Provincializing Rome: The Indian Ocean Trade Network and Roman Imperialism." 22 *Journal of World History* 27–54.

Goitein, Shelomo Dov, and Mordechai Akiva Friedman. 2007. *India Traders of the Middle Ages: Documents from the Cairo Geniza "India Book."* Leiden: Brill.

Gurukkal, Rajan. 2013. "Classical Indo-Roman Trade: A Historiographical Reconsideration." 40 *Indian Historical Review* 181–206.

Hansmann, Henry, Reiner Kraakman, and Richard Squire. 2006. "Law and the Rise of the Firm." 119 *Harvard Law Review* 1333–1403.

Harrauer, Hermann, and Pieter J. Sijpesteijn. 1986. *Ein neues Dokument zu Roms Indienhandel: P. Vindob. G 40822.* Vienna: Verlag der Österr. Akad. d. Wiss.

Harris, Ron. 2005. "The Formation of the East India Company as a Cooperation-enhancing Institution." Available at: http://dx.doi.org/10.2139/ssrn.874406.

Harris, Ron. 2009. "The Institutional Dynamics of Early Modern Eurasian Trade: The *Commenda* and the Corporation." 71 *Journal of Economic Behavior & Organization* 606–22.

Harris, Ron. 2010. "Law, Finance and the First Corporations," in James J. Heckman, Robert L. Nelson, and Lee Cabatingan, eds, *Global Perspectives on the Rule of Law.* Abingdon: Routledge, 145–71.

Harris, Ron. (2020). *Going the Distance: Eurasian Trade and the Rise of the Business Corporation, 1400–1700*. Princeton: Princeton University Press.

Harris, Ron, and Asher Meir. 2013. "Non-Recourse Mortages—A Fresh Start." 21 *American Bankruptcy Institute Law Review* 119–279.

Hoover, Calvin B. 1926. "The Sea Loan in Genoa in the Twelfth Century." 40 *The Quarterly Journal of Economics* 495–529.

Jongman, Willem M. 2014. "Re-constructing the Roman Economy," in Larry Neal and Jeffrey Williamson, eds, *The Cambridge History of Capitalism*. Cambridge: Cambridge University Press, 1.75–100.

Khalilieh, Hassan S. 2006. *Admiralty and Maritime Laws in the Mediterranean Sea (ca. 800–1050): The "Kitāb Akriyat al-Sufun" vis-à-vis the "Nomos Rhodion Nautikos."* Vol. 64. Leiden: Brill.

Knopf, Ellen 2005. "Contracts in Athenian Law." Diss., The City University of New York. Available at: https://academicworks.cuny.edu/cgi/viewcontent.cgi?article=2845&context=gc_etds.

Lanni, Adriaan 2006. *Law and Justice in the Courts of Classical Athens*. Cambridge/New York: Cambridge University Press.

Libingier, Charle Sumner. 1935. "The Maritime Law of Rome." 47.1 *Juridical Review* 1–32.

Lopez, Robert S., and Raymond, Irving W. 1955. *Medieval Trade in the Mediterranean World: Illustrative Documents Translated with Introductions and Notes*. New York: Columbia University Press.

Malmendier, Ulrike. 2009. "Law and Finance 'at the Origin.'" 47 *Journal of Economic Literature* 1076–1108.

Manning, Joseph G. 2003. "Demotic Law." 2 *A History of Ancient Near Eastern Law* 819–62.

Maxfield, Valerie A. 2003. "Ostraca and the Roman Army in the Eastern Desert." 46 *Bulletin of the Institute of Classical Studies* 153–73.

McLaughlin, Raoul. 2010. *Rome and the Distant East: Trade Routes to the Ancient Lands of Arabia, India and China*. London: Continuum.

Meyer, Carol. 1992. *Glass from Quseir al-Qadim and the Indian Ocean Trade*. Chicago: Oriental Institute of the University of Chicago.

Millett, Paul. 2002. *Lending and Borrowing in Ancient Athens*. Cambridge: Cambridge University Press.

Morelli, Federico 2011. "Dal Mar Rosso ad Alessandria. Il verso (ma anche il recto) del 'papiro di Muziris' (SB 18, 13167)." 26 *Tyche. Contributions to Ancient History, Papyrology and Epigraphy* 199–233. Available at: https://doi.org/10.15661/tyche.2011.026.10.

Nappo, Dario. 2007. "The Impact of the Third Century Crisis on the International Trade with the East," in Olivier Hekster, Gerda de Kleijn, and Daniëlle Slootjes, eds, *Crises and the Roman Empire: Proceedings of the Seventh Workshop of the International Network Impact of Empire*. Leiden/Boston: Brill, 232–44.

Pavlov, Andrey, and Susan Wachter. 2004. "Robbing the Bank: Non-recourse Lending and Asset Prices." 28 *Journal of Real Estate Finance & Economics* 147–60.

Randazzo, Salvo. 2005. "The Nature of Partnership in Roman Law." 9 *Australian Journal of Legal History* 119–29.

Rathbone, Dominic. 2000. "The 'Muziris' Papyrus (SB XVIII 13167): Financing Roman Trade with India." *Alexandrian Studies II in Honor of Mostafa el Abbadi, Bulletin de la Société Archéologique d'Alexandrie* 4–6.

Rathbone, Dominic. 2007. "Merchant Networks in the Greek World: The Impact of Rome." 22 *Mediterranean Historical Review* 309–20.

Ray, Himanshu Prabha. 2003. *The Archaeology of Seafaring in Ancient South Asia.* Cambridge: Cambridge University Press.

Riggsby, Andrew M. 2010. *Roman Law and the Legal World of the Romans.* Oxford: Oxford University Press.

Rowlandson, Jane. 2010. "Administration and Law: Graeco-Roman," in A. B. Lloyd, ed., *A Companion to Ancient Egypt*, vol. 1. Oxford: Wiley-Blackwell, 237–54.

Ruffing, Kai. 2013. "The Trade with India and the Problem of Agency in the Economy of the Roman Empire," in Silvia Bussi, ed., *Egitto dai faraoni agli Arabi.* Pisa/Rome, 199–210.

Schulz, Fritz. 1951. *Classical Roman Law.* Oxford: Oxford University Press.

Sidebotham, Steven E. 2011. *Berenike and the Ancient Maritime Spice Route.* Berkeley/Los Angeles: University of California Press.

Taubenschlag, Rafael. 1944–8. *The Law of Greco-Roman Egypt in the Light of the Papyri 332 BC–640 AD.* New York: Herald Square Press.

Tomber, Roberta 2012. "From the Roman Red Sea to beyond the Empire: Egyptian Ports and Their Trading Partners." 18 *British Museum Studies in Ancient Egypt and Sudan* 201–15.

Thür, Gerhard. 1987. "Hypotheken-Urkunde eines Seedarlehens für eine Reise nach Muziris und Apographe für die Tetarte in Alexandreia (zu P. Vindob. G. 40.822)." 2 *Tyche, Contributions to Ancient History, Papyrology and Epigraphy* 229–45. Available at: https://doi.org/10.15661/tyche.1987.002.23.

Udovitch, Abraham L. 1962. "At the Origins of the Western Commenda: Islam, Israel, Byzantium?" 37.2 *Speculum* 198–207.

Warmington, Eric Herbert. 1974. *The Commerce between the Roman Empire and India.* 2nd edn. London: Curzon Press.

Watson, Alan. 1961. *Contract of Mandate in Roman Law.* Oxford: Clarendon Press.

Wilson, Andrew. 2015. "Red Sea Trade and the State," in F. De Romanis and M. Maiuro, eds, *Across the Ocean: Nine Essays on Indo-Mediterranean Trade.* Leiden: Brill, 13–32.

Yiftach-Firanko, Uri. 2009. “Law in Graeco-Roman Egypt: Hellenization, Fusion, Romanization,” in Roger S. Bagnall, ed., *The Oxford Handbook of Papyrology*. Oxford: Oxford University Press, 541–60.

Young, Gary K. 2001. *Rome's Eastern Trade: International Commerce and Imperial Policy 31 BC–AD 305*. Abingdon: Routledge.

Zimmermann, Reinhard. 1996. *The Law of Obligations: Roman Foundations of the Civilian Tradition*. Oxford: Oxford University Press.

Ziskind, Jonathan R. 1974. “Sea Loans at Ugarit.” 94 *Journal of the American Oriental Society* 134–7.

Part III

Organizing Business

8

Incomplete Organizations

Legal Entities and Asset Partitioning in Roman Commerce

Henry Hansmann, Reinier Kraakman, and Richard Squire

Economic activity in modern societies is dominated by organizations. In nearly all commercial transactions, at least one party is a firm organized as a distinct legal entity such as a corporation, trust, or limited liability company. The Roman economy was strikingly different. Across its millennium of history, ancient Rome saw the rise of both sophisticated legal institutions and a vibrant economy. With scattered exceptions, however, Roman commerce managed to flourish without the benefit of entities that were legally distinct from their human owners. While Romans were familiar with all the legal and economic building blocks of workable commercial entities, they surprise the modern observer for generally failing to take the next developmental step of assembling those blocks into the types of organizations that dominate economies today.

In this chapter we examine the structure of the various legal forms through which the Romans conducted business, emphasizing their rationales and economic consequences. For an analytic framework, we draw on recent scholarship (by us and others) that seeks to identify the defining elements of a legal entity and the dimensions along which entities can differ—topics that, despite a voluminous literature on business organizations since the nineteenth century,

Henry Hansmann, Reinier Kraakman, and Richard Squire, *Incomplete Organizations: Legal Entities and Asset Partitioning in Roman Commerce* In: *Roman Law and Economics: Institutions and Organizations, Volume I.* Edited by: Giuseppe Dari-Mattiacci and Dennis P. Kehoe, Oxford University Press (2020). © Oxford University Press. DOI: 10.1093/oso/9780198787204.003.0008 have remained surprisingly vague. An important aspect of our analysis is the relationship between Rome's *legal* institutions and its *commercial* structures. The question that drives our analysis is this one: why did the ancient Romans not develop the law of commercial entities that we might expect given the sophistication of their legal system and the complexity of their economy?[1]

An important caveat: our object here is not to bring to light previously unknown facts about business in ancient Rome or the legal environment that governed it. Classicists (which we are not) have already unearthed a rich body of facts for us to draw upon. Our aim is instead to examine what is known through the lens of modern theory, employing the law and economics of enterprise organization to clarify our understanding of those institutions and the forces affecting their development. Of necessity, our characterization of Roman institutions is schematic and summary, as we highlight those refinements, ambiguities, and temporal variations that appear to us most important to the questions we hope to answer.

8.1. THE FAMILY

If business organizations are like molecules, then in modern economies it is individual humans who serve as the atoms. Our legal systems grant each adult the right to own (and hence control) property and to bind herself by contract. Contracts are credible because a person's property backs her promises unless the contract says otherwise. If she fails to perform the contract as promised, the other party can sue her for damages and then seize enough of her assets to satisfy the judgment.

In our terminology, these legal rules make each individual a distinct "legal entity," meaning that she has the authority to enter into contracts in her own name, and that she owns a pool of assets (her

[1] In this chapter, we draw heavily on the discussion of Roman law and practice in our earlier article on the historical evolution of the law of legal entities over the last two millennia (Hansmann et al. 2006). We are aware of little subsequent scholarship that inclines us to deviate from the facts and analysis we offer there. The major exceptions are the important recent work of Dufour (2010, 2012) and Fleckner (2010, 2011, 2014).

property) that bonds her performance of those contracts. Indeed, "contracting entity" might be a more appropriate name than "legal entity" (or "juridical person"), as the critical factor is the entity's ability to enter into contracts in its own right. Today, it is common to reserve the term "legal entity" (or "juridical person") for "artificial" persons—such as business corporations, limited liability companies, nonprofit corporations, or municipalities—as opposed to "natural" persons. But there is nothing inevitable about endowing individual human beings with the powers to own assets and make contracts. Rather, individuals have these powers only if the law recognizes them. And often it has not. Ancient Rome is an example.

In ancient Rome, it was the family rather than the individual that was the most basic legal entity—the "atom" from which larger arrangements might be constructed. The Roman *familia* was, moreover, much broader than today's simple "nuclear" family, extending from the oldest living male in the male line of descent (the *paterfamilias*) to include his minor children, his slaves, and all his adult male descendants and their households. Formally, the *paterfamilias* owned all of the family property, even if others in the family acquired it.[2] And he alone had the authority to approve, and thus make effective, contracts that his family members had negotiated. Only if he specifically delegated that authority would the family's property bind contracts made by other family members, and his delegation power was tightly circumscribed by law (Johnston 1999: 31–2; Aubert 2013: 193).

These attributes made the Roman family both large and, from the point of view of someone who might make contracts with it, robust. It had an indefinitely long lifespan, remaining intact over multiple generations. There was great clarity as to who did and did not have authority to commit the family to contractual obligations. And those people to whom family members might be most tempted to convey property to keep it away from creditors—close relatives and especially descendants—were themselves part of the same legal entity and thus already liable for its debts.

[2] Under the most common form of marriage, however, the wife's assets, including those she brought into the marriage and those subsequently acquired, were not merged with those of the *paterfamilias* of her husband's family except for the dowry; technically, they still belonged to her father's family (Kirschenbaum 1987: 12; Frier and McGinn 2004: 121–38).

The wealth of a single, prosperous Roman family appears to have been sufficient to finance the typical commercial enterprise (Crook 1967: 229; Kehoe 2007: 559–66).[3] Thus, most Roman industry was small in scale, with the production of ceramic lamps, ironware, lead pipes, jewelry, and clothing occurring in small workshops or the homes of craftsmen (Frank 1927: 220–44, 261–4; Aubert 1994: 301; Hawkins 2016). To be sure, large-scale production was not unknown: brickmaking, bronze smelting, glass blowing, and copperware manufacturing often happened in extensive urban factories (Frank 1927: 223–38).[4] But even these factories appear to have derived their scale economies from labor specialization rather than from capital intensity. For this reason, most of the large workshops in the more capital-intensive brickmaking industries were located on the estates of landowning families that had made fortunes in agriculture and then diversified (Kehoe 2007: 560–4).

This evidence suggests that the legal attributes of the patriarchal *familia* made it an effective legal entity for conducting the typical Roman business. And its capacity to finance and manage enterprise was enhanced by Rome's peculiar rules for slave-managed businesses, a subject to which we will turn after considering Rome's version of a more modern legal form, the partnership (Harris 2011: 284–5).

8.2. THE *SOCIETAS*

Beyond the *familia*, ancient Rome's principal legal arrangement for organizing businesses was the *societas*, a term commonly translated as "partnership" because it described an arrangement between two or more citizens to share the profits and losses from a joint enterprise (Buckland 1921: 504–7; Kaser 1971: 572–6; Zimmermann 1996: 451–76). Beyond an agreement to share the fortunes of a business, however, the *societas* had little in common with the modern partnership. Most importantly for our purposes, it lacked both of the principal attributes of a legal entity: (1) a partitioned pool of assets; and

[3] Wealth seems to have been concentrated in particular in families that owned extensive landed property (Aubert 1994: 301).

[4] For the *terra sigilliata* industry, see Fülle (1997). See the study of the Roman terracotta lamp industry in Harris (2011: 113, 134–5).

(2) a well-defined delegation of authority to pledge those assets. We discuss these attributes in turn, illuminating them by comparing the *societas* with the modern partnership.[5]

8.3. ASSET PARTITIONING

A legal entity as we have defined it (Hansmann and Kraakman 2000) must have a pool of assets that serves to bond its contractual obligations. To be meaningful, this requires that persons who transact with the entity must, if the entity breaks its contract, have a claim on the pool of assets that is prior to the claims of people who transact with the entity's owners in their individual capacities. We see this quality in the general partnership as it took form in the Middle Ages and has continued to the present day.

A modern partnership has a designated pool of assets, contributed by the partners and augmented by retained earnings, that it holds in its own name. Pursuant to the partnership agreement, the partners can enter into contracts that bind the partnership and thus commit this pool of partnership assets. This asset pool is "partitioned" in the sense that it must be used for paying the partnership's debts before it can be claimed by creditors who transacted with partners in their personal affairs (or in their other business activities, which may involve other firms in which they have invested). Put another way, partnership creditors have priority over partners' personal creditors in the division of partnership assets. We have elsewhere termed this form of asset partitioning "entity shielding," because it shields the assets of business entities (such as partnerships) from the creditors of business owners (such as partners), at least until the entity's own creditors have been paid in full (Hansmann et al. 2006).

[5] In this chapter, we emphasize the role of legal entities in organizing the claims of creditors. Legal entities also offer the important advantage of permitting transfer (assignment), from one person to another, of the benefits and burdens of a whole class of related contracts without having to obtain approval for the transfer from the counterparties to those contracts (Ayotte and Hansmann 2013). Ancient Rome seems to have endowed the limited shares in the *societas publicanorum* with this capacity by making them tradable, as discussed below, §8.8. We will not further pursue here, however, the Roman law on contract assignability and its relationship to Roman legal entities.

In contrast to the modern partnership, the Roman *societas* seems not to have featured entity shielding. Assets held by the *societas* were simply considered to be owned in common by the partners (Buckland 1921: 504–7), and creditors of the *societas* were treated just like personal creditors of the partners (or their families). If, for example, persons A and B formed a *societas* to which A contributed one-third of the assets and B contributed two-thirds, A would continue to be considered the owner of his one-third of the partnership's assets. Creditors of the *societas* and A's personal creditors could claim on equal footing against both A's one-third share of the *societas*'s assets and A's personal assets.

Lacking the form of asset partitioning—namely, entity shielding—that characterizes a legal entity, the *societas* could not offer the important benefits that entity shielding affords. The principal benefits are reductions in the information costs of creditors and in the administrative costs of bankruptcy. Entity shielding can also have offsetting costs, principally in the form of debtor opportunism. We discuss each of these in turn.

8.3.1. Informational Benefits

Asset partitioning, and particularly entity shielding, can allow creditors to economize on their *information costs*, meaning the costs they incur when evaluating a debtor's creditworthiness (Posner 1976; Hansmann and Kraakman 2000: 399–402). Because unpaid creditors compete for a debtor's assets, the nonpayment risk that each creditor bears is a function of the value of the debtor's assets and the amount of its other liabilities. When a firm fails and its creditors are paid pro rata regardless of which was first to give credit—the default payout rule in most contemporary bankruptcy systems, as it was in ancient Rome (Abatino and Dari-Mattiacci in this volume)—the ratio of assets to liabilities determines how much each creditor recovers on his claim.[6] Creditors are willing to bear some default risk so long as they are compensated for it, typically through the interest rate they charge when extending credit. Thus, in order to know what interest rate to

[6] However, when one of several creditors of a slave doing business with a *peculium* chose to sue the master introducing an action on the *peculium*, the rule applied was "first come first serve" (Aubert 2013: 198–9, 202–3).

charge (and other forms of protection to insist upon), a creditor must evaluate the debtor's existing and expected assets and liabilities.

Without entity shielding, recoveries for business creditors would depend heavily on the assets and liabilities not only of the firm but also of all its individual owners. By giving the firm's creditors priority over personal creditors in the division of the firm's assets, entity shielding allows the firm's creditors to focus their appraisal efforts principally on the firm's own balance sheet. By making it cheaper for creditors to lend, entity shielding reduces the interest rate that creditors can charge and still expect to turn a profit. In this way, the informational benefits of entity shielding can reduce a firm's borrowing costs, thereby increasing returns for its owners.

8.3.2. Bankruptcy Efficiencies

A further benefit of asset partitioning is that it can simplify the bankruptcy proceedings that many legal systems—including the Roman (Solazzi 1937: 43; Arangio Ruiz 1966: 145–7; Crook 1967: 174–8)—employ when an individual or business firm becomes insolvent. As noted above, the default payout rule in modern legal systems is the pro rata rule, which pays each of a debtor's creditors a percentage of his claim equal to the ratio between the debtor's total assets available to creditors and the debtor's total liabilities. This is a slow rule to administer, because it means that no assets can be distributed to creditors until the total, legally enforceable amount of the debtor's liabilities is known. Entity shielding, by contrast, allows a bankruptcy court to distribute the entity's assets to its creditors once the amount of its liabilities are known, regardless of the amount of the owners' personal liabilities (Hansmann et al. 2006: 1346; Squire 2009: 835).[7]

[7] As an example, consider the partnership. When a partnership becomes bankrupt, its partners typically become bankrupt as well. With entity shielding, the partnership's assets will be divided among the partnership creditors without concern for the partners' various personal creditors. If, as is usual in bankruptcy, the partnership does not have enough assets to pay off all of its creditors, then it will be dissolved and its bankruptcy proceeding finished. Unsatisfied partnership creditors then become creditors in the partners' individual bankruptcy proceedings, which can proceed on their own. Absent entity shielding, it would be necessary to resolve all of the claims of the partnership's creditors as well as those of the partners' personal creditors before any payouts could be made (Squire 2009: 835).

8.3.3. Debtor Opportunism

As against these potential forms of economic efficiency, asset partitioning can also generate costs. In particular, while asset partitioning can reduce creditors' informational costs, it can also increase their costs of *supervision*, meaning the costs they incur from debtor misconduct and from efforts to deter that misconduct (Posner 1976: 507–8; Hansmann et al. 2006: 1351–2).

For example, if one or more partners in a partnership face a strong probability of personal bankruptcy while the partnership remains relatively solvent, they may be tempted to invest their remaining liquid assets in the partnership, thereby giving the partnership creditors priority in those assets over the claims of the owners' personal creditors. They can then use those assets as collateral for further borrowing by the firm on better terms than they could have received from personal creditors. By thus increasing their total leverage, they may increase the chances that firm profits will be high enough to pay off their personal creditors, while leaving their personal creditors with lower priority claims and a higher risk of nonpayment.

The example illustrates a general point: any asset partition invites opportunistic smuggling of assets across it (as well as other types of debtor misconduct). Smuggling is particularly likely if the same persons control, or have equity claims on the assets on both sides of the partition. The implication is that the optimal amount of asset partitioning—that is, the optimal size of the asset pool that unpaid creditors can recover from—reflects a context-specific tradeoff between informational and bankruptcy benefits on the one hand, and the costs of debtor opportunism on the other.[8] That trade-off limits the amount of asset partitioning that is efficient within any given economy and legal system. But, given the overall level of economic development in ancient Rome, it seems odd that, for the principal business unit beyond the *familia*, the efficient amount of partitioning—and, in particular, entity shielding—should have been none.

[8] Over time, legislatures have created devices—such as the rules against fraudulent transfers—designed to deter debtor misconduct and hence decrease supervision costs.

8.4. DELEGATED AUTHORITY

The other respect in which the Roman *societas* fell short of being a legal entity concerns the delegation of authority. As we have said, for an organization to be a distinct legal entity requires that there be at least one person with the authority to enter into contracts that legally bind the entity, and in particular with the authority to commit the assets of the entity to bond those contracts. That is, there must be someone who can act as the entity's agent. In the modern general partnership, each partner has this authority when acting within the ordinary scope of the partnership's business activities unless creditors are on notice that such authority has been specifically withheld.

The Roman *societas*, by contrast, lacked the mutual agency among partners that characterizes the modern partnership. No member of the *societas* had authority to bind other members—and hence their share of the business assets—to contracts. Rather, each member had to endorse a contract to be bound by it.[9] The consequence would have been higher transaction costs in contracting—indeed, costs that must have been about the same as if the firm did not exist and each of its members had to be dealt with individually.

8.5. THE ROLE OF LAW

In sum, the Roman *societas* was essentially just an agreement between two or more persons to do business together. It thus did little to make it easier for those persons to do business with third parties, which is the important role of true legal entities.

But, we might ask, why was a special legal form necessary for the creation of an effective legal entity? Couldn't partners simply have used contract law to add to a *societas* the attributes of entity shielding and delegated authority? The answer is no, because both entity shielding and delegated authority affect the interests of third parties

[9] As Roman law developed, members of a *societas* eventually could act for each other, although for most of Roman history this innovation applied only to large banking firms, and may not have applied to the regular *societas* until the sixth century CE under the Eastern (Byzantine) emperor Justinian (Buckland 1921: 507; Crook 1967: 233).

who are not, initially, in privity of contract with the firm or its members (Hansmann and Kraakman 2000).

First, consider authority. Suppose that a vendor wishes to enter into a supply contract to deliver goods to a three-member firm organized as a *societas*. The default rule is that all three members must sign a contract to be bound by it. Suppose one member, however, tells the vendor that he and his two co-venturers have agreed that all three are bound by supply contracts made by any of them individually, so long as the contract is related to the firm's business. Such an agreement among the members has obvious advantages if effective, as it would eliminate the bother of obtaining three signatures on many supply contracts. But will the vendor be willing to rely on it? If the vendor is being deceived and the agreement does not in fact exist, the vendor may lack recourse against two of the three partners. And even if the agreement does exist, the vendor is not a party to it, and thus may not be able to use it to force the other members to pay their share of the vendor's bill. It requires a legal rule to establish that agreements to delegate authority—what we call agency agreements and partnership agreements—create enforceable rights for people who are not parties to them.

Second, consider entity shielding. As we have said, the default legal rule in ancient Rome was that, when a person entered into a contract, all property belonging to that person served as collateral to bond his performance of the contract. And this rule was extended to creditors of the *societas*: a member of a *societas* in effect entered into a contract on the same terms that would apply to any other contract. In particular, the counterparty to a contract with the *societas* would have a claim on the member's personal assets equal to that of the member's personal creditors, and vice versa: the member's personal creditors would have a claim on the member's share of the firm's assets equal to that of the firm's creditors.

To alter that rule by contract so as to give firm creditors priority over personal creditors with respect to firm assets would be complicated. It would require that each member of the firm insert into each personal contract a provision by which the counterparty agreed to subordinate, to all firm creditors past and future, his claim to the member's share of the firm's assets. The cumulative transaction costs to the members of securing these subordination clauses would have been high—prohibitively so in a firm with any substantial number of members. Moreover, there would be an inescapable problem of moral hazard: each member would have faced a strong temptation to omit the clauses from personal creditors, especially when the member was near insolvency, when the waiver would be most important. And the firm's creditors would find it extremely difficult—often impossible—to know if the firm's members had in fact secured such waivers. Nor would a damage action for breach of contract provide a sufficient remedy against a member who omitted a waiver clause from a personal contract. Absent entity shielding by legal rule, the damage claim awarded by a court would presumably lack seniority with respect to the member's assets.

Again, the underlying problem is to align the expectations of third parties. Here, in contrast to the case of authority to bind the firm, the problem is not to coordinate the expectations of third parties with those of the firm and its members, but rather to coordinate the expectations of third parties who contract with the firm with the expectations of third parties who contract with the members of the firm as individuals. This coordination can be provided only by a legal rule. In this important respect, organizational law is property law (Hansmann and Kraakman 2002). It establishes rules that create common expectations about who has the right to use assets and who has the right to transfer use rights in assets—that is, who owns assets, in whole or in part. In particular, organizational law coordinates expectations as to who can transfer to a creditor a contingent claim on an asset—in effect a security interest, representing partial ownership of the asset—that can be converted to full ownership if the creditor's claim goes unpaid.

8.6. TYPES OF LEGAL ENTITIES

The general partnership did not become part of European law until the Middle Ages (Hansmann et al. 2006), after which it served as the basic entity form for organizing commercial firms through the Industrial Revolution and up to the late nineteenth century, when it began to be displaced—ultimately for small as well as large firms—by the business corporation.

The undeveloped status of the Roman *societas*, in comparison with these subsequent organizational forms—the general partnership and the business corporation—was compensated for in part by reliance on other forms of organization for general business activity. Chief among these alternatives was an intra-*familia* business arrangement based on the *peculium*, and a limited-use quasi-corporate form termed the *societas publicanorum*. These entities featured forms of asset partitioning, beyond simple entity shielding, that we summarize next.

8.6.1. Owner Shielding

We referred above to entity shielding, our term for legal rules that give a business's creditors priority over the owners' personal creditors in the division of the business's assets. By definition—in our terminology—all legal entities provide entity shielding. Most modern entities also feature what is effectively the reverse rule: that each owner's personal creditors have a claim on the owner's personal assets that is prior to the claims of the firm's creditors. This rule is a form of asset partitioning that we call *owner shielding* because it shields a firm owner's personal assets from the claims of the creditors of the firm.

For example, in Anglo-American law the general partnership has featured owner shielding as well as entity shielding for most of the past three hundred years (Hansmann et al. 2006). The consequence is that if, as is common, a partnership and its partners go bankrupt at the same time, the partnership creditors get the first claim to partnership assets, and the personal creditors of each partner get the first claim to the partner's personal assets.

Owner shielding has economic benefits analogous to those of entity shielding. First, it economizes on the information and monitoring costs facing the personal creditors of a firm's owners, and further reduces those costs for the firm's creditors as well. Second, it adds further economies to resolution of claims in bankruptcy. In particular, in a partnership with both entity shielding and owner shielding, if each of the individual partners, and the partnership itself, all have debts that exceed the value of their assets, then the bankruptcies of the individual partners and of the partnership can all be settled separately from each other. Each partner's remaining assets can simply be divided up among the individual partners' personal creditors, while the partnership assets can simultaneously be divided among the partnership creditors. If one of the bankruptcies proceedings becomes especially time-consuming to resolve, it need not hold up the others.

In sum, entity shielding and owner shielding are complementary, working together to reduce the cost of credit for firms endowed with these features. The Roman *societas* evidently lacked both forms of asset partitioning, and thus could not offer their associated efficiencies.

8.6.2. Strong Asset Partitioning

The type of asset partitioning described above and found in the modern partnership is what we term "weak" asset partitioning. Other types of asset partitioning are found in other legal entities. In particular, the modern business corporation replaces the "weak" entity shielding and "weak" owner shielding of the partnership with what we term "strong" entity shielding and "strong" owner shielding.

Strong entity shielding features the same rule of priority in firm assets for firm creditors that constitutes the "weak" entity shielding of the partnership but also prohibits the individual owner of a firm and her personal creditors from seizing her share of firm assets even if she is personally insolvent. Thus, the creditors of an insolvent shareholder in a business corporation can only seize the shareholder's shares in the firm, supplanting her as a shareholder. Nor can an individual shareholder herself force the firm to pay out her pro rata share of the firm's assets. The consequences are that runs on the firm's assets by anxious shareholders are avoided, that individual shareholders cannot hold up their fellow shareholders by threatening to dissolve their investment in the firm at a time when the firm itself is highly illiquid, and that creditors of the firm have assurance that their claims on the firm will not be compromised by an untimely liquidation.

Strong owner shielding, in turn, is simply the rule of limited shareholder liability that is a familiar characteristic of the modern business corporation. It provides that personal creditors of an owner of the firm have a claim over the owner's personal assets that is not only prior to that of the firm's creditors, as in weak owner shielding, but that is exclusive. That is, creditors of the firm have no claim on the personal assets of the firm's owners.

8.6.3. Weak and Strong Entities

There is a clear complementarity among forms of asset partitioning. In modern legal entities, weak entity shielding is generally accompanied by weak owner shielding, as in the partnership, while strong entity shielding is generally accompanied by strong owner shielding, as in the business corporation. There are important efficiencies underlying this complementarity (Squire 2009). As we have seen, when weak owner shielding is added to weak entity shielding, administration of bankruptcy proceedings is greatly simplified, and creditor information costs are greatly reduced.

Likewise, strong entity shielding pairs well with strong owner shielding (limited liability). Strong entity shielding serves to lock in a firm's capital by preventing individual owners and their creditors from forcing partial or complete liquidation of the owner's share in the firm. In so doing, however, strong entity shielding in itself makes the owner's investment illiquid. Strong owner shielding restores liquidity by making the value of an owner's share in the firm independent of the owner's personal wealth, and hence more easily traded.

By contrast, in a partnership or other firm with weak entity shielding, the value of a share depends on the personal wealth of the owner: rich individuals place more personal wealth at risk when buying into the firm and thus will be less willing to do so. We can thus predict that shares in such a firm will tend to be transferred to poorer investors. But the partners have a collective incentive to prevent such transfers, which reduce the total assets backing the firm's contracts and thus will drive up the firm's cost of credit. Consequently, shares in a general partnership are not usually tradable; a partnership is an association among specific individuals, each of whose personal identity is important to the others.

Table 8.1 displays the Roman *societas*, the modern partnership, and the modern business corporation together with their respective degrees of asset partitioning (entity shielding and owner shielding). These three types of organization are arrayed along the diagonal of the matrix formed by the table: the *societas* with no entity shielding and no owner shielding; the partnership with weak entity shielding and weak owner shielding, and the business corporation with strong entity shielding and strong owner shielding. The correlation between degrees of owner and entity shielding allows us to classify these organizational forms, respectively, simply as "non-entities," "weak entities," and "strong entities," as shown in the table.

This is not to say that all legal entities lie on the diagonal of the matrix in Table 8.1. Among modern entities, for example, the general partnership in the United States was stripped of its weak owner

Table 8.1. Legal entities organized by asset partitioning. Roman organizational forms are indicated in italics; other forms are modern.

		ENTITY SHIELDING			
		NONE	WEAK	STRONG	SUPER-STRONG (OR "COMPLETE")
OWNER SHIELDING	NONE	NON-ENTITIES *Societas*	U.S. Partnership after 1978		
	WEAK		WEAK ENTITIES *Societas Publicanorum—Socii*; Limited Partnership—General Partners; General Partnership		
	STRONG	*Peculium*?		STRONG ENTITIES *Societas Publicanorum—Adfines* and *Participes*; Limited Partnership—Limited Partners; Business Corporation; Limited Liability Company; Cooperative Corporation	
	SUPER-STRONG ("COMPLETE")				COMPLETE ("AUTONOMOUS") ENTITIES *Familia*; *Collegium*; Individual; Nonprofit Corporation (European Foundation)

shielding through bankruptcy reform in 1978, so that it lies off-diagonal as shown in Table 8.1. But these asymmetric entities are unusual. For example, the general partnership has become largely vestigial in the United States in recent decades, having been almost entirely displaced by a variety of very flexible strong entities such as the limited liability company and the business trust. The result is that it is employed only in unusual circumstances (Hansmann et al. 2006), and even then the efficiency of its asymmetry is subject to debate (Squire 2009). It is therefore of particular interest that commercial firms in Rome so commonly took the form of a slave-managed *peculium* business—a distinctly asymmetric entity which we analyze below.

8.6.4. Super-Strong ("Autonomous" or "Complete") Entities

Table 8.1 also displays a "super-strong" (or "complete") level of asset partitioning, which takes the specific forms of super-strong entity shielding and super-strong owner shielding.

In an organization with super-strong entity shielding, personal creditors of the organization's owners have no claim on the organization's assets whatsoever: they cannot establish a right to appropriate future distributions that an indebted beneficiary might receive from the organization, nor can they appropriate, even after the dissolution of the organization, any portion of the net assets that might remain after all of the organization's creditors have been repaid. Super-strong owner shielding, in turn, is close to strong owner shielding (limited liability), but goes even further in protecting the personal assets of the organization's owners by eliminating exceptions to limited liability such as the doctrine of veil-piercing.

A familiar contemporary example of a legal form for establishing super-strong entities is the U.S. nonprofit corporation (or the European foundation), which is characterized, not by an inability to earn a profit from its activities, but rather by a "non-distribution constraint" that bars distribution of any such profit to persons who control the organization, such as directors or managers. The persons who control a nonprofit corporation can receive from the organization nothing more than compensation that is reasonable for the services they render and that is not tied to the organization's net earnings. The reason for the nondistribution constraint is to deprive managers of an incentive to take advantage of customers or donors who are poorly situated to determine the quality or quantity of services provided to or for them, and hence are vulnerable to exploitation by a proprietary provider (Hansmann 1980).

By its nature, a nonprofit corporation has no true owners, since owners are by definition persons who have (some share in) both the right to control the organization and the right to appropriate its net earnings. Rather, in a nonprofit the attributes of ownership are divided between trustees and managers (who control the organization) and a designated class of beneficiaries who receive the goods or services produced by the organization (such as the patients in a nonprofit hospital or the storm victims who receive aid from the Red Cross). The nonprofit form provides some assurance, where information is radically asymmetric, that donations to the organization will ultimately aid their intended beneficiaries, and that amounts paid for services rendered by the organization will not opportunistically be diverted by those who control the organization.

In short, there is no one associated with the organization who has a claim on the organization's net assets, much less whose personal creditors can establish such a claim. In a sense, a super-strong organization owns itself. Hence these "super-strong" or "complete" entities might more intuitively be termed "autonomous" entities.

Autonomous entities appear in the lower right-hand cell of the diagonal in Table 8.1. As reflected there, ancient Rome appears to have had several well-established institutional forms for autonomous entities. One of these, quite close to the modern nonprofit corporation, was the *collegium*, which was used by guilds, social clubs, or burial societies.[10] Two other examples were a mixed class of religious and charitable organizations (Duff 1971: 177–9) and the municipal corporation (*municipium*) (Duff 1971: 70–94).

The most important autonomous entity in ancient Rome, however, was one we have already discussed: the patriarchal *familia*. The Roman *familia* was a fully autonomous legal entity with no outside owners, much less owners having their own personal creditors with

[10] "[I]t is almost certain that the property of a corporate college was protected against the creditors of individual members . . ." (Duff 1971: 152, 155–8; Berger 1953). For the organization and economic significance of *collegia* in the Roman world, see Liu (2009) and Hawkins (2016: 66–129).

contingent claims on its assets; direct creditors of the *familia* were the sole outside claimants to its property. Analogously, as reflected in Table 8.1, the individual adult is the basic autonomous legal entity in modern economies.

As Table 8.1 shows, the forms of business organization that have dominated commercial activity for the better part of a millennium—the general partnership and, subsequently, the business corporation—exhibit weak and strong entities, respectively. Ancient Rome, in contrast, principally employed organizations at the extremes of asset partitioning: either none or complete. If Rome could create successful super-strong (autonomous) entities, why couldn't—or didn't—it develop general-purpose weak and strong entities as well?

Part of the answer presumably lies in the structure of the *familia.* As we have noted, the patriarchal Roman *familia* was a large entity which—unlike a partnership—could survive over generations as individual members were born and died. Moreover, the economic reach and flexibility of the *familia* was importantly enhanced by the *peculium.*

8.7. THE *PECULIUM*

Slaveholding was extensive in ancient Rome, and it was to their slaves that Roman families frequently delegated the responsibility for managing commercial activity. The slave-run business was congenial to Roman social mores, under which trade was considered demeaning (D'Arms 1981). Moreover, Rome's slaves often exhibited substantial commercial talent, in important part because they frequently were captured in overseas wars with societies, such as Greece, in which commercial activity was held in less disdain.

It was common practice for a master to provide his slave (or his own son) with a set of assets, termed a *peculium*, for use in a business venture (Kirschenbaum 1987: 33–7; Frier and Kehoe 2007: 131–3). The *peculium* and any profits it generated formally remained the property of the master. A slave was not permitted to dispose of *peculium* assets for personal benefit, and upon his death these assets reverted entirely to the master (Fleckner 2014: 216–17). To incentivize the slave who managed such a business, the master would sometimes promise manumission if the slave grew the *peculium* by a specified amount (Kirschenbaum 1987: 33). In theory, multiple masters who jointly owned a slave could also create a co-owned *peculium* business. Whether *peculia* were commonly used to create joint ventures of this sort is a contested issue in the literature (compare Fleckner 2014: 221–3 with Di Porto 1992: 231–60).

The assets comprising the *peculium* were partitioned to a degree from the master's other assets. Although default on *peculium* debt enabled creditors of the *peculium* enterprise to sue the managing slave's master, the master's liability was capped at the value of the *peculium*, plus any distributions or benefits he had received from it, so long as he had not participated actively in the management of the enterprise (Crook 1967: 187–9; Serrao 2002: 60–4; Abatino et al. 2011). That is, a *peculium* business provided a version of strong owner shielding (like corporate-type limited liability, except that corporate shareholders are normally not liable for lawfully received distributions).

On the other hand, the typical *peculium* business, like the *societas*, appears not to have provided even weak entity shielding. That is, the personal creditors of a slaveholder seem to have enjoyed a claim to all his assets, including those managed by his slaves as *peculia*, equal in priority to the claims of the *peculium* creditors. The available sources are unclear on the issue (Di Porto 1984: 52 n. 41; Fleckner 2010: 420–41). We only know for certain that a special type of *peculium* first introduced during Emperor Augustus' reign (27 BCE to 14 CE)—the *peculium castrense—did* provide a degree of entity shielding to peculium creditors.[11]

The *peculium castrense* initially consisted of all sums earned or otherwise acquired by a son in the power of a *paterfamilias* while on active military service. Creditors of the *peculium* evidently *did* enjoy a prior claim on *peculium* assets over the creditors of the *paterfamilias* (Solazzi 1940: 200–3).[12] The son was initially a quasi-owner of his *peculium castrense* in the sense that he had the legal power to dispose of its assets while he remained in active service and the power to provide for their distribution by will if he died in the course of his service (Fleckner 2014: 228). Thus the *peculium castrense* in its

[11] A privilege similar to the *peculium castrense*—the *peculium quasi castrense*—was extended by the emperor Constantine to a son active in civil service; see Mastrangelo (2005).

[12] We are particularly indebted to Bruce Frier for help in researching this issue.

Augustan incarnation provided something more than weak entity shielding.[13] This explicit recognition of priority for the creditors of a son's *peculium castrense* suggests that the background rule for *peculium* creditors in general was the contrary. If that inference is correct,[14] then slave-managed *peculium*-financed businesses, which were a mainstay of Roman commerce, were endowed with a highly anomalous form of asset partitioning: strong owner shielding (limited liability) but no entity shielding at all.

This is a pattern of asset partitioning that, to our knowledge, cannot be found in the organizational law of modern economies. The pattern is unusual because, in general, entity shielding lays a necessary foundation for owner shielding, and particularly for the strong owner shielding reflected by limited liability. Providing for limited liability alone, without even weak entity shielding, requires that business creditors share their claims on the business assets (the *peculium*) with the (perhaps numerous and difficult to monitor) personal creditors of the owner of the business (the *paterfamilias*), while at the same time renouncing to those creditors any recourse against the *paterfamilias*'s assets beyond those constituted by the *peculium*. In short, the pattern of asset partitioning provided for *peculium* businesses appears to create a sort of anti-entity that puts business creditors in a worse position than they would be without any asset partitioning at all.[15]

Absence of entity shielding in Roman *peculium* businesses may nonetheless have made sense in the Roman context, reinforcing the inference that this may well have been the rule. The fact that the typical *peculium* business had a single owner would have increased the risk of opportunism toward creditors because a single owner need not coordinate with others the transfer of assets into and out of the entity. If the *peculium* had provided entity shielding, a *paterfamilias*

[13] Legal power to dispose of *peculium castrense* assets was extended to retired military veterans during Hadrian's reign (117–38 CE), giving creditors the full protection of strong entity shielding (Fleckner 2010: 230).

[14] Both Di Porto and Solazzi speculate that *peculium* creditors had priority of claim in ordinary *peculia* as well as in the *peculium castrense*, evidently because they feel that the result would be logical (Solazzi 1940: 200–3; Di Porto 1984: 52–3). But they do not confront the contrary logic we offer here.

[15] Indeed, if the master had no knowledge that his slave was using a *peculium* for business purposes, then the master's credits against the *peculium* had to be paid before the claims of other creditors (Abatino et al. 2011).

facing potential insolvency may have been tempted to assign personal assets to *peculia* and to encourage his slaves (or sons) to borrow further against those assets and invest in speculative ventures. Success in such ventures would have redounded to the ultimate benefit of the *paterfamilias* while the cost of failure would have fallen on his personal creditors.[16] The *peculium castrense* may have been a less tempting vehicle for such opportunism, and hence endowed with entity shielding, because it was principally comprised of the son's own earnings and not those of his *paterfamilias* (or more accurately, the latter's slaves).

In addition, the single-owner nature of a *peculium* business would have limited the benefits that entity shielding could have offered in reducing creditor monitoring costs. As we note above, the absence of entity shielding in a multi-owner firm requires a prospective firm creditor to evaluate the personal creditworthiness of each firm owner. A prospective creditor of a slave's *peculium* business, however, needed to evaluate only the creditworthiness of the single slaveholder who owned it to establish appropriate terms of credit.

The limited liability that *peculium* businesses exhibited, moreover, would have provided each of those businesses with de facto strong entity shielding against the creditors of the master's other *peculium* businesses. Limited liability in one *peculium* business would have prevented the creditors of that business from levying upon assets committed to other *peculia* of the same slave-holder. The result would be, in effect, a privileged claim for creditors of one *peculium* business, in the assets comprising that particular *peculium*, over the creditors of other *peculia* established by the same *paterfamilias* (Hansmann et al. 2006).

Such de facto entity shielding would have been only partial, since it would not have excluded creditors of businesses in which the master played an active managerial role, or debts incurred directly by the *paterfamilias*. It is quite possible, however, that it was rare for a slaveholder to engage actively in businesses managed by his slaves. Moreover, while it was evidently not uncommon for prosperous Romans to incur substantial debts directly, and for those debts sometimes to lead to bankruptcy, such borrowing was typically used

[16] Roman law did provide creditors with a remedy for fraudulent conveyances, though how effective that remedy was in contexts such as the *peculium* is unclear (Serrao 2002: 26; Getzler and Macnair 2005: 267, 272).

to finance personal obligations, including, for example, campaigns for political office, rather than business ventures. And for such special purposes the borrower may well have found it advantageous to pledge as much of his commercial wealth as was feasible. This means that there would be an advantage to giving his personal creditors a claim on his commercial assets—including particularly amounts he had invested in *peculia*—that was equal to the claims of his various commercial *peculium* creditors. The latter creditors, in turn, might not have suffered much from such parity in claims, since it would presumably be public knowledge that a given rich Roman was engaged in, or was likely to engage in, an expensive political campaign, thus making him and all of his *peculium* businesses less attractive as credit risks.

The usefulness of the de facto entity shielding enjoyed by creditors of slave-managed businesses was reinforced by the fact that Roman law would further partition a *peculium* for liability purposes if a slave used it to manage multiple businesses.[17] The implications of this rule of weak entity shielding intra-*peculium* is that the Romans often took a practical approach to their creditor priority rules, and that they were aware of the costs of forcing creditors to bear losses resulting from risks the creditors could not easily monitor. Interestingly, ancient Rome's rule of business-specific asset partitioning anticipated a similar rule developed in medieval Italy whereby the business creditors of a merchant who operated in multiple locations enjoyed the first claim to the assets at the specific location where they had transacted (Hansmann et al. 2006).

In sum, the partial, de facto entity shielding Roman law provided for slave-managed businesses, although technically falling short of rendering those businesses true legal entities, might have been well suited to the particular needs of prosperous and prominent Romans.

The three business forms we have surveyed here—the *familia* (a super-strong entity), the *peculium* (a de facto weak entity), and the *societas* (a non-entity)—were evidently the principal organizational

[17] See Abatino and Dari-Mattiacci in this volume (internal citations omitted): "The principle expressed [by the jurist Ulpian, D. 14.4.5.15; 29 *ad ed.*] is that creditors of one business should be allowed to seize the assets pertaining to that business prior to the creditors of the other business, and vice-versa. The same principle applied to a business run in two different locations. The reason given [is that] it is 'fairest to have separate distributions; otherwise, some people might be able to satisfy themselves out of the assets of others and so shift their losses to them.'"

forms employed in Roman private commerce. For the purpose of executing public contracts, however, a fourth form was deployed—the *societas publicanorum*—which appears to have been more like a modern business entity than any of its private counterparts.

8.8. THE *SOCIETAS PUBLICANORUM*

The *societas publicanorum* was an apparent exception to the general lack of legal entities in Roman commerce beyond the extended family. Dating from the third century BCE, the *societas publicanorum* consisted of a consortium of investors, known as *publicani*, who assembled to bid on and perform state contracts. Regrettably, little is known for certain about the rules governing these organizations. Firms organized as *societates publicanorum* flourished during the years of the Roman Republic, and then fell into desuetude under the Empire. But it is from the late Empire, rather than the Republic, that most of our knowledge of Roman law derives. Consequently, what is known of the *societas publicanorum* comes largely from references in private correspondence and other non-legal sources.

Under the Republic, the Roman state contracted out to private parties a substantial portion of its activities, such as the construction of public works, the provision of armaments, the operation of state-owned mines, and tax collection (Badian: 1983: 68–9).[18] The contracts were awarded by bid at auction. The consortia that bid on these contracts—presumably following requirements set by law—were organized as *societates publicanorum*. Similar forms were evidently employed in other sectors of private commerce such as banking, shipping, and trading in slaves. We focus here principally on the public works contractors formed as *societates publicanorum*.

From the available sources, these organizations appear to have had roughly the characteristics of a modern limited partnership with tradable shares. The lead investor in the group, the *manceps*, pledged

[18] Dufour (2012: 53–130) provides a chronological survey of the publicans' business activities. The *societates publicanorum* were evidently numerous (see the table in Dufour 2012: 681–2), though it seems that the actual contract of association for only one such firm has been found (Badian 1983: 68–9; Vighi 1900: 38–46).

his landed estates as security for performance of the contract (Malmendier 2002: 273–4).[19] Other investors could act either as "general partners" (*socii*), who exercised control and were fully liable for firm debts, or as "limited partners" (*adfines* and *participes*), who lacked control but enjoyed limited liability (that is, liability limited to specific assets, such as estates, that they pledged to the organization) (Malmendier 2002: 261–8). Consequently, the *societas publicanorum*—like the modern limited partnership—was, as reflected in Table 8.1, a hybrid entity in our terms: a strong entity for the limited partners, and a weak entity for the general partners.

The *societas publicanorum* reached its peak in the first century BCE. It is unclear how many members the largest of them had. Some sources suggest widespread investment among Romans in these firms, which seems to imply large membership for at least a subset of them. However, Fleckner (2010: 214) reports that, in all the surviving documents, the largest explicit figure for the number of full members (i.e. *socii*) is nineteen, and it is unclear whether that figure is the number of members of a single *societas publicanorum* or the aggregate membership of three such firms. We can safely conclude, therefore, only that participation in a single *societas publicanorum* reached at least as high as seven "general partners."[20] There is no evidence bearing on the number of limited partners that might have been associated with a large *societas publicanorum* (Nicolet 2000: 301–4).

There is substantial evidence that shares of limited partners in a *societas publicanorum* were tradable (Malmendier 2002: 249–51), although there is no direct historical evidence supporting the existence of an institutionalized market for trading shares (Fleckner 2010: 471; Poitras 2011: 100–13; Dufour 2012: 359–76). While we lack direct evidence of the form of entity shielding provided by the *societas publicanorum*, tradability of shares would in turn imply strong entity shielding with respect to the limited partners: as we emphasize above,

[19] A short description of the *societas publicanorum* is also provided in Malmendier (2005). Fleckner (2010) provides a detailed review of the historical sources on the *societas publicanorum*. Dufour (2012: 399–683) provides a detailed compilation of the surviving sources from the time of the Republic, when the *societas publicanorum* played its largest economic role.

[20] Dividing nineteen members across three firms in the manner that minimizes the membership of the largest firm results in firms with six, six, and seven members.

tradability of shares is difficult to sustain without strong entity shielding, while tradability in turn provides the liquidity that strong entity shielding would otherwise deny to the firm's shareholders by depriving them of the ability to withdraw the funds they've invested before the entity is dissolved. Less contested evidence of strong entity shielding is that, unlike a simple *societas*, a *societas publicanorum* survived the death of any of its members (i.e. "general partners"). Indeed, Fleckner conjectures that it could even survive the death of its lead investor whose name appeared on the contract with the state (Fleckner 2010: 383). When a member other than the *manceps* died, his heir assumed his financial rights and obligations, although he became a full member only if there was a prior agreement to that effect (Crook 1967: 234; Duff 1971: 160; Malmendier 2002: 243–7). Still further evidence for strong entity shielding is that the *societas publicanorum* appears to have had the capacity to own property and transact in its own name, although this privilege may have been used only by the larger firms (Badian 1983: 69).[21]

In sum, there is substantial reason to believe that, by the last days of the Republic, the Romans had developed and used widely a type of legal entity rather similar to the modern limited partnership (Dufour 2012: 695), which is characterized by strong entity shielding and limited liability (strong owner shielding) for the limited partners, and weak entity shielding and weak owner shielding for the general partners. This is a hybrid form of entity that is reasonably close to the modern business corporation, and in fact was widely used in France through the nineteenth and into the twentieth century as an alternative to the business corporation by large-scale enterprises such as railways (Lamoreaux and Rosenthal 2004). The last days of the Republic, however, also marked the beginning of the end for the *societas publicanorum* (Malmendier 2009: 1090–2) By the time that the Empire collapsed several centuries later, the *societas publicanorum* had largely disappeared from Roman law and practice (Dufour 2012: 139–43).[22]

[21] Fleckner (2010: 413) notes the lack of evidence for the claim that the *societas publicanorum* could own property as a matter of law, but argues that legal protection of the firm's common property was unnecessary for social reasons (418).

[22] The chronology of the demise of the *societas publicanorum* is controversial, as surveyed in Dufour (2012: 139–43).

This leaves us with two broad questions. The first is why the Romans failed to develop a weak entity such as the general partnership, the legal workhorse throughout Europe during its period of economic development from the Middle Ages through the Industrial Revolution. The second is why the Romans failed to maintain the *societas publicanorum*, much less develop it into a full strong entity like the modern business corporation.

To address these questions, it helps to situate Roman law and the Roman economy in a broader developmental context.

8.9. PERSPECTIVES AND PROBLEMS

In archaic societies, the family, clan, or other kinship-based organization was apparently the main organizational unit for commerce, as for other activities. Viewed in terms of legal entities, evolution toward a sophisticated, modern market economy has involved two basic developments. The first is the creation of legal entities that can combine the talents and wealth of individuals from more than one family or clan. The second is to liberate individuals from forced economic membership in the extended family by making the individual, not the family or clan, society's basic legal entity.

These developments typically take place in tandem, and in stages. Innovation in commercial entities begins with weak entities, such as the general partnership, in which a degree of personal liability continues to be borne by the active members of the business to avoid opportunistic transfers of assets across the boundary that partitions business assets from personal assets. Only later do strong commercial entities such as the business corporation emerge, in response to demand by private, capital-intensive firms that own large fixed assets that are not easily dissipated, making the firms' creditors willing to part with their claims to the owners' personal assets. Subsequent improvement in capital markets then permit strong entities to displace weak entities even in smaller-scale firms and firms that have highly liquid assets.

In Western Europe, we see these two developments taking place simultaneously from the Middle Ages to the present. For an Italian merchant in the early Middle Ages, the household—rather like the patrilineal family in ancient Rome—constituted the basic entity for commercial purposes. This entity included the merchant's workplace—usually located in his home—plus servants and apprentices who (as was common) also lived in the merchant's home. This arrangement gradually evolved into one in which a merchant's adult sons were effectively treated as autonomous entities on their own, while two or more merchants who (post-apprenticeship) worked together in a trade were considered partners in a general partnership with the attributes of a weak entity. With minor exceptions, strong commercial entities did not emerge until the early seventeenth century, with the governmental chartering of the joint stock companies that were the precursors of the modern business corporation.

This evolution was not rapid. The modern business corporation emerged in England and Continental Europe as a well-formed legal entity that could be established without a discretionary governmental charter only in the late nineteenth century, and recent decades have brought further experimentation with much more flexible types of strong entities. Meanwhile, although adult men gained autonomy from their fathers as legal persons by the time of the Renaissance, it is only more recently that adult women have generally come to be treated as autonomous legal entities separate from their fathers or husbands.

Viewed from this perspective, Roman commercial entities seem paradoxical. Despite the sophistication of Roman law, and the scope and prosperity of Roman commerce, the Romans continued to rely upon the patriarchal *familia* as their basic commercial entity. Indeed, they embedded it deeply in formal law, and elaborated on it by providing for multiple, subsidiary slave-managed *peculium* businesses that were apparently endowed with an idiosyncratic anti-entity type of asset partitioning. In contrast to this complex legal structure for the *familia*, the Romans did not take the seemingly straightforward step of providing for a general partnership or any other weak entity that could be used in creating a business entity outside the *familia*. Yet for large projects of special types the Romans seem to have created a hybrid weak/strong (or "semi-strong") entity with the attributes of a modern tradable limited partnership. And then, instead of taking the next—seemingly modest—step and developing strong commercial entities such as the business corporation, the Romans went the other direction and abandoned the form.

We have seen that there was substantial internal logic to the forms of asset partitioning exhibited by each of ancient Rome's best-developed enterprise forms: the *familia*, the *peculium*, and the *societas publicanorum*. What is odd is the entity forms that were missing.

Although the broadly conceived Roman *familia*, supplemented with slave-managed *peculia*, may have been an adequate vehicle for much of Roman commerce, it is hard to imagine that developing the *societas* into a general partnership with weak entity shielding would not have been advantageous. The costs seemingly would have been modest. If Roman courts were capable of sorting out creditors and assets based on the distinction between a slave's *peculium* and the other affairs of the master, as was required by the limited liability that came with the *peculium*, then presumably they could have done the same with the creditors and assets of a partnership and those of its various partners.[23]

It is difficult to believe that the development of legal entities in Rome was inhibited by lack of imagination.[24] For example, limited liability (strong owner shielding) has often been described as an inspired invention of recent centuries that was vital to the sustained economic growth characteristic of modern societies. But limited liability is not a complicated concept, and the Romans were not only aware of it but made clear use of it in both the *peculium* and the *societas publicanorum*. More importantly, the Romans clearly understood the concept of a legal entity, and employed entity shielding in all its principal forms. Thus, late in the first century BCE, the Romans evidently employed a kind of weak entity shielding in the *peculium castrense*,[25]

[23] To be sure, ancient Rome lacked double-entry bookkeeping, a development which—along with the replacement of Roman numerals with Hindu-Arabic digits (including the zero)—contributed to the development of sophisticated forms of commercial asset partitioning in Renaissance Italy (Hansmann et al. 2006: 1367). Abatino et al. (2011: 21–2) cite the lack of sophisticated accounting methods as one of the main reasons that ancient Rome did not develop general-purpose business entities resembling the modern corporation.

[24] Finley (1999: 144) draws, in more general terms, a similar conclusion.

[25] Rome also had a law of secured transactions sophisticated enough to handle floating liens on commercial assets (Leage 1937: 190–6). Because it generally bonds only named creditors, and not a shifting group of creditors, a security interest is a much more restrictive device than a legal entity (Hansmann and Kraakman 2000: 418). But floating liens certainly signify a system of commercial law with a sophisticated approach to creditors' rights. (At the same time, we note that the availability of floating liens might have reduced somewhat the demand for weak entities, for which they can serve as something of a substitute.)

strong entity shielding in the *societas publicanorum*, and super-strong (complete) entity shielding in extra-*familia* noncommercial legal entities such as the *collegium* and the *municipium*.

Nor did the Romans lack experience with the other major law-created element of a legal entity, namely delegated authority to bind the firm contractually. Although the Romans famously lacked a general concept of contractual agency, they developed specific forms of agency when necessary. Thus, a slave could bind his master by contract up to the extent of his *peculium*. And the *manceps* of a *societas publicanorum* apparently could bind the entity and the invested assets of all of its members in contracts with the state.

Evidently one must turn to noncommercial aspects of Roman culture to understand the paradoxical characteristics of Roman commercial entities. While this is not our area of expertise, we can offer some conjectures.

Roman society seems to have had substantial disdain for personal participation in commercial activity. In this respect, it contrasted dramatically with the later Italian society of the Middle Ages and Renaissance, which was dominated by merchants. This may explain the strongly contrasting development of the family in these societies. As we observed above, the medieval Italian household, already conceived as a productive commercial unit, had by the fifteenth century evolved into three different types of entities—the individual, the general partnership, and the limited partnership—that provided even further flexibility in organizing entrepreneurial activity.[26] Roman law, in contrast, seems to have been designed to keep Roman citizens *out* of active participation in commerce, and to protect the stability and status of prominent Roman families from the vicissitudes of economic activity.

Hence Roman law concentrated all power over the wealth of a *familia* in the hands of the *paterfamilias* and limited his capacity to delegate it—for example by providing for no general form of agency. The persons whom the *paterfamilias* could make agents—sons, slaves, and the managers of a *societas publicanorum*—could commit only the specific assets placed in their possession. The lack of mutual agency among participants in a *societas* is consistent with this more

[26] This is not to imply that the limited partnership had only the household as a predecessor; its origins lay, in important part, in the *commenda* and related earlier commercial forms (Hansmann et al. 2006).

general pattern. Perhaps the same conservatism about committing wealth belonging to the *familia* that seems to have been reflected in ancient Rome's limits on agency authority discouraged a grant of priority to business creditors over other creditors of the *familia* with respect to *any* assets belonging to it. For the Romans, the risks of commercial credit may have been more salient than its advantages, and hence they were not eager to facilitate it.

The Romans seem to have viewed commerce as a means of reinforcing the extended family, while the Italians of the Middle Ages, though much in awe of Roman culture, took the reverse approach by viewing the family as an institution for promoting commerce. While Roman law provided business entities—the *peculium* and *societas publicanorum*—for investing the wealth of a *familia* with limited liability, unlimited liability came only if the *paterfamilias* actively engaged in management of a business (Johnston 1995). Thus the family could prosper from business investments without the stigma of engaging in commerce—much as the French nobility did with the limited partnership in the seventeenth century (Kessler 2003; cf. D'Arms 1981). At the same time, families less concerned with social status were free to engage in commercial activity, though the entity forms available to them were not as convenient as they might otherwise have been.

Rather different considerations arguably explain why the Romans not only failed, after the fall of the Republic, to go beyond the *societas publicanorum* and develop a strong entity form on the model of the business corporation, but in fact went in the other direction and gradually abandoned the *societas publicanorum* itself. When Rome transformed itself from Republic to Empire, the wealth and influence of the *publicani* drew jealous attention from the emperors, who responded by having the state take over activities, such as the construction of public works, that it had previously contracted out. The *publicani* persisted for a time as tax collectors, but repeated clampdowns eliminated them from even this role by the end of the second century CE (Crook 1967: 234).

By the last years of the Republic, Roman law and the Roman economy had arguably evolved to the point where they were quite capable of establishing commercial legal entities of the character found in eighteenth-century England. And perhaps if Rome had evolved further toward an open society, its economic institutions would have taken that direction. But social and political developments ultimately blocked Rome's evolution from dependence on the *familia* as the basic legal entity to a society with legal entities suited to efficient general commerce and freedom of enterprise.

To be sure, the family continues to play a strong role today in the organization of enterprise. Even in the most economically advanced societies, the family's affective bonds, continuity, and reputation commonly provide a strong foundation for successful commercial firms. The important difference in this respect between Roman society and contemporary society is that, while the latter provides a number of general legal entity forms that can be used to create an effective business firm comprising any desired combination of family and non-family members, Roman law compelled the family to act as a commercial entity, providing very limited alternatives and ultimately abandoning even the best of those.[27]

REFERENCES

Abatino, Barbara, Giuseppe Dari-Mattiacci, and Enrico Perotti. 2011. "Depersonalization of Business in Ancient Rome." 31 *Oxford Journal of Legal Studies* 365–89.

Arangio Ruiz, Vincenzo. 1966, repr. 1984. *Istituzioni di diritto romano*. Naples: Jovene.

Aubert, Jean-Jacques. 1994. *Business Managers in Ancient Rome: A Social and Economic Study of Institores, 200 B.C.–A.D. 250*. Leiden: Brill.

Aubert, Jean-Jacques. 2013. "Dumtaxat de peculio: What's in a Peculium, or Establishing the Extent of the Principal's Liability," in Paul J. du Plessis, ed., *New Frontiers: Law and Society in the Roman World*. Edinburgh: Edinburgh University Press, 192–206.

Ayotte, Kenneth, and Henry Hansmann. 2013. "Legal Entities as Transferable Bundles of Contracts." 111 *Michigan Law Review* 715–58.

Badian, E. 1983. *Publicans and Sinners: Private Enterprise in the Service of the Roman Republic*. Ithaca: Cornell University Press.

Berger, Adolf. 1953, repr. 1991. *Encyclopedic Dictionary of Roman Law*. American Philosophical Society Transactions, new ser., v. 43, pt 2.

Buckland, William Warwick. 1921. *A Text of Roman Law from Augustus to Justinian*. Cambridge: Cambridge University Press.

[27] For invaluable research assistance, we are indebted to Alissa Abrams and, especially, Marina Santilli.

Crook, John. 1967. *Law and the Life of Rome.* Ithaca: Cornell University Press.

D'Arms, John H. 1981. *Commerce and Social Standing in Ancient Rome.* Cambridge: Harvard University Press.

Di Porto, Andrea. 1984. *Impresa Collettiva e Schiavo "Manager" in Roma Antica.* Milan: Giuffré.

Di Porto, Andrea. 1992. "Filius, servus e libertus. Strumenti dell'imprenditore romano," in M. Marrone, ed., *Imprenditorialità e diritto nell'esperienza storica.* Palermo: Pubblicazioni della Società italiana di Storia del diritto, 231–60.

Duff, Patrick William. 1938, repr. 1971. *Personality in Roman Private Law.* Cambridge: Augustus M. Kalley, Publishers/Rothman Reprints.

Dufour, Genevieve. 2010. "Les societates publicanorum de la République romaine: des ancêtres des sociétés par actions modernes?" 57 *Revue Internationale des droits de l'Antiquité* 145–95.

Dufour, Genevieve. 2012. *Les societates publicanorum de la République romaine: ancêtres des sociétés par actions?.* Montréal/Geneva: Éditions Thémis/Schulthess.

Finley, Moses. 1999. *The Ancient Economy.* Berkeley/Los Angeles: University of California Press.

Fleckner, Andreas. 2010. *Antike Kapitalvereinigungen: Ein Beitrag zu den konzeptionellen und historischen Grundlagen der Aktiengesellschaft* (Forschungen zum Römischen Recht 55). Cologne/Weimar/Vienna: Böhlau.

Fleckner, Andreas. 2011. "Corporate Law Lessons from Ancient Rome," in *The Harvard Law School Forum on Corporate Governance and Financial Regulation.* Available at http://blogs.law.harvard.edu/corpgov/2011/06/19/.

Fleckner, Andreas. 2014. "The Peculium: A Legal Device for Donations to personae alieno iuri subiectae?," in Filippo Carlà and Maja Gori, eds, *Gift Giving and the "Embedded" Economy in the Ancient World*, Akademiekonferenzen, 17. Heidelberg: Universitätsverlag Winter, 213–39.

Frank, Tenney. 1927. *An Economic History of Rome.* 2nd edn. London: Jonathan Cape.

Frier, Bruce W., and Thomas A. J. McGinn. 2004. *A Casebook on Roman Family Law.* Oxford: Oxford University Press.

Frier, Bruce W., and Dennis P. Kehoe. 2007. "Law and Economic Institutions," in Scheidel et al., eds, 113–43.

Fülle, Gunnar. 1997. "The Internal Organization of the Arretine Terra Sigillata Industry: Problems of Evidence and Interpretation." 87 *Journal of Roman Studies* 111–55.

Getzler, Joshua, and Mike Macnair. 2005. "The Firm as an Entity before the Companies Acts," in Paul Brand, Kevin Costello, and W. N. Osborough, eds, *Adventures of the Law: Proceedings of the Sixteenth British Legal History Conference*, Dublin 2003. 267–72. Available at http://www.law.cam.ac.ukldocs/view.php?doc=2365.

Hansmann, Henry. 1980. "The Role of Nonprofit Enterprise." 89 *Yale Law Journal* 835–901.

Hansmann, Henry, and Reinier Kraakman. 2000. "The Essential Role of Organizational Law." 110 *Yale Law Journal* 387–440.

Hansmann, Henry, and Reinier Kraakman. 2002. "Property, Contract, and Verification: The *Numerus Clausus* Problem and the Divisibility of Rights." 31 *Journal of Legal Studies* 373–420.

Hansmann, Henry, Reinier Kraakman, and Richard Squire. 2006. "Law and the Rise of the Firm." 119 *Harvard Law Review* 1333–1403.

Harris, William V. 2011. *Rome's Imperial Economy: Twelve Essays*. Oxford: Oxford University Press.

Hawkins, Cameron. 2016. *Roman Artisans and the Urban Economy*. Cambridge: Cambridge University Press.

Johnston, David. 1995. "Limiting Liability: Roman Law and the Civil Law Tradition." 70 *Chicago-Kent Law Review* 1515–38.

Johnston, David. 1999, repr. 2002. *Roman Law in Context*. Cambridge: Cambridge University Press.

Kaser, Max. 1971. *Das Römische Privatrecht. Erster Abschnitt, Das altrömische, das vorklassische und klassische Recht*. 2nd edn. Munich: Beck.

Kehoe, Dennis P. 2007. "The Early Roman Empire: Production," in Scheidel et al., eds, 543–69.

Kessler, Amalia D. 2003. "Limited Liability in Context: Lessons from the French Origins of the American Limited Partnership." 32 *Journal of Legal Studies* 511–48.

Kirschenbaum, Aaron. 1987. *Sons, Slaves and Freedmen in Roman Commerce*. Jerusalem: Magnes Press.

Lamoreaux Naomi R., and Jean-Laurent Rosenthal. 2004. "Legal Regime and the Business's Organizational Choice: A Comparison of France and the United States During the Mid-Nineteenth Century." National Bureau of Economics Research Working Paper No. 10288. Available at http://www.nber.org/papers/wr0288.

Leage, R. W. 1937. *Roman Private Law*. London: Macmillan.

Liu, Jinyu. 2009. *Collegia Centonariorum: The Guilds of Textile Dealers in the Roman West*. Leiden/Boston: Brill.

Malmendier, Ulrike. 2002. *Societas Publicanorum: Staatliche Wirtchaftsaktivitaten in Den Handen Privater Unternehmer*. Cologne/Vienna: Böhlau.

Malmendier, Ulrike. 2005. "Roman Shares," in William N. Goetzmann and K. Geert Rouwenhorst, eds, *The Origins of Value: The Financial Innovations That Created Modern Capital Markets*. Oxford: Oxford University Press, 31–42.

Malmendier, Ulrike. 2009. "Law and Finance 'at the Origin.'" 47 *Journal of Economic Literature* 1076–1108.

Mastrangelo, Luigi. 2005. "Il peculium quasi castrense Privilegio dei palatini in età tardo antica." 52 *Revue Internationale des droits de l'Antiquité* 261–308.

Nicolet, Claude. 2000. *Censeurs et publicains: économie et fiscalité dans la Rome antique*. Paris: Librairie Arthème Fayard.

Poitras, Geoffrey. 2011. *Valuation of Equity Securities: History, Theory and Application*. London: World Scientific Publishing.

Posner, Richard. 1976. "The Rights of Creditors of Affiliated Corporations." 43 *University of Chicago Law Review* 499–526.

Scheidel, Walter, Ian Morris, and Richard Saller, eds. 2007. *The Cambridge Economic History of the Greco-Roman World*. Cambridge: Cambridge University Press.

Serrao, Feliciano. 2002. *Impresa e responsabilità a Roma nell'età commerciale*. Pisa: Pacini Editore.

Solazzi, Siro. 1937–40. *Il concorso dei creditori nel diritto romano*, vol. I (1937), vol. II (1938), vol. III (1940). Naples: Jovene.

Squire, Richard. 2009. "The Case for Symmetry in Creditors' Rights." 118 *Yale Law Journal* 806–67.

Vighi, Alberto. 1900. *La personalità giuridica delle società commerciali: studio*. Verona/Padua: Drucker.

Zimmerman, Reinhard. 1996. *The Law of Obligations: Roman Foundations of the Civilian Tradition*. Oxford: Oxford University Press.

9

Roman Business Associations

Andreas Martin Fleckner

9.1. INTRODUCTION: LAW, HISTORY, AND THE THEORY OF THE FIRM

A well-known literature explores why firms exist and why they have a certain size.[1] In recent years, scholars have become increasingly interested in how the *legal* setting affects the rise and structure of firms. Some have mulled over the minimum set of rules, if any, that jurisdictions must provide for firms to flourish.[2] Others have tried to link a nation's corporate and securities law to the maturity of its capital market.[3] Still others have turned to the social and political environment to explain persisting differences in corporate law and practice around the world.[4]

While theories have been formulated, models developed, and empirical data collected, one great source of knowledge and wisdom

[1] Coase (1937); Williamson (1971); Alchian and Demsetz (1972); Jensen and Meckling (1976); Klein, Crawford, and Alchian (1978); Grossman and Hart (1986); Hart and Moore (1990); Aghion and Bolton (1992); Hart and Holmstrom (2010); Hart (2017).

[2] Easterbrook and Fischel (1991); Hansmann and Kraakman (2000); Armour and Whincop (2007); Armour, Hansmann, Kraakman, and Pargendler (2017).

[3] La Porta, Lopez-de-Silanes, Shleifer, and Vishny (1997, 1998); La Porta, Lopez-de-Silanes, and Shleifer (1999, 2006); Djankov, La Porta, Lopez-de-Silanes, and Shleifer (2008); but Spamann (2010).

[4] Roe (1994); Licht (2001); Roe (2003); Stulz and Williamson (2003); Pagano and Volpin (2005); Roe (2006); Zingales (2017).

Andreas Martin Fleckner, *Roman Business Associations* In: *Roman Law and Economics: Institutions and Organizations, Volume I.* Edited by: Giuseppe Dari-Mattiacci and Dennis P. Kehoe, Oxford University Press (2020).

DOI: 10.1093/oso/9780198787204.003.0009

has received little attention so far: *history*.[5] This is the motivation for the present chapter and for the book it draws on.[6]

The chapter proceeds as follows. Section 9.2 ("Overview") presents three general observations from ancient Rome. The essence of these observations is that Roman business associations were surprisingly small (often limited to two partners, the absolute minimum of an "association" or a "joint" business venture). Section 9.3 ("Focus") identifies the high level of instability as one of the factors that help explain why business associations did not become larger in Rome. Here and elsewhere (for instance with respect to the liability regime), Roman law appears to be unfavorable for joint business ventures. However, and this will be a recurring theme throughout the chapter, it seems that the law merely reflects reservations in the social and political setting, rather than oddities of Roman legal doctrine. This is an important lesson from history, both for the theory of the firm and for the role that law plays in it.

9.2. OVERVIEW: JOINT BUSINESS VENTURES IN ANCIENT ROME

How did the Romans finance capital-intensive projects such as the erection of temples, the pavement of roads, or the trading of goods from overseas? This problem has fascinated generations of classical scholars, but it is also of interest to the modern lawyer and economist. To be sure, ancient sources will not directly answer our present-day questions about the functions of corporate law, about its role within the broader economic, social, political, and legal setting, or about the factors that determine the rise and structure of firms—the past just differs too much from the present. But history will teach us lessons that can help find answers to contemporary questions and, equally importantly, history will often point us to new questions and issues that have escaped our attention thus far.

Three general observations from ancient Rome will be presented here: there were no shareholder companies or other large capital

[5] Exceptions in recent years: Blair (2003); Hansmann, Kraakman, and Squire (2006); Malmendier (2009).

[6] Fleckner (2010).

associations (§9.2.1); for smaller joint business ventures, Roman businessmen could choose among three legal forms (§9.2.2); private capital accumulation was met with skepticism by the public (§9.2.3).

9.2.1. Absence of Evidence: No Shareholder Companies

For more than 180 years, historians, lawyers, and economists have speculated or even claimed that, as early as the Roman Republic, businessmen formed large firms with publicly traded shares similar to modern stock corporations.[7] Only a decade ago, a longer *Journal of Economic Literature* article suggested that there was evidence of "an early form of shareholder company, the *societas publicanorum*."[8]

Two recent books have come to the conclusion that any such claims are unwarranted.[9] The first book (on which this chapter is based) considers all legal and literary sources, both in Latin and Greek, that have come down to us, such as the works of Polybius (second century BC), Cicero (first century BC), Livy (first century BC–first century AD), Pliny the Elder (first century AD), or Plutarch (second century AD), as well as great collections like the New Testament (first/second century AD) or the *Digest* (sixth century AD).[10] None of these sources brings to light evidence of large "capital associations" (i.e. entities that help finance projects that, due to their scope, duration, or risk, exceed the capacity of individual businessmen),[11] let alone stock corporations with publicly traded shares.[12]

[7] Starting with Orelli (1835: 10–11); additional references in Fleckner (2010: 88–102, 451–62).

[8] Malmendier (2009: 1076).

[9] Fleckner (2010) and Dufour (2012), written independently of one another.

[10] All sources taken into consideration are recorded in the book's appendix (Fleckner 2010: 657–778).

[11] Fleckner (2010) uses *Kapitalvereinigung* (capital association) throughout the book to shield the historical analysis from the modern ideas unconsciously associated with the more common terms (such as "company," "corporation," or "business firm" in English). A theory of the *Kapitalvereinigung* (capital association) is developed at the outset of the book (ibid.: 37–86). "Capital" refers to all types of financing, including those forms that are known as "debt" and "equity" today.

[12] That many other scholars, most recently Ulrike Malmendier, have come to the opposite conclusion is partly the result of differing interpretations, partly the result of factual mistakes. Two examples of the latter: Malmendier frequently claims that ancient shareholders were referred to as *participes* by Cicero (Malmendier 2002: 250; 2005: 38; 2009: 1089; 2013: 5659–60). This is factually wrong because in the whole work of Cicero, the term *participes* is not used once in connection with a capital

Of course, the mere lack of evidence does not suffice to conclude that large capital associations did not exist in ancient Rome. *Absence of evidence is not evidence of absence.* Theoretically, all evidence could be buried in the scores of sources that have been lost. However, an evaluation of the structural features that would have supported capital associations and an analysis of the general economic, social, political, and legal setting indicate that the absence of evidence is not an irony of fate but rather a reflection of the fact that ancient Rome indeed never witnessed anything similar to the modern stock corporation. Section 9.3 will give an example of arguments that help corroborate this impression from the sources. The best reason, though, for doubting the idea that large capital associations *did* exist in ancient Rome, and only the corresponding sources have been lost, is that there is plenty of evidence for other—smaller—business entities (which brings us to the second observation).

9.2.2. Three Legal Forms: *societas, societas publicanorum, peculium*

Roman businessmen eager to launch a joint business venture could choose among three legal forms: the *societas* (§9.2.2.1), the *societas publicanorum* (§9.2.2.2), and the *peculium* of a commonly held slave (§9.2.2.3).[13]

9.2.2.1. Societas: *An Association to Pursue Any Goal*

The *societas* allowed two or more individuals to team up and pursue any goal, ranging from personal affairs under one roof to for-profit trading overseas. Examples of businesses organized as a *societas*

association or a joint business venture (Fleckner 2010: 466–7). A similar mistake lies in Malmendier's claim that Cicero spoke of shares as *partes societatum publicanorum* (Malmendier 2002: 248; 2005: 38). Again, in the whole work of Cicero, there is no single mention of *partes societatum publicanorum*, nor in any other ancient source that has survived (Fleckner 2010: 471). While these and similar mistakes put a question mark behind some of Malmendier's conclusions, they do not change the fact that she raises many interesting questions and provides lots of ideas for further research.

[13] Surveyed in Fleckner (2010: 119–43, 145–215, 217–37). Excluded hereinafter are joint businesses based on status rather than contract; for references, especially with respect to family businesses, see Fleckner (2010: 111–12; 2011a: 677–8).

include the provision of financial services (as an *argentarius*),[14] maritime transport (as an *exercitor*), cattle breeding (*pecus*), the cultivation of land (*ager*), the construction and sale of tombs (*monumentum*), the operation of sales shops (*taberna*), the rental of apartment buildings (*insula*), grammar lessons (*grammaticam docere*), the training and education of slaves (*puerum docere/nutrire*), as well as joint trading in oil (*oleum*), wine (*vinum*), grain (*frumentum*), slaves (*mancipium*), pearls (*margarita*), or clothes (*sagaria*).

To the surprise of the modern reader, all sources about the *societas* have one thing in common: despite the astonishing diversity of business objectives, no *societas* seems to have consisted of more than a few partners, and most sources provide evidence of only two partners (which is, naturally, the absolute minimum to form a *societas*).[15]

9.2.2.2. Societas publicanorum: *An Association to Carry Out State Contracts*

The *societas publicanorum* was a special form of *societas* limited to carrying out state contracts (along with ancillary services). Such contracts covered an impressive range of activities, as wide as the tasks and items the government put out to tender: the collection of taxes (*vectigalia*);[16] the lease of mines and quarries for gold (*aurum*), silver (*argentum*), iron (*ferrum*), lead (*plumbum*), tin (*minium*), salt (*sal*), chalk (*creta*), or pitch (*pix*); the lease of public lands (*ager publicus*), fisheries (*lacus*), water pipes (*aqua*), or canals (*rivus*); the erection and maintenance of public infrastructure like temples (*templum*), wells (*lacus*), water pipes (*aqua*), canals (*rivus*), sewers (*cloaca*), urinals (*forica*), roads (*via*), bridges (*pons*), walls (*murus*), colonnades (*porticus*), waterways (*flumen*), harbors (*portus*), theaters (*theatrum*), retail shops (*taberna*), or markets (*macellum*); the support of the army (*exercitus*); or the import of grain (*frumentum*).

Of all the ancient institutions that modern scholarship knows about, the *societas publicanorum* would have been best suited to finance capital-intensive projects, prompting many observers to call

[14] Here and elsewhere, Latin nouns appear in the nominative singular and Latin verbs appear in the infinitive, i.e. the forms under which most terms can be found in a Latin dictionary (unless another form is more common, below n. 16).

[15] Fleckner (2010: 135–43) and, for inscriptions and papyri featuring the terms κοινωνέω, κοινωνός, or κοινωνία (below n. 31), Fleckner (2018: 695–700).

[16] Nominative plural (see generally above, n. 14).

the *societas publicanorum* an early form (or even a predecessor) of the stock corporation (as seen above). However, it is again remarkable that there is hardly any evidence of a *societas publicanorum* consisting of more than a few *socii* or other capital providers. Despite the abundance of references to the *societas publicanorum*, only one ancient author provides a concrete figure: Livy, writing under emperor Augustus, mentions a group of *nineteen* state contractors who formed, separately or together, *three* associations to support the Roman armies in the Second Punic War (third century BC).[17] Overall, it appears from the sources that the *societas publicanorum* was typically not much larger than the standard *societas*.[18] Nor was its structure fundamentally different.[19]

9.2.2.3. Peculium: *A Category of Property in the Hands of Slaves and Others*

The *peculium* was a category of property in the hands of slaves and other individuals who were subject to the authority of someone else (usually the *pater familias*, the head of the *familia*). If several businessmen had vested a commonly held slave with their capital and instructed him to run a business on their behalf, some of the structural disadvantages of the *societas* would have been mitigated.[20] This is why the idea that the *peculium* was used to fund large firms has become so popular among modern scholars. It is, however, not supported by the sources. First, no traces of large joint business ventures based on *peculia* have come down to us; and second, those

[17] Liv. 23.49.1: *ubi ea dies venit, ad conducendum tres societates aderant hominum undeviginti*.

[18] Fleckner (2010: 207–15).

[19] Between the *socii* of a standard *societas* and the *socii* of a *societas publicanorum*, there were probably no major differences as to the separation of ownership from control (Fleckner 2010: 262–92), the protection of private assets (325–35), the protection of common assets (372–420), and the transferability of shares (450–94). Only if we suppose that the *societas publicanorum* could apply for corporate rights (below §9.3.1.1) and/or typically included a second type of contributors ("financiers"), i.e. passive investors who gave capital without becoming *socii* (below n. 76 and accompanying text), its regime would have been more favorable toward large capital associations (but there is still no evidence of such associations). On the four structural features (separation of ownership from control, the protection of private assets, the protection of common assets, and transferability of shares), see also below (§9.3.3.2).

[20] Especially the impossibility of combining separation of ownership from control with limited liability (generally discussed below, §9.3.3.2).

sources that have survived suggest that the *peculium*'s legal regime was not tailored to funding such enterprises.[21] As a result, the *peculium*'s role in Roman society remains a puzzle.[22]

9.2.3. Obstacles: Social Reservations and Political Constraints

At first glance, the second observation (above §9.2.2) seems to be incompatible with the first one (above §9.2.1): Romans knew how to combine capital for joint business ventures (as the *societas*, the *societas publicanorum*, and the *peculium* demonstrate); they were aware of projects that demanded greater sums of capital (such as overseas trading or state contracts); and they also had a basic understanding of the structural features that help fund capital-intensive enterprises (resulting, most importantly, in the emergence of the *societas publicanorum*). But why, then, the modern observer wonders, did Roman businessmen refrain from establishing shareholder companies or other large capital associations?

An interdisciplinary analysis of Roman society suggests that the main obstacles are to be found in the social and political rather than in the economic or legal setting.[23] To begin with, there is little, if any, doubt that the Roman economy was advanced enough to create a demand for capital-intensive projects, i.e. projects that exceeded the financial capacity of individual businessmen. The main examples come from the list of services that the *societas publicanorum* provided (above §9.2.2.2). Overseas trading is another area that would have benefited from the formation of large capital associations. How many of these associations were needed, and how capital-intensive their business would have been, is difficult to estimate. Any answer heavily depends on the centuries-old controversy over the size and nature of the ancient economy. Yet, even under the most pessimistic assumptions about the level of economic activity, it will be difficult to deny that there was *some* form of economic demand for large capital

[21] For agency problems, see Abatino and Dari-Mattiacci in this volume; for stability concerns, see below (§9.3.2); for other obstacles, see Fleckner (2010: 229–37; 2014: 218–25).

[22] This puzzle is discussed by Bürge (2010) and Fleckner (2014).

[23] The economic, social, political, and legal setting is surveyed (mainly based on literary and legal sources) in Fleckner (2010: 499–518, 519–88, 589–606, 607–23).

associations, starting as early as in the midst of the Roman Republic.[24] The ultimate reasons for the absence of large capital associations must therefore lie outside the economic sphere.

Was the legal regime too restrictive? This is a common supposition.[25] It is true that Roman law could have made capital associations more attractive to entrepreneurs, for instance by protecting their private assets ("limited liability"), and more appealing to third parties, such as by reserving common assets for business creditors ("entity shielding"). However, the large number of special rules for trade and commerce—e.g. on the *merx peculiaris* (merchandise), on the *institor* (sales clerk), or on the *magister navis* (ship captain)—suggests that Roman law usually did not fail to respond to new business needs (or to broader changes in society). And given the complex design of the *peculium*, there are no grounds to believe that certain rules, for instance those that separate private from common assets, were too sophisticated for that period.[26]

Instead, the fact that apparently no such rules emerged indicates that obstacles in the social and political environment, rather than oddities of Roman jurisprudence and law-making, stifled the economic demand for large capital associations. Military, political, or artistic activities brought more prestige and recognition than running a business or participating in a joint venture. Even worse, those engaged in commercial activities were often met with indifference and disrespect (especially the public contractors, i.e. the *publicani*, who formed the *societas publicanorum*). This can be observed both across time and space, as the works of the most influential ancient authors reveal, among them Homer (probably eighth century BC), Plato (fourth century BC), Aristotle (fourth century BC), Cicero (first century BC), Livy (first century BC–first century AD), Pliny the Elder (first century AD), Seneca (first century AD), Plutarch (first century AD), and the Evangelists (first century AD). Against this background, it is anything but far-fetched to assume that social reservations caused many potential businessmen and investors to steer clear of commercial activities, thereby reducing both the demand for and the supply of capital, respectively.

The ill repute of commerce went hand in hand with an unfavorable political environment. In accordance with social attitudes, members

[24] An example is given by Liv. 23.49.1 (above n. 17).

[25] References in Fleckner (2010: 610–15).

[26] For an illustration of the *peculium*'s complexity, see the diagrams in Fleckner (2010) on the liability regime (303) and on the separation of assets (423).

of the upper class, i.e. those who would have had the means to commit capital for the long term, were often explicitly barred from capital-intensive businesses such as overseas trading or state contracting. Another impediment was the ever-increasing share of the government in the gross domestic product. Through the end of the Roman Republic, the state sector had stayed small and lean. Most capital-intensive projects had been put out to tender, and the *societas publicanorum* flourished (first century BC). This changed following the collapse of the old order. More and more capital-intensive projects were undertaken by state authorities, rather than put out to tender, and the market share of private capital associations shrank. This is why the *societas publicanorum* began to disappear in the Principate (first century BC through third century AD). To be sure, those who came into power were interested in a thriving economy, both to prevent unrest and to increase their personal income. But they either did not fully appreciate the benefits of large capital associations, or those benefits were trumped by overriding social and political considerations, e.g. by the ethical reservations noted above or by the fear that private capital accumulation might lead to unwanted political clout.

On balance, blaming Roman law as the main reason for the small size of Roman business associations would miss the point. The law merely reflects the social and political skepticism prevalent at the time. Ancient Rome would not have been the hotbed of publicly traded shareholder companies if only the legal framework had been different. Unless public attitudes had changed as well, capital supply and demand would still have been low, even under the most favorable legal regime. This historical insight is grist to the mill of those who feel that today's scholarship overestimates economic and legal factors and fails to appreciate how much corporate law and practice owe to their social and political environment. While the situation today obviously differs from antiquity, ancient Rome at least provides anecdotal evidence that the social and political setting *can* be decisive.

9.3. FOCUS: LEVEL OF STABILITY

Why were Roman business associations so small? There are many approaches to tackle this question, and the previous section has already presented some general factors that help explain the picture we find in the sources. Among the more subtle explanations for the absence of large firms, the first that come to mind are probably liability risks or limits to monitoring and control. Another factor that could have tipped the balance against large firms, despite their benefits (such as risk diversification or economies of scale), is the *level of stability*. The stability or instability, respectively, of joint business ventures has never been separately dealt with in the Roman context, allowing the remainder of the chapter to turn from general observations to a very specific problem.

How does stability influence size? At first view, the answer is trivial: firms will only become large if they grow, and they will only grow if they last for some time. If they are unstable, in contrast, i.e. face a high risk of untimely termination, then their founders will be very hesitant to expand the business (or launch the firm in the first place), given that start-up costs are typically recovered over a long period of time rather than at the commencement of services. The same holds true for investors pondering to commit capital, due to the large discrepancy between liquidation and going-concern values. But size and stability are even more closely connected, because in some respects, size and stability run into opposite directions, i.e. firms become less stable as they grow. Take mandatory dissolution of the firm upon the death of a partner.[27] With an annual mortality rate of, say, 1 percent,[28] there is a probability of roughly 2 percent that a firm of two partners will be dissolved within the next year; with ten partners, the probability rises to almost 10 percent; with one hundred partners, to 63 percent; with five hundred partners, to 99 percent.[29]

[27] "Mandatory" due to a statutory provision, a clause in the bylaws, or for other reasons (e.g. when each partner's input is indispensable).

[28] 1 percent is a very conservative estimate, i.e. the annual mortality rate among Roman businessmen was probably much higher (and, as a consequence, the risk of dissolution). Ancient mortality rates, along with the many uncertainties surrounding them, are discussed e.g. by Frier (1982; 1983; 2000: 788–97); Scheidel (2001: 13–32); Woods (2007).

[29] If the number of partners is denoted with n, it follows that the probability of dissolution within the next year (i.e. at least one of the partners dies) is: $p(\textit{dissolution}) = 0.01 + 0.01 * 0.99 + 0.01 * 0.99^2 + \ldots + 0.01 * 0.99^{n-1} = 0.01 * \sum_{k=1}^{n} 0.99^{k-1} = 0.01 * \frac{0.99^n - 1}{0.99 - 1} = 1 - 0.99^n$. Or, from a different perspective (calculating the complementary probability, i.e. no partner dies): $p(\textit{dissolution}) = 1 - p(\textit{no dissolution}) = 1 - (1 - 0.01)^n = 1 - 0.99^n$. More generally: if the annual mortality rate is denoted with q (rather than estimated to be 0.01), the probability of dissolution within the next year is: $p(\textit{dissolution}) = 1 - (1 - q)^n$. To simplify matters, it is assumed that each partner's life expectancy is independent of the other partners' life expectancy.

How stable, then, were Roman business associations? This is an empirical question, and under ideal circumstances, one would resort to actual records and data to answer it. However, while joint business ventures are sometimes mentioned in documentary sources, especially inscriptions and papyri, there is almost no information on the structure, the operations, and the fate of the joint ventures.[30] From these sources, it is virtually impossible to estimate the stability of Roman business associations, let alone calculate their average or median life span.[31] In the absence of better evidence, the following discussion will therefore have to focus on the legal sources, and what can be inferred from them, only occasionally corroborated by other evidence.[32]

The legal sources suggest, with all their limits and caveats, that the level of stability varied from the *societas* to the *societas publicanorum* to the *peculium*, but overall, all three were quite unstable (§§9.3.1 and 9.3.2). Why did Roman law tolerate (or even create)

[30] Fleckner (2010: 115, 121, 134–5, 140–1, 149–50, 203–6, 208, 220, 230, 266, 284, 293, 328, 331, 356, 371, 406, 408, 417, 496, 504–5, 557; 2018: 695–700); Broekaert (2012: 232–3).

[31] The most comprehensive study is Ogereau (2014), taking into account all inscriptions and papyri featuring the terms *κοινωνέω*, *κοινωνός*, and *κοινωνία* (meticulously recorded in an appendix: 351–499), the terms that are most closely related to *societatem coire*, *socius*, and *societas* (Fleckner 2010: 400–7; 2018: 691; Ogereau 2014: 169–83, 198–209, 209–15, 215–19, 326–29). However, even if one ignores the fact that the material collected by Ogereau originates from many different places and a period spanning an entire millennium, almost nothing turned up that would help estimate the stability of Roman (or other cultures') business associations: the 461 sources recorded in the appendix provide evidence for sixty-one joint business ventures, but only eight sources (all papyri) specify the (planned) duration of the joint business venture: in four cases a single year; once at least one year; once one and a half years; once five years; and once forever (Fleckner 2018: 699). – Most of the sources (*tituli picti*) discussed by Broekaert (2012: 230–48) do not explicitly mention a *societas* (or a related term such as *socius*), and even where the terminology is used, it is unclear whether or not it refers to a joint business venture constituting a *societas* in the legal sense.

[32] *IKilikiaBM* 1.34 (Adanda, first century AD?), below n. 71; *P.Oxy.* XXII 2342 (Oxyrhynchos, AD 102), below n. 52; *P.Flor.* III 370 (Hermopolis Magna, AD 132), below n. 41; *SB* XVI 13008 = *SB* XVI 13009 (Arsinoites, AD 144), below n. 41; *P.Par.* 17 (Elephantine, AD 153), below n. 53; *CIL* III 950–1 = *FIRA*² III 157 (Dacia, AD 167), below nn. 41 and 71; *BGU* XI 2067 (Theadelphia, AD 173?), below n. 53; *P.Amh.* II 94 = *W.Chr.* 347 (Hermopolis Magna, AD 208), below n. 41; *P.Köln* II 101 = *SB* XII 11238 (Oxyrhynchos, AD 274/280?), below n. 41; *P.Lond.* V 1794 (Hermopolis Magna, AD 488), below n. 41; *P.Cair.Masp.* II 67159 (Antinoopolis, AD 568), below nn. 41 and 71. The aforementioned inscriptions and papyri overlap with those mentioned above, n. 31, and are subject to the same caveats (i.e. that they originate from many different places and span a long period of time).

such a high level of instability? Once again, it seems that the law merely reflects the public skepticism about joint business ventures, rather than oddities of Roman legal doctrine (§9.3.3).

9.3.1. *societas* and *societas publicanorum*: Dissolution, Withdrawal, Seizure

Societas and *societas publicanorum* were more alike than earlier scholarship has made us believe. This is the key result of the book that forms the basis of the present chapter.[33] The level of stability is the main exception: the *societas publicanorum* was more stable than the *societas*. But even where they differed, the two forms were still united by a common legal regime: the *societas publicanorum*'s increased stability was the result of exceptions from the standard *societas* rules and not the consequence of a distinct legal nature. Hence, *societas* and *societas publicanorum* are considered together rather than separately here.

That the *societas publicanorum* was more stable, at least in theory, than the *societas* has always been known.[34] One of the best comparisons appeared as early as four centuries ago.[35] However, those interested in the history and the theory of the firm have missed some of the legal nuances so far, leading to over-optimistic assumptions about the stability of Roman business associations.[36] The following paragraphs aim to set the record straight and provide a more accurate account.[37]

9.3.1.1. General Dissolution Principles

Nulla societatis in aeternum coitio est—no *societas* is established for eternity.[38] The colorful bouquet of events triggering the dissolution

[33] Fleckner (2010), in various contexts (such as size, legal regime, or structural features).

[34] Monographs on the *societas* and *societas publicanorum*, respectively, in recent decades: Cimma (1981); Hernando Lera (1992); Santucci (1997); Malmendier (2002); Meissel (2004); Fleckner (2010); Dufour (2012); Mattiangeli (2017).

[35] Matthaeus (1653: 428–32).

[36] A recent example is Broekaert (2012: 229–30).

[37] Extending the discussion of Fleckner (2010: 340–6, 355–72, 372–86, 413–20; 2018: 693–5).

[38] D. 17.2.70 (Paul. 33 [or 32] *ad ed.*); also D. 17.2.1 pr. (Paul. 32 *ad ed.*): *societas coiri potest vel in perpetuum, id est dum vivunt* [!], *vel ad tempus vel ex tempore vel sub condicione.*

of the *societas* is testament to this principle.[39] The most concise synopsis comes from Ulpian: *societas solvitur ex personis, ex rebus, ex voluntate, ex actione*—the *societas* is dissolved following changes in persons and things, when the consensus among the *socii* ends, and in the case that a *socius* files a lawsuit.[40]

From the perspective of capital commitment and stability, some dissolution events pose no problems because they are in line with the contractual agreement among the *socii* or subject to each *socius*'s consent: the *societas* will end when the contract has run its term,[41] when the *societas* has reached or missed its goal,[42] or when the *socii* unanimously decide to dissolve the *societas*.[43] Both the *socii* and, to some extent, third parties can anticipate these situations and plan accordingly. The other dissolution events are more difficult to control. They will be examined in detail below (§§9.3.1.2/3/4),[44] along with the withdrawal and seizure of common assets (which is not an event that

[39] The central reference points are D. 17.2.4.1 (Mod. 3 *reg.*): *dissociamur renuntiatione morte capitis minutione et egestate* and D. 17.2.63.10 (Ulp. 31 *ad ed.*): *societas solvitur ex personis, ex rebus, ex voluntate, ex actione. ideoque sive homines sive res sive voluntas sive actio interierit, distrahi videtur societas. intereunt autem homines quidem maxima aut media capitis deminutione aut morte: res vero, cum aut nullae relinquantur aut condicionem mutaverint, neque enim eius rei quae iam nulla sit quisquam socius est neque eius quae consecrata publicatave sit. voluntate distrahitur societas renuntiatione.*

[40] D. 17.2.63.10 (Ulp. 31 *ad ed.*); a slightly different synopsis is given in D. 17.2.4.1 (Mod. 3 *reg.*). Both fragments are reproduced above (n. 39).

[41] D. 17.2.1 pr. (Paul. 32 *ad ed.*) (above n. 38); D. 17.2.70 (Paul. 33 [or 32] *ad ed.*) (above n. 38 and accompanying text). Term limits also appear in other sources; e.g. *P.Flor.* III 370 (Hermopolis Magna, AD 132) (one year); *SB* XVI 13008 = *SB* XVI 13009 (Arsinoites, AD 144) (one year); *CIL* III 950–1 = *FIRA*² III 157 (Dacia, AD 167) (four months); *P.Amh.* II 94 = *W.Chr.* 347 (Hermopolis Magna, AD 208) (five years); *P.Köln* II 101 = *SB* XII 11238 (Oxyrhynchos, AD 274/280?) (one year and six months); *P.Lond.* V 1794 (Hermopolis Magna, AD 488) (one year); *P.Cair.Masp.* II 67159 (Antinoopolis, AD 568) (one year).

[42] D. 17.2.58 pr. (Ulp. 31 *ad ed.*); D. 17.2.63.10 (Ulp. 31 *ad ed.*) (above n.39); D. 17.2.65.10 (Paul. 32 *ad ed.*). Iust., *Inst.* 3.25.6.

[43] D. 17.2.65.3 (Paul. 32 *ad ed.*), perhaps D. 17.2.64 (Call. 1 *quaest.*); generally (without explicit reference to the *societas*) Iust., *Inst.* 3.29.4 (contrary agreements terminate contractual relationships formed by consent alone).

[44] With the exception of dissolution following "changes in things" (D. 17.2.63.10 [Ulp. 31 *ad ed.*]: *societas solvitur . . . ex rebus*; above n. 39), since the problems it raises are easier to manage (generally discussed in the text accompanying n. 41–43). Note that dissolution upon legal action (ibid.: *societas solvitur . . . ex actione*) will be discussed earlier than in Ulpian's synopsis (§9.3.1.3) because there is an explicit exception for the *societas publicanorum* (at least for its main field of application).

triggers dissolution, but nonetheless a serious threat to the long-term success of business ventures) (§9.3.1.5).

The dissolution rules under Roman law were mandatory. If, for example, a *socius* died, the *societas* of which he had been a member was dissolved, no matter what the initial contract said or the *socii* agreed upon later. In a two-member *societas*, the second *socius* would wind up the joint business venture or invite others to launch a new *societas*. In a multi-member *societas*, the remaining *socii* could decide to carry on the business among themselves. But since the old *societas* was irreversibly dissolved, they too had to set up a new *societas*.[45] This discontinuity is frustrating because dissolution and liquidation alter the appropriation of assets and the priority of claims. Even if all remaining *socii* and all third parties agreed upon the establishment of an identical copy of the old *societas*, it is unlikely that the allocation of debit and credit would remain unaffected, given the many uncertainties surrounding the winding up of the old and the launch of the new *societas*. Mandatory discontinuity is hard (or virtually impossible) to contract around.[46]

Subject to the exceptions below, all that has been said so far also applied to the *societas publicanorum*. This would only be different if one believed that the *societas publicanorum*, unlike the standard *societas*, sometime in history was given the option to apply for corporate rights. In that case, the point of departure would no longer be the law of the *societas* but the law of the various corporate forms that Roman law began to recognize, such as municipalities, crafts, guilds, clubs, or churches. However, the idea that the *societas publicanorum* was a corporation is one of the many myths surrounding it, with no sound basis in the sources.[47] The present context supports the skepticism: the only way to explain

[45] Death: D. 17.2.37 (Pomp. 13 *ad Sab.*) (for an exception in later periods, see below n. 50 and accompanying text); individual insolvency: Iust., *Inst.* 3.25.8; status deterioration: Gai., *Inst.* 3.153.

[46] The uncertainties surrounding the winding up of the old and the launch of the new *societas* have not been fully appreciated in the existing literature (e.g. Broekaert 2012: 229–30, 245–6). The main challenge was that all assets and all liabilities rested with the individual *socii*. As a result, any change in the composition of the *socii* affected the credit of all other *socii*, and therefore of the joint business venture, unless the departing and the entering *socius* had exactly the same financial standing (which is virtually impossible).

[47] Fleckner (2010: 386–413), critically evaluated by Meissel (2014b) and Mattiangeli (2017).

the various exemptions, discussed below, of the *societas publicanorum* from the standard *societas* regime is that without the exemptions, the law of the *societas* would have applied (suggesting that the *societas publicanorum* was considered to be a *societas* rather than a corporation).

9.3.1.2. societas solvitur ex personis: *Dissolution Following Changes in Personal Circumstances*

The *societas* did not survive changes in personal circumstances, i.e. when a *socius* died, when a *socius* became insolvent, and when a *socius* lost his personal freedom or his civil rights.

Death. The *societas* was dissolved upon the death of one of its members.[48] The remaining *socii* could not continue the *societas* among themselves, nor with the heir of the deceased *socius.*[49] The law of later periods let the *socii* of multi-member *societates* contract around mandatory dissolution,[50] but it is very unlikely that this option was available before.[51] In any case, the law might have been less severe in practice than the legal sources suggest.[52]

Unlike the standard *societas*, a *societas publicanorum* engaged in tax farming, known as *societas vectigalium*, apparently survived the death of its members.[53] The details rank among the most difficult

[48] Gai., *Inst.* 3.152: *solvitur adhuc societas etiam morte socii* = Iust., *Inst.* 3.25.5 (below n. 106); *Gai inst. epit.* 2.9.17. D. 17.2.65.9 (Paul. 32 *ad ed.*): *morte unius societas dissolvitur*. Additional evidence: Gai., *Inst.* 3.153. D. 3.2.6.6 (Ulp. 6 *ad ed.*); D. 17.2.4.1 (Mod. 3 *reg.*) (above n. 39); D. 17.2.35 (Ulp. 30 *ad Sab.*); D. 17.2.36 (Paul. 6 *ad Sab.*); D. 17.2.37 (Pomp. 13 *ad Sab.*); D. 17.2.40 (Pomp. 17 *ad Sab.*); D. 17.2.52.9 (Ulp. 31 *ad ed.*); D. 17.2.59 pr. (Pomp. 12 *ad Sab.*) (below n. 53); D. 17.2.60 pr. (Pomp. 13 *ad Sab.*); D. 17.2.62 (Pomp. 13 *ad Sab.*); D. 17.2.63.8 (Ulp. 31 *ad ed.*) (below n. 53); D. 17.2.63.10 (Ulp. 31 *ad ed.*) (above n.39); D. 17.2.65.10 (Paul. 32 *ad ed.*); D. 17.2.65.11 (Paul. 32 *ad ed.*) (below n. 107).

[49] D. 17.2.35 (Ulp. 30 *ad Sab.*); D. 17.2.52.9 (Ulp. 31 *ad ed.*); D. 17.2.59 pr. (Pomp. 12 *ad Sab.*) (below n. 53).

[50] Iust., *Inst.* 3.25.5: *sed et si consensu plurium societas coita sit, morte unius socii solvitur, etsi plures supersint, nisi si in coeunda societate aliter convenerit.*

[51] As indicated by the lack of an exception in Gai., *Inst.* 3.152 (below n. 106), the basis of Iust., *Inst.* 3.25.5 (the addendum is reproduced above in n. 50).

[52] Two oft-discussed examples (both ambiguous) are Cic., *Quinct.*, esp. 4.14–15, 24.76, and *P.Oxy.* XXII 2342 (Oxyrhynchos, AD 102).

[53] The two main sources are D. 17.2.59 pr. (Pomp. 12 *ad Sab.*): *adeo morte socii solvitur societas, ut nec ab initio pacisci possimus, ut heres etiam succedat societati. haec ita in privatis societatibus ait: in societate vectigalium nihilo minus manet societas et post mortem alicuius, sed ita demum, si pars defuncti ad personam heredis eius*

questions in the law of the *societas publicanorum* and would easily fill a separate chapter. All in all, the most plausible interpretation of the ancient records is that the *societas vectigalium*, and possibly other types of the *societas publicanorum* too, lived on if one of its members died, including the person who concluded the contract with the state.[54] However, it is unclear from these sources whether the exception from the law of the standard *societas* was already available when it was most needed, i.e. at the end of the Republic when the *societas publicanorum* hit its peak (first century BC).

Individual insolvency. The *societas* was dissolved when one of its members became insolvent.[55] Many legal details have remained in the dark, but the main consequence, mandatory dissolution, is well-established.[56]

No rule is known that would have saved the *societas publicanorum* from dissolution upon individual insolvency. However, two provisions in the Customs Law of Asia (*νόμος τέλους Ἀσίας* = *lex portorii Asiae*, first century AD), along with a cryptic remark attributed to Paul (third century AD), suggest that the *societas publicanorum* might have survived some forms of individual insolvency (at least in later periods).[57]

Status deterioration. The *societas* was dissolved when one of its members lost his personal freedom (*capitis deminutio maxima*) or his

adscripta sit, ut heredi quoque conferri oporteat: quod ipsum ex causa aestimandum est. quid enim, si is mortuus sit, propter cuius operam maxime societas coita sit aut sine quo societas administrari non possit? and D. 17.2.63.8 (Ulp. 31 *ad ed.*): *in heredem quoque socii pro socio actio competit, quamvis heres socius non sit: licet enim socius non sit, attamen emolumenti successor est. et circa societates vectigalium ceterorumque idem observamus, ut heres socius non sit nisi fuerit adscitus, verumtamen omne emolumentum societatis ad eum pertineat, simili modo et damnum adgnoscat quod contingit, sive adhuc vivo socio vectigalis sive postea: quod non similiter in voluntaria societate observatur.* Perhaps *P.Par.* 17 (Elephantine, AD 153) and *BGU* XI 2067 (Theadelphia, AD 173?) (death of a fellow tax collector); unclear C. 4.37.3 (Diocl./Max., ca. AD 300).

[54] Fleckner (2010: 373–83).

[55] Gai., *Inst.* 3.154: *item si cuius ex sociis bona publice aut privatim venierint, solvitur societas.* D. 17.2.4.1 (Mod. 3 *reg.*): *dissociamur . . . egestate* (above n. 39); D. 17.2.65.1 (Paul. 32 *ad ed.*): *item bonis a creditoribus venditis unius socii distrahi societatem Labeo ait*; D. 17.2.65.12 (Paul. 32 *ad ed.*): *publicatione quoque distrahi societatem diximus.* Iust., *Inst.* 3.25.7: *publicatione quoque distrahi societatem manifestum est, scilicet si universa bona socii publicentur: nam cum in eius locum alius succedit, pro mortuo habetur*; Iust., *Inst.* 3.25.8: *item si quis ex sociis mole debiti praegravatus bonis suis cesserit et ideo propter publica aut propter privata debita substantia eius veneat, solvitur societas.*

[56] Fleckner (2010: 369–71).

[57] Fleckner (2010: 384, 486–8).

civil rights (*capitis deminutio media*),[58] but remained in place when merely the *familia* changed (*capitis deminutio minima*).[59]

Following the explicit exception for the death of a *socius* and the possible exception for cases of individual insolvency, it would be logical to assume (*argumentum a maiore ad minus*) that a *societas publicanorum*, unlike a standard *societas*, also survived the other two status deteriorations (*capitis deminutio maxima* and *media*).[60] But there is no direct or indirect evidence of an exception from the standard *societas* regime to corroborate this very plausible assumption.

9.3.1.3. societas solvitur ex actione: *Dissolution upon Legal Action*

Scholars of Roman law are still undecided whether the *societas* was inevitably dissolved when one *socius* filed the *actio pro socio*, the main legal remedy given to the members of a *societas*. All rules related to the *societas* seem to mandate dissolution in these cases.[61] If this was the final word of Roman law, it would have been impossible to bring conflicts before a judge without discontinuing the joint venture, forcing the *socii* to sort it out among themselves or to dissolve the *societas*—often a choice between a rock and a hard place. Did Rome's law of procedure open up an alternative path, for instance by allowing a *socius* to restrict his *actio pro socio* to a single controversy? The sources give no direct answer, and the discussion is still in full swing.[62]

[58] Gai., *Inst.* 3.153: *dicitur etiam capitis deminutione solvi societatem*; *Gai inst. epit.* 2.9.17. D. 17.2.4.1 (Mod. 3 *reg.*): *dissociamur ... capitis minutione* (above n. 39); D. 17.2.63.10 (Ulp. 31 *ad ed.*): *... distrahi videtur societas. intereunt autem homines quidem maxima aut media capitis deminutione aut morte* (above n. 39).

[59] D. 17.2.63.10 (Ulp. 31 *ad ed.*) (above n. 58, *argumentum e contrario*); also D. 17.2.58.2 (Ulp. 31 *ad ed.*) and D. 17.2.65.11 (Paul. 32 *ad ed.*).

[60] Wieacker (1936: 162, 290); Fleckner (2010: 385). The affected *socius* probably would have lost his membership position, as in the case of death and insolvency.

[61] D. 17.2.63.10 (Ulp. 31 *ad ed.*): *societas solvitur ... ex actione* (above n. 39); D. 17.2.65 pr. (Paul. 32 *ad ed.*): *actione distrahitur, cum aut stipulatione aut iudicio mutata sit causa societatis. Proculus enim ait hoc ipso quod iudicium ideo dictatum est, ut societas distrahatur, renuntiatam societatem, sive totorum bonorum sive unius rei societas coita sit.* Additional evidence: D. 17.2.52.14 (Ulp. 31 *ad ed.*) as well as (less restrictive) D. 17.2.65.15 (Paul. 32 *ad ed.*) (below n. 63) and (unclear) C. 4.37.5 (Diocl./Max., AD 294).

[62] Meissel (2004: 24–5, 38–9, 41–5, 284–6); Fleckner (2010: 345–6); Müller-Kabisch (2011: 91–3); Kaser, Knütel, and Lohsse (2017: 281–2). Important earlier

Interestingly, it seems that the *societas publicanorum*, unlike the standard *societas*, was not dissolved following legal disputes among its members (again at least for those associations engaged in tax farming). Paul states that it was sometimes necessary to file an action during ongoing business operations (*manente societate agi pro socio*), and mentions the example of a *societas* that has been founded for the purpose of tax farming (*societas vectigalium causa coita est*).[63] As always, it remains unclear how early this legal innovation was available (Paul wrote at the beginning of the third century AD, when the *societas publicanorum* had long lost its former relevance).[64]

9.3.1.4. societas solvitur ex voluntate: *Dissolution When the Consensus Ends*

Manet autem societas eo usque, donec in eodem ‹con›sensu perseverant—the *societas* continues to exist as long as its members remain in agreement.[65] Put negatively, if there is no longer a consensus among the *socii*, the *societas* comes to an end.[66] The key consequence of this principle is that each *socius* could unilaterally terminate the *societas* at any time.[67] This includes cases of bad faith and fraud on the part of the terminating *socius*: the other *socii* may claim for

accounts include Matthaeus (1653: 431); Wieacker (1936: 9–12, 166–9); Arangio-Ruiz (1950: 172–82); Schulz (1951: 552–3); and Zimmermann (1990: 457, 460, 465, 470–1).

[63] D. 17.2.65.15 (Paul. 32 *ad ed.*): *nonnumquam necessarium est et manente societate agi pro socio, veluti cum societas vectigalium causa coita est propterque varios contractus neutri expediat recedere a societate nec refertur in medium quod ad alterum pervenerit.*

[64] The general controversies surrounding this fragment can be ignored here because the exception for the *societas publicanorum* (or *vectigalium*) is widely recognized (Kniep 1896: 297–305; Cimma 1981: 221–5; Malmendier 2002: 245–7; Meissel 2004: 44–5, 211–12; Fleckner 2010: 383–4).

[65] Gai., *Inst.* 3.151 ≈ *Gai inst. epit.* 2.9.17 ≈ Iust., *Inst.* 3.25.4. C. 4.37.5 (Diocl./Max., AD 294): *tamdiu societas durat, quamdiu consensus partium integer perseverat.*

[66] *Gai inst. epit.* 2.9.17: *sicut consensu contrahitur, etiam dissensu dissolvitur.*

[67] Gai., *Inst.* 3.151: *at cum aliquis renuntiaverit societati, societas solvitur* ≈ Iust., *Inst.* 3.25.4; *Gai inst. epit.* 2.9.17. D. 17.2.4.1 (Mod. 3 *reg.*): *dissociamur renuntiatione* (above n. 39). The key source is D. 17.2.65.3–8 (Paul. 32 *ad ed.*). Additional evidence: D. 17.2.14 (Ulp. 30 *ad Sab.*); D. 17.2.15 (Pomp. 13 *ad Sab.*); D. 17.2.16 pr. (Ulp. 30 *ad Sab.*); D. 17.2.17.1/2 (Paul. 6 *ad Sab.*); D. 17.2.18 (Pomp. 13 *ad Sab.*); D. 17.2.63.10 (Ulp. 31 *ad ed.*) (above n. 39); D. 17.2.65 pr. (Paul. 32 *ad ed.*) (above n. 61); perhaps (unless there is a *consensus*) D. 17.2.64 (Call. 1 *quaest.*). C. 3.37.5 (Diocl./Max., AD 294) (below n. 113 and accompanying text); C. 4.37.5 (Diocl./Max., AD 294) (above n. 65).

damages, but the *societas* was still dissolved.[68] A termination was effective even when the *socii* had explicitly excluded it.[69] Some of the details are very controversial.[70]

Nothing in the sources suggests that the *socii* typically used other mechanisms to make their capital commitment more binding. The most obvious method would have been to stipulate prohibitively high contractual penalties.[71] But then again, such penalties would have made unilateral withdrawal only costly, without removing the right to pull out of the joint venture at will.

Could the members of a *societas publicanorum* unilaterally terminate their joint business venture? The sources are silent, but especially in this context, it is important to recall the large time lag between the peak of the *societas publicanorum* (first century BC), the zenith of legal reasoning (second century AD), and the compilation of the *Corpus iuris civilis* (sixth century AD). The silence of the sources is therefore no conclusive evidence that the standard regime—allowing unilateral termination—applied in earlier periods without modification. Instead, given the *societas publicanorum*'s public function and the exemptions from other dissolution events, it is not far-fetched to assume that the members of a *societas publicanorum* had no unilateral dissolution powers, or were at least restricted in exercising their rights.[72] But it has to be emphasized that this is only speculation, based on plausibility and policy considerations rather than direct or indirect evidence. In addition, it is again uncertain whether any

[68] Gai., *Inst.* 3.151 ≈ Iust., *Inst.* 3.25.4. D. 17.2.14 (Ulp. 30 *ad Sab.*); D. 17.2.17.2 (Paul. 6 *ad Sab.*).

[69] Most instructive are (in direct sequence) D. 17.2.14 (Ulp. 30 *ad Sab.*); D. 17.2.15 (Pomp. 13 *ad Sab.*); D. 17.2.16 pr. (Ulp. 30 *ad Sab.*). Additional evidence: D. 10.3.14.2–4 (Paul. 3 *ad Plaut.*); D. 17.2.17.2 (Paul. 6 *ad Sab.*); D. 17.2.65.6 (Paul. 32 *ad ed.*).

[70] Fleckner (2010: 343, 356; 2011a: 692). The most recent monograph is Müller-Kabisch (2011), critically reviewed by Meissel (2014a) and Schermaier (2015).

[71] In the section on the *societas*, the following fragments refer to stipulations: D. 17.2.41 (Ulp. 20 *ad ed.*); D. 17.2.42 (Ulp. 45 *ad Sab.*); D. 17.2.65 pr. (Paul. 32 *ad ed.*) (above n.61); D. 17.2.71 pr. (Paul. 3 *epit. Alf. dig.*). But none of these fragments describes a situation where the *socii* use stipulations to make their (capital) commitment more binding. A better example, but from a different period and place, is *P.Cair.Masp.* II 67159 (Antinoopolis, AD 568) (exclusion of withdrawal, stipulation of contractual penalties, provision of collateral); perhaps *IKilikiaBM* 1.34 (Adanda, first century AD?) (penalty for withdrawal), but the reading and the context are unclear (Ogereau 2014: 366); generally *CIL* III 950–1 = *FIRA*² III 157 (Dacia, AD 167) (stipulation of contractual penalties).

[72] Kniep (1896: 254, 269–70, 298, 300); Fleckner (2010: 385).

possible exception from the standard *societas* regime was already available when it was most needed, i.e. during the peak of the *societas publicanorum* at the end of the Republic (first century BC).

9.3.1.5. *Withdrawal and Seizure of Common Assets*

A fundamental threat to joint business ventures is that the *socii* unilaterally withdraw capital or that their private creditors seize common assets ("private" creditors because their claims are unrelated to the joint business venture). Unlike the dissolution events discussed so far, unilateral withdrawal and seizure do not automatically dissolve the *societas* or *societas publicanorum*. But if the outflow of funds renders it impossible to continue the business, the result will be the same: dissolution. And similar to the dissolution events, the risk of untimely termination increases with the number of *socii* (at least if their private creditors have access to all common assets), so entrepreneurs again have to find a trade-off between maximizing size and stability. Despite the importance of the issue, no sources directly address the protection of common assets, making it one of the most ambiguous features of both the *societas* and the *societas publicanorum*.[73]

The assets of joint business ventures organized as a *societas* were apparently almost unprotected.[74] All assets were owned by the *socii*, either collectively or individually (in the latter case, the *socius* who was the owner of the asset allowed the others to use it, without granting them co-ownership). There was no "corporate property" or the like because the *societas* lacked legal capacity to hold assets on its own. Each *socius* was free to transfer his share in the assets at any time to third parties (who became owners but not *socii*). A *socius* could also terminate the *societas* (above §9.3.1.4) and claim his share in the liquidation proceeds. Contractual restrictions typically affected only what the *socii* were *allowed* to do internally, without confining what they were *able* to do externally; violations gave fellow *socii* claims for damages but no remedies to rescind the transaction. Likewise, it seems that the private creditors of the *socii* had unrestricted access to the common assets.

[73] Recent studies include Hansmann, Kraakman, and Squire (2006: 1356–7, 1360–1) and Fleckner (2010: 339–420); earlier scholarship is surveyed in Fleckner (2010: 355–6, 362–8, 413–19).

[74] Fleckner (2010: 355–72).

The *societas publicanorum* offered only slightly better protection.[75] As discussed in previous sections, the members of a *societas publicanorum* had fewer opportunities to terminate the joint venture and reclaim their money. In addition, the *societas publicanorum* was apparently open to passive investors who provided only capital, similar to money-lenders, without becoming *socii* (referred to e.g. as *adfines* or as owners of *partes*).[76] These "financiers" had probably no powers to advance repayment, and their private creditors could not seize the assets of the joint venture. But apart from that, the regime of the standard *societas* applied, giving the private creditors of the *socii* unrestricted access to the common assets.

9.3.2. *peculium*: Death, Withdrawal, Seizure

The instability of the *peculium* has been neglected or overlooked by many scholars so far.[77] Otherwise, the myth that Roman businessmen employed the *peculia* of common slaves to fund large business ventures could never have become so popular.[78]

In a joint business venture based on the *peculium* of a common slave, there were three sources of instability that an individual business partner could not control: dissolution events resulting from internal relationships (§9.3.2.1), the death of the slave who held the *peculium* (§9.3.2.2), and withdrawal or seizure of common assets (§9.3.2.3).[79]

[75] Fleckner (2010: 413–420).

[76] The role of the various stakeholders surrounding the *societas publicanorum* (*socii*, bidders, capital providers, guarantors) is difficult to decipher, given the available evidence (surveyed by Fleckner 2010: 185–207).

[77] Exceptions include Bürge (1988: 860; 1999: 199; 2010: 385) and Fleckner (2010: 227–8, 236, 424; 2014: 217, 225–34).

[78] The discussion is still ongoing; some authors vehemently support the idea, others dismiss it outright, still others explore its limits. Main monographs: Di Porto (1984); Serrao (1989); Aubert (1994); Cerami and Petrucci (2010). Important papers: Földi (1996); Hansmann, Kraakman, and Squire (2006: 1358–60); Abatino, Dari-Mattiacci, and Perotti (2011); Abatino and Dari-Mattiacci in this volume. Additional references (including pioneering works from the nineteenth century) are provided in Fleckner (2010: 221–2; 2014: 222). The principal accounts of the *peculium* (in general) are Mandry (1876); Micolier (1932); Buti (1976); Brinkhof (1978); and Żeber (1981).

[79] Not covered hereinafter are ransom and other forms of manumission (because they are easy to avoid).

9.3.2.1. Internal Dissolution Events

Many proponents of *peculium*-based businesses think of the *peculium* as an alternative to the *societas*, to overcome the latter's structural challenges for large firms. Yet, the very first source of the *peculium*'s own instability was, in cases of joint business ventures, again the law of the *societas*. The reason is that holding common assets (like a slave entrusted with a *peculium*) is the classic example of a *societas*. In fact, there are good reasons to believe that it is *this* situation—holding common assets—that (co)triggered the emergence of the *societas* in the first place.[80]

To be sure, several individuals could make use of a *peculium* without forming a *societas*.[81] However, the *societas* contract did not require a certain form or format; an informal agreement sufficed.[82] How would a third person have interpreted the situation where several individuals, without a word on their internal relationships, teamed up to launch a joint business venture through a common slave? The most plausible assumption, given the historical development and the broad scope of the *societas* rules, would have been that those business partners founded a *societas* to administer their internal relationships.[83] The common slave who held the *peculium* became an asset that the *socii* jointly managed, governed by the standard *societas* regime. As a "by-product" of this regime, the *socii* also imported the dissolution events of the *societas* (such as the death of a *socius*), making their joint venture subject to the same level of instability that any firm organized as a *societas* faced (plus the instability inherent to the *peculium*, discussed in the next two subsections).[84]

[80] Fleckner (2010: 123–6, 398–9; 2011a: 680) and (published in the meantime) Müller-Kabisch (2011: 39–73); see also below n. 109 and accompanying text.

[81] D. 15.1.19.2 (Ulp. 29 *ad ed.*); generally (joint ownership with no *societas* among the co-owners) e.g. D. 9.4.10 (Paul. 22 *ad ed.*); D. 17.2.31 (Ulp. 30 *ad Sab.*); Iust., *Inst.* 3.27.3.

[82] D. 17.2.4 pr. (Mod. 3 *reg.*): *societatem coire et re et verbis et per nuntium posse nos dubium non est*; generally Gai., *Inst.* 3.135–8 ≈ Iust., *Inst.* 3.22 (*de consensu obligatione*) with explicit reference to the *societas* in Gai., *Inst.* 3.135 ≈ Iust., *Inst.* 3.22 pr.; also Gai., *Inst.* 3.154: *societas . . . , quae nudo consensu contrahitur.* But see Gai., *Inst.* 3.154b: *alii quoque, qui volebant eandem habere societatem, poterant id consequi apud praetorem certa legis actione.*

[83] Fleckner (2010: 229, 292, 335). This is even acknowledged (albeit very cautiously) by one of the main proponents of *peculium*-based businesses: Di Porto (1984: 161–7, 255, 379).

[84] The details, especially the scope of the *actio pro socio* and its relation to the *actio communi dividundo*, must be reserved for further research; see generally Drosdowski (1998), along with Bürge (2000) and Meissel (2004: 281–308).

9.3.2.2. *Death of the Slave*

Notwithstanding the fact that the masters transferred all business assets to the *peculium* of the common slave, all these assets remained part of their property. The masters, not the *peculium* holders, were the owners of the *peculium* items.[85] The reason is that slaves lacked legal capacity to hold assets in their own name.[86]

If the slave passed away, all assets belonging to the *peculium* reverted back to the masters, thanks to their continuing ownership position. This result is well documented in the sources.[87] It is also indirectly confirmed (*argumentum e contrario*) by the creation of two *peculium* variants that avoided the reversion: the *peculium castrense* (for sons in military service) and the *peculium quasi castrense* (for sons in civil service).[88] Neither of the two was available for joint business ventures.[89]

9.3.2.3. *Withdrawal and Seizure of Common Assets*

An important consequence of the masters' continuing ownership position was that they could reclaim *any* item belonging to the *peculium* at *any* time and for *any* reason.[90] Among the proponents of *peculium*-based businesses, many seem to have missed this source of instability. But the absolute powers of the *peculium* holder's master or father have always been present in other strands of the literature.[91] In fact, there is

[85] The general principle is succinctly summarized in Iust., *Inst.* 2.12 pr.: *iure civili omnium qui in potestate parentum sunt peculia perinde in bonis parentum computantur, ac si servorum peculia in bonis dominorum numerantur.*

[86] Gai., *Inst.* 2.87: *ipse enim, qui in potestate nostra est, nihil suum habere potest* ≈ D. 41.1.10.1 (Gai. 2 *inst.*); also e.g. Gai., *Inst.* 2.96; D. 50.16.182 (Ulp. 27 *ad ed.*); Iust., *Inst.* 2.12 pr. (above n. 85).

[87] D. 15.2.1.3 (Ulp. 29 *ad ed.*): *cum morte vel alienatione extinguitur peculium* and D. 15.2.3 (Pomp. 4 *ad Q. Muc.*): *desiit morte servi vel manumissione esse peculium*, and generally D. 15.2: *quando de peculio actio annalis est*; also D. 15.3.1.1 (Ulp. 29 *ad ed.*): *morte servi exstinctum est peculium*. Indirectly Gai., *Inst.* 3.56/58/59; Iust., *Inst.* 3.7.4.

[88] On the long process (fueled by various constitutions of Roman emperors and changes in Roman legal doctrine) that led to more financial independence of sons in military and civil service, see Fleckner (2014: 227–32).

[89] Fleckner (2010: 222–3; 2014: 232).

[90] D. 15.1.8 (Paul. 4 *ad Sab.*): *contra autem simul atque noluit* [sc. *dominus*], *peculium servi desinit peculium esse*. Additional evidence: D. 15.1.4 pr. (Pomp. 7 *ad Sab.*); D. 15.3.1.1 (Ulp. 29 *ad ed.*); D. 15.3.5.3 (Ulp. 29 *ad ed.*). Iust., *Inst.* 2.12 pr. (below n. 96) (*argumentum e contrario*).

[91] An early example is Mandry (1876: 170).

even a discussion among modern scholars about the existence of *social* restrictions on the principal's far-reaching *legal* powers.[92]

Another threat to the common assets, besides unilateral withdrawal by the masters, was seizure by the latter's private creditors.[93] As for the *societas* and the *societas publicanorum*, no definitive answer is provided by the sources that have come down to us. But those sources that have survived suggest that *peculium* items were *not* protected against seizure by private creditors.[94] While the issue is highly controversial, there are two strong arguments to support the view presented here. First, as the reversion following the death of the *peculium* holder and as the withdrawal powers of his masters show (two well-documented cases), the fact that the masters remained the owners of all *peculium* items continued to be decisive for the allocation of assets in cases of doubt or conflict. If a master defaulted on a debt and his creditors seized his assets, it would have been inconsistent with the general regime to exclude his share in the *peculium* assets from seizure. Second, there are two provisions (apparently unknown to many observers) that explicitly address the issue for specific situations and thereby provide an *argumentum e contrario* for the standard *peculium* regime. The first of these exceptions shields the son's regular *peculium* from confiscations of his father's property;[95] the second saves the son's *peculium castrense* from withdrawal by his father and seizure by the latter's creditors.[96] Neither of the two exceptions applied to slaves holding assets of a joint business venture.[97]

[92] For references, see Fleckner (2010: 227–8; 2014: 225). Note that social restrictions would predominantly affect fathers with regard to the (standard) *peculia* of their sons; masters of a common slave would not face the same level of social scrutiny when they reclaim business assets.

[93] Recent studies include Hansmann, Kraakman, and Squire (2006: 1358–60); Fleckner (2010: 420–41); and Abatino, Dari-Mattiacci, and Perotti (2011: 379–81); the older literature is surveyed in Fleckner (2010: 424–7).

[94] Fleckner (2010: 420–41; 2014: 225–6, 232).

[95] D. 4.4.3.4 (Ulp. 11 *ad ed.*): *ut puta si patris eius bona a fisco propter debitum occupata sunt: nam peculium ei ex constitutione Claudii separatur*. On this fragment, see (in general) e.g. Brinkhof (1978: 175–6) and (in the present context) Fleckner (2010: 228, 236, 423, 425–6, 428, 436–7; 2014: 226–7).

[96] Iust., *Inst.* 2.12 pr.: *ex hoc intellegere possumus, quod in castris adquisierit miles, qui in potestate patris est, neque ipsum patrem adimere posse neque patris creditores id vendere vel aliter inquietare*; also D. 49.17.18.4 (Maec. 1 *fideic.*): *hoc peculium a patris bonis separetur*. For additional references, see Fleckner (2010: 430–7).

[97] Fleckner (2014: 226, 232, 233).

9.3.3. Explanations: Public Sentiment, Structural Features, and the Theory of the Firm

The sources presented so far suggest that Roman business associations faced a high risk of untimely termination. What factors help explain this inherent instability (§9.3.3.1)? How does the lack of stability fit into the general structure of Roman business associations (§9.3.3.2)? And, finally, are there any lessons to draw from the Roman experience for the theory of the firm (§9.3.3.3)?

9.3.3.1. Stability and the Public Sentiment

At first glance, the notorious conservatism of Roman jurists and lawmakers may appear as the main culprit for the many uncertainties to which Roman business associations were exposed.

Following the typical stereotypes, one could be tempted to argue that Roman lawyers lacked the courage, or the vision, to draft a more favorable legal regime, and as a result, joint business ventures remained small. But even the dissolution rules themselves show that Roman law was more accommodating than many modern observers are willing to concede: the standard *societas* did not survive the death of a *socius* or the filing of an action; the *societas publicanorum* apparently did.[98] Multi-member *societates* were dissolved, even if the remaining *socii* wanted to carry on the joint venture; the law of later periods let them contract around this rule.[99] *Peculium* assets were generally not protected against seizure by the master's private creditors; the *peculia* of sons increasingly were, thanks to interventions by various emperors and a shift in legal doctrine that made sons more independent of their father's influence and fortune.[100] Another feature that may be added in this context is that the assets of a slave who ran two different stores were separated.[101] Ulpian's reasoning would

[98] D. 17.2.59 pr. (Pomp. 12 *ad Sab.*) and D. 17.2.63.8 (Ulp. 31 *ad ed.*) (both above n. 53), plus D. 17.2.65.15 (Paul. 32 *ad ed.*) (above n. 63).

[99] Iust., *Inst.* 3.25.5 (above n. 50).

[100] D. 4.4.3.4 (Ulp. 11 *ad ed.*) (above n. 95) as well as D. 49.17.18.4 (Maec. 1 *fideic.*) and Iust., *Inst.* 2.12 pr. (both above n. 96).

[101] D. 14.4.5.15/16 (Ulp. 29 *ad ed.*), discussed in more detail by Fleckner (2010: 437–41; 2011a: 686; 2014: 233); for a diagram, see Fleckner (2010: 423). Whether or not the commercial goods (*merx peculiaris*) were protected against withdrawal by the masters and seizure by the latter's private creditors is uncertain (probably not).

pass the peer review of a modern law and economics journal: *unusquisque enim eorum merci magis quam ipsi credidit*—the creditors of both stores have put their trust more in the assets than in the slave.[102]

All four innovations have in common that they remove some of the uncertainties surrounding the *societas* and the *peculium*. This makes it difficult to argue that Roman jurists and law-makers failed to appreciate the positive effects of more stable business associations. It would be equally unconvincing to assume that Roman lawyers did not know how to draft succession and continuation rules, given the explicit exceptions for the *societas publicanorum* and provisions in other areas that let contractual relationships pass on to the heirs.[103] Nor were restrictions on unilateral termination powers a foreign concept.[104] That the rules on the *societas*, the *societas publicanorum*, and the *peculium* did not provide for a higher level of stability has to be the result of factors outside the legal sphere. Was it just the aforementioned dislike of commercial activities? This is unlikely, considering the many areas where Roman lawyers *did* respond to business needs. Was it a discomfort with *large* business organizations? Again, this is unlikely, given the favorable treatment of family businesses that allowed them to grow and prosper over many generations. There must be something specifically inherent to *joint business ventures among strangers* (as opposed to family businesses) that stopped Roman jurists and law-makers from developing a more stable regime. What was it? The "characteristically Roman aversion to associations"?[105]

Curiously enough, our best evidence of the *non-legal* factors that shaped the law of joint business ventures comes again from the *legal* sources. While other sources are mostly silent, the jurists reveal, directly and indirectly, some of the non-legal factors in their reasoning. Note how both Gaius and Justinian justify the dissolution of the *societas* upon the death of a *socius*: *qui societatem contrahit, certam personam sibi eligit*—when someone enters into a *societas* contract,

[102] D. 14.4.5.15 (Ulp. 29 *ad ed.*).

[103] For the *societas publicanorum*, see D. 17.2.59 pr. (Pomp. 12 *ad Sab.*) and D. 17.2.63.8 (Ulp. 31 *ad ed.*), both reproduced above (n. 53); other examples include Iust., *Inst.* 3.19.25 (*stipulatio*), 3.20.2 (*fideiussor*), 3.24.6 (*locatio conductio*), and Gai., *Inst.* 3.160 ≈ Iust., *Inst.* 3.26.10 (*mandatum*).

[104] See e.g. Iust., *Inst.* 3.26.11 (*mandatum*).

[105] Schulz (1951: 553).

he selects a certain individual (i.e. as his partner).[106] Continuing a *societas* with the heir of a deceased *socius* would run counter to this idea because, as Paul explains, it could make someone (the remaining partner) a *socius* of an individual (the heir) with whom he does not want to be affiliated.[107] It is reasonable to assume that this is also the rationale for dissolving the *societas* following other changes in personal matters (instead of e.g. letting the creditor of an insolvent *socius* assume the latter's position and become a member of the *societas*).[108] Not allowing membership transfers *inter vivos* (below §9.3.3.2) is another consequence that fits into this picture.

But why did Romans object to the idea of becoming the *socius* of a stranger? The most plausible explanation combines two closely related considerations. The first is that Roman elites were generally rather reluctant to enter into contractual relationships with their peers. The reason is the legendary—and often somewhat overstated—individualism of Roman housefathers (*patres familias*). They valued their freedom above all else, so the legend goes, and avoided restricting it through contractual mechanisms. If they were faced with a task that called for the collaboration of several individuals, they would assign it to their fellow *familia* members. If special skills were required, they would buy a slave who had the skills. They would do the same if more manpower was needed—all without sacrificing one iota of freedom.

The second element of the explanation is that the *societas* emerged, at least partly, from the community of heirs and related family relationships.[109] In public perception, the *societas* apparently never gave up its intimate familial character. The law is testament to this: the *societas* was associated with *fraternitas* (brotherhood); the *socius*'s

[106] Gai., *Inst.* 3.152: *solvitur adhuc societas etiam morte socii, quia, qui societatem contrahit, certam personam sibi eligit* = Iust., *Inst.* 3.25.5. Another consequence of this principle is the lower standard of liability (since *qui parum diligentem sibi socium adquirit, de se queri debet*): D. 17.2.72 (Gai. 2 *cott.*) ≈ Iust., *Inst.* 3.25.9.

[107] D. 17.2.65.11 (Paul. 32 *ad ed.*): *societas quemadmodum ad heredes socii non transit, . . . , ne alioquin invitus quis socius efficiatur cui non vult.* While Wieacker (1936: 163) believed this passage to be interpolated, more recent scholarship no longer doubts its authenticity (Zimmermann 1990: 456; Fleckner 2010: 447).

[108] Iust., *Inst.* 3.25.7 (above n. 55) suggests this rationale by comparing an insolvent *socius* with a dead *socius*; Gai., *Inst.* 3.153 makes the same comparison for a *socius* whose status deteriorates (*capitis deminutio*), following similar rules elsewhere (see e.g. Gai., *Inst.* 3.101 and 4.88).

[109] The details are highly controversial. The most interesting source is Gai., *Inst.* 3.154a/154b, found as late as 1933; for additional references, see Zimmermann (1990: 451–4) and Fleckner (2010: 123–6); see also above n. 80 and accompanying text.

duty of care was limited to the *diligentia quam in suis* (the level that he applied in his own affairs); one important variation of the *societas* united all assets of the *socii* (*societas omnium bonorum*); the *actio pro socio* belonged to the *bona fides* (good faith) remedies; and the conviction under the *actio pro socio* led to *infamia*, i.e. the loss of civil rights.[110] Non-legal sources, including various works of Cicero, confirm that a close and intimate relationship among the members of a *societas* was generally assumed.[111]

The most important expression of both—individualism and intimacy—is the fact that a *socius* could unilaterally terminate the *societas* at any time.[112] Diocletian and Maximian coined the underlying reason: *in . . . societatem nemo compellitur invitus detineri*—no one will be forced to remain in a *societas* against his will.[113] As the *societas* continued to be associated with intimacy, Romans were reluctant to use it for associations with strangers. But since they would avoid contractual relationships anyway, they had no reason to press for political reforms that would have made the *societas* less personal, for instance by separating ownership from control, by allowing membership transfers, or by cutting back on the various dissolution reasons.

While individualism and intimacy go a long way in explaining why Roman business associations remained unstable, some doubts remain because the legally imposed instability seems to exceed what public sentiment called for. Why was dissolution *mandatory*, no matter what the *socii* agreed upon? *Volenti non fit iniuria* is the obvious objection to this regime.[114] In addition, the various safeguards overlap. Had the heir of a deceased *socius* automatically assumed the latter's membership position, the remaining *socii* would still have

[110] Fleckner (2010: 126–7, 340–2; 2011a: 680, 692).

[111] Fleckner (2010: 340–2).

[112] For the details, see above (§9.3.1.4). The unilateral termination powers of the *socii* have been explained with both Roman individualism (Schulz 1936: 149–51, 155, 227; 1951: 553) and the traditional intimacy of the *socii* (Wieacker 1936: 105). As shown in the text (and also by Zimmermann 1990: 457), both explanations complement one another (too restrictive Fleckner 2010: 343–4).

[113] C. 3.37.5 (Diocl./Max., AD 294).

[114] Non-mandatory rules were not unknown in the law of the *societas*: Gai., *Inst.* 3.150, D. 17.2.29 pr. (Ulp. 30 *ad Sab.*), and Iust., *Inst.* 3.25.1/3 (allocation of profits and losses); Iust., *Inst.* 3.25.5 (continuation of multi-member *societates*; above nn. 50 and 99 and accompanying text).

had the power to unilaterally terminate the *societas* if the heir turned out to be inapt or inept. These mysteries are difficult to unravel.[115]

9.3.3.2. *Stability and the Structure of Roman Business Associations*

The instability inherent to the *societas*, the *societas publicanorum*, and the *peculium* is, without doubt, just one factor among many that explain why Roman business associations remained small. But instability is a major obstacle, and it is symptomatic of other problems that can be observed.

The broader picture, and the role of instability therein, is best understood by turning to those structural features that, over various periods and across multiple jurisdictions, have proven to be critical for capital associations to accomplish their goals (i.e. to finance projects that, due to their scope, duration, or risk, exceed the capacity of individual businessmen). Four structural features stand out: the separation of ownership from control, the protection of the capital providers' private assets ("limited liability"), the protection of the capital providers' common assets ("entity shielding"), and the transferability of the capital providers' shares in the association.[116] How does the stability or instability, respectively, of Roman business associations relate to these four features?

[115] As in other areas, Roman jurists focused on discussing concrete legal problems rather than on developing a general theory of the *societas*. The *natura societatis* is mentioned only once, and without any further elaboration: Iust., *Inst.* 3.25.2 ($\approx$ Gai., *Inst.* 3.149?), citing Quintus Mucius (not necessarily his term). Note that Gaius, in a very famous passage (above n. 109), calls the community of heirs a *naturalis societas*: Gai., *Inst.* 3.154a.

[116] Fleckner (2010: 47–62) discusses these four features as part of a general theory of the capital association (above nn. 11 and 19). While all four features are necessary to make capital associations work, the second feature (limited liability) and the third feature (entity shielding) are key for accomplishing the capital association's primary goal, i.e. long-term capital accumulation, by separating private from common assets. Fleckner (2010) calls this the *Prinzip beidseitiger Vermögenstrennung*, i.e. the "principle of bi-directional asset separation." (The literal translation, "both-sided" instead of "bi-directional," would be more precise, but unlike "beidseitig" in German, "both-sided" is not very common in English; other possible translations include "bilateral," "double-sided," "two-sided," or "two-way." The author wishes to thank Henry Smith for discussing at great length the pros and cons of the various translations.) Whether or not the capital association is considered a legal person is irrelevant, provided that the four structural features can be achieved.

Separation of ownership from control. The first feature, separation of ownership from control, in many ways mirrors the stability concerns. Rome never developed a general agency regime, and much ink has been spilled to figure out why. That the use of slaves and their *peculia* led to similar consequences, or even to outcomes that go beyond the effects of modern agency regimes, is probably the main explanation. But it is equally plausible that the very same attitude that kept Romans from forming associations with peers let them remain skeptical of hiring peers or acting on behalf of peers. From this perspective, the lack of agency and the absence of stable business associations go hand in hand. For the *societas publicanorum*, literary sources suggest a wider separation of ownership from control, but even here, the legal texts offer little to corroborate a departure from the standard *societas* regime.[117]

Limited liability. Closely connected to the agency problem is the protection of the capital providers' private assets, the second structural feature ("limited liability"), because the special circumstances under which management may be separated from ownership are the same situations in which Roman law imposes personal liability on the principals. In other words, without a general agency regime, separation of ownership from control and limited liability were difficult to achieve at the same time.[118] If the *socii*, for instance, decided to appoint an *institor* and let him manage their retail business, the *socii* were liable under the *actio institoria* for the contracts the *institor* entered into. This is true for both the standard *societas* and the *societas publicanorum*. Only the financiers of the *societas publicanorum*, i.e. those who provided capital without becoming *socii*, seem to have escaped liability (similar to money-lenders). The *peculium* offered some, but not complete, protection from the claims that the business partners faced.[119] What was the rationale for this regime? Readers of today will be surprised to learn that it was nothing less than the "modern" idea that risk and reward should be carefully balanced.[120] This rationale is different from the instability reasons,

[117] Fleckner (2010: 241–94). [118] Fleckner (2010: 295–337).

[119] There are few, if any, areas of Roman law that are more complicated than the interplay between the *peculium* and the various liabilities arising from the activity of slaves and other personnel. For surveys (from different perspectives), see Di Porto (1984: 257–341); Földi (1996: 179–211); and Fleckner (2010: 317–22).

[120] D. 14.3.1 (Ulp. 28 *ad ed.*): *aequum praetori visum est, sicut commoda sentimus ex actu institorum, ita etiam obligari nos ex contractibus ipsorum et conveniri.*

but both are linked through the first feature, the separation of ownership from control.

Entity shielding. The third feature, the protection of the capital providers' common assets ("entity shielding"), is most directly related to the stability discussion. In fact, as seen above (§§9.3.1.5, 9.3.2.3), if common assets are not protected against withdrawal by the business partners or seizure by their private creditors, then business associations will remain unstable and, as a consequence, it will be very difficult to fund capital-intensive projects. From this perspective, the protection of common assets is just one important aspect of a much broader issue, to wit, stability.

Transferability of shares. Finally, membership in a standard *societas* was not transferable, rendering it impossible to implement the fourth structural feature. The underlying reason is well known from the stability discussion: Roman businessmen objected to the idea of letting heirs take the position of deceased *socii* (above §9.3.3.1); the transfer of membership *inter vivos* was met with similar reservations and, accordingly, remained a foreign concept to them.[121] Nevertheless, many observers still believe that the aforementioned "financiers" of the *societas publicanorum* could freely transfer their stake in the joint venture. Some have even argued that these stakes resembled modern "shares" and were publicly traded.[122] The sources that have come down to us do not support these claims.[123] Among the many references to the *societas publicanorum*, there is only one single sentence that provides (weak) evidence of a transfer from one person to another.[124] And this transfer is not a voluntary sale on a market but a forced transaction in secrecy.[125]

The four structural features—separation of ownership from control, limited liability, entity shielding, and transferability of shares—raise a multitude of additional questions that are unrelated to the

Similarly *Pauli sent.* 2.8.1: *sicut commoda sentimus ex actu praepositi institoris, ita et incommoda sentire debemus.*

[121] Fleckner (2010: 444–50).

[122] Most prominently in recent years Malmendier (2002, 2005, 2009, 2013), as indicated above (n. 12); for additional references, see Fleckner (2010: 451–62).

[123] Fleckner (2010: 462–92).

[124] Cic., *Vatin.*, 12.29: *eripuerisne partis illo tempore carissimas partim a Caesare, partim a publicanis?* This is only "weak" evidence, as noted in the main text, because there is no proof that the *partes* indeed changed hands.

[125] Fleckner (2010: 473–80).

stability or instability of Roman business associations. For some of these questions, the sources give an almost definitive answer; the liability regime surrounding the employment of slaves comes to mind. For others, we have ample evidence in the legal sources but lack information from elsewhere to verify their relevance in practice; this is most obvious for the separation of ownership from control in *peculium*-based businesses. For still other questions, non-legal sources suggest business practices that are difficult to explain with the legal sources; the management of the *societas publicanorum* is one of those puzzles.

9.3.3.3. *Stability and the Theory of the Firm*

Finding answers to these and similar questions is important for several reasons. First, it will help us corroborate the impression from the sources that there were no shareholder companies or other large business associations in ancient Rome (recall that *absence of evidence is not evidence of absence*). Second, the more we learn about the reasons why Roman business associations remained small, the better we will understand the Roman economy and, by extension, Roman society in general. Third, and this brings us back to the chapter's outset: knowing more about the *history* of the firm may inspire those struggling to refine the *theory* of the firm.

Take the observation that in ancient Rome, large firms were typically based on status rather than contract, i.e. formed among kinsmen rather than among strangers. This underscores the importance of social factors, one of the threads running through this chapter. But the prevalence of family businesses is also interesting from an economic perspective. Coase (1937) thought that the key feature of firms, the feature that sets them apart and prompts their rise, is that within firms, bargaining is replaced by authority. The Roman experience seems to confirm this view. In a Roman *familia*, there was typically a clear hierarchy, along with strong mechanisms that ensured compliance and continuity. Among strangers, in contrast, no such "natural" order existed, and much less among *patres familias* who were used to giving and not receiving orders. Many would rather have withdrawn from the joint business venture than knuckled down. As a consequence, we would expect business associations among strangers to be small and unstable, subject to termination at will and with very limited powers of those in leadership positions, leaving capital-intensive projects to firms run by members of the same *familia*. In fact, that is exactly what can be observed in the sources.[126] And its implications go much further: the anecdotal evidence from Rome also supports the hypotheses of Williamson (1971), Klein, Crawford, and Alchian (1978), and others who resort to transaction costs, relationship-specific investments, and the incompleteness of contracts to explain the rise of firms. These scholars assume that under ideal circumstances, business partners would negotiate long-term contracts with provisions for all possible states of the world, thereby eliminating the need to ever haggle over them again. In practice, however, any attempt to draft "complete" contracts is doomed to fail, so individuals form firms to avoid costly renegotiations each time something unexpected happens. The crucial factor, then, is how good a framework for settling disputes the firm is. The *societas* fares badly here, as explained above, because any lawsuit would dissolve it, and each *socius* had extensive hold-up powers. The Roman *familia*, in contrast, was much better suited to handle conflicts, given its clear hierarchy. From this perspective, it is again no surprise that in ancient Rome, businesses among kinsmen seem to have typically been larger than associations among strangers.

Another, more general lesson from ancient Rome is that the structure of firms is not only a function of the preferences *inside* the firm but also driven by the expectations of *outsiders* who maintain contacts with the firm. The reason is that third parties will not enter into contracts with the firm or its agents unless they can rest assured that their claims will be honored. Offering joint and several liability will ease any such concerns, and will significantly enhance the firm's credit in the market. But it can also transform the firm's *internal* organization, since the entrepreneurs may decide to manage their liability risks by limiting each other's activities and powers. This, of course, runs counter to the idea of replacing bargaining with authority, as explained above, and makes it impossible to fully implement the first two structural features, i.e. separation of ownership from control and limited liability.

A second example where outside factors influence the firm's inner dynamics is the allocation of assets. The property rights theory of

[126] A recent confirmation of this old insight (above n. 13) may be seen in the material discussed by Broekaert (2012: 233–43).

Grossman and Hart (1986) and of Hart and Moore (1990) focuses on the physical (nonhuman) assets of a firm, such as land and machinery, and asks who should "own" them, i.e. who should have the final say over them. The main idea is to avoid hold-up situations, and to allocate the assets accordingly. But the allocation of assets has many additional implications, e.g. for the firm's credit, for the ability and willingness of entrepreneurs to commit capital, or for the protection of common assets. At the end, the optimal ownership structure will be a tradeoff between several factors, accounting for both the interests inside the firm and its standing in the market. Ancient Rome is an example of a compromise that favors the individual *socii* and their private creditors rather than "the firm" and its business creditors. This underscores the diversity and plurality of the interests at stake, and suggests that entrepreneurs will look beyond the firm when they allocate assets, to please third parties they hope to interact with (in private or commercial affairs).

* * *

How does the legal setting affect the rise and structure of firms? This question was posed at the outset of the chapter, and the study of Roman business associations has unearthed new material to answer it. That the law will have a decisive influence where it effectively precludes certain structural features, e.g. limited liability or transferability of shares, will come as no surprise. The Roman experience confirms here what common sense would tell anyway. But there are more subtle mechanisms at work. The impossibility for Roman businessmen to achieve, at the same time, the first two structural features, separation of ownership from control and limited liability, comes to mind. Or the very focus of this chapter, stability: if the genius of firms lies in the substitution of authority for bargaining, then unilateral withdrawal rights, as in ancient Rome, will be an important impediment, given the hold-up powers that come with them. Entity shielding is another example: in Rome as well as in many modern jurisdictions, business partners lack the power to bar private creditors from seizing common assets, i.e. the most efficient allocation of assets may be impossible to attain without the "help" of law-makers or judges.

Including these and similar considerations into a more advanced theory of the firm will be a challenge. Formalizing them will be even more difficult. But economists, historians, and lawyers should team up and give it a try. Otherwise, the theory of the firm may miss important factors and remain "one of the less developed and agreed-upon areas of economics."[127]

REFERENCES

Abatino, Barbara, Giuseppe Dari-Mattiacci, and Enrico Perotti. 2011. "Depersonalization of Business in Ancient Rome." 31 *Oxford Journal of Legal Studies* 365–89.

Aghion, Philippe, and Patrick Bolton. 1992. "An Incomplete Contracts Approach to Financial Contracting." 59 *The Review of Economic Studies* 473–94.

Alchian, Armen A., and Harold Demsetz. 1972. "Production, Information Costs, and Economic Organization." 62 *The American Economic Review* 777–95.

Arangio-Ruiz, Vincenzo. 1950. *La società in diritto romano*. Naples: Jovene.

Armour, John, Henry Hansmann, Reinier Kraakman, and Mariana Pargendler. 2017. "What Is Corporate Law?," in John Armour, Luca Enriques, et al., *The Anatomy of Corporate Law: A Comparative and Functional Approach*, 3rd edn. Oxford: Oxford University Press 1–28.

Armour, John, and Michael J. Whincop. 2007. "The Proprietary Foundations of Corporate Law." 27 *Oxford Journal of Legal Studies* 429–65.

Aubert, Jean-Jacques. 1994. *Business Managers in Ancient Rome: A Social and Economic Study of Institores (200 B. C.–A. D. 250)*. Leiden/New York/Cologne: Brill.

Blair, Margaret M. 2003. "Locking in Capital: What Corporate Law Achieved for Business Organizers in the Nineteenth Century." 51 *University of California Los Angeles Law Review* 387–454.

[127] Hart (2011: 102); from a finance perspective Rajan (2012: 1176) ("a very rewarding area of research in the years to come will be to open up the black box of the corporation so as to link its inner functioning to its financing needs").

For many valuable comments and suggestions, the author is indebted to Amin Kachabia as well as to Felix Bassier, David Ciepley, Corinna Coupette, Giuseppe Dari-Mattiacci, Andreas Engert, Miguel Gimeno Ribes, Alexander Hellgardt, Dennis Kehoe, Daniel M. Klerman, Egbert Koops, Thilo Kuntz, Philipp Aron Leimbach, Johannes Liefke, Erik Röder, Daniel Schwander, Henry E. Smith, and Adam Winkler, also to participants at the eighteenth annual Conference of the International Society for New Institutional Economics (Duke University, Durham, 2014) and to participants in the Werkstattseminar Antike Rechtsgeschichte und Römisches Recht (Ludwig-Maximilians-Universität, Munich, 2017). The usual disclaimers apply. Some sections of the chapter are based on Fleckner (2010) and Fleckner (2011b), an English introduction to Fleckner (2010).

Brinkhof, Johannes J. 1978. *Een studie over het peculium in het klassieke Romeinse recht*. Meppel: Krips.

Broekaert, Wim. 2012. "Joining Forces: Commercial Partnerships or Societates in the Early Roman Empire." 61 *Historia* 221–53.

Bürge, Alfons. 1988. "Book review: Andrea Di Porto, Impresa collettiva e schiavo 'manager' in Roma antica." 105 *Zeitschrift der Savigny-Stiftung für Rechtsgeschichte (Romanistische Abteilung)* 856–65.

Bürge, Alfons. 1999. *Römisches Privatrecht: Rechtsdenken und gesellschaftliche Verankerung—Eine Einführung*. Darmstadt: Wissenschaftliche Buchgesellschaft.

Bürge, Alfons. 2000. "Book review: Thomas Drosdowski, Das Verhältnis von actio pro socio und actio communi dividundo im klassischen römischen Recht." 117 *Zeitschrift der Savigny-Stiftung für Rechtsgeschichte (Romanistische Abteilung)* 546–54.

Bürge, Alfons. 2010. "Lo schiavo (in)dipendente e il suo patrimonio," in Alessandro Corbino, Michel Humbert, and Giovanni Negri, eds, *Homo, caput, persona: La costruzione giuridica dell'identità nell'esperienza romana*. Pavia: IUSS Press 369–91.

Buti, Ignazio. 1976. *Studi sulla capacità patrimoniale dei "servi"*. Naples: Jovene.

Cerami, Pietro, and Aldo Petrucci. 2010. *Diritto commerciale romano*, 3rd edn. Turin: Giappichelli.

Cimma, Maria R. 1981. *Ricerche sulle società di publicani*. Milan: Giuffrè.

Coase, Ronald H. 1937. "The Nature of the Firm." 4 *Economica* 386–405.

Di Porto, Andrea. 1984. *Impresa collettiva e schiavo "manager" in Roma antica*. Milan: Giuffrè.

Djankov, Simeon, Rafael La Porta, Florencio Lopez-de-Silanes, and Andrei Shleifer. 2008. "The Law and Economics of Self-dealing." 88 *Journal of Financial Economics* 430–65.

Drosdowski, Thomas. 1998. *Das Verhältnis von actio pro socio und actio communi dividundo im klassischen römischen Recht*. Berlin: Duncker & Humblot.

Dufour, Geneviève. 2012. *Les societates publicanorum de la République romaine: Ancêtres des sociétés par actions?* Montréal: Thémis; Geneva/Zurich/Basel: Schulthess.

Easterbrook, Frank H., and Daniel R. Fischel. 1991. *The Economic Structure of Corporate Law*. Cambridge/London: Harvard University Press.

Fleckner, Andreas M. 2010. *Antike Kapitalvereinigungen: Ein Beitrag zu den konzeptionellen und historischen Grundlagen der Aktiengesellschaft*. Cologne/Weimar/Vienna: Böhlau.

Fleckner, Andreas M. 2011a. "Book review: Barbara Stelzenberger, Kapitalmanagement und Kapitaltransfer im Westen des Römischen Reiches." 128 *Zeitschrift der Savigny-Stiftung für Rechtsgeschichte (Romanistische Abteilung)* 677–95.

Fleckner, Andreas M. 2011b. "Corporate Law Lessons from Ancient Rome," in *The Harvard Law School Forum on Corporate Governance and Financial Regulation* (June 19, 2011). Available at http://blogs.law.harvard.edu/corpgov/2011/06/19/.

Fleckner, Andreas M. 2014. "The Peculium: A Legal Device for Donations to personae alieno iuri subiectae?," in Filippo Carlà and Maja Gori, eds, *Gift Giving and the "Embedded" Economy in the Ancient World*. Heidelberg: Winter 213–39.

Fleckner, Andreas M. 2018. "Book review: Julien M. Ogereau, Paul's Koinonia with the Philippians." 135 *Zeitschrift der Savigny-Stiftung für Rechtsgeschichte (Romanistische Abteilung)* 685–700.

Földi, András. 1996. "Remarks on the Legal Structure of Enterprises in Roman Law." 43 *Revue Internationale des Droits de l'Antiquité* 179–211.

Frier, Bruce. 1982. "Roman Life Expectancy: Ulpian's Evidence." 86 *Harvard Studies in Classical Philology* 213–51.

Frier, Bruce. 1983. "Roman Life Expectancy: The Pannonian Evidence." 37 *Phoenix* 328–44.

Frier, Bruce W. 2000. "Demography," in Alan K. Bowman, Peter Garnsey, and Dominic Rathbone, eds, *The Cambridge Ancient History*. Vol. 11: *The High Empire, A.D. 70–192*, 2nd edn. Cambridge: Cambridge University Press 787–816.

Grossman, Sanford J., and Oliver D. Hart. 1986. "The Costs and Benefits of Ownership: A Theory of Vertical and Lateral Integration." 94 *Journal of Political Economy* 691–719.

Hansmann, Henry, and Reinier H. Kraakman. 2000. "The Essential Role of Organizational Law." 110 *Yale Law Journal* 387–440.

Hansmann, Henry, Reinier H. Kraakman, and Richard Squire. 2006. "Law and the Rise of the Firm." 119 *Harvard Law Review* 1333–1403.

Hart, Oliver. 2011. "Thinking about the Firm: A Review of Daniel Spulber's The Theory of the Firm." 49 *Journal of Economic Literature* 101–13.

Hart, Oliver. 2017. "Incomplete Contracts and Control." 107 *The American Economic Review* 1731–52.

Hart, Oliver, and Bengt Holmstrom. 2010. "A Theory of Firm Scope." 125 *Quarterly Journal of Economics* 483–513.

Hart, Oliver, and John Moore. 1990. "Property Rights and the Nature of the Firm." 98 *Journal of Political Economy* 1119–58.

Hernando Lera, Julio. 1992. *El contrato de sociedad: La casuística jurisprudencial clásica*. Madrid: Dykinson.

Jensen, Michael C., and William H. Meckling. 1976. "Theory of the Firm: Managerial Behavior, Agency Costs and Ownership Structure." 3 *Journal of Financial Economics* 305–60.

Kaser, Max, Rolf Knütel, and Sebastian Lohsse. 2017. *Römisches Privatrecht*, 21st edn. Munich: Beck.

Klein, Benjamin, Robert G. Crawford, and Armen A. Alchian. 1978. "Vertical Integration, Appropriable Rents, and the Competitive Contracting Process." 21 *The Journal of Law and Economics* 297–326.

Kniep, Ferdinand. 1896. *Societas Publicanorum*. Vol. 1. Jena: Fischer.

La Porta, Rafael, Florencio Lopez-de-Silanes, and Andrei Shleifer. 1999. "Corporate Ownership Around the World." 54 *The Journal of Finance* 471–517.

La Porta, Rafael, Florencio Lopez-de-Silanes, and Andrei Shleifer. 2006. "What Works in Securities Laws?" 61 *The Journal of Finance* 1–32.

La Porta, Rafael, Florencio Lopez-de-Silanes, Andrei Shleifer, and Robert W. Vishny. 1997. "Legal Determinants of External Finance." 52 *The Journal of Finance* 1131–50.

La Porta, Rafael, Florencio Lopez-de-Silanes, Andrei Shleifer, and Robert W. Vishny. 1998. "Law and Finance." 106 *Journal of Political Economy* 1113–55.

Licht, Amir N. 2001. "The Mother of All Path Dependencies: Toward a Cross-Cultural Theory of Corporate Governance Systems." 26 *Delaware Journal of Corporate Law* 147–205.

Malmendier, Ulrike. 2002. *Societas Publicanorum: Staatliche Wirtschaftsaktivitäten in den Händen privater Unternehmer*. Cologne/Weimar/Vienna: Böhlau.

Malmendier, Ulrike. 2005. "Roman Shares," in William N. Goetzmann and K. Geert Rouwenhorst, eds, *The Origins of Value: The Financial Innovations That Created Modern Capital Markets*. Oxford: Oxford University Press 31–42, 361–5.

Malmendier, Ulrike. 2009. "Law and Finance 'at the Origin.'" 47 *Journal of Economic Literature* 1076–1108.

Malmendier, Ulrike. 2013. "Publicani," in Roger S. Bagnall, Kai Brodersen, Craige B. Champion, Andrew Erskine, and Sabine R. Huebner, eds, *The Encyclopedia of Ancient History*. Vol. 10: *Pl–Ro*. Chichester: Wiley-Blackwell 5658–60.

Mandry, Gustav. 1876. *Das gemeine Familiengüterrecht mit Ausschluss des ehelichen Güterrechtes*. Vol. 2. Tübingen: Laupp.

Matthaeus, Antonius. 1653. *De auctionibus libri duo*. Utrecht: Waesberge.

Mattiangeli, Daniele. 2017. *Societas und corpus: Auf den Spuren einer Handelsgesellschaft als juristische Person im römischen Recht*. Vienna: facultas.

Meissel, Franz-Stefan. 2004. *Societas: Struktur und Typenvielfalt des römischen Gesellschaftsvertrages*. Frankfurt am Main: Lang.

Meissel, Franz-Stefan. 2014a. "Book review: Simon Müller-Kabisch, Die Kündigung bei societas und locatio conductio rei." 131 *Zeitschrift der Savigny-Stiftung für Rechtsgeschichte (Romanistische Abteilung)* 473–83.

Meissel, Franz-Stefan. 2014b. "Constat enim societas ex societatibus? Zur 'Körperschaftlichkeit' und [zu] anderen Besonderheiten der

Publikanengesellschaften," in Jan Hallebeek, Martin Schermaier, Roberto Fiori, Ernest Metzger, and Jean-Pierre Coriat, eds, Inter cives necnon peregrinos: *Essays in honour of Boudewijn Sirks*. Göttingen: V&R unipress 513–31.

Micolier, Gabriel. 1932. *Pécule et Capacité Patrimoniale: Étude sur le pécule, dit profectice, depuis l'édit "de peculio" jusqu'à la fin de l'époque classique*. Lyon: Bosc & Riou.

Müller-Kabisch, Simon. 2011. *Die Kündigung bei societas und locatio conductio rei: Zur Frage ihrer rechtsgeschäftlichen Natur in vorklassischer und klassischer Zeit*. Baden-Baden: Nomos.

Ogereau, Julien M. 2014. *Paul's Koinonia with the Philippians: A Socio-Historical Investigation of a Pauline Economic Partnership*. Tübingen: Mohr Siebeck.

Orelli, Johann Caspar von. 1835. "M. Tullii Ciceronis In P. Vatinium testem interrogatio," in *Index Lectionum in Academia Turicensi inde a die XXVI. mensis Octobris M. DCCC. XXXV. usque ad diem XX. mensis Martii M. DCCC. XXXVI. habendarum*. Zurich: Ulrich 1–16.

Pagano, Marco, and Paolo F. Volpin. 2005. "The Political Economy of Corporate Governance." 95 *The American Economic Review* 1005–30.

Rajan, Raghuram G. 2012. "Presidential Address: The Corporation in Finance." 67 *The Journal of Finance* 1173–1217.

Roe, Mark J. 1994. *Strong Managers, Weak Owners: The Political Roots of American Corporate Finance*. Princeton: Princeton University Press.

Roe, Mark J. 2003. *Political Determinants of Corporate Governance: Political Context, Corporate Impact*. Oxford: Oxford University Press.

Roe, Mark J. 2006. "Legal Origins, Politics, and Modern Stock Markets." 120 *Harvard Law Review* 460–527.

Santucci, Gianni. 1997. *Il socio d'opera in diritto romano: Conferimenti e responsabilità*. Padua: CEDAM.

Scheidel, Walter. 2001. "Progress and Problems in Roman Demography," in Walter Scheidel, ed, *Debating Roman Demography*. Leiden/Boston/Cologne: Brill 1–81.

Schermaier, Martin. 2015. "Book review: Simon Müller-Kabisch, Die Kündigung bei societas und locatio conductio rei." 132 *Zeitschrift der Savigny-Stiftung für Rechtsgeschichte (Romanistische Abteilung)* 590–2.

Schulz, Fritz. 1936. *Principles of Roman Law*. Oxford: Oxford University Press.

Schulz, Fritz. 1951. *Classical Roman Law*. Oxford: Oxford University Press.

Serrao, Feliciano. 1989. *Impresa e responsabilità a Roma nell'età commerciale: Forme giuridiche di un'economia-mondo*. Pisa: Pacini.

Spamann, Holger. 2010. "The 'Antidirector Rights Index' Revisited." 23 *The Review of Financial Studies* 467–86.

Stulz, René M., and Rohan Williamson. 2003. "Culture, Openness, and Finance." 70 *Journal of Financial Economics* 313–49.

Wieacker, Franz. 1936. *Societas: Hausgemeinschaft und Erwerbsgesellschaft—Untersuchungen zur Geschichte des römischen Gesellschaftsrechts*. Vol. 1. Weimar: Böhlau.

Williamson, Oliver E. 1971. "The Vertical Integration of Production: Market Failure Considerations." 61 *The American Economic Review* 112–23.

Woods, Robert. 2007. "Ancient and Early Modern Mortality: Experience and Understanding." 60 *Economic History Review* 373–99.

Żeber, Ireneusz. 1981. *A Study of the Peculium of a Slave in Pre-classical and Classical Roman Law*. Wrocław: Wydawnictwo Uniwersytetu Wrocławskiego.

Zimmermann, Reinhard. 1990. *The Law of Obligations: Roman Foundations of the Civilian Tradition*. Cape Town/Wetton/Johannesburg: Juta Reprint Oxford: Oxford University Press 1996.

Zingales, Luigi. 2017. "Towards a Political Theory of the Firm." 31 *Journal of Economic Perspectives* 113–30.

10

Agency Problems and Organizational Costs in Slave-Run Businesses

Barbara Abatino and Giuseppe Dari-Mattiacci

10.1. INTRODUCTION

Starting in the 1980s, the literature on Roman law focusing on the period between the second century BC and the second century AD has shown that a business could be organized as a *plurium exercitio negotiationum per servos*. This format included a slave, in some cases co-owned (Di Porto 1984: 371–7),[1] and the assets entrusted to him by his master(s) (the *peculium*; Micolier 1932; La Rosa 1965; Amirante 1983),[2] with which the slave managed a business.

This way of organizing individual or collective enterprises[3] had some advantages over the mere partnership contract (*societas*

[1] Whether the slave was owned by only one or by several masters does not seem to be relevant: Di Porto (1984: 259); see below n. 24. On co-owned slaves, see Micolier (1932) and Bretone (1958).

[2] On the etymology of "*peculium*," see Varr., *De ling. Lat.* V.19.95. Cf. Ceci (1892: 166 n. 1).

[3] Di Porto (1984: 386) (emphasizing that the most distinctive feature of this format was the possibility to organize both individual and collective limited-liability enterprises by means of the *peculium*); Di Porto (1997: 421–2) (stressing that the fundamental elements of the organizational modes of businesses through the use of slaves are independent of the fact that the slave and the *peculium* were co-owned; in fact, co-ownership only added a layer of complexity to the business structure without affecting its characteristics in terms of liability and governance); Lawson (1969: 134–41) (showing the level of complexity that slave-run businesses could reach).

Barbara Abatino and Giuseppe Dari-Mattiacci, *Agency Problems and Organizational Costs in Slave-Run Businesses*
In: *Roman Law and Economics: Institutions and Organizations, Volume I.* Edited by: Giuseppe Dari-Mattiacci and Dennis P. Kehoe, Oxford University Press (2020). © Oxford University Press.
DOI: 10.1093/oso/9780198787204.003.0010

consensu contracta).[4] It provided masters with the ability to delegate the management of business activities to a slave and benefit from a de facto limitation of their liability, a limited measure of location-based entity shielding, direct agency,[5] and mechanisms to guarantee the continuity of business activities in the event of relevant changes in ownership and management (Hansmann et al. 2006; Fleckner 2010: 299–325, 420–41, 495; Abatino et al. 2011; cf. Serrao 2000). Nevertheless, in practice, businesses organized in this way were relatively small (Andreau 2001: 131–2; 2004: 124; Fleckner 2010: 654). Scholars have considered size to be an indication of the limited relevance of these businesses within the Roman economy.[6] In this chapter, we argue that questions about the size of slave-run businesses can only be answered after another, more fundamental question has been posed: what are the determinants of the (optimal) size of slave-run businesses?

Slave-run businesses may have been small in the sense that they involved a limited number of individuals or in the sense that they employed limited amounts of capital.[7] We argue that economic importance is only a secondary factor affecting the size of these businesses. First-order effects are produced by the inherent characteristics of such business organizations and their relations to the markets in which they operated.

[4] Guarino (1972); Talamanca (1990: 814–60, 827–8). With regard to the possibility that the partnership contract had effects for third parties, see Sanfilippo (1951: 159–61); Arangio-Ruiz (1965: 62, 78–92, 84 n. 1, 142–4); Serrao (1971: 743–67).

[5] Concerning direct agency under Roman law, see Gordon (1983); Wacke (1997); Miceli (2008).

[6] An exception to this trend is Hansmann et al. (2006: 1356) noting that "the *societas* lack[ed] strong entity shielding: although partners could agree not to withdraw firm assets before the expiration of a term, Roman law enforced such contracts through damages rather than specific performance, making a partner just one among many potential creditors grappling for his copartner's assets when that copartner fell insolvent. Consistent with their lack of entity shielding, most commercial *societates* had no more than a few members."

[7] Evidence provided by literary sources lets us indirectly presume the limited size of the *peculium* (see Plaut., *Stichus* 751). They are in accordance with the etymologies provided by Varro, *De ling. Lat.* 5.19.95 (cf. Varro, *Rer. rust.* I.2.17); Colum., *De agric.* 6.4; and Fest., *De verborum significatione* 290; and confirmed also by Plaut., *Merc.* v. 523; Cic., 2 Verr. 3.86. Cf. Plaut., *Asin.* 496 and *Merc.* 96; see also the adjective *peculiosus* in Plaut., *Rud.* v. 112 and *peculiatus* in Apul. 10.17.

A business organization[8] is a governance institution for economic activities, some of which could alternatively take place in the market. Running economic activities through an organization has the benefit of saving the costs of using the market (transaction costs), but in turn also involves organization costs (Coase 1937). Organization costs mainly derive from the fact that the hierarchical structure governing a business organization requires a constant flow of information to function properly. Incomplete or asymmetric information generates monitoring costs or foregone opportunities, which amount to organization costs. An organization can grow only as long as the additional savings in transaction costs are greater than the increment in organization costs. In the following, we emphasize two broad categories of problems that, contributing to create organization costs, might have constrained the size of Roman slave-run businesses: governance problems and limited access to finance, of which Figure 10.1 provides a graphical illustration.

First, governance problems can help explain the limited number of individuals involved. We will examine three sets of governance problems: those deriving from the principal-agent relationship between the owner(s) and the slave managing the *peculium*, those deriving from the mutual principal-agent relationships among owners, and

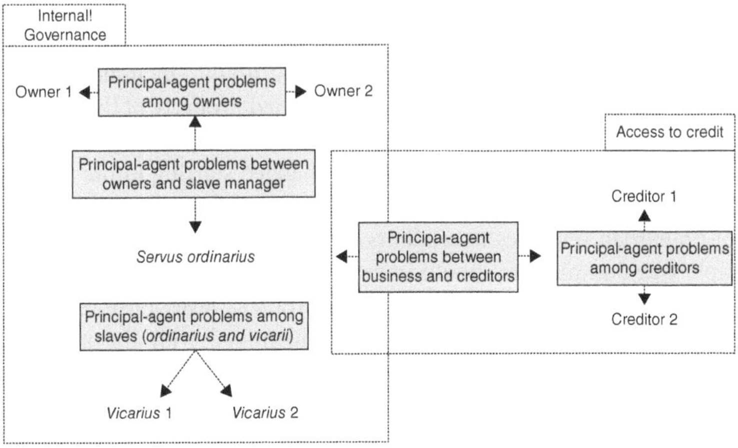

Figure 10.1. Principal-agent problems in slave run-businesses.

[8] For a broad view on instability concerning Roman business associations, see Fleckner in this volume.

those arising within the management due to the employment of underslaves. Second, limited access to finance sheds light on the limited amounts of capital involved. We examine two sets of problems relating to access to external credit and access to equity, respectively. Access to both forms of capital depends not only on the existence of a capital market external to the business organization, but also on the ability to tackle the principal-agent problems arising between creditors and owners, in addition to the principal-agent problems arising among owners, which we examine under the heading of internal governance. While the former limited the owners' ability to finance their enterprises through credit, the latter diminished their willingness to commit their own capital.

Institutions, both public and private, are endogenous to an economy in that they develop within it in response to its specific characteristics (cf. North and Weingast 1989; Frier and Kehoe 2007: 113). We show that business organizations in the Roman economy developed endogenously in response to agency problems and the available technology to solve them. Clues can be found in the writings of the jurists Gaius, Ulpian (often quoting Julian), and to a more limited extent, Paul. By systematically analyzing both the problems presented to them and the solutions they proposed, we are able to identify several specific agency problems that were at work in slave-run businesses.

These businesses operated within a legal framework based on the traditional *ius civile* but enriched by innovations produced within the formulary system. Both the slave and his *peculium*, (including subsequent acquisitions; Gai., *Inst.* 3.167) remained property of the master. In addition, under the *ius civile*, contracts entered into by slaves did not bind their masters. This situation changed starting in the second century BC,[9] in a period of economic expansion, with the recognition of praetorian remedies to creditors of the slave. The underlying principle was that masters should internalize both the profits (*commoda*) and the losses (*incommoda*) deriving from their slaves' business activities.[10] The praetorian remedies—later identified with the name of *actiones adiecticiae qualitatis* (Wacke 1997: 614–15)—extended the

[9] Guarino, (1957: 271); Arangio-Ruiz (1965: 7); Kaser (1971: 605); Aubert (1994: 70). See also de Ligt (1999: 206; 2007: 13) arguing for an earlier introduction (third century BC).

[10] D. 14.3.1 (Ulp. 28 *ad ed.*). See also Cerami and Petrucci (2010: 47–9); cf. Cerami et al. (2004: 45–7).

liability of the master for transactions by his slaves, making the master's liability increase in accordance with his involvement in the businesses.[11] The praetorian remedies de facto made the contracts concluded by a slave enforceable against his master(s), under certain conditions. This development crucially improved the willingness of third parties to rely on the slaves' commitment to repay debts and honor the obligations contracted and, in turn, made it easier for masters to delegate economic activities to their slaves (Frier and Kehoe 2007: 128; cf. Watson 1987: 91). Furthermore, the use of slaves (as opposed to free individuals) as business managers[12] could mitigate the governance problems arising between owners and management (Frier and Kehoe 2007: 131–2), while the possibility for the slave-manager to purchase slaves of his own allowed for a hierarchical structure with different levels of management.[13] Against this background, we explain why slave-run businesses involved limited numbers of individuals and limited capital.

10.2. ANALYTICAL FRAMEWORK

This chapter touches upon several issues that are controversial in the literature.[14] In particular, studies on slave-run businesses have

[11] The chronology of the praetorian remedies is controversial: Micolier (1932: 11, 63) and Miceli (2008, 49) refer to the second and first century BC; Aubert (1994: 414) refers to the late second century BC; Guarino (2001: 336–7), refers more generally to a time between the late pre-classical and the classical periods. The order in which these remedies were created is also debated: Aubert (1994: 78–84); Wacke (1997: 587); de Ligt (1999: 205–26).

[12] On the term "slave manager" proposed by Di Porto (1984), see Andreau (2004: 111). Note that the fact that a slave could be assigned managerial tasks can also be inferred by the fact that the law recognized the possibility that a *peculium* could be directly managed by the slave without any involvement by the master (and, in this case, granted the master limited liability and priority for his credits under the *actio de peculio*). On the coexistence of *peculium* and *praepositio*, see Andreau and Descat (2009: 109–14); cf. Stolfi (2009: 25–6) and Ligios Garbarino (2013).

[13] See n. 39.

[14] Debated issues include different and more or less modernist views of ancient economies, the chronology of the *actiones adiecticiae qualitatis* and of the *obligationes naturales servorum*, the formulary structure of the *actiones*, the legal capacity to own assets of individuals *alieni iuris*, the coexistence of partnership and co-ownership, and the importance of accounting techniques for a distinction between *rationes servi* and *ratio dominica*.

stimulated a vigorous scholarly debate, which continues today.[15] Critics have especially emphasized that comparisons between slave-run businesses and modern notions of economic organizations may fail to consider very significant differences in the respective legal systems, economic and technological development, and economic thinking.[16] Roman jurists did not think about those issues in the same terms used in twenty-first-century economics (see Melillo 2005).[17] Rather, they used their experience with the practice of law to propose solutions that seemed to fit the problems they faced. Yet, the problems they analyzed were economic in nature when they emerged, as we will explain, in situations characterized by asymmetric information. Historians have observed that "there is still ample room for studying in more detail, and through an analysis specifically oriented by the conceptualizations of the New Institutionalism, both the emergence and the diffusion of what we may call Roman commercial law: [...] the effects of the rules which govern the

[15] Recently, criticisms to Di Porto's analysis (see n. 3) have been voiced by Chiusi (2007a); Fleckner (2010: 230, 234 ff.); and Bürge (2010: 384), expanding on Bürge (1988: 857, 860, 862) (emphasizing that slaves endowed with a *peculium* cannot be seen as an organizational tool of business activity). Cf. also Bürge (1999: 197). See the different opinion of Cerami (2008: 96–8) and Pesaresi (2008). Cf. also Cerami (2010: 336–4). Finally, see Polara (2010: 61–2).

[16] See in particular Andreau (1999: 69–70; 2001: 131–5; 2004: 114, 123–5) (also observing that the *peculium* cannot be considered as a partnership's assets although it is separated from the *dominus*'s assets). Additional criticisms concern the use of modern concepts to describe ancient economies, the difficulties in assessing the prevalence of this format in practice, and the fact that *servi communes* were often workers instead of managers: Mayer-Maly (1984: 117) (arguing that it is difficult to assess how widespread the *negotiatio per servos communes* was); Bürge (2012: 45–7 and 2010: 857, 860, 862) (arguing that *servi communes* were often workers rather than managers and that slave-run businesses were unstable in that they were vulnerable to the *actio communi dividundo*); Montanari (1990: 5–6 n. 7) (arguing that the *negotiatio per servos communes* did not seem to be widespread and that technically the co-owners' liability cannot be considered as limited since creditors could take legal steps against masters through the *actio de in rem verso* in case of unjust enrichment); M. Talamanca (1990: 814 n. 8); Andreau (2004: 114–15, 125) (arguing that the analysis is methodologically incorrect); Labruna (1994: 129); Meissel (2004: 65) (concurring with the interpretation of other scholars). In favor of Di Porto: Burdese (1986: 204); Asser (1988: 371–2) (inviting more research on the economic context in which the *negotiatio per servos communes* took place).

[17] Cf. Maucourant (2004: 227, 235–6); Frier and Kehoe (2007: 114) (emphasizing that economics "can be applied to come to a deeper understanding of economic organization and the possibilities for economic growth in the Greek and Roman worlds"). On the economic approach in Celsus' *Rationes decidendi* and on a comparison of costs and revenues in *Scriptores de re rustica*, see Cerami (2008: 81–2).

relationship between principal and agent" (Lo Cascio 2006: 223; cf. also Lo Cascio in this volume).[18] Accordingly, we draw *functional* parallels between ancient and modern solutions to similar problems and we use modern economic theory to shed light on the question to what extent a certain solution solved a particular problem and with what consequences.[19]

The literature on slave-run businesses has been traditionally divided into two main camps. One view recognizes the advantages of such businesses over other organizational forms, such as partnerships, and stresses the fact that they allowed for a better management of the risks deriving from shifts in profitability and exposure to liabilities. Another view emphasizes the limited scope of this phenomenon in terms of capital employed and individuals involved, and implicitly suggests that size was "pathologically" limited. Our approach could be situated at the interface of these previous theories as we try to relate costs and benefits of business organizations based on the employment of (possibly co-owned) slave managers and show that such businesses were "physiologically" small. That is, we suggest that the observed size was a result of forces operating both internally (organization costs related to governance) and externally (transaction costs related to access to credit) and was not necessarily related to the economic importance of these businesses.[20]

Understanding the interplay between transaction costs and organizational costs means addressing questions as to the optimal boundaries, scope, legal configuration, and size of business organizations[21] and has been a challenge for economists since the seventies (see Hart 1989; Holmström and Tirole 1989; Milgrom and Roberts 1992; Foss et al. 2000). Three theories come to the fore. The property rights theory of the firm stresses the optimal *use* of available resources (Grossman and Hart 1986; Hart and Moore 1990). In contrast, the bundled assignability theory of the firm emphasizes the optimal *transfer* of resources (Ayotte and Hansmann 2013). Finally, the agency theory focuses on the conflicts of interests arising within the

[18] Cf. Carlsen (2010: 89) and Zimmermann (2012: 554–70). On professional associations in the Roman economy, see also Verboven (2011: 188). Cf. Maragno (2013: 1425–6).

[19] See also Frier (1989/90: 239); Morris and Weingast (2004: 702–3).

[20] The size of slave-run businesses might have been also affected by additional political or ideological factors (Schiavone 1996: 192–4).

[21] See Fleckner in this volume.

firm and with creditors (Alchian and Demsetz 1972; Ross 1973; Jensen and Meckling 1976). The property rights and bundled assignability theories provide fundamental tools for a mature understanding of the scope of business organizations and of the strategic choices involved, as they explain which sets of activities are most likely to be carried out within a business organization (boundaries of the firm) rather than through market exchange.[22] However, for our purposes, the necessary building block for an economic perspective on ancient and modern businesses is an examination of the costs generated by the functioning of the organization. In this respect, agency theory plays a major role. Agency costs are the costs generated by the simple fact that the parties involved in a business organization will typically have different sources of information and hence information available to one party may not be available to another. This perspective provides guidance for our analysis.

We first analyze governance problems—the agency problems arising within the business organization—and show that they constrained the expansion of these business organizations in terms of the number of individuals involved. Then, we examine limited access to credit—mainly focusing on agency problems between business and creditors and among creditors—and emphasize that limited access to credit constrained the expansion of these business organizations in terms of amount of capital invested.

10.3. LIMITS TO THE NUMBERS OF INDIVIDUALS INVOLVED

10.3.1. Governance Problems

Agency costs may affect the relationships among the various individuals within the business—owners and (slave-)managers—and act as a constraint on the expansion of the firm in terms of individuals

[22] The property rights theory sees the firm as a bundle of assets under unified ownership and stresses that the economic boundaries of the firm correspond with those resources that are best used if placed under unified ownership. The bundled assignability theory sees the firm as a bundle of contracts that can be transferred in block if the firm is organized as a legal entity, which in turn identifies the legal boundaries of the firm.

involved. In the next subsections, we review several types of such agency problems emerging from cases discussed in the writings of Roman jurists and then examine the legal remedies offered to reduce them. Besides legal remedies, two other forces can also keep principal-agent problems under control: external market forces and internal monitoring by the principal. We will also review these two mechanisms and show that they faced limitations in the Roman economy.

10.3.1.1. Agency Problems among Owners

A slave and possibly, but not necessarily, his *peculium* could either be owned by one master or be co-owned by several masters.[23] Co-owned slave-run businesses involving the use of the *peculium* show organizational patterns—of which we can find evidence in several texts in the *Digest*[24]—featuring principal-agent problems among the various masters. Since each master can make decisions that affect the others, each master is, in this sense, an agent of the others, who assume (for the purpose of the analysis) the role of principals. Each slaveowner has an interest in making sure that none of the others put his personal gain before the common good of the business. Obviously, the problem is reciprocal so that each slaveowner is both an agent of the others and a principal. Among the cases reported by legal sources we discuss those in which a master is in a position to exploit private information or externalize costs by imposing on the other masters.

A first set of agency problems arises from the fact that the masters could be differently informed about the slave's actions and dealings. In this regard, in D. 14.4.3 pr. (Ulp. 29 *ad ed.*), Ulpian is concerned with the limits of application of the *actio tributoria* and its relationship with the *actio de peculio*, but he discusses a more general case of

[23] See Di Porto (1984: 259, 297–300), who points out that the *exercere negotiationes per servos* implied a multiplicity of *negotiationes* organized in an autonomous way and the existence of a unique residual claimant (an individual or a group) of profits and losses. On legal sources concerning co-ownership by more than two masters, see Fleckner (2010: 234 n. 77).

[24] This case is attested in D. 14.4.3 pr. (Ulp. 29 *ad ed.*); D. 14.4.5.10 (Ulp. 29 *ad ed.*); D. 15.1.7.1 (Ulp. 29 *ad ed.*); D. 15.1.11.9 (Ulp. 29 *ad ed.*); D. 15.1.19.2 (Ulp. 29 *ad ed.*); D. 15.1.20 (Paul. 30 *ad ed.*); D. 15.1.27.8 (Gai. 9 *ad ed. prov.*) and D. 15.1.28 (Iul. 12 *dig.*); D. 15.1.37.2 (Iul 12 *dig.*); D. 15.1.51 (Scaev. 2 *quaest.*); D. 15.3.14 (Iul. 11 *dig.*) and marginally also by D. 14.1.6 pr.–1 (Paul. 6 *brev.*).

two masters who are asymmetrically informed about the activities of their commonly owned slave. One of them knows that the slave is trading with funds pertaining to the *merx peculiaris* while the other does not. Besides its legal implications,[25] asymmetric information has profound economic implications. Different knowledge of the slave's activities could induce the masters to form different expectations about the future returns of the business or to make different decisions concerning their participation in the business that the slave is running or in connected businesses. Therefore, asymmetric information on the slave's activities may allow the informed master to exploit such information to his own advantage.

Moreover, co-owners of a slave could affect each other's positions through hidden actions. In the interest of creditors, if a slave was owned by two or more masters and he was engaged in a common trade on the basis of the *merx peculiaris*, the creditor could sue one of the masters for the full amount of his credit;[26] this was possible even if the co-owners had unequal shares in the business.[27] It was a later worry for the individual owners to recover from each other what was due according to their shares.[28] *Prima facie*, co-ownership of a slave created a common-pool problem with masters facing joint liability. The fact that such liability was only later apportioned generated a risk for solvent masters, who bore liability in excess of their shares if one of the others became insolvent. Since one's own solvency is a variable

[25] Cf., among others, Chiusi (1993: 385).

[26] This is stated in analogy with the action against the shipowner and the action on the *peculium* (Gaurier 2004: 79–95). With regard to the *actio de peculio* Ulpian (29 *ad ed.*; D. 15.1.11.9, D. 15.1.13 and 15) emphasizes that each owner can be sued for the full amount, with relevant implications for the *deductio peculii*.

[27] This was the case when the masters had different shares in the *merx peculiaris* (D. 14.3.13.2; Ulp. 28 *ad ed.*).

[28] In this respect, Julian, quoted by Ulpian in D. 14.3.13.2, raised the question whether each owner should be liable in full, in equal shares, or in proportion to his share in the slave or in the *merx peculiaris*. As Julian's opinion is that each *dominus* may be sued for the full amount due to the creditor, Ulpian adds that "the person sued can recover part of what he is made to pay by an action on the partnership or for the division of property" (*iudicium societatis vel communi dividundo*). Cf. also D. 15.1.27.8 (Gai. 9 *ad ed. prov.*): "Nor will the defendant be harmed by being held liable, because if he pays more than his portion, he may recover the balance from his partner or partners by suing the partnership or bringing a divisory action" (trans. Watson, 1985 vol. 1: 443); D. 14.3.14 (Paul. 4 *Plaut.*) and D. 14.4.5.10 (Ulp. 29 *ad ed.*). Note that the latter text applies the same rules to cases without *praepositio*. On the relation between co-ownership of a slave and partnership contract, see Di Porto (1984: 377–9). Cf. also the criticism by Bürge (1988) towards Di Porto's opinion.

that can be affected by one's financial decisions, each owner could expose the others to the risk of insolvency.[29]

Another case concerns problems that could arise from an authorization (*iussum domini*) given to the slave by one of the owners only. Here the legal question is whether creditors could also sue the other masters (D. 15.4.5.1; Paul. 4 *ad Plaut.*).[30] This case evidences a potential agency problem, due to the effects of a master's instructions to the slave for other masters of the same slave.

10.3.1.2. Agency Problems between Management and Owners

A second set of agency problems could arise between the owner (or the owners) and their slave. In this case the slave (the agent) might act to his own benefit, thereby sometimes disregarding the owners' (principals') interests.

On the one hand, from a legal standpoint, the lack of awareness of slaves' business activities could be seen as strengthening (instead of weakening) the master's position towards external creditors, since less control meant less liability. This is the case of the *privilegium deductionis*—which gave the master priority over other creditors of the slave—granted to owners only if the slave had acted outside the master's control (*insciente domino*). Conversely, under certain circumstances, if the master had knowledge of dependents' dealings and did not distance himself from the slave's management of the *peculium*, he was liable to an *actio tributoria*. In other words, we are dealing here with cases where more information expands the slave-owner's liability.[31]

On the other hand, lack of information could result in adverse consequences for the slaveowner. The case mentioned in D. 14.4.5.1 (Ulp. 29 *ad ed.*) concerns asymmetry of information between a slave and his master about the activities of underslaves (*servi vicarii*); this

[29] As we will examine, such risks were mitigated by the limited liability arising from the use of a *peculium*.

[30] Paulus notes that creditors could act only against the authorizing master. If the authorization had been given by two masters, then both of them were jointly liable vis-à-vis creditors.

[31] It has been recently remarked that the control of the owner on slaves' activities and his liability towards creditors proportionally increased in case of *voluntas*, *praepositio* or *iussum domini*. Cf. Chiusi (2007b).

text evidences that the slave could be more informed than the master and offers a mirror image of the case of differently informed masters reported in D. 14.4.3 pr. (Ulp. 29 *ad ed.*) and commented on above.

Several other texts[32] offer examples of hidden actions by the slave that could, absent legal correctors, negatively affect the master: disregard for the master's instructions or misuse of funds. Concerning the first issue, in D. 15.1.37.1 (Iul. 12 *dig.*) Julian considered the case of a slave who, having been permitted to buy an underslave for eight *aurei* with his master's money, disregarded his master's instructions and bought a more expensive underslave. The slave's purchase could in theory expose the master to additional liability toward the seller, corresponding to the different amount due.[33]

Concerning the second problem (misuse of funds), in D. 15.3.3.9 (Ulp. 29 *ad ed.*) a slave received a loan from a creditor on the assumption that he would use it in the interest of his master. Instead, the slave used the amount he borrowed for other purposes. Plausibly, the slave (ab)used the owner's position in order to credibly commit to repay or to obtain more favorable conditions from the lender. The master could be personally liable towards the creditor for the benefit he should have received (but did not in fact receive) or, alternatively, the creditor could be exposed to a loss should the master not be held liable. In other cases, harm to the masters could derive from theft committed or damage caused by slaves[34] or by activities of the underslaves.[35] Underslaves often benefited from substantial autonomy, as we explain below. In turn, the possibility of such events and the difficulties encountered in monitoring slaves amounted to agency problems.

10.3.1.3. Agency Problems within the Management

The management of businesses run by slaves endowed with a *peculium* could be organized as a hierarchy, where the slave could acquire several underslaves, who, in principle, could also have their own underslaves (Di Porto 1984; cf. Földi 1996). Therefore, within the management, agency problems could arise, with the upper layer of

[32] See also D. 2.13.4.3 (Ulp. 4 *ad ed.*); D. 3.5.41 (42) (Paul. 32 *ad ed.*).

[33] In this case, the passage states that this additional liability should be imputed to the business assets (*peculium*) rather than to the owner's personal assets (*ratio dominica*). Cf. D. 15.1.4 pr. (Pomp. 7 *ad Sab.*).

[34] D. 15.1.9.1 (Ulp. 29 *ad ed.*).

[35] D. 15.1.38.2 (Afr. 8 *quaest.*); D. 15.3.17.1 (Afr. 8 *quaest.*).

the organization being the principal of the lower layer. In D. 14.4.5.1 (Ulp. 29 *ad ed.*), we have the case of a business hierarchically structured, with the different layers having different information about the activities of the underslave.[36] From this case it is clear that the underslave could be involved in business activities of which slave and master had no knowledge.[37]

Moreover, both slaves and underslaves could have debts towards each other or towards the master (D. 15.1.17, Ulp. 29 *ad ed.*). These relationships were internal to the business organization and gave rise to the question whether the master could keep his *privilegium deductionis* and from which *peculium* (of the slave, of the underslave, or both) should be deducted what was owed to the master.[38] Deductions implied that a master's credit would be satisfied prior to other claims.[39] Next to their impact on creditors, these scenarios expose the complexity of the relationships internal to the business organization, underscore the degree of autonomy that underslaves had, and hence suggest that there must have been relevant agency problems within the business' management. As several texts show, the activity of underslaves could be relevant not only for the legal position of the master but also for the solvency of the *peculium* of the slave (D. 15.1.38.2; Afr. 8 *quaest.*,[40] and D. 15.3.17.1; Afr. 8 *quaest.*). Thus, decisions taken by underslaves—for instance, incurring a debt or entering into a contract—could potentially harm the interests of the slave if they were computed in his *peculium* and not only in the *peculium* of the underslave.

10.3.2. Mitigating Governance Problems

The praetorian remedies offered various solutions to the agency problems emphasized above and, although unable to solve them completely, helped to reduce the impact of those problems that could not be addressed directly by the parties. Again, the *Digest* offers

[36] See below §10.3.3. Cf. also the case described by Di Porto (1984: 303–8).

[37] See the case mentioned in D. 9.4.19.2 (Paul. 22 *ad ed.*).

[38] Such arrangements have also been interpreted as a way to spread business risk; see Cerami et al. (2010). Cf. D. 15.3.17.1 (Afr. 8 *quaest.*).

[39] Presumably, Servius was the first jurist to deal with the problem of whether the master could deduct from the *peculium* what the slave (*ordinarius*) owed to the underslaves (*vicarii*). See Reduzzi Merola (1990; 2007). Cf. Földi (1996) and Micolier (1932).

[40] Cf. D. 15.1.18 (Paul. 4 *quaest.*).

several examples of this trend. We will first examine how the praetorian remedies addressed agency problems among owners. Then, we will analyze the solutions provided by these remedies to address problems arising with or within management of a business.

When the co-owners had jointly employed their slave in a business, all of them shared liability towards third parties, as can be inferred by several fragments of the *Digest* such as D. 15.1.27.8 (Gai. 9 *ad ed. prov.*) discussing the *actio de peculio*. The same solution applied if a defendant had been sued by way of the *actio exercitoria* (D. 14.1.1.25; Ulp. 28 *ad ed.*; D. 14.1.2, Gai. 9 *ad ed. prov.* and D. 14.1.3, Paul. 29 *ad ed.*)[41] or the *actio institoria* (as can be deduced from D. 14.3.13.2; Ulp. 28 *ad ed.*; Di Porto 1984: 207–9, 214). Notably, this liability was joint in that creditors had an action for the entire amount of their credit against all of the masters[42] regardless of their respective parts in the business (which did not need to be equal). Each master could be sued in full by creditors even though any acquisition by the slave would enrich each co-owner *pro parte*, depending on the share he had in the slave.[43]

This solution served a commercial interest as it prevented "a person who dealt with a single contractor" having to "split his suit between several defendants" (D. 15.1.27.8; Gai. 9 *ad ed. prov.*, consistently with D. 14.1.1.24; Ulp. 28 *ad ed.*),[44] thereby reducing

[41] In D. 14.1.5 (Paul. 29 *ad ed.*), an individual employed in his maritime business a *servus alienus*. In this case, the *dominus servi* was allowed to act with the *actio exercitoria* against the *exercitor navis* if a contract he had concluded with the slave was not honored. It is worth noting that the passage reports a case in which a master is allowed a remedy for dealings he had with his own slave in account of the economic nature of the transaction and of the asymmetric information and control powers between the master and the individual employing the slave. Doing otherwise would have inevitably exacerbated agency problems by allowing the managing party to generate negative externalities for the slave master. More broadly, this solution recognizes that a slave may be an agent of a different individual from his own master. The same solution applied to a co-owned slave whom only one of the masters employs in a maritime business. In cases, in which the common business was run by a slave not commonly owned (as in the example above), the available actions were the *actiones ex locato* or *ex conducto* for compensated services and the *actio mandati* for gratuitous services. With regard to agency problems, the peculiarity of maritime business shows other cases relevant for our purpose. See Gaurier (2004: 91).

[42] As can be inferred from D. 15.1.27.8 (Gai. 9 *ad ed. prov.*), D. 14.1.1.25 (Ulp. 28 *ad ed.*), and D. 14.3.13.2 (Ulp. 28 *ad ed.*). Cf. Gaurier (2004: 85).

[43] See the general principle deducible from D. 45.3.5 (Ulp. 48 *ad Sab.*).

[44] Cf. also D. 14.1.2 (Gai. 9 *ad ed. prov.*) *ne in plures adversarios distringatur qui cum uno contraxerit* (for otherwise a person who dealt with a single contractor would have to split his suit between several defendants).

transaction costs and facilitating business. However, at the same time, joint liability generated an agency problem among owners, as the master who had been sued also faced liability on account of the others. The natural option open to the master who bore liability was to seek compensation from the others. If this attempt failed, different remedies were available. The master could resort to an *actio communi dividundo*, based on the co-ownership of the slave, or to an *actio pro socio*,[45] based on the partnership contract.

An additional problem is examined in D. 15.1.11.9 (Ulp. 29 *ad ed.*) and concerns whether a defendant sued for the full amount could deduct what was due by his partner. Julian's opinion, shared by Ulpian, is in favor of the deduction, as confirmed by D. 15.1.13 (Ulp. 29 *ad ed.*) and indirectly by D. 15.1.15 (Ulp. 29 *ad ed.*). Ulpian explains that "if the *peculium* is held in common, an action will lie for the full amount, and deduction may be made of what is owed to the other." This type of approach was not applicable—and was indeed not necessary—when a co-owned slave had been given two separate *peculia* by the two masters. If each master kept his *peculium* separate neither of them could be sued on the other's *peculium*.[46]

The posture of the praetorian remedies vis-à-vis other agency problems among owners may be seen as an attempt to keep the positions of the different owners legally separated when this was possible. In D. 14.4.3 pr. (Ulp. 29 *ad ed.*), we have the case of two masters: one of them knew that the slave was trading with funds

[45] See D. 14.3.13.2 (Ulp. 28 *ad ed.*) and D. 14.3.14 (Paul. 4 *ad Plaut.*), where the *servus alienus* is appointed to manage a common *merx peculiaris*. Cf. D. 15.1.19.2 (Ulp. 29 *ad ed.*) emphasizing that *in duobus dominis sufficiat pro socio vel communi dividundo actio* (between two owners the need met by an action on the partnership or on a divisory action) and, with regards to the *iudicium societatis*, see also D. 14.1.3 (Paul. 29 *ad ed.*). See also D. 45.3.28.1 (Gai. 3 *de verb. oblig.*) and D. 41.1.45 (Gai. 7 *ad ed. prov.*).

[46] D. 15.1.15 (Ulp. 29 *ad ed.*). Cf. D. 45.3.1.2 (Iul. 52 *dig.*): *Si servus communis meus et tuus ex peculio, quod ad te solum pertinebat, mutuam pecuniam dederit, obligationem tibi adquiret et, si eandem mihi nominatim stipulatus fuerit, debitorem a te non liberabit, sed uterque nostrum habebit actionem, ego ex stipulatu, tu quod pecunia tua numerata sit: debitor tamen me doli mali exceptione summovere poterit* (If a slave belonging to you and me in common has made a loan from his *peculium*, which belongs exclusively to you, he acquires the obligation for you, and even if he has stipulated for the same sum in my name, he will not release the debtor from his obligation. Each of us will have an action, I on the stipulation and you because it is your money that has been paid over; however, the debtor will be able to defeat me with the defense of fraud [trans. Watson 1985, vol. 4: 680].)

pertaining to the *merx peculiaris* while the other did not. Knowledge of this type also had consequences for the liability of the masters: a knowing master could be sued by way of the *actio tributoria*, while a non-knowing master also enjoyed an additional protection related to the *deductio peculii*.[47] The problem incidentally discussed in this text is whether knowledge on the part of one of the masters could (negatively) affect the liability regime of the other (non-knowing) master; the solution given by Ulpian, in line with Julian's opinion, is that two different regimes should apply to the two masters. This solution shields the non-knowing master from increases in liability arising from the fact that the other master was more involved in the trading activity of the slave. As a result, distinguishing the liability regime applicable to the two masters, this rule removes this specific agency problem as it prevents a master's knowledge of the slave's trading from having legal effects on the other masters. By analogy, Ulpian (D. 14.4.5.1; 29 *ad ed.*) adopts a similar solution, proposed by the jurist Pomponius, for the case of a business hierarchically structured, involving both slaves and underslaves managing a *merx peculiaris* (Di Porto 1984: 307–30).

Against the master who knew that his underslaves were engaged in a trade, Ulpian holds that the appropriate remedy is the *actio tributoria*. By contrast, if the slave had knowledge of the underslave's trading, although the master did not, the suit should be brought against the master by way of an *actio de peculio*.[48] Thereby, a softer

[47] D. 14.4.1 pr. (Ulp. 29 *ad ed.*): one of the advantages of this edict is that it treats the master as an external creditor if he was aware that his slave was trading with the stock of the *peculium*, whereas in other cases he is privileged in respect of his slave's contracts, being liable only for what remains in the *peculium* after everything due to himself has been deducted. Thus, as considered in D. 14.4.3 pr. (Ulp. 29 *ad ed.*), the defendant *sciens* was subject to a deduction of all that is owed to the master who did not know. But if the suit was brought against the *dominus ignorans*, "it must be by way of the *actio de peculio*: so a full deduction must be made of anything owed to the master with knowledge, just as it would be if he himself had been sued on the *peculium*."

[48] In this case, from the *peculium* of the underslave the master was allowed to deduct what was owed to him, but not what was owed to the slave. See Chiusi (1993: 382–4). Pomponius' advice quoted in D. 14.4.5.1 (Ulp. 29 *ad ed.*) is that in case of knowledge of both the master and the slave, the *dominus* should be liable not only to an *actio tributoria*, but also to an *actio de peculio*, "the former in respect of the underslave, the latter in respect of the *peculium* of the slave"; debts due to the master and debts due to the slave "will both qualify for proportional deduction 'in respect of the *merx*.'" With regard to the different case of the maritime trade, cf. D. 14.1.1.22 (Ulp. 28 *ad ed.*).

liability regime is applied to a master who is less involved in the business.

Most likely, agency problems arising with or within the management left fainter traces in the legal sources because slaves were not considered persons before the law and the use of force was a readily-available disciplining device. One exception is D. 15.1.38.2 (Afr. 8 *quaest.*). Here Africanus examines a case in which the slave was endowed with a *peculium*, which included an underslave. In turn, the underslave owed the master a sum equal to half of the underslave's value. The case involves a creditor's suit brought against the master in respect to the slave's *peculium*. The jurist considers the question whether the credit that the master had towards the underslave should be deducted from the *peculium* of the slave. Not doing so causes the master to suffer a loss equal to the value of the underslave's debt. In principle, the liability of the owner under the *actio de peculio* was net of the credits he had with the slave—that is, for his credits towards the *peculium*, he had priority over other creditors. However, in this case, the credit does not pertain to the slave's *peculium*, to which the suit refers, but to the underslave's *peculium*. The jurist states that the whole value of the underslave should be taken into account without deducting his debt to the master, according to the principle that "no one can be treated as forming part of his own *peculium*." From the slave's perspective, this solution enhances his solvency and shields him from over-indebtedness of his own underslave even in cases when he contracted debts with their common master.

Finally, from D. 15.1.17 (Ulp. 29 *ad ed.*) it emerges that creditors of the slave could seize assets pertaining to the *peculium* of the underslaves of the said slave, but, in contrast, creditors of an underslave could not seize assets pertaining to the slave's *peculium* (beyond the underslave's *peculium*).

10.3.3. Governance Problems as a Constraint

Governance problems within the business increased as the number of individuals involved increased. Adding one additional individual to the business entity does not simply add one measure of monitoring costs. The total increase in monitoring is much larger, as every addition to the partnership imposes a monitoring cost on all pre-existing partners. Since each additional partner brings about a greater increase in monitoring costs, monitoring costs increase faster than the number of partners. A natural boundary on the size of ordinary businesses arises at the point where increasing marginal governance costs meet decreasing marginal returns to scale.[49]

The optimal size of businesses is a matter of empirical investigation that cannot possibly fall within the scope of this chapter; however, the balance of costs and benefits depends heavily on the baseline cost of monitoring. The greater this cost, the smaller the optimal size of businesses. In turn, this cost can be seen as a proxy of the importance of agency problems that were not completely addressed by the law and were left to be solved by the masters themselves. Such residual governance problems have been identified in several cases described in the *Digest*, which give important hints as to why masters had to monitor each other to a substantial extent.

A similar logic also applies to increases in size due to an increment at the bottom of the hierarchical structure of the business organization through the employment of underslaves. As in the case of several masters, the law cannot remove all adverse effects and there remain agency problems to be solved. The activities of the underslave can have a potentially negative impact on the master's (or masters') position, even if liability is confined to the *peculium*. It is in the interest of the master and, to a large extent, also of the slave to ensure that the capital invested in the *peculium* is not affected by business decisions taken by the underslaves. A slave endowed with a *peculium* could delegate certain activities to underslaves[50] or could rent the underslave's services to a third party; moreover, the underslaves could be engaged in dealings of their own (D. 14.4.5.1; Ulp. 29 *ad ed.*),[51] contract debts with their own masters (D. 15.1.17; Ulp. 29 *ad ed.*;[52] D. 15.1.38.2; Afr. 8 *quaest.*), or enter into contracts with third parties to the benefit of the slave or of the master (D. 15.3.17.1; Afr. 8 *quaest.*).

Economists have identified mechanisms, other than legal remedies, that keep the interests of the various participants in a business venture aligned, principally with reference to management and owners (Easterbrook and Fischel 1991). In particular, the market

[49] Coase (1937: 386–405).

[50] The sources envision cases of underslaves appointed as managers of maritime businesses (D. 14.1.1.22; Ulp. 28 *ad ed.*) or of a store (D. 14.3.11.8; Ulp. 28 *ad ed.*).

[51] See above §§10.3.1.2 and 3.

[52] See above §10.3.1.3.

for corporate control (which entails the possibility that a potential acquirer could take control of the business and replace management: Manne 1965), the market for managerial services (Fama 1980), the financial market (Jensen 1986: 323–9), and the product market (Hart 1983) have been advocated as forms of indirect control on management in modern corporations. The market for corporate control and the financial market were probably not sufficiently developed to exert substantial control over managers in ancient Rome.[53] A market for managerial services existed to a certain extent only in the form of the slave market, which, however, cannot be compared to a modern labor market for managers. The product market did exercise a certain degree of control on managerial performance, especially by providing masters with imperfect but nevertheless valuable signals. However, transportation costs and product perishability severely constrained trade both in size and in reach. Market discipline was certainly not enough to remove agency problems completely.

In addition, modern businesses rely on sophisticated forms of accounting, auditing, and certification, so that information can be reliably transmitted from management to owners, potential investors, and creditors (Littleton 1953). Accounting in the Roman world between the second century BC and the second century AD was based on the recording of a limited amount of information concerning capital assets and (only marginally) income (Rathbone 1991: 396–401; Rathbone 1994; Andreau and Maucourant 1999; Minaud 2005).

The main purpose of accounts (*rationes*) was to record events chronologically in terms of debts and credits per activity,[54] without a system of double-entry bookkeeping.[55] Moreover, there is no evidence of any statistical aggregation of data or certification by an independent agency. As a result, ancient accounting provided far

[53] For a discussion of the stage of development of the Roman financial market, see Temin (2001: 178).

[54] See the interesting observations by Bürge (2010: 380–1) (emphasizing the conflicts of interest among the owner, the slave, and creditors; the owner had an interest in understating the size of the *peculium* and overstating the debts that the slave had towards him; the slave had an interest in overstating his credits towards the master; in contrast, creditors, had an interest in overstating the size of the *peculium*).

[55] de Sainte Croix (1956); Thilo (1980: 40–1); Macve (1985); Jouanique (1986); Minaud (2005); Bürge (2010: 385). Waelkens (2000: 352) is more open towards the existence of a double-entry bookkeeping technique.

less reliable information and could be used to convey information to third parties only to a limited extent.[56]

10.4. LIMITS TO THE AMOUNTS OF CAPITAL INVESTED

10.4.1. Limits to Access to Credit

Modern firms can finance their activities by means of equity—thereby extending the ownership base—or debt. We have already examined the agency problems generated by an expansion in the number of owners; the same problems limited the amount that each owner was willing to invest. Here we emphasize that agency problems may also have constrained the second source of finance for firms: debt. We will analyze the agency problems that arose between the business and its creditors and emphasize that such problems may have curbed the ability of business managers to raise needed capital by borrowing.

10.4.1.1. Agency Problems between Business and Creditors

Evidence of agency problems between creditors and business could be inferred from the fact that the business—which can be seen as an agent of the creditors—could incur losses that, in case of insolvency, were externalized on creditors, a possibility that has been attested in the *Digest* (D. 15.1.30 pr.; Ulp. 29 *ad ed.*). In addition, under the *actio de peculio*, the credits of the master had priority over other credits and hence had to be deducted from the *peculio*. Deductions could also occur as a result of more complex operations, such as when the slave promised to take over the liability of a debtor toward his master (D. 15.1.56; Paul. 2 *ad Ner.*), or when the master promised to take over the liability of his slave (D. 15.1.11.1; Ulp. 29 *ad ed.*). Such

[56] Andreau (2001: 125–35, in particular 134). It has been recently observed that the simplicity of Roman accounting techniques does not represent proof of "primitivism" of the economic system. Rather, the rudimentary accounting method could be explained by way of elementary means for financing production and exchange activities (Bresson and Bresson 2004: 5; cf. Giliberti 1984).

deductions limited the assets that creditors could seize and generated agency costs.

Other passages of the *Digest* indicate that payments made to the slave became part of the *peculium* unless the master had disposed otherwise, in which case they had to be deducted even if the master had debts toward the *peculium* (D. 15.1.7.6; Ulp. 29 *ad ed.*). Somewhat similarly, in case the slave had stood surety for a third party or had given guarantee for a debt, the creditor had an action against the *peculium* only if the slave had done so in the interest of the *peculium* (D. 15.1.3.5–6; Ulp. 29 *ad ed.*). Therefore, one may infer that creditors were required to have access to a substantial amount of information in order to assess the solvency of the *peculium*.

Several other events could result in a detriment for creditors.[57] In some cases, the creditor could have to split his suit between several defendants for the same credit if a slave was co-owned by several masters and endowed with a *peculium* or appointed to a common business.[58] Finally, the slave could in various ways transfer resources pertaining to the *peculium* into the personal assets of the owner, thereby causing a potential detriment to the creditors (D. 15.3.13; Ulp. 29 *ad ed.*).

Further problems could emerge from the hierarchical organization of the business, as reported in D. 15.1.17 (Ulp. 29 *ad ed.*) and D. 15.1.38.2 (Afr. 8 *quaest.*). Finally, even without the intermediation of slaves, the master could directly harm his business creditors if he tried to reduce his liability exposure (D. 15.2.1 pr.; Ulp. 29 *ad ed.*) by reducing or subtracting funds from the *peculium* (D. 15.1.21 pr.–2; Ulp. 29 *ad ed.*; D. 15.1.26; Paul. 30 *ad ed.*).

10.4.1.2. Agency Problems among Creditors

A subtler but not less important set of agency problems concerns the relationship among the different creditors of the same business. Quite clearly, each additional creditor potentially reduces the solvency of the *peculium* for the other creditors. In this sense, each creditor is an

[57] For instance, the master or fellow slave could cause damage to the slave (D. 15.1.9 pr.–3; Ulp. 29 *ad ed.*), the master could sell, manumit, or give the slave as a gift or dowry to someone else, or the slave could die (D. 15.2.1.1–2, 6; Ulp. 29 *ad ed.*).

[58] See D. 15.1.27.8 and D. 14.1.1.24 (Gai. 9 *ad ed. prov.*), discussed above (§10.3.2). Likewise, the creditor also had to pursue multiple lawsuits for the same credit in the case discussed by Ulpian in D. 15.1.32 pr. (Ulp. 2 *disp.*).

agent of the others. Problems among creditors could arise especially when a slave conducted, with *merces peculiares* pertaining to the same *peculium*, different business activities, such as for instance a garment factory and a textile workshop (D. 14.4.5.15; Ulp. 29 *ad ed.*), or the same activity in different locations (one in *Bucinum* and one across the Tiber: D. 14.4.5.16; Ulp. 29 *ad ed.*; Chiusi 1993: 287). These situations created potential conflicts between two distinct sets of creditors with a claim on the same *peculium*. Time could also serve as a confounding factor, in all those cases in which a creditor came forward after the distribution had taken place (D. 14.4.5.19; Ulp. 29 *ad ed.*).

The potential for conflicts among creditors is evidenced by the considerations made on the optimal choice of remedy (D. 14.4.11; Gai. 9 *ad ed. prov.*; cf. Gai., *Inst.* 4.74a). It could happen that creditors had a choice between the *actio de peculio* and the *actio tributoria* (see also D. 14.4.5.1, Ulp. 29 *ad ed.*, discussed above), in that the necessary conditions for the two *actiones* were partially overlapping. While the former allowed creditors to seize a larger set of assets, it obliged them to deduct the master's credits towards the slave. In contrast, the latter remedy did not give priority to the master's credits (*privilegium deductionis*; Bürge 2010: 379–80). In turn, the balance affected the total amount of debt to which the *peculium* (or the *merx peculiaris*) was exposed. Thus, it was crucial for a creditor to have a good picture of the total exposure of the *peculium* both in its entirety and concerning an individual *merx peculiaris*, before making a strategic choice of remedy. In turn, total exposure was a common-pool problem, with no creditor in a position to control or limit the amount of debt that a slave was contracting (Chiusi 1993: 380–2).

10.4.2. Fostering Access to Credit

Given the chilling effect that agency problems could have on access to credit, the *ius honorarium* developed remedies designed to grapple with them. In economic terms, addressing the agency problems between business and creditors with respect to access to credit means increasing the probability of repayment, which in turn positively affects creditworthiness and improves businesses' ability to obtain credit.

A first step in this direction could be made by removing unnecessary procedural hurdles, which could make it more difficult for creditors to seize business assets in order to satisfy debt. In case of *negotiationes per servos communes*, in principle, unsatisfied creditors would have to sue all the co-owners, so that doing business with a co-owned slave would have resulted in substantially higher ex post litigation costs for the creditors than doing business with a slave with only one master. This hurdle was removed by allowing creditors to sue one of the masters for the entire amount (under the *actiones institoria*, *exercitoria*, and *de peculio*)[59] and then let the co-owners deal with the internal apportionment of the losses.[60] Likewise, time could also be a confounding factor on account of the natural variability of business yields.[61]

A second important feature of the rules fostering access to credit is the definition ex ante (before credit is extended) of the extent that the master would be liable ex post. Different remedies define different measures of the master's liability and it was crucial for the creditors to be able to anticipate under which remedy they could sue, should it be necessary. In turn, the choice of remedy was a function of the master's involvement in the slave's business.[62] In a nutshell, the larger the degree of the master's involvement, the broader the scope of his liability towards creditors (cf. Chiusi 2007b).

A third step in the direction of removing obstacles to access to credit is preventing certain actions by the slave or the masters that would hurt creditors and, consequently, providing for adequate remedies should these actions nevertheless be taken. The fraudulent alienation of the slave could be one of the actions that could possibly hurt the interests of creditors. "As long as the slave remains in power,

[59] See D. 14.3.13.2 (Ulp. 28 *ad ed.*); D. 14.1.1.25 (Ulp. 28 *ad ed.*); D. 14.1.2 (Gai. 9 *ad ed. prov.*); D. 15.1.27.8 (Gai. 9 *ad ed. prov.*). Cf. D. 14.1.1.24 (Ulp. 29 *ad ed.*) and D. 15.1.32 pr. (Ulp. 2 *disp.*).

[60] See also D. 15.3.13 (Ulp. 29 *ad ed.*) stating the general rule for benefits conferred to one of two co-owners at the expense of the *peculium*. In this case, the creditor could only sue the owner to whom the benefit had been conferred. D. 15.3.14 (Iul. 11 *dig.*) contains an exception to this principle.

[61] Thereby, it was believed that if a creditor had sued with the *actio de peculio* and the *peculium* was insufficient for the satisfaction of debt, the creditor should not be precluded a new trial with the same *actio* if the *peculium* had successively grown (D. 15.1.30.4, Ulp. 29 *ad ed.*).

[62] The sources describe this situation as "not being contrary to" (*non nolle*), "knowledge of" (*scientia*), "not objecting to" (*non protestatur*), "the master does not say he is against" (*dominus non dicit se contra*) the trading by the slave; D. 14.4.1.3 (Ulp. 29 *ad ed.*). See Chiusi (1993).

there is no time limit on the *actio de peculio*,"[63] but the sale of the slave with *peculium* could have in principle nullified creditors' claims. To correct for this problem the praetorian remedies extended the liability of the seller to one year after the sale, so that creditors could seize the assets that were originally in the *peculium*.[64]

The slave could to be sold with or without the *peculium*.[65] If the *peculium* had been transferred together with the slave, a series of specific rules tried to give some economic continuity to the business even after a change in ownership. Significantly, the *actio de peculio annalis* was not available if the seller had handed over the *peculium* to the purchaser in exchange for a price;[66] however, creditors could sue the seller if the price received for the *peculium* by the seller had been intended to take the place of the *peculium* (D. 15.1.33; Iav. 12 *ex Cass.*; D. 15.1.34; Pomp. 12 *ex var. lect.*).[67]

Likewise, in line with the goal of assuring economic continuity despite the transfer of ownership, the jurists advocated remedies preventing various parties from engaging in opportunistic behavior. Thus the seller could not deduct his credits towards the *peculium* twice (once at the moment of the sale and again when sued by the creditor under the *actio de peculio annalis*: D. 15.1.11.7; Ulp. 29 *ad ed.*).[68] Similarly, purchasers were not to sell the slave strategically pending trial (D. 15.1.43; Paul. 30 *ad ed.*). The purchaser (if he were sued) could not deduct increments to the *peculium* that had occurred after the sale (D. 15.1.32.1; Ulp. 2 *disp.*), while the creditor could not sue both the seller and the purchaser at the same time

[63] D. 15.2.1.1 (Ulp. 29 *ad ed.*).

[64] D. 15.2.1 pr. (Ulp. 29 *ad ed.*); D. 15.2.1.5 (Ulp. 29 *ad ed.*).

[65] D. 18.1.29 (Ulp. 43 *ad Sab.*); D. 21.1.18.2 (Gai. 1 *ad ed. cur.*); D. 21.1.33 pr. (Ulp. 1 *ad ed. cur.*).

[66] D. 15.1.32.2 (Ulp. 2 *disp.*).

[67] Cf. D. 15.1.27.2 (Gai. 9 *ad ed. prov.*). See also D. 15.1.30.5 (Ulp. 29 *ad ed.*). Understandably, the purchaser of a slave could not be sued in the *actio tributoria* (D. 14.4.10; Paul. 30 *ad ed.*). This rule seems to be in line with the fact that such an action presupposes knowledge by the master of the slave's trade, which the seller could not have.

[68] Since what is owed to the master formed no part of the *peculium*, the master could reclaim these funds through *condictio*. If the slave had been sold without *peculium*, the deductions of pre-existing debts toward the seller were allowed, plausibly because there was no risk of double deductions due to the fact that the *peculium* had not been sold. Debts incurred after the sale, instead, could not be deducted because at that point the seller was no longer the master of the slave and hence had a claim on such deductions (D. 15.1.47.5; Paul. 4 *ad Plaut.*).

(D. 15.1.47.3; Paul. 4 *ad Plaut.*). More complex cases arose when either the seller or the purchaser was a creditor of the slave prior to the sale. In general, the seller could not sue the purchaser with an *actio de peculio* for such credits (D. 15.1.27.4; Gai. 9 *ad ed. prov.*; D. 15.1.38.3; Afr. 8 *quaest.*). By barring such suits, this rule forced the seller to reveal the value of his credits to the purchaser prior to the sale so that the price could be adjusted and the debts deducted from the *peculium*. In contrast, the purchaser was allowed to sue the seller with respect to previous dealings just like any other creditor could (D. 15.1.47.4; Paul. 4 *ad Plaut.*). This possibility probably stemmed from the fact that the *peculium* was not necessarily transferred to the purchaser.[69]

A related set of rules concerns the *actio de in rem verso*, through which a creditor could recover from the slave owner to the extent that this person benefited from actions taken by a slave. Ulpian in D. 15.3.13 (Ulp. 29 *ad ed.*) mentions conferrals of benefits (at the expense of the *peculium*) to one of the co-owners only. Such conferrals could be undone with an *actio de in rem verso*. The question arose if the *actio de in rem verso* was available only against the master who had received the benefit or also against a co-owner. Although in general the *actio* was thought to be available only against the master to whom the benefits had been conferred (D. 15.3.13; Ulp. 29 *ad ed.*), in some cases the *actio* could also be used against the other master. In this case, the defendant could reclaim from his partner what he had been held liable to pay (D. 15.3.14; Iul. 11 *dig.*).

Not only could the slave confer *peculium* assets to his master, but the master could also fraudulently reduce the *peculium* by withdrawing assets from it,[70] in order to reduce his liability exposure. Creditors could then sue the master for fraud.[71]

Balancing the interests of creditors with the general advantages given by limited liability, the praetorian remedies protecting creditors found a natural limit in the need to protect the master during

[69] See also D. 15.1.27.5–8 (Gai. 9 *ad ed. prov.*) concerning the sale of a slave to whom the seller had previously extended a loan.

[70] It was within the powers of the master to reduce and even withdraw the entire *peculium* (D. 15.1.8; Paul. 4 *ad Sab.*).

[71] D. 15.1.9.4 (Ulp. 29 *ad ed.*); D. 15.1.26 (Paul. 30 *ad ed.*); D. 15.2.1 pr. (Ulp. 29 *ad ed.*); D. 15.1.30.6 (Ulp. 29 *ad ed.*); D. 15.1.30.7 (Ulp. 29 *ad ed.*); D. 15.1.31 (Paul. 30 *ad ed.*).

bankruptcy, so that he did not have to compute credits not yet paid in the *peculium* assets, since execution could be costly, uncertain, and lengthy (D. 15.1.51; Scaev. 2 *quaest.*).

So far we have focused on the legal solutions for agency problems between business and creditors, but praetorian remedies were also available to mitigate agency problems among creditors, mainly in respect to (potential) conflicts among different creditors who tried to seize the same assets for the satisfaction of debt. The general principle seems to have been that, if possible, creditors should be allowed to rely on the assets more strictly related to the business to which they extended credit. As we have seen above,[72] Ulpian deals with cases in which a slave ran two different businesses with the same *peculium*. The principle expressed is that creditors of one business should be allowed to seize the assets pertaining to that activity prior to the creditors of the other business, and vice versa. The same principle applied to a business run in two different locations (D. 14.4.5.16; Ulp. 29 *ad ed.*). The reason given in the latter text quite explicitly refers to the agency problems that we have identified: it is "fairest to have separate distributions; otherwise, some people might be able to satisfy themselves out of the assets of others and so shift their losses to them."

Similar concerns were voiced in the case of one creditor's obtaining payment in full, to the potential disadvantage of creditors who came forward later. It is well known that under the *actio tributoria* all creditors were treated equally irrespective of the timing of their claims (D. 14.4.6; Paul. 30 *ad ed.*). In order to prevent unjust distributions, if a creditor had obtained full payment, he had to give a *cautio* guaranteeing that he would give a *pro rata* refund to creditors coming forward after the proceeding (D. 14.4.5.19; Ulp. 29 *ad ed.*; D. 14.4.7 pr.; Ulp. 29 *ad ed.*). This solution not only guaranteed fairness but also prevented potentially inefficient early liquidations of businesses due to a creditors' run, motivated by the fear of being late. In addition, creditors could ask for secured credit (D. 13.7.18.4; Paul. 29 *ad ed.*) and, in that case, were to be privileged even vis-à-vis the master (D. 14.4.5.8; Ulp. 29 *ad ed.*).[73]

[72] See above §10.4.1.2. Cf. D. 14.4.5.15 (Ulp. 29 *ad ed.*).

[73] See also D. 14.4.5.11–13 (Ulp. 29 *ad ed.*) and D. 14.4.5.17–18 (Ulp. 29 *ad ed.*) specifying what assets could be seized.

10.4.3. Limited Access to Credit as a Constraint

As we have observed with respect to governance problems, agency problems relating to access to external finance grew with the number of parties involved. The text in D. 14.4.5.19 (Ulp. 29 *ad ed.*) requiring a guarantee from the satisfied creditor in order to protect other creditors coming forward later is a testament to this effect. Moreover, the risk of insolvency borne by creditors increased with the amount lent to the business, so that there was a natural limit to the size of loans. Although the law tried to grapple with these problems, many unresolved issues remained, partially also due to the limits of the Roman accounting system, which we have already evidenced above (§10.3.3).

Creditors could use two readily available ways to protect themselves from the risk of insolvency, beyond the protection afforded by the law. One way was to apply high interest rates in order to compensate for the high probability of default. A second strategy was to require secured credit in order to cover against the probability of default. Both strategies clearly reduced the ability of businesses to raise external capital, given the natural limits to the amount of interest a business could afford to pay and the assets that could be pledged as security. The result of these factors is a constraint on the size of businesses in terms of capital employed.

10.5. CONCLUSIONS

In this chapter, we have examined the economic organization of slave-run businesses and showed that numerous problems discussed by Roman jurists—principally, by Ulpian in his commentary to the Edict—can be interpreted as agency problems.[74] This analytical tool allows for a re-examination of the solutions proposed by the jurists and for the identification of a functional connection between these solutions and the goals of mitigating governance problems within the business and facilitating access to external finance. Despite these

[74] As we have stressed, we do not claim that Roman jurists conceptualized such problems in the same terms as we do.

efforts, agency problems could not be completely removed, and agency costs generated relevant diseconomies of scale, resulting in a constraint on the growth of slave-run businesses both in terms of people involved and in terms of capital invested. These observations call for a rethinking of the notion of (optimal) size of Roman slave-run businesses. The evidence we analyze does not imply that the jurists were necessarily aware of the economic rationale of the solutions adopted. However, further research could shed light on the degree of sophistication of the jurists' analytical tools.[75]

REFERENCES

Abatino, Barbara, Giuseppe Dari-Mattiacci, and Enrico Perotti. 2011. "Depersonalization of Business in Ancient Rome." 31 *Oxford Journal of Legal Studies* 365–89.

Alchian, Armen A., and Harold Demsetz. 1972. "Production, Information Costs, and Economic Organization." 62 *American Economic Review* 777–95.

Amirante, Luigi. 1983. "Lavoro di giuristi sul peculio: le definizioni da Quinto Mucio ad Ulpiano," in 3 *Studi in onore di Cesare Sanfilippo*. Milan: Giuffrè, 1–15.

Andreau, Jean, and Jérôme Maucourant. 1999. "À propos de la rationalité économique dans l'antiquité gréco-romaine: une interprétation des thèses de D. Rathbone (1991)." 9 *Topoi* 47–102.

Andreau, Jean, and Raymond Descat. 2009. *Gli schiavi nel mondo greco e romano*. Trans. Raffaella Biundo. Bologna: Il Mulino.

Andreau, Jean. 1999. *Banking and Business in the Roman World*. Cambridge: Cambridge University Press.

Andreau, Jean. 2001. *Banque et affaires dans le monde romain (IVᵉ siècle av. J.-C.–IIIᵉ siècle ap. J.-C.)*. Paris: Editions du Seuil.

Andreau, Jean. 2004. "Les esclaves 'hommes d'affaires' et la gestion des ateliers et des commerces," in Jean Andreau, Jérôme France, and Sylvie Pittia, eds, *Mentalités et choix économiques des Romains*. Bordeaux: Ausonius, 111–25.

Arangio-Ruiz, Vincenzo. 1965. *La società in diritto romano*. Naples: Jovene.

[75] The authors would like to thank Kenneth Ayotte, Pietro Cerami, Bruce Frier, and Rick Verhagen for helpful comments, and Sander Verrips for excellent editorial assistance. The authors gratefully acknowledge the financial support by the Netherlands Organisation for Scientific Research (NWO grant 016.075.332).

Asser, Daan H. 1988. "Book review: Impresa collettiva e schiavo 'manager' in Roma antica (II sec. a.C. - II sec. d.C.)." 56 *Tijdschrift voor Rechtsgeschiedenis* 371–2.

Aubert, Jean-Jacques. 1994. *Business Managers in Ancient Rome: A Social and Economic Study of* Institores, *200 B.C.–250 A.D.* Leiden: Brill.

Ayotte, Kenneth, and Henry B. Hansmann. 2013. "Legal Entities as Transferable Bundles of Contracts." 111 *Michigan Law Review* 715–58.

Bresson, Alain, and François Bresson. 2004. "Max Weber, la comptabilité rationnelle et l'économie du monde gréco-romain." 34 *Cahiers du Centre de Recherches Historiques* 91–114.

Bretone, Mario. 1958. *Servus communis: contributo alla storia della comproprietà romana in età classica*. Naples: Jovene.

Burdese, Alberto. 1986. "Book review: Impresa collettiva e schiavo 'manager' in Roma antica (II sec. a.C. - II sec. d.C.)." 32 *Labeo. Rassegna di diritto romano* 204–15.

Bürge, Alfons. 1988. "Book review: Impresa collettiva e schiavo 'manager' in Roma antica (II sec. a.C. - II sec. d.C.)." 105 *Zeitschrift der Savigny Stiftung für Rechtsgeschichte* 856–65.

Bürge, Alfons. 1999. *Römisches Privatrecht*. Darmstadt: Wissenschaftliche Buchgesellschaft.

Bürge, Alfons. 2010. "Lo schiavo (in)dipendente e il suo patrimonio," in Alessandro Corbino, Michel Humbert, Giovanni Negri, eds, *Homo, caput, persona: la costruzione giuridica dell'identità*. Padua: IUSS Press, 369–91.

Bürge, Alfons. 2012. "Synchronische und diachronische Rechtsvergleichung als Instrument zur Gewinnung von Tiefenschärfe," in Tomasz Giaro, ed., *Roman Law and Legal Knowledge. Studies in Memory of Henryk Kupiszewski*. Warsaw: Warsaw University Press, 37–49.

Carlsen, Jesper. 2010. "Recruitment and Training of Roman Estate Managers in a Comparative Perspective," in Ulrike Roth, ed., *By the Sweat of Your Brow: Roman Slavery in Its Socio-Economic Setting*. London: Institute of Classical Studies, 75–90.

Ceci, Luigi. 1892. *La lingua del diritto romano*. Vol. 1: *Le etimologie dei giureconsulti romani*. Turin: Loescher.

Cerami, Pietro. 2008. "Impresa e *societas* nei primi due secoli dell'impero." 52 *Annali dell'Università di Palermo* 75–132.

Cerami, Pietro. 2010. "Book review: Ricerche sul peculio imprenditoriale." 58 *Iura* 336–44.

Cerami, Pietro, Andrea Di Porto, and Aldo Petrucci. 2004. *Diritto commerciale romano*, 2nd edn. Turin: Giappichelli.

Cerami, Pietro, and Aldo Petrucci. 2010. *Diritto commerciale romano: profilo storico*, 3rd edn. Turin: Giappichelli.

Chiusi, Tiziana J. 1993. "Contributo allo studio dell'editto *de tributoria actione*." 34 *Memorie dell'Accademia del Lincei series 9 vol. 3 fasc. 4* 277–399.

Chiusi, Tiziana J. 2007a. "Zum Zusammenspiel von Haftung und Organisation im römischen Handelsverkehr: *scientia, voluntas* und *peculium* in D. 14.1.19–20." 124 *Zeitschrift der Savigny-Stiftung für rechtsgeschichte RA*. 94–112.

Chiusi, Tiziana J. 2007b. "Diritto commerciale romano? Alcune osservazioni critiche," in Cosimo Cascione and Carla Masi Doria, eds, 2 *Fides Humanitas Ius. Studii in onore di L. Labruna*. Naples: Editoriale scientifica, 1025–41.

Coase, Ronald H. 1937. "The Nature of the Firm." 4 *Economica* 386–405.

de Ligt, Luuk. 1999. "Legal History and Economic History: The Case of the *actiones adiecticiae qualitatis*." 67 *Tijdschrift voor Rechtsgeschiedenis* 205–26.

de Ligt, Luuk. 2007. "Roman Law and the Roman Economy: Three Case Studies." 66 *Latomus* 11–23.

de Sainte Croix, Geoffrey E. M. 1956. "Greek and Roman Accounting," in Ananias C. Littleton and Basil S. Yamey, eds, *Studies in the History of Accounting*. London: Sweet and Maxwell, 14–74.

Di Porto, Andrea. 1984. *Impresa collettiva e schiavo "manager" in Roma antica (II sec. a.C. – II sec. d.C.)*. Milan: Giuffrè.

Di Porto, Andrea. 1997. "Il diritto commerciale romano. Una 'zona d'ombra' nella storiografia romanistica e nelle riflessioni storico-comparative dei commercialisti," in 3 *Nozione, formazione e interpretazione del diritto dall'età romana alle esperienze moderne. Ricerche dedicate al prof. F. Gallo*. Naples: Jovene, 413–52.

Easterbrook, Frank H., and Daniel R. Fischel. 1991. *The Economic Structure of Corporate Law*. Cambridge: Harvard University Press.

Fama, Eugene F. 1980. "Agency Problems and the Theory of the Firm." 88 *Journal of Political Economy* 288–307.

Fleckner, Andreas M. 2010. *Antike Kapitalvereinigungen: Ein Beitrag zu den konzeptionellen und historischen Grundlagen der Aktiengesellschaft*. Cologne: Böhlau.

Földi, András. 1996. "Remarks on the Legal Structure of Enterprises in Roman Law." 43 *Révue internationale des droits de l'antiquité* 179–211.

Foss, Nicolai J., Henrik Lando, and Steen Thomsen. 2000. "The Theory of the Firm," in Boudewijn Bouckaert and Gerrit De Geest, eds, 3 *Encyclopedia of Law and Economics*. Cheltenham: Edward Elgar, 631–58.

Frier, Bruce W. 1989/90. "Law, Economics and Disasters. Down on the Farm: *Remissio mercedis* revisited." 31/32 *Bullettino dell'Istituto di diritto romano* 237–70.

Frier, Bruce W., and Dennis P. Kehoe. 2007. "Law and Economic Institutions," in Walter Scheidel, Ian Morris, and Richard Saller, eds, *The Cambridge Economic History of the Greco-Roman World*. Cambridge: Cambridge University Press, 113–43.

Gaurier, Dominique. 2004. *Le Droit maritime romain*. Rennes: Presses Universitaires de Rennes.

Giliberti, Giuseppe. 1984. *Legatum kalendarii: mutuo feneratizio e struttura contabile del patrimonio nell'età del principato*. Naples: Jovene.

Gordon, William. 1983. "Agency and Roman Law," in 3 *Studi in Onore di Cesare Sanfilippo*. Milan: Giuffrè, 339–49.

Grossman, Sanford J., and Oliver D. Hart. 1986. "The Costs and Benefits of Ownership: A Theory of Vertical and Lateral Integration." 94 *Journal of Political Economy* 691–719.

Guarino, Antonio. 1957. "Actiones adiecticiae qualitatis," 1 *Novissimo Digesto Italiano*. Turin: Giappichelli, 271–5.

Guarino, Antonio. 1972 [reprint 1988]. *Societas consensu contracta*. Naples: Jovene.

Guarino, Antonio. 2001. *Diritto privato romano*, 12th edn. Naples: Jovene.

Hansmann, Henry B., Reinier Kraakman, and Richard Squire. 2006. "Law and the Rise of the Firm." 119 *Harvard Law Review* 1333–1403.

Hart, Oliver D. 1983. "The Market Mechanism as an Incentive Scheme." 14 *Bell Journal of Economics* 366–82.

Hart, Oliver D. 1989. "An Economist's Perspective on the Theory of the Firm." 89 *Columbia Law Review* 1757–74.

Hart, Oliver D., and John Moore. 1990. "Property Rights and the Nature of the Firm." 98 *Journal of Political Economy* 1119–58.

Holmström, Bengt, and Jean Tirole. 1989. "The Theory of the Firm," in Richard Schmalensee and Robert D. Willig, eds, 1 *Handbook of Industrial Organization*. Amsterdam: Elsevier, 61–133.

Jensen, Michael C., and William H. Meckling. 1976. "Theory of the Firm: Managerial Behavior, Agency Costs and Ownership Structure." 3 *Journal of Financial Economics* 305–60.

Jensen, Michael C. 1986. "Agency Costs of Free Cash Flow, Corporate Finance and Takeovers." 76 *American Economic Review* 323–9.

Jouanique, Pierre. 1986. "A propos de Digeste 35.1.82: survivances antiques dans la comptabilité moderne." 64 *Revue historique du droit français et étranger* 533–48.

Kaser, Max. 1971–5. 1–2 *Das Römische Privatrecht*. Munich: Beck.

La Rosa, Franca. 1965. "Peculium." 12 *Novissimo Digesto Italiano*. Turin: Giappichelli 755–7.

Labruna, Luigi. 1994. "Il diritto mercantile dei romani e l'espansionismo," in Alessandro Corbino, ed., *Le strade del potere. Maiestas populi romani. Imperium, coercitio, commercium*. Catania: Libreria editrice Torre, 115–29.

Lawson, Frederick H. 1969. *The Roman Law Reader*. New York: Oceana Publications.

Ligios Garbarino, Maria Antonietta. 2013. *Nomen negotiationis: profili di continuità e di autonomia della negotiatio nell'esperienza giuridica romana*. Turin: Giappichelli.

Littleton, Ananias C. 1953. *Structure of Accounting Theory*. Urbana: American Accounting Association.

Lo Cascio, Elio. 2006. "The Role of the State in the Roman Economy," in Peter Fibiger Bang, Mamoru Ikeguchi, and Harmut G. Ziche, eds, *Ancient Economies, Modern Methodologies: Archeology, Comparative History, Models and Institutions*. Bari: Edipuglia, 215–34.

Macve, Richard H. 1985. "Some Glosses on Greek and Roman Accounting," in Paul A. Cartledge and F. D. Harvey, eds, *Crux: Essays in Greek History*. London: Duckworth, 233–61.

Manne, Henry G. 1965. "Mergers and the Markets for Corporate Control." 73 *Journal of Political Economy* 110–20.

Maragno, Giorgia. 2013. "Diritto romano e economia: due modi di pensare e organizzare il mondo." 79 *Studia et documenta historiae et iuris* 1425–31.

Maucourant, Jérôme. 2004. "Rationalité économique ou comportements socio-économiques," in Jean Andreau, Jérôme France, and Sylvie Pittia, eds, *Mentalités et choix économiques des Romains*. Bordeaux: Ausonius, 227–38.

Mayer-Maly, Theo. 1984. "Book review: Impresa collettiva e schiavo 'manager' in Roma antica (II sec. a.C. – II sec. d.C.)." 35 *Iura* 115–17.

Meissel, Franz-Stefan. 2004. *Societas: Struktur und Typenvielfalt des römischen Gesellschaftvertrage*. Frankfurt am Main: Peter Lang.

Melillo, Generoso. 2005. "La giurisprudenza romana tra le sistematiche e la riflessione economica." 71 *Studia et documenta historiae et iuris* 565–83.

Miceli, Maria. 2008. *Studi sulla rappresentanza nel diritto romano*. Milan: Giuffrè.

Micolier, Gabriel. 1932. *Pécule et capacité patrimoniale: étude sur le pécule, dit profectice, depuis l'édit de peculio jusqu'à la fin de l'époque classique*. Lyon: Bosc frères et L. Riou 371–448.

Milgrom, Paul, and John Roberts. 1992. *Economics, Organization, and Management*. Englewood Cliffs: Prentice-Hall.

Minaud, Gerard. 2005. *La comptabilité à Rome: essai d'histoire économique sur la pensée comptable commerciale et privée dans le monde antique romain*. Lausanne: Presses polytechniques et universitaires Romandes.

Montanari, Massimo. 1990. *Impresa e responsabilità: sviluppo storico e disciplina positiva*. Milan: Giuffrè.

Morris, Ian, and Barry R. Weingast. 2004. "Views and Comments on Institutions, Economics and the Ancient Mediterranean World: Introduction." 160 *Journal of Institutional and Theoretical Economics* 702–8.

North, Douglass C., and Barry R. Weingast. 1989. "Constitutions and Commitment: The Evolution of Institutions Governing Public Choice in Seventeenth-Century England." 49 *Journal of Economic History* 803–32.

Pesaresi, Roberto. 2008. *Ricerche sul peculium imprenditoriale*. Bari: Cacucci.

Polara, Giovanni. 2010 "Autonomia, controllo del mercato e regola giuridica nell'esperienza storica del commercio," in Carmela Russo Ruggeri, ed., 5 *Studi in onore di Antonino Metro*. Milan: Giuffrè, 1–72.

Rathbone, Dominic. 1991. *Economic Rationalism and Rural Society in Third-Century A.D. Egypt: The Heroninos Archive and the Appianus Estate*. Cambridge: Cambridge University Press.

Rathbone, Dominic. 1994. "Accounting on a Large Estate in Roman Egypt," in Robert H. Parker and Basil S. Yamey, eds, *Accounting History: Some British Contributions*. Oxford: Clarendon Press, 13–56.

Reduzzi Merola, Francesca. 1990. *Servo parere: studi sulla condizione giuridica degli schiavi vicari e dei sottoposti a schiavi nelle esperienze greca e romana*. Naples: Jovene.

Reduzzi Merola, Francesca. 2007. "Servi ordinari e schiavi vicari nei *responsa* di Servio e nel teatro di Plauto," in Francesca Reduzzi Merola, ed., *Forme non convenzionali di dipendenza nel mondo antico*. Naples: Satura, 21–9.

Ross, Stephen A. 1973. "The Economic Theory of Agency: The Principal's Problem." 63 *American Economic Review* 134–9.

Sanfilippo, Cesare. 1951. "Sulla irrilevanza esterna del rapporto di società." 2 *Iura* 159–61.

Schiavone, Aldo. 1996. *La storia spezzata: Roma antica e Occidente modern*. Bari: Laterza.

Serrao, Feliciano. 1971. "Sulla rilevanza sterna del rapporto di società in diritto romano," in 5 *Studi in onore di Edardo Volterra*. Milan: Giuffrè, 743–67.

Serrao, Feliciano. 2000. "Impresa, mercato, diritto, Riflessioni minime," in Elio Lo Cascio, ed., *Mercati permanenti e mercati periodici nel mondo romano. Atti degli Incontri capresi di storia dell'economia antica. Capri 13–15 ottobre 1999*. Bari: Edipuglia, 31–67.

Stolfi, Emanuele. 2009. "La soggettività commerciale dello schiavo: soluzioni greche e romane." 2 *Teoria e Storia del Diritto Privato* 33–47.

Talamanca, Mario. 1990. *Società (diritto romano)*. 42 *Enciclopedia del diritto*. Milan: Giuffrè 814–60.

Temin, Peter. 2001. "A Market Economy in the Early Roman Empire." 91 *Journal of Roman Studies* 169–81.

Thilo, Ralf M. 1980. *Der Codex accepti et expensi im Römischen Recht: Ein Beitrag zur Lehre von der Litteralobligation*. Göttingen: Muster-Schmidt.

Verboven, Koenraad. 2011. "Professional *collegia*: Guilds or Social Clubs?" 41 *Ancient Society* 187–93.

Wacke, Andreas. 1997. "Alle origini della rappresentanza diretta: le azioni adiettizie," 2 *Nozione, formazione e interpretazione del diritto dall'età romana alle esperienze moderne. Ricerche dedicate a F. Gallo*. Naples: Jovene, 583–615.

Waelkens, Laurent. 2000. "Gaius IV, 73: debet ou debetur?" 68 *Tijdschrift voor Rechtsgeschiedenis* 347–56.

Watson, Alan, ed. 1985 (rev. edn, 2009). *The Digest of Justinian*. Philadelphia: University of Pennsylvania Press.
Watson, Alan. 1987. *Roman Slave Law*. Baltimore: Johns Hopkins University Press.
Zimmermann, Martin. 2012. "Die Haftung des Reeders mit der *actio exercitoria*: Ein Beitrag zur ökonomischen Analyse des römischen Rechts." 129 *Zeitschrift der Savigny-Stiftung für Rechtsgeschichte RA* 554–70.

11

Mandate and the Management of Business in the Roman Empire

Dennis P. Kehoe

A major debate about the economy of the Roman Empire has focused on the question of economic growth. The question is whether the Roman Empire achieved economic growth beyond what could be accounted for by an increase in population alone. It would have done so at least in part by developing legal institutions surrounding the economy that would have encouraged productive economic relationships among people, so that resources could be used "efficiently," by finding their highest valued use.[1] The alternative is that law and legal institutions served primarily to protect the interests of a well-connected elite, which was able to capture the lion's share of the surplus produced by an increasing rural population.[2] In this circumstance, there would be little capacity for innovation and growth in the Roman economy, and little possibility for significant changes in the economy that would have made possible a more broadly shared prosperity. One crucial and vast area of the law that potentially affected the organization of the economy to a significant degree is agency, since in virtually all sectors of the economy Roman property owners had to rely on others to manage their property or to carry out significant transactions on their behalf.[3] As is commonly pointed out,

[1] For the relationship between urbanism and economic growth in the Roman Empire, see Wilson (2009), commenting on Scheidel (2009); as well as Temin (2013: 195–219).

[2] On the first theme in medieval and early modern Europe, see Ogilvie (2007).

[3] For general theoretical discussion of the problem of agency, see Furubotn and Richter (2005: 162–70).

Dennis P. Kehoe, *Mandate and the Management of Business in the Roman Empire* In: *Roman Law and Economics: Institutions and Organizations, Volume I.* Edited by: Giuseppe Dari-Mattiacci and Dennis P. Kehoe, Oxford University Press (2020). © Oxford University Press.
DOI: 10.1093/oso/9780198787204.003.0011

Roman law had no provision for the type of agency relationship that is fundamental to modern commerce, since it was not possible for one person to engage in direct representation by creating obligations between a principal and a third party, as a designated employee of a modern firm can. This lack of direct agency was long thought to be a major impediment to the development of long-lasting commercial enterprises.[4] Even so, it is clear that in the Roman Empire complex agency relationships did exist, and in recent years, scholars have used increasingly sophisticated methodologies to examine how property owners used social dependents, slaves and freedmen, to perform important commercial functions.

Analyzing a system of agency relying primarily on social dependents, however, only tells part of the story of the organization of commercial life in the Roman Empire, since there were numerous undertakings for which the use of social dependents did not provide an appropriate solution to agency problems. Roman property owners tended to rely on people of their own social class to perform many important functions, including guaranteeing the performance of contracts, standing surety in credit arrangements, buying and selling estates, and serving as a general manager of one's property. This type of agency, which was in theory gratuitous, was defined in terms of the Roman contract of mandate, *mandatum*, or, in some cases, "unauthorized administration," *negotia gesta*.[5] The form of gratuitous agency encompassed under mandate presents particular analytical problems, since it is difficult to identify the incentives that could help to align the interests of the agents with those of the principals. Still, the type of agency legally defined as mandate remained an important institution throughout the period of classical and post-classical Roman law, and so provided an important complement to other forms of agency in Roman commerce. As I will argue, its duration as an institution resulted from its success in facilitating economic activity by helping people overcome deficiencies

[4] For Roman definitions of agency, see Plescia (1984), discussed in Frier and Kehoe (2007: 127–34).

[5] Another form of agency, involving prosecuting or defending against lawsuits on behalf of another in a court of law also involved the contract of mandate, but since it was not directly linked with the management of property, it deserves a separate treatment. For discussion of the economic significance of the legal rules surrounding tutorship, another significant form of agency, see Kehoe (2013); as well as Saller (1994: 181–203).

in information that otherwise would have imposed serious impediments to providing credit or undertaking other economically significant investments. At the same time, the contract of mandate imposed potential costs on transactions, since it favored the interests of the principal over those of the agent and the third party doing business with the agent.[6]

11.1. MANDATE AS A CONTRACT

Mandate is defined as a contract in which an agent, the *mandatarius*, obligated himself to carry out a financial function on behalf of another, the principal, or *mandator*, on that person's instruction.[7] The services that the agent in mandate performed could encompass just about any type of financial transaction, but to judge by its treatment by the Roman jurists, as well as by the imperial chancery when it responded to petitions, these services commonly involved purchasing land, slaves, or other valuable commodities, making loans, paying off loans, and serving as a guarantor or surety, *fideiussor*, for a loan. The business involved could be that of the mandator or a third party, or that of the agent and the mandator, but never the agent's own. As the jurist Gaius (D. 17.1.2 pr.–6; 2 *rer. cottid. sive aureorum*) emphasizes, the mandate cannot simply be for the interest of the agent; if a person instructed another to take some financial action that would be to the latter's benefit, this would simply be "advice," *consilium*.

Mandate was a consensual contract, like sale, lease, and partnership, and it probably became defined as a contract and therefore actionable in the courts in the late second century BCE. Like other consensual contracts, it was based on the good faith of both of the parties. In a trial arising from mandate, the *iudicium mandati*, a

[6] In a second paper, Kehoe (2017), I address more directly the policy considerations of the Roman legal authorities in treating mandate and unauthorized administration. All translations from Book IV of the Code of Justinian are taken from my translations in Frier (2017). All other translations of legal sources are my own.

[7] For general discussion of mandate, see Kaser (1971: 577–83); Zimmermann (1996: 413–32); as well as Randazzo (2005). For a concise overview of mandate and related agency relationships in Roman law, see Aubert (1994: 100–14). The basic definition is in Gai., *Inst.* 3.155, and 3.161.

judgment against the agent or mandatary could involve *infamia*, a very serious penalty.[8] But in contrast to the other consensual contracts, it was not an altogether bi-lateral relationship, since the performance of the mandate was to be completely gratuitous. Any benefit arising from the actions taken by the agent was to accrue to the mandator. The mandator could sue for this through the *actio mandati*, whereas the agent was entitled to recover any expenses that he undertook while performing the mandate through the *actio mandati contraria*. A person asked to perform a mandate had the right to refuse to do so, but once he accepted it, he was obliged to see his assignment to its completion in accordance with good faith (D. 17.1.22.1; Paul. 32 *ad ed.*).[9] When the performance of business was without the principal's knowledge or authorization, the contractual relationship between the parties was defined as "unauthorized administration," *negotia gesta*, in which the same rules about good faith applied.[10]

Mandate originated as a contract between parties of an equal social status, although, as I will argue later (§§11.3, 4), in the imperial period it could be applied flexibly to a variety of situations. As Randazzo (2005) argues, the contract of mandate developed out of reciprocal relationships among Roman property owners based on *fides*, *amicitia*, and *officium*, upper-class values that find their origin in archaic and Republican Rome. Romans traditionally viewed the violation of a mandate as a great disgrace.[11] It is debatable whether its creation is

[8] See Kaser (1971: 274–5): the disabilities might include restrictions on the capacity to bring and plead cases in court. See also Nörr (1993: 15 n. 10). For the process by which the legal disabilities in the Praetor's Edict and legislation in the late Republic and early Principate evolved into the concept of *infamia*, see Wolf (2010).

[9] D. 17.1.22.1 (Paul. 32 *ad ed.*): "Just as one is free not to take up a mandate, so too must a mandate, once taken up, be completed, unless it has been renounced..." (*Sicut autem liberum est mandatum non suscipere, ita susceptum consummari oportet, nisi renuntiatum sit....*)

[10] For *negotia gesta*, see Kaser (1971: 586–90); and Zimmermann (1996: 433–50).

[11] Randazzo (2005: 84–5), based on Cicero, *Pro Roscio Amerino* 111–14. For exploration of the relationship between the services commonly provided through mandate and the Roman conception of the reciprocal obligations arising out of friendship, see Nörr (1993). Mandate and *negotia gesta* are likely to have developed from the services provided by friends representing one another in court as procurators or cognitors: see Nörr (1993: 26), with Kaser (1971: 587), and Kaser and Hackl (1996: 211–12). Another theory is that mandate developed from Roman public law, when individuals acted on behalf of the community; see Winkel (1993), with discussion of previous theories.

directly comparable to that of the other consensual contracts, which have been viewed by many scholars, and most recently Schiavone, as connected with the efforts of the praetors in the second century BCE to incorporate the "law of nations," or *ius gentium*, into Roman law to facilitate commerce and other economic relationships with non-citizens.[12] The (at least originally) reciprocal nature of mandate and its role as an upper-class institution excluded the possibility of direct compensation; the performance of a financial transaction or another service in exchange for pay was considered a work contract, falling under the category of *locatio-conductio*.[13] As the early third-century jurist Paul emphasized: "There is no mandate unless it is gratuitous, for it draws its origin from duty and friendship, and payment is contrary to duty. So when money is involved the matter looks rather toward lease and hire" (D. 17.1.1.4; Paul. 32 *ad ed.*).[14] The one type of compensation that could be claimed was the honorarium, which, perhaps fictitiously, was not interpreted as direct compensation for work, but instead as a recognition of the agent for his services rendered. But the honorarium was formally distinct from the contract of mandate. Thus, by the Severan period, the honorarium was recoverable through the law courts, but the agent had to pursue it through *cognitio extraordinaria*, rather than through an action on mandate. Accordingly, in a rescript, the emperors Septimius Severus and Caracalla emphasized that the petitioner was entitled to seek the expenses he incurred in performing the business of another, whether they were from his own funds or he had to borrow to meet them, through the action on mandate, but he had to seek the salary promised by the mandator separately (Severus and Caracalla, C. 4.35.1).[15] That some kind of compensation was commonly associated with mandate in the Severan age is strongly suggested in a text from Papinian, who

[12] Schiavone (2012: esp. 142).

[13] On the payment of honoraria in mandate, see Verboven (2002: 246–9).

[14] D. 17.1.1.4 (Paul. 32 *ad ed.*): *Mandatum nisi gratuitum nullum est: nam originem ex officio atque amicitia trahit, contrarium ergo est officio merces: interveniente enim pecunia res ad locationem et conductionem potius respicit.*

[15] C. 4.35.1: "You can sue a person whose affairs have been managed (by you) for the money you have spent from your own resources or received on loan from others, in an action on mandate for the principal and interest; a hearing will be offered by the provincial governor concerning the honorarium (*salarium*) he promised." (*Adversus eum cuius negotia gesta sunt, de pecunia, quam de propriis opibus vel ab aliis mutuo acceptam erogasti, mandati actione pro sorte et usuris potes experiri: de salario quod promisit a praeside provinciae cognitio praebebitur.*)

distinguishes between a salary sought through *cognitio ordinaria* by a procurator (here pleading a case on a mandate) and someone purchasing the outcome of a lawsuit; only in the former case would there be any need to abide by the faith of the agreement (D. 17.1.7; Papin. 3 *resp.*).[16] Ulpian, moreover, distinguishes between a procurator receiving a salary from one acting simply on the mandate; the former would follow different rules for seeking to recover his expenses, since he could be expected to cover them from his salary (D. 17.1.10.9; Ulp. 31 *ad ed.*).

As in other Roman contracts, the penalty that arose from an adverse judgment in the *iudicium mandati* was monetary; there was no provision for specific performance. In addition, the successful plaintiff was entitled to his interest in the contract's being performed. Thus, for example, a property owner who had mandated the purchase of property would be entitled to receive the value of the property if the agent did not provide him with it, as well as the value of any crops harvested from it, together with any interest that might be due for any delay in providing these items. Likewise, the agent would be entitled to any expenditures that he had made in good faith, as well as interest. Thus Ulpian, quoting Labeo, includes, among the expenses that a procurator acting on a mandate might claim, the costs of harvesting the crops that were to be turned over to the owner, as well as his transportation costs in traveling to the property (D. 17.1.10.9; Ulp. 31 *ad ed.*).[17] The principle that the mandator or agent was entitled to

[16] D. 17.1.7 (Papin. 3 *resp.*): "If an honorarium (*salarium*) established for a procurator is sought in an extraordinary procedure, it will have to be considered whether the owner wanted to provide remuneration for work and for that reason faith must be kept for what has been agreed upon, or whether he purchased the outcome of lawsuits with a reward of greater money in violation of good morals." (*Salarium procuratori constitutum si extra ordinem peti coeperit, considerandum erit, laborem dominus remunerare voluerit atque ideo fidem adhiberi placitis oporteat an eventum litium maioris pecuniae praemio contra bonos mores procurator redemerit.*)

[17] D. 17.1.10.9 (Ulp. 31 *ad ed.*): "Labeo also says and it is true that this judgment also admits computations, and just as the one who serves as procurator is compelled to restore fruits, so too must he deduct the expense that he made in capturing the fruits. But if he incurred an expense for his transportation while he ran forth to the estate, I think he must also take consideration of these expenses, unless he was under salary and this was agreed that he cover the expenses from his own money, that is from his honorarium (*salarium*)." (*Idem Labeo ait et verum est reputationes quoque hoc iudicium admittere et, sicuti fructus cogitur restituere is qui procurat, ita sumptum, quem in fructus percipiendos fecit, deducere eum oportet: sed et si ad vecturas suas, dum excurrit in praedia, sumptum fecit, puto hos quoque sumptus reputare eum oportere,*

recover his interest in an action on mandate makes the damages from this contract, as with other Roman consensual contracts, similar to modern "expectation" damages, so that the successful plaintiff would receive not only any expenses he had made in connection with the contract, but also any lost profits.[18] This is illustrated in a text from Ulpian concerning a mandate to purchase property (D. 17.1.12.9; Ulp. 31 *ad ed.*; also discussed below, §11.5). The agent would not only be entitled to recover what he had spent on purchasing the property, but also interest. The interest would not simply be calculated on the basis of any delay in payment; in addition, the agent would be entitled to foregone interest if he called in his own loans, or had to borrow money at interest, to come up with funds to make the purchase for the mandator. Similarly, the agent would be liable to pay interest if, having received a mandate to do so, he failed to use funds that he received from the mandator to pay off that person's debt (D. 17.1.12.10; Ulp. 31 *ad ed.*).

In late classical jurisprudence, the agent was defined as liable to the mandator in the *actio mandati directa* for deliberate misconduct (*dolus*) and for fault (*culpa*). For example, when discussing a mandate to purchase a slave, Ulpian emphasizes the principle that the agent was responsible to restore the slave to the mandator when he purchased him (D. 17.1.8.10; Ulp. 31 *ad ed.*). If the agent failed to purchase the slave, he would be liable to the mandator if his failure resulted from his deliberate misconduct, or *dolus*, say if he had accepted money to allow someone else to buy the slave, or his "broad negligence," or *lata culpa*, if, for example, someone's influence, *gratia*, led him to allow that person to buy the slave.[19] But after purchasing the slave the agent would be liable to deliver him, unless the slave escaped without his deliberate misconduct or fault.[20] Later,

nisi si salariarius fuit et hoc convenit, ut sumptus de suo faceret ad haec itinera, hoc est de salario.)

18 Mahoney (2000: 121); Frier and White (2005: 468–545), discussed further in Kehoe (2015: 237).

19 "Broad negligence," or *lata culpa*, refers to a failure to do what any reasonable person would do.

20 See D. 17.1.8.10 (Ulp. 31 *ad ed.*): "Accordingly if I have given a mandate to you that you buy a person, and you bought him, you are liable to me to restore him. But if you neglected to buy him out of deliberate misconduct (*dolus*) (say perhaps, after taking money you yielded to another so that he might buy him), or out of broad negligence (say if induced by influence you allowed another to buy him), you are held liable. But if the slave you bought flees, if this is as a result of your own deliberate misconduct, you are

in a rescript concerning the responsibilities of a procurator serving in his post pursuant to a mandate, the emperor Diocletian stated that the procurator was liable both for actions that he took, such as enforcing debts owed to the principal, as well as for action not taken, such as failing to enforce debts, whether as a result of deliberate misconduct or *culpa* (C. 4.35.11, Sirmium, 293 CE).[21] The agent's liability would be balanced against the expenses that he had made in good faith in performing his office.[22] Similarly, in another constitution of the same year, Diocletian ruled that a procurator was responsible for *culpa* and *dolus* but not for an unforeseen accident (*inprovisum casum*; C. 4.35.13). As Zimmermann argues, the notion of "fault", or *culpa*, was different from the rather precise definitions of *culpa* that the jurists developed for delicts, as with the *lex Aquilia* on damage to property, and it was likely judged on a case-by-case basis what constituted the good faith administration of his duties by the agent.[23] Thus an agent who failed to carry out a mandate to purchase

liable, but if neither misconduct nor fault is involved, you are not liable unless to this extent, that you promise to restore him if he in comes into your power." (*Proinde si tibi mandavi, ut hominem emeres, tuque emisti, teneberis mihi, ut restituas. Sed et si dolo emere neglexisti (forte enim pecunia accepta alii cessisti ut emeret) aut si lata culpa (forte si gratia ductus passus es alium emere), teneberis. Sed et si servus quem emisti fugit, si quidem dolo tuo, teneberis, si dolus non intervenit nec culpa, non teneberis nisi ad hoc, ut caveas, si in potestatem tuam pervenerit, te restituturum.*)

[21] As Klinck (2007) argues, the term procurator in classical Roman law has no specific, overarching legal significance. In the Republic and the early classical period, the term encompassed a range of functions, including persons legally authorized to pursue a case in court on behalf of another, the *procurator omnium bonorum*, managing all of the property of another and on that basis having the authority to appear in court, and the *procurator absentis*, who appeared in court on behalf of a person who was away and unable to appear personally. The procurator acting as a business manager pursuant to a mandate was a development of classical jurisprudence in the second century. See also Wittmann (1993) 43: originally freedmen appointed as procurators would be liable (and also could make claims) under *negotia gesta*. For procurators managing property on the basis of a mandate, see Schäfer (1998).

[22] C. 4.35.11: "A procurator must be responsible not only for those things that he has managed, but also for those things that he has undertaken to manage, both for the money exacted on the basis of his mandate as well as money not exacted, and also for deliberate misconduct as well as fault, with account taken for his expenses in accordance with good faith." (*Procuratorem non tantum pro his quae gessit, sed etiam pro his quae gerenda suscepit, et tam propter exactam ex mandato pecuniam quam non exactam, tam dolum quam culpam, sumptuum ratione bona fide habita, praestare necesse est.*)

[23] Zimmermann (1996: 426–8). See also Finazzi (2010: 794–9), who discusses the view that in classical law agents acting on mandate were liable for *dolus* alone and only in the late classical period were they considered liable for *culpa*.

property would be liable if he failed to renounce the mandate as a result of his own *culpa* (D. 17.1.22.11; Paul. 32 *ad ed.*).

It is important to emphasize that neither mandate nor unauthorized administration represented direct agency in the modern sense, in that the agent acted on behalf of a principal and created reciprocal obligations between the principal and the third party with whom he did business. Instead, all obligations existed between the agent and the third party or between the agent and the principal. To some extent the Roman agent acting under mandate could more approximate a modern agent when he ceded actions against the third party to the principal (see below, §11.5). In addition, as Wacke (1994) argues, the origins of modern agency can be seen in the late classical treatment of the *actio institoria* (one of the *actiones* discussed in the next section), when a free person was appointed as a manager of a business; the late classical jurists under certain circumstances allowed claims directly between the principal and a third party, while the *institor* or manager, when acting in accordance with what the principal had assigned him to do, would assume no personal liability. But the "seeds" for modern agency that Wacke sees in the *actio institoria* were not to be found in mandate or unauthorized administration.

11.2. AGENCY THROUGH SLAVES AND FREEDMEN

The type of agency represented by mandate appears to contrast very distinctly from agency involving the hierarchical system represented by the Roman *familia*, which included both slaves and freedmen dependent on the property owner.[24] This type of agency involved setting up a slave as a business manager operating with some degree of autonomy. Endowed with a *peculium*, the slave agent would have every incentive to run his business productively, since he would be a kind of "residual claimant," able to retain some portion of the profits that he made. The property owner employing such an agent was to some extent shielded from the risk resulting from the activities of his slave agent, since the legal remedies by which a third party dealing

[24] For discussion of this aspect of agency, see Frier and Kehoe (2007: 130–4), and Kehoe (2015: 244–9); and for economic analysis of the incentives inherent in this system, Dari-Mattiacci (2013).

with an agent, the *actiones adiecticiae qualitatis*, established probably in the second century BCE, tended to limit the liability of the principal to the slave's *peculium* or the agent's profit from any transaction undertaken by the agent.[25] The property owner had a great deal of leverage over the slave agent, since he could use the decision whether to provide or withhold eventual freedom as a major incentive to align the agent's interests reasonably with his own. At the same time, as Mouritsen (2011) shows in his recent study of freedmen, freedmen often continued to perform similar economic functions within an aristocratic household as they had done as slaves. Since freedmen often undertook duties that involved a great deal of discretion and over which the patron could exercise little control, Roman property owners buttressed the very real leverage that they could exercise over their slaves and freedmen with an ideology that privileged a set of virtues, all centering around loyalty, that characterized the ideal freedman.[26]

The reliance on the inherently hierarchical structure of Roman slavery surely had important implications for the ways in which businesses were organized in the Roman world. Arguably, the use of agents who were residual claimants in their own right tended to make businesses decentralized. Agents in this situation would have a great deal of latitude to manage businesses independently, and the property owner's profit would depend on their providing him some remittance from their own profits; in some cases they would use their profits to purchase their freedom. Arguably, this system of agency made it difficult to maintain enterprises for the long-term as entities independent from the individuals who created them. However, in a recent article, Abatino et al. (2011) argue that a business run through slaves owned in a partnership, *negotiatio per servos communes*, created a structure to sustain long-term enterprises. This form of business organization provided the most important characteristics of modern firms, including continuity in spite of changes in personnel, direct agency, and the protection of the assets of the business's owners. But if, in theory, Roman property owners could achieve many of the

[25] On the *actiones adiecticiae qualitatis*, see Aubert (1994: 46–91); de Ligt (1999); and, for a thorough discussion of the appointment of an agent as a manager or a business, or *institor*, and of a ship's captain, or *exercitor*, see Wacke (1994). Wacke dates the *actiones adiecticiae* somewhat later, to the end of the second century BCE or the beginning of the first.

[26] Mouritsen (2011: 206–47).

advantages connected with modern firms by using slaves owned in common to manage businesses, relying on a slave with a *peculium* does not appear to be a convenient way to engage in many large-scale, high-stakes transactions, such as those involving the purchase or sale of land or lending substantial amounts of money. In this situation, using trusted friends or business acquaintances to undertake such transactions provided a potentially valuable solution, and the contract of mandate (and under some circumstances unauthorized administration) defined the rights and obligations of both parties in the relationship.[27]

11.3. AGENCY THROUGH MANDATE

To be sure, there were contracts of mandate that simply involved a trusted friend carrying out the wishes of the mandator. One example, commented on by the jurist Gaius (D. 17.1.13; Gai. 10 *ad ed. prov.*), involved purchasing land for the heirs of the mandator after his death. This mandate was enforceable, since the mandator's intention survived his death, but its origin lies in a concern for estate planning rather than in a commercial arrangement.[28] Similarly, the jurist Marcellus (D. 17.1.12.17; Ulp. 31 *ad ed.*) allowed the enforcement of a contract of mandate when it involved building a monument after the mandator's death. It was also possible to rely on personal friends to oversee the management of one's property. This possibility is suggested in a text of Ulpian, concerning the liability of a person who oversaw the actions of a property owner's procurator and slaves (D. 17.1.10.7; Ulp. 31 *ad ed.*).[29] The property owner mandated that

[27] On the important role of social relationships in the commercial life of the late Republic, see Verboven (2002: esp. 227–74 for the use of the contracts of mandate and unauthorized administration in these relationships).

[28] Normally the mandate was extinguished with the death of the mandator or the agent.

[29] D. 17.1.10.7 (Ulp. 31 *ad ed.*): "If someone mandated that those things that his procurator or slaves were managing be ratified only if they were carried out on the supervision of Sempronius, and the money was loaned out badly, Sempronius, who did nothing by deliberate fault, is not liable. And it is true that the one who intervened not with the intention of a procurator, but promised his friendly affection in in admonishing the procurators and managers and in guiding them with advice is not liable for mandate, but if he did anything out of deliberate misconduct, he is not liable for mandate, but rather for deliberate misconduct." (*Si quis ea, quae procurator suus et servi gerebant, ita demum rata esse mandavit, si interventu Sempronii gesta essent, et*

the actions taken by his procurator and slaves would only be considered ratified if they were carried out under the supervision (*interventu*) of a trusted person.[30] But then Ulpian goes on to distinguish between such a business manager who acts on mandate and a person who intervenes not as a procurator, but as someone providing friendly advice. In this case, the trusted person would not be liable under mandate (although he could be liable under a separate action for deliberate misconduct). The trusted person envisioned by Ulpian is reminiscent of Alypios, a landowner in his own right who played an important role in the management of the estate owned by the third-century Egyptian magnate Aurelius Appianus, as documented in the Heroninos archive.[31] It is hard to imagine that Alypios was an "employee" of Appianus in any meaningful sense. It seems more likely that he was performing a gratuitous service for Appianus, one that was essential to a long-term relationship that involved the reciprocal exchange of services.[32] This may be the type of arrangement that Paul imagined when he discussed the wide latitude of action for a procurator with the "free administration", *libera administratio*, of the principal's property (D. 3.3.58–9; Paul. 71 *ad ed.* and Paul. 10 *ad Plaut.*).

The reciprocity that provided the impetus for people to take on a gratuitous assignment to serve as large-scale business managers stood behind many contracts on mandate, but certainly not all. The Roman chancery interpreted as mandates a wide variety of business arrangements. We can see this in a response from Diocletian in 294 CE (C. 4.35.14, Sirmium): "If, in accordance with the mandate of Trypho and Felix, you have given to one of these, with the consent of both, horses purchased with your money or delivered to you as payment by your debtor, good faith compels them, when sued in a judgment on

male pecunia credita sit, Sempronium, qui nihil dolo fecit, non teneri. Et est verum eum, qui non animo procuratoris intervenit, sed affectionem amicalem promisit in monendis procuratoribus et actoribus et in regendis consilio, mandati non teneri, sed si quid dolo fecerit, non mandati, sed magis de dolo teneri.)

[30] In this case, the issue was whether the trusted friend would be liable for a loan that went bad. On this passage, see Finazzi (2010: 737–8, 756): the property owner and the friend could choose to maintain their relationship purely on a social rather than legal level.

[31] On the Heroninos archive, see Rathbone (1991: esp. 58–71) on the high social ranks of upper administrators of the estate.

[32] On this point, see Verboven (2002: 256–8).

the mandate, to comply with their agreement."[33] In this case, the petitioner, Hermianus, apparently had the task of acquiring horses for two individuals, Trypho and Felix, and he delivered some to them. In this circumstance, in the emperor's interpretation, Trypho and Felix would be compelled by good faith, essential to the contract of mandate, to compensate Hermianus for his expenses. Here, the chancery interpreted as an agreement to do business on behalf of another as a contract of mandate, even if the parties involved did not explicitly conceive of themselves as bound in this way or, for that matter, even if they were not aware that a contract of mandate existed.

The gratuitous nature of the mandate contract raises questions about the role that it played in the economic life of the empire. If the person performing the mandate was not supposed to profit from his service, under what conditions would it be advantageous to accept the responsibility to perform a mandate? In this connection, we might consider two rescripts issued by the emperor Gordian to soldiers. One of these (C. 4.35.6, 238 CE) concerns a person serving as a surety for someone who is defendant in a lawsuit. The rescript of the emperor affirmed that the surety would be able to regain from the defendant any expenditures on his part through an action on mandate.[34] In the second case (C. 4.35.7, undated), the petitioning soldier received a letter from an acquaintance to lend money to a third party. Apparently the petitioner had not been paid back, and so his petition concerned what recourse he might have to collect on his loan. The answer is that he has an action on mandate against the author of the letter, as well as an action (presumably on loan, *mutuum*) against the borrower.[35] Under ordinary circumstances, one would expect that

[33] C. 4.35.14: *Si secundum mandatum Tryphonis ac Felicis equos tua pecunia comparatos vel in solutum a proprio debitore tibi traditos uni de his utriusque voluntate dedisti, ad parendum placitis eos mandati iudicio conventos bona fides urguet.*

[34] C. 4.35.6: "If a surety, with the permission of the defendant, has bound his faith, he can bring an action for mandate against him after payment of the money or a condemnation has occurred." (*Si fideiussor pro reo patiente fidem suam adstrinxit, mandati cum eo post exsolutam pecuniam vel factam condemnationem potest exercere actionem.*)

[35] C. 4.35.7: "If, following the instructions in letter of the person who was its author, you lent funds to the person who handed the letter over to you, an action on mandate is available to you both against the person who received money on loan from you and against the person whose mandate you followed." (*Si litteras eius secutus, qui pecuniae auctor fuerat, ei qui tibi litteras tradidit pecunias credidisti, tam adversus eum, qui a te mutuam sumpsit, quam adversus eum, cuius mandatum secutus es,*

the soldier who made the loan would have been confident in the ability of the principal, the author of the letter, to repay him, or at least to protect him against any loss arising from the borrower's failing to repay. The services that the agents were performing for the mandators in these cases are unlikely to have been one-off transactions, but instead stemmed from ongoing relationships. Upper-class Roman notions of duty and reciprocity may help to account for the origins of the contract of mandate, but they do not provide an adequate explanation for the endurance of mandate as a social institution and a major component of Roman financial life. Rather, the explanation is to be found in a different type of reciprocity, one that involved people who were bound by enduring business relationships performing services for one another to promote their mutual interests.

11.4. MANDATE AND CREDIT

We can trace some of the essential features of mandate as an economic institution by considering its role in the provision of credit, which seems to have represented perhaps its most common use.[36] In credit, the contract of mandate could play two functions. One was that, in order presumably to receive credit or at least to receive it on more favorable terms, the borrower would request through a mandate that another person stand surety for him, that is, to serve as a *fideiussor*. The task of the *fideiussor* was to guarantee a loan by providing a formal promise to pay it off if the principal debtor defaulted.[37] The other major function of mandate in credit involved a person providing another with a mandate to provide credit, called the *mandatum credendae pecuniae*. In this case, the mandator would by law become a surety for the borrower.

To consider the role of the surety, this service potentially involved serious costs and risks, even when the original borrower was not in danger of defaulting. From one perspective, providing people to stand

mandati actio tibi competit.) There are some problems with the text: *mandati* in the last clause should perhaps be deleted, since the petitioner could not have any action on mandate against the borrower.

[36] On this point in general, see Wolf (2010: 548–49).

[37] On *fideiussio*, see Kaser (1971: 660–67).

as sureties for loans helped to speed the flow of credit, since the personal guarantee helped to overcome problems of information about the creditworthiness of the borrower, or about the possibility to make a profit from a business venture for which credit was being provided. The provision of credit under these conditions would form part of a system of a kind of "relational" contracting, in which business arrangements are commonly created within communities in which people have personal ties to one another.[38] Having a personal guarantor for a loan would make it possible to broaden the business community, and thus to speed the flow of capital, by overcoming some of the obstacles to lending money for potentially profitable business ventures, when the creditor might otherwise be deterred from doing so because he was not sufficiently familiar with the borrower. As Harris points out, *fideiussores* provided the principal form of security for the loans recorded in the Murecine tablets from Pompeii. The Murecine tablets are documents that come from the archive of Sulpicii, a group of moneylenders active at Puteoli in the first century CE; the tablets document a wide range of business activities, particularly loans.[39] In view of his overall argument about the widespread use of credit across all levels of Roman society, this situation suggests that the requests to stand surety or to provide credit are likely to have played an important role in facilitating credit arrangements across Roman society.[40] One of the documents from this collection (*TPSulp.* 45), preserves an arrangement that a merchant named C. Iulius Prudens arranged with a partner in the circle of the Sulpicii, C. Sulpicius Cinnamus, to provide for continuing credit to his agents or employees, including a freedman, Suavis, a slave, Hyginus, and any other persons who might be involved in the future. The document includes a mandate to provide funds to these personnel, either as loans or as guarantees for loans, as well as a stipulation to repay any funds expended under these circumstances. As Wolf argues, the mandate, because of its faulty formulation, would have been only enforceable in part.[41] However, the document does indicate how merchants and a group of professional moneylenders sought to

[38] See Dixit (2004).

[39] See especially Wolf (2001), as well as Lerouxel (2016: 193–244).

[40] Harris (2006: 9), as well as Camodeca (2003: 90). For an analysis of the trading community at Puteoli traceable in the Murecine tablets, see Terpstra (2013: 9–49), discussed in Ratzan et al. (2015: 20–25).

[41] Wolf (1993).

use mandate and suretyship as part of an enduring business relationship. As Granovetter argues, the existence of "dense" networks of people involved in related commercial activities, such as among the people involved in commerce documented in the Murecine tablets, can reduce information costs. In his analysis of the medieval trading networks, Greif argues that the Jewish merchants documented in the medieval Cairo Geniza relied on a tight network of merchants across the Mediterranean and created their own merchants law to enforce obligations.[42] However, access to such networks, as Granovetter points out, could encourage people to depend on familiar trading partners, and so diminish their incentive to seek new opportunities.[43] To return to the Roman world, the contract of mandate provided a way to describe such arrangements in terms of formal Roman legal conventions.

The role that mandates to guarantee loans played in Rome's credit market can be traced in a text from Ulpian (D. 46.1.10 pr., Ulp. 7 *disput.*), concerning the creditor's uncertainty about the insolvency of the sureties. In the scenario discussed by Ulpian, one of the sureties was prepared to offer a formal promise that the other sureties would be liable at his risk. In Ulpian's view, this provision would be binding for the creditor, as long as the surety making the offer provided suitable security (*satisdationes*) and the co-sureties who were solvent were present.[44] The point is that the formal promise by the one surety and the process that was to accompany it provided a way of reducing risk for a creditor in a transaction in which the creditor's knowledge about the people from whom he would potentially be seeking to recover his loan was imperfect. Having the solvent sureties present was important because it might otherwise be very difficult for the creditor to determine whether they had other obligations that might prevent them from fulfilling their potential obligations towards him.

[42] Greif (2006: 59–90). [43] Granovetter (2005).

[44] D. 46.1.10 pr. (Ulp. 7 *disput.*): "If the creditor should doubt whether the sureties are solvent, and one chosen by him should be prepared to offer a formal promise that his co-sureties might be sued at his risk, in part I say that he should be heard, but only if he both offers security and all the co-sureties, who are said to be solvent, are present. For the purchase of a debt is not always easy, when the payment of the entire debt is not at hand." (*Si dubitet creditor, an fideiussores solvendo sint, et unus ab eo electus paratus sit offerre cautionem, ut suo periculo confideiussores conveniantur, in parte dico audiendum eum esse, ita tamen, et si satisdationes offerat et omnes confideiussores, qui idonei esse dicuntur, praesto sint: nec enim semper facilis est nominis emptio, cum numeratio totius debiti non sit in expedito.*)

Having multiple sureties obviously reduced the risk for the creditor, but it might be demanded in a credit arrangement because of the difficulties involved in determining the credit-worthiness of business partners. A seemingly wealthy guarantor, for example, might face financial catastrophe because of debts to the Fiscus arising from a civic liturgy.

Sureties provided an additional advantage, because they made it easier for creditors to pursue informal means, or "private ordering," that is, seeking payment by means other than suing the debtor or confiscating the property pledged and selling it. Thus a number of legal texts indicate that borrowers regularly provided sureties even when they also pledged property to secure loans. Thus Papinian (D. 46.1.51.2, Papin. 3 *resp.*) remarks that the creditor, when the borrower had not paid off the loan, need not sell the pledged property and use the proceeds from such a sale to cover the loan, if he preferred to sue the surety. The creditor might choose to proceed against the surety rather than taking the seemingly more obvious step of selling the pledges because the latter step could be require a great deal of time and have an uncertain result, especially if the value of the property pledged as security had declined. To judge by a series of constitutions on this issue in the third century,[45] it must have been quite common for creditors to prefer the simpler procedure of exacting payment from sureties rather than selling the borrower's pledges. This does not mean that creditors would necessarily have to sue to recover loans that otherwise would have gone bad. Rather, the creditor could negotiate about repayment with a solvent surety, and leave him the task of recovering from the original borrower on an action on mandate. Having multiple parties involved and potentially liable in a high-stakes credit arrangement afforded much more flexibility in finding a way in paying off the loan. This had the added advantage of protecting a defaulting borrower from *infamia*, which would be the result in an adverse judgment.[46]

The mandate to lend money (*mandatum pecuniae credendae*) also provided a contractual method to create complex credit relationships, and thus also to help speed the flow of capital. In this arrangement,

[45] C. 8.40.2 pr.–1 (207 CE), 8.40.5 (214 CE), 8.40.17 (242 CE), 8.40.19 (293 CE), and 8.40.20 (293 CE).

[46] For discussion of the significance of private ordering to resolve disputes in the archive of the Sulpicii, see Broekaert (2017).

the mandator would request that an agent provide a loan to a third party, and by law the mandator would stand surety for the loan. One can imagine that there would be many circumstances under which such an arrangement might be viewed as advantageous. The mandator would in all likelihood have a direct interest in the credit's being extended, and so would be willing to back up any loan. However, the creditor still bore some costs and risks. This can be seen in a rescript concerning a person who received a mandate to provide a loan but failed to accept pledges, in violation of the mandate (C. 8.40.7, 215). In this case, the creditor had no claim against the mandator in an action on mandate, since the mandator was interpreted as not having obligated himself unless that loan had been contracted with property pledged as security. The question is what incentives existed for the lender to take up a mandate under these circumstances. A hint to the possible answer can be found in a rescript from Valerian and Gallienus (C. 4.35.8, 259 CE). In this case, the petitioner had a mandate from a now deceased person to lend money to that person's slaves for his benefit, and, on the mandator's instructions, property was pledged as security. In the emperors' ruling, the petitioner had the right to sue the mandator's heirs, who were pupils (wards), on mandate, and to pursue the pledges, if the loan was not repaid.[47] In this case, the original principal in this arrangement used a mandate to lend because the agent was in a position to advance money to his slaves more quickly than he could himself. Whatever the precise circumstances were that stood behind this arrangement, the mandate to lend money facilitated arranging credit when the principal had liquidity problems or perhaps the loan was for a transaction to occur in a place where the principal could not be present.

The important role that providing sureties acting under a mandate played in overcoming information problems in the credit market can also be seen in other types or transactions. Certainly a transaction

[47] C. 4.35.8: "If (before his death) the father of the wards gave a mandate to you to lend money to his slaves for his benefit and pledges were given also for this purpose at his own instruction, you will be able both to sue the wards on an action on mandate after the death of their father and, if they fail to pay, to enforce your right from the obligation of the pledges." (*Si tibi pupillorum pater, ut pecuniam in rem suam servis eius crederes, mandavit et in hanc rem aeque ipso praecipiente pignora sunt obligata, et mandati actione pupillos post mortem patris convenire et exsequi ius obligationis pignorum poteris, si in solutione cessabitur.*)

that involved significant risk was the purchase of land; because of the lack of complete and up to date records and the possibility of contesting wills, the precise, legally binding title to a property might be uncertain. Customarily sellers of real estate had to guarantee against the eviction of the buyer by offering a stipulation to pay double the purchase price in this event.[48] When selling land, a property owner could offer added assurance to the buyer by providing a *fideiussor*. Thus Scaevola discusses the ability of a surety to recover from the heir of the seller of two farms when the buyer was evicted from one of them (D. 46.1.45, Scaev. 6 *dig.*). The involvement of sureties could help to overcome information problems and thus to lower transaction costs in many types of arrangements.

11.5. COSTS ON AGENTS AND THIRD PARTIES

The importance of mandate as a social institution is suggested by the way in which the advantages gained from reciprocity outweighed the potential costs and risks imposed on both on the agent and on the third party who did business with the agent. We can gain a better understanding of mandate as a social institution by considering in detail the types of transactions for which it seems typically to have been used, and then to consider how Roman law defined the rights and obligations of the parties to the contract. The point of this investigation will be to come to a better understanding of the likely incentives that arose from a contract of mandate, as well as to understand how and to what extent the Roman legal authorities formulated rules surrounding mandate to promote these putative incentives. Certainly a person could issue a mandate for just about any type of transaction, but the types of transactions that seem to loom largest in the legal sources, as mentioned above, perhaps because of the legal complications that arose in connection with them, concern, in addition to the provision of credit, purchasing property and managing businesses for the mandator as a procurator.

[48] On the *stipulatio duplae*, see Kaser (1971: 555–56). For analysis of the role of records for land in encouraging economic activity, see Lerouxel (2015), with Dari-Mattiacci (2015: 283–84).

To begin with the purchase of land, a mandate to perform this task posed potentially serious problems for the agent. These included the likelihood of having to spend substantial funds of his own to purchase the property and then to have to wait for compensation long after the fact, and the possibility that unanticipated circumstances might complicate the transaction, and thus put at risk the agent's legal claim for compensation for his expenses. At the same time, in most circumstances, there would be substantial asymmetries of information between the agent and the mandator, and the agent would potentially be in a position of taking advantage of his immediate knowledge of the business he was transacting to collude with the seller of the property by raising the purchase price in exchange for a kickback. Alternatively, the agent could simply be incompetent, and negotiate a purchase price that was far too high and so disadvantageous to the mandator. The problem of the agent's expenditures underlies a text of Paul, who affirms the right of the agent to recover his expenses when he had purchased a farm pursuant to a mandate, only to learn, after the fact, that the mandator rescinded his order (D. 17.1.15, Paul. 2 *ad Sab.*).[49] Disputes could arise when the mandator and agent did not share an explicit understanding about the price at which the purchase was to be made. When there was no explicit provision about the purchase price, as Paul states, both the agent and the mandator would be liable, the agent to perform the mandate and the mandator to compensate the agent (D. 17.1.3.1; Paul. 32 *ad ed.*). More controversial was the situation in which the agent purchased the property in question at a price higher than the mandator had ordered. As Paul describes, some jurists, including Sabinus, held that the agent had no action on mandate, even if the agent were willing to remit his claim on that part of the purchase price that exceeded the mandator's instruction (D. 17.1.3.2; Paul. 32 *ad ed.*).[50] However, Gaius quotes

[49] D. 17.1.15 (Paul. 2 *ad Sab.*): "If I had mandated to you that you buy a farm and afterward I wrote that you not buy it, but you bought it before you knew that I had forbidden it, I will be obligated to you on mandate, lest the person who undertakes a mandate be affected by a loss." (*Si mandassem tibi, ut fundum emeres, postea scripsissem, ne emeres, tu, antequam scias me vetuisse, emisses, mandati tibi obligatus ero, ne damno adficiatur is qui suscipit mandatum.*)

[50] This case stems from the famous controversy between the Sabinians and Proculians discussed by Gaius (*Inst.* 3.161) whether, if a person exceeds his mandate by purchasing a farm at a higher price than he was mandated to do, he has violated the faith of the mandate. On this controversy, see Nörr (1993: 15–20).

the view of first-century jurist Proculus that the agent would have a claim to recover his expenses up to the specified price (D. 17.1.4, Gai. 2 *rer. cottid. sive aur.*). The right of the mandator to recover after the fact did not eliminate the inconvenience that many agents would have to spend substantial funds of their own up front.

Proculus' solution raises an important question about mandate, since one can imagine that an agent could act in good faith by paying a higher purchase price than what the mandator had in mind; for example, if with changing market circumstances, in the agent's judgment the mandator retained his interest in acquiring the property in spite of a higher price. Presumably most principals in these arrangements would stand behind the actions of their agents and compensate them for expenses without delay, but the possibility of having to pay money in advance posed significant risks for the agent in mandate. For example, what would happen if the mandator were insolvent and so unable to pay the agent back?

One solution to the problem of compensating the agent for costs was to have the mandator take over any rights and obligations that the agent gained by carrying out his mandate, a solution that Paul discusses in connection with a mandate to purchase a farm (D. 17.1.45 pr.; Paul. 5 *ad Plaut.*).[51] The problem that Paul addresses concerns the outlays that the agent might have to make in fulfilling the mandate, which could impose a substantial burden. One possibility would be that the agent pay the purchase price and then recover this from the mandator in an action on mandate, but Paul also approves of the principle by which the agent sue on mandate to compel the mandator to take over the agent's obligations toward the seller. In this case, the mandator would become a *procurator in rem suam*, which would mean that he could be sued in his own name to pay off the purchase price of the farm.[52] But suing on mandate

[51] D. 17.1.45 pr. (Paul. 5 *ad Plaut.*): "If you buy a farm on my mandate, might you have an action against me on mandate when you have given the price, or also before you give it, so that you not need to sell your own property? And it is said correctly that the action on mandate consists in this, that I take up the obligation that is available to the seller against you; for I can also pursue an action with you that you provide me with your causes of action on purchase against the seller." (*Si mandatu meo fundum emeris, utrum cum dederis pretium ageres mecum mandati, an et antequam des, ne necesse habeas res tuas vendere? Et recte dicitur in hoc esse mandati actionem, ut suscipiam obligationem, quae adversus te venditori competit: nam et ego tecum agere possum, ut praestes mihi adversus venditorem empti actiones.*)

[52] See Kaser (1971: 655 and n. 28).

would in most cases represent an extreme step, one that would fracture the trust that presumably made possible the relationship between the mandator and the agent in the first place. Much more common, apparently, was the scenario in which the agent paid up front and then expected compensation from the mandator.

Perhaps a more troublesome question concerns the asymmetries of information inherent in a mandate contract, just as in other agency arrangements. Ulpian provides an important discussion of the rights and obligations accruing to the agent acting on such a mandate (what type of property was to be purchased is not specified):

> "If you mandate to me that I buy some piece of property for you, and I buy it at my price, I will have an action on mandate to recuperate the price. But if (you mandate the purchase of property) at your price, and I spend something in good faith toward the purchase of the item, there will be a contrary action on mandate, or if you should be unwilling to take back the item purchased. A similar principle will apply if you mandate something else and I make an expenditure towards it. I will gain not only what I have spent but also interest."[53]

In this text, Ulpian presents the basic principles underlying the claims of the agent acting under a mandate, under the *actio mandati contraria*. The essential problem is that once the agent accepted the mandate, he then had a great deal of freedom in performing his duties, because of his inevitably superior knowledge of the business he was transacting. Thus in the first part of the text, if the mandate was open-ended, the agent would have the right to recover whatever he spent on the purchase of the property. But this circumstance could put the mandator in a vulnerable position, even if the agent did not engage in deliberate misconduct (*dolus*), say, by colluding with the seller to raise the price of the property, or otherwise failed in obtaining an appropriate price, say, by overestimating the value of the property. Consequently, it is likely that many people would set a price at which the agent could purchase the property, as in the second part of the text from Ulpian. In this circumstance, the mandator would not be obliged to accept the property if the agent overpaid for it, but he would be obligated to compensate the agent for

[53] D. 17.1.12.9 (Ulp. 31 *Ad ed.*): *Si mihi mandaveris, ut rem tibi aliquam emam, egoque emero meo pretio, habebo mandati actionem de pretio reciperando: sed et si tuo pretio, impendero tamen aliquid bona fide ad emptionem rei, erit contraria mandati actio: aut si rem emptam nolis recipere: simili modo et si quid aliud mandaveris et in id sumptum fecero. Nec tantum id quod impendi, verum usuras quoque consequar . . . .*

expenditures made in good faith. As the early third-century jurist Paul emphasizes, contract of mandate is never supposed to make the situation of the mandator worse (D. 17.1.3 pr.; Paul. 32 *ad ed.*).[54]

The point is that in the law on mandate, despite provisions to compensate the agent for the expenses that he undertook in good faith, the interests of the mandator rather than the agent take priority over all others, including third parties. The privileging of the interests of the mandator over those of the agent can be seen in a case commented on by Scaevola, in which a property owner assigned a mandate to two people to manage his business (D. 17.1.60.2; Scaev. 1 *resp.*). In this situation, each of the agents was liable to the mandator for the whole amount connected with the business. If the mandator sued one of them on mandate, it was up to that person to bring proceedings to recover from the other.

To understand how conflicts between the mandator and agent might be resolved, it will be helpful to consider a case discussed by the jurists Neratius and Iavolenus, concerning a complicated situation in which an agent took up a mandate to purchase land (a *fundus*) of which he was part owner. For Neratius, this mandate was to be understood as requiring the agent to turn over to the mandator the entire farm, including the part that he owned (D. 17.1.35; Nerat. 5 *membran.*).[55] If the mandate was to acquire

[54] D. 17.1.3 pr. (Paul. 32 *ad ed.*): "Besides in a case of mandate this is also a consideration, that sometimes the situation of the mandator might not be able to become better, sometimes better, but never worse." (*Praeterea in causa mandati etiam illud vertitur, ut interim nec melior causa mandantis fieri possit, interdum melior, deterior vero numquam.*)

[55] D. 17.1.35 (Nerat. 5 *membran*), and D. 17.1.36 (Iav. 7 *ex Cass.*): "If I have mandated to you to buy for me a farm that it partly yours, it is true that a mandate can consist in this, that after purchasing the other shares you be obligated also to provide yours. But if I mandate that you buy them (the shares) at a certain price, for however much you bought the shares of the others, (the price of) your share will be reduced, so that it not exceed the amount of the mandate for which I mandated to you to buy the whole. But if I mandated to you to buy it without establishing a certain price and you have bought the shares of the other owners at different prices, your share must be given with the price appraised at the judgment of a good man, (Iav.) in such a way that it combine together all the greater and lesser sums and thus provide the portion to the one who has undertaken the mandate. Most (authorities) approve this." (*Si fundum, qui ex parte tuus est, mandavi tibi ut emeres mihi, verum est mandatum posse ita consistere, ut mihi ceteris partibus redemptis etiam tuam partem praestare debeas. Sed si quidem certo pretio emendas eas mandaverim, quanticumque aliorum partes redemeris, sic et tua pars coartabitur, ut non abundet mandati quantitatem, in quam tibi emendum totum mandavi: sin autem nullo certo pretio constituto emere tibi mandaverim tuque ex*

the farm at a set price, the agent's compensation for his own share of the farm would be limited by this overall amount, but if there were no set price, and the agent acquired others shares at differing prices, what he would be able to claim for his share would be on the basis of the "standards of an upright man" (*viri boni arbitratu*). In Iavolenus' discussion of the same scenario, if the agent was able to buy shares from the other owners at a more favorable price than the mandator had specified, this situation was not to prejudice the right of the agent to full compensation for his own share, as long as this did not exceed the originally mandated price (D. 17.1.36.1; Iav. 7 *ex Cass.*).[56] Thus if some of the co-owners were forced by circumstances to sell cheap, this did not mean that the agent also had to do so. At the same time, the agent was not to profit from this situation by holding up the sale of the land to the mandator if he should sense that the latter would be willing to pay a higher price. The agent could be in a position to engage in opportunistic behavior at the expense of the mandator, but the law sought to prevent this.

If jurists construed mandate as privileging the interests of the mandator over those of the agent, this principle also applied in relationship to third parties dealing with the agent. This could

diversis pretiis partes ceterorum redemeris, et tuam partem viri boni arbitratu aestimato pretio dari oportet, (36) ita ut omnes summas maiores et minores coacervet et ita portionem ei qui mandatum suscepit praestet. Quod et plerique probant.)

[56] D. 17.1.36.1 (Iav. 7 *ex Cass.*): "In a similar fashion and in this notion, when I have mandated to you to buy at a certain price and as regard the other shares you have managed the business favorably and bought cheaply, for your share you will be provided what is in your interest, as long as it is within the price that is contained in the mandate. For what will happen, if some of those with whom the farm was owned in common with you are forced to throw their property away for a small price, either because of financial necessity or some other reason? For you are not brought to the same loss. But you are not to gain for yourself any profit from this account, since a mandate ought to be gratuitous; nor is it to be allowed to you to impede the sale on this account, that you know that there is a more enthusiastic buyer of this thing than was mandated to you." (*Simili modo et in illa specie, ubi certo pretio tibi emere mandavi et aliarum partium nomine commode negotium gessisti et vilius emeris, pro tua parte tantum tibi praestatur, quanti interest tua, dummodo intra id pretium, quod mandato continetur. Quid enim fiet, si exiguo pretio hi, cum quibus tibi communis fundus erat, rem abicere vel necessitate rei familiaris vel alia causa cogerentur? Non etiam tu ad idem dispendium deduceris. Sed nec lucrum tibi ex hac causa adquirere debes, cum mandatum gratuitum esse debet: neque enim tibi concedendum est propter hoc venditionem impedire, quod animosiorem eius rei emptorem esse quam tibi mandatum est cognoveris.*) Finazzi (2010: 739) discusses the philosophical underpinnings of the interpretation of the agent's rights and obligations in D. 17.1.36.2 (Iav. 7 *ex Cass.*).

especially be an issue when the agent took actions that could be interpreting as exceeding his mandate. For his part, the principal could avoid any liability for such an undertaking on the part of the agent by not ratifying it, in which case the agent would sustain the full liability toward the person with whom he was doing business. The precedence accorded to the interests of the principal can be seen in a rescript from Diocletian, who ruled that a mandator was protected when he did not ratify the sale of his land by his procurator (C. 4.35.12, Sirmium, 293 CE): "Since you assert the contract for the mandate of a business involved specific terms (*certam legem*), it is accepted that these terms be observed fully in accordance with good faith. Therefore if, contrary to the tenor of the mandate, the procurator sold a farm belonging to you and afterwards you did not ratify the sale, he could not take ownership away from you."[57] The principal's refusal to ratify the sale could impose significant expenses on the agent, since he would be liable to the purchaser in an action on sale, and so would be obligated not only to return the purchase price to the buyer but also to compensate him for his interest in the sale's not going through. Indeed, as the jurist Paul emphasizes, if the agent sold the property at a price beneath that specified in the mandate, the mandator would not be prevented from claiming back ownership—the fact that the would-be buyer had paid money for this would not prevent him from doing so (D. 17.1.5.3; Paul. 32 *ad ed.*).[58] The agent would have to indemnify the mandator against any loss, at his own expense. On the other side of the coin, as outlined in another rescript of Diocletian, if the property owner took steps to show her ratification of a sale of property that took place without a mandate, she would assume liability for everything connected with the sale, including the possibility that the buyer might be evicted by the true owner (C. 4.5.9.1, 294 CE).

[57] C. 4.35.12: *Cum mandati negotii contractum certam accepisse legem adseveres, eam integram secundum bonam fidem custodiri convenit. Unde si contra mandati tenorem procurator tuus ad te pertinentem fundum vendidit nec venditionem postea ratam habuisti, dominium tibi auferre non potuit.*

[58] D. 17.1.5.3 (Paul. 32 *ad ed.*): "Also if I mandate to you that you sell my farm for one hundred, and you sell it for ninety and I seek the farm, a defense will not impede me, unless you also provide the remaining sum that is missing from my mandate and keep me indemnified through everything." (*Item si mandavero tibi, ut fundum meum centum venderes tuque eum nonaginta vendideris et petam fundum, non obstabit mihi exceptio, nisi et reliquum mihi, quod deest mandatu meo, praestes et indemnem me per omnia conserves.*)

The third party dealing with an agent faced potential costs arising from the possibility of the mandator's unwillingness to ratify what the agent had done. In other words, when entering into a contract with someone acting on a mandate, the third party would have to assess the likelihood that the agent was acting in accordance with a mandate and not somehow exceeding it. In the rescript of Diocletian mentioned above (C. 4.35.12), the ruling that the property owner would not be bound by the actions of his agent if they contradicted the terms of the mandate meant that the buyer could face eviction from the property. The buyer's right to sue the agent as seller in this situation would not necessarily provide a full solution. Quite apart from the fact that he wanted to buy the property in the first place and that lawsuits are costly, he would also face the possibility of the agent's insolvency. The general problem for third parties dealing with agents apparently acting on a mandate is expressed in a rescript from Diocletian to a father whose son (in his power) had taken some action contrary to the father's interest (C. 4.1.7, 293 CE). Diocletian ruled that if the son had acted without a mandate, the father had no obligation to ratify what the son had done, and if the father did not ratify, he would not be bound to the third party. In this case, the obligations that would arise between the son in power and the third party with whom he transacted business would be limited in accordance with the prescriptions of the various remedies included in the *actiones adiecticiae qualitatis*. However, the same principle about ratification applied if the agent were not in the father's power, say, if he were a procurator managing someone's business pursuant to a mandate. The question is how much would a third party dealing with an agent acting on mandate know the extent of the agent's instructions or the limitations imposed on him by the mandator. We can see a different aspect of this problem in a text from the jurist Paul, in which a person who was standing surety for a loan (a common assignment with mandate; see §11.4) erroneously paid the principal's debt to someone with no connection to the creditor (D. 17.1.26.5; Paul. 32 *ad ed.*). If the surety had paid this debt to the creditor's procurator, he would be able to recover this in an action on mandate, but since he did not, the principal assumed no liability to the surety. It would be left up to the surety to seek to recover what he paid in claim for restitution (*condictio*) of a sum not owed (*indebitum*).

From the point of view of liability, property owners might well prefer to undertake large-scale transactions through a free agent acting on a mandate rather than through a slave agent. In the latter case, the property owner would be able to exercise the type of leverage connected with a master-slave relationship, and so would be able to enforce good behavior on the part of the slave agent, or competent administration of his business interests, ex ante. But the property owner would have little capacity to recover from the slave agent if the agent entered into a business deal wrongly with serious financial consequences, since by necessity the property owner's recovery would be limited to the *peculium*. In assigning a major transaction to a free person under mandate, by contrast, the property owner would in theory have a greater capacity to recover any losses in full. When a third party entering into business with an agent on mandate as opposed to a slave, the third party would have to be confident that he would be able to recover from the agent if something went wrong. In cases in which the agent was acting as a *procurator ad litem* to argue a case in court on behalf of the principal, he would have to provide, through a stipulation, a formal guarantee that the mandator would ratify the action.[59] But when the mandate involved a financially significant transaction like the sale of property or the extension of credit, the third party's knowledge of the financial situation of the agent would be crucial.

11.6. CONCLUSION

To conclude, the contract of mandate evolved from one originally based on upper-class notions of reciprocity to an important instrument for property owners engaging in large-scale transactions involving significant risks. In the broader Roman commercial world, mandate represented the contractual relationship among property owners and "agents" of various classes who carried significant tasks, involving considerable expenses and financial exposure, on their behalf.[60] To judge by the frequency of rescripts concerning mandate in the Code of Justinian, mandate remained a versatile contract throughout the period of classical Roman law and afterwards.

[59] On the stipulations connected with the *procurator ad litem*, see Kaser and Hackl (1996: 214–18).

[60] A point emphasized by Verboven (2002) 260–4.

Its importance as an economic institution derived from its role in overcoming knowledge problems in a commercial world in which business revolved around personal relationships and contacts. In the credit market, this reciprocity involved overcoming problems of information to make it easier for people to lend and borrow. In all likelihood, people involved in the credit market would play the role of both creditor and surety, and perhaps perform this service for one another. But it seems also likely that many of the other types of enterprises involving mandate would involve similar reciprocity. The complex commercial world of the Roman principate required cooperation and flexibility, and business relationships involving the contract of mandate provided an important supplement to the type of agency arising from the hierarchical structure of the *familia*.

REFERENCES

Abatino, Barbara, Giuseppe Dari-Mattiacci, and Enrico C. Perotti. 2011. "Depersonalization of Business in Ancient Rome." 31 *Oxford Journal of Legal Studies* 365–89.

Aubert, Jean-Jacques. 1994. *Business Managers in Ancient Rome: A Social and Economic Study of Institores, 200 B.C.–A.D. 250*. Leiden: Brill.

Broekaert, Wim. 2017. "Conflict, Contract Enforcement, and Business Communities in the Archive of the Sulpicii," in Miko Flohr and Andrew Wilson, eds, *The Economy of Pompeii*. Oxford: Oxford University Press, 387–414.

Camodeca, Giuseppe. 2003. "Il credito negli archive campani: il caso di Puteoli e di Herculaneum," in Elio Lo Cascio, ed., *Credito e moneta nel mondo romano*. Bari: Edipuglia, 69–98.

Dari-Mattiacci, Giuseppe. 2013. "Slavery and Information." 73 *Journal of Economic History* 79–116.

Dari-Mattiacci, Giuseppe. 2015. "The Economic Perspective: Demand and Supply in the Reduction of Transaction Costs in the Ancient World," in Dennis P. Kehoe, David M. Ratzan, and Uri Yiftach-Firanko, eds, *Law and Transaction Costs in the Ancient Economy*. Ann Arbor: University of Michigan Press, 273–92.

de Ligt, Luuk. 1999. "Legal History and Economic History: The Case of the *actiones adiecticiae qualitatis*." 67 *Tijdschrift voor Rechtsgeschiedenis* 205–26.

Dixit, Avinash. 2004. *Lawlessness and Economics: Alternative Modes of Governance*. Princeton: Princeton University Press.

Finazzi, Giovanni. 2010. "Amicitia e doveri giuridici," in Alessandro Corbino, Michel Humbert, and Giovanni Negri, eds, *Homo, caput, persona: la costruzione giuridica dell'identità*. Padua: IUSS Press, 633–861.

Frier, Bruce W., ed. 2016. *The Codex of Justinian: A New Annotated Translation with Parallel Latin and Greek Text*. 3 vols. Cambridge: Cambridge University Press.

Frier, Bruce W., and Dennis P. Kehoe. 2007. "Law and Economic Institutions," in Walter Scheidel, Ian Morris, and Richard Saller, eds, *The Economic History of the Greco-Roman World*. Cambridge: Cambridge University Press, 113–43.

Frier, Bruce W., and James J. White. 2005. *The Modern Law of Contracts*. St. Paul: Thomson/West.

Furubotn, Eirik G., and Rudolf Richter. 2005. *Institutions and Economic Theory: The Contribution of New Institutional Economics*, 2nd edn. Ann Arbor: University of Michigan Press.

Granovetter, Marc. 2005. "The Impact of Social Structure on Economic Outcomes." 19 *The Journal of Economic Perspectives* 33–50.

Greif, Avner. 2006. *Institutions and the Path to the Modern Economy: Lessons from Medieval Trade (Political Economy of Institutions and Decisions)*. Cambridge: Cambridge University Press.

Harris, William V. 2006. "A Revisionist View of Money." 96 *Journal of Roman Studies* 1–24.

Kaser, Max. 1971. *Das Römische Privatrecht. Erster Abschnitt, Das altrömische, das vorklassische und klassische Recht*, 2nd edn. Munich: Beck.

Kaser, Max, and Karl Hackl. 1996. *Das Römische Zivilprozessrecht*. Munich: Beck.

Kehoe, Dennis P. 2013. "Law, Agency, and Growth in the Roman Economy," in Paul J. du Plessis, ed., *New Frontiers: Law and Society in the Roman World*. Edinburgh: Edinburgh University Press, 177–91.

Kehoe, Dennis P. 2015. "Contracts, Agency, and Transaction Costs in the Roman Economy," in Dennis P. Kehoe, David M. Ratzan, and Uri Yiftach-Firanko, eds, *Law and Transaction Costs in the Ancient Economy*. Ann Arbor: University of Michigan Press, 231–52.

Kehoe, Dennis P. 2017. "Agency, Roman Law, and Roman Social Values," in Dennis P. Kehoe and Thomas A. J. McGinn, eds, *Ancient Law, Ancient Society*. Ann Arbor: University of Michigan Press, 105–32.

Klinck, Fabian. 2007. "Zur Bedeutung des Wortes procurator in den Quellen des klassischen Rechts." 124 *Zeitschrift der Savigny-Stiftung für Rechtsgeschichte: Romanistische Abteilung* 25–52.

Lerouxel, François. 2015. "The βιβλιοθήκη ἐγκτήσεων and Transaction Costs in the Credit Market of Roman Egypt," Dennis P. Kehoe, David M. Ratzan, and Uri Yiftach-Firanko, eds, *Law and Transaction Costs in the Ancient Economy*. Ann Arbor: University of Michigan Press, 162–84.

Lerouxel, François. 2016. *Le marché du crédit dans le monde romain*. Rome: École française de Rome.

Mahoney, Paul G. 2000. "Contract Remedies: General," in Boudewijn Bouckaert and Gerrit De Geest, eds, *Encyclopedia of Law and Economics*. Vol. 3. Cheltenham: Edward Elgar, 117–40.

Mouritsen, Henrik. 2011. *The Freedman in the Roman World*. Cambridge: Cambridge University Press.

Nörr, Dieter. 1993. "Mandatum, fides, amicitia," in Dieter Nörr and Shigeo Nishimura, eds, *Mandatum und Verwandtes: Beiträge zum römsichen und modernen Recht*. Berlin: Springer-Verlag, 13–37.

Ogilvie, Sheilagh. 2007. "'Whatever Is, Is Right'? Economic Institutions in Pre-industrial Europe." 60 *Economic History Review* 649–84.

Plescia, Joseph. 1984. "The Development of Agency in Roman Law." 30 *Labeo* 171–90.

Randazzo, Salvo. 2005. *Mandare: radici della doverosità e percorsi consensualistici nell'evoluzione del mandato Romano*. Milan: Giuffrè.

Rathbone, Dominic. 1991. *Economic Rationalism and Rural Society in Third-Century A.D. Egypt: The Heroninos Archive and the Appianus Estate*. Cambridge: Cambridge University Press.

Ratzan, David, Dennis Kehoe, and Uri Yiftach. 2015. "Transaction Costs, Ancient History, and the Law," in Dennis P. Kehoe, David M. Ratzan, and Uri Yiftach-Firanko, eds, *Law and Transaction Costs in the Ancient Economy*. Ann Arbor: University of Michigan Press, 1–35.

Saller, Richard P. 1994. *Patriarchy, Property and Death in the Roman Family*. Cambridge: Cambridge University Press.

Schäfer, Christof. 1998. *Spitzenmanagement in Republik und Kaiserzeit. Die Prokuratoren von Privatpersonen im Imperium Romanum vom 2. Jh. v. Chr. bis zum 3. Jh. n.Chr*. St. Katharinen: Scripta Mercaturae.

Scheidel, Walter. 2009. "In Search of Roman Economic Growth." 22 *Journal of Roman Archaeology* 46–70.

Schiavone, Aldo. 2012. *The Invention of Law in the West*. Trans. Jeremy Carden and Antony Shugaar. Cambridge: Harvard University Press.

Temin, Peter. 2013. *The Roman Market Economy*. Princeton: Princeton University Press.

Terpstra, Taco. 2013. *Trading Communities in the Roman World: A Micro-Economic and Institutional Perspective*. Leiden/Boston: Brill.

Verboven, Koenraad. 2002. *The Economy of Friends: Economic Aspects of Amicitia and Patronage in the Late Republic*. Brussels: Latomus.

Wacke, Andreas. 1994. "Die adjektizischen Klagen im Überblick." 111 *Zeitschrift der Savingy-Stiftung für Rechtgeschichte: Romanistische Abteilung* 280–362.

Wilson, Andrew I. 2009. "Indicators for Roman Economic Growth: A Response to Walter Scheidel." 22 *Journal of Roman Archaeology* 71–82.

Winkel, Laurens. 1993. "*Mandatum* im Römsichen öffentlichen Recht?" in Dieter Nörr and Shigeo Nishimura, eds, *Mandatum und Verwandtes: Beiträge zum römsichen und modernen Recht*. Berlin: Springer-Verlag, 53–66.

Wittmann, Roland. 1993. "Die Prozeßformeln der actio mandati. Ein Beitrag zur Geschichte des prätorischen Edikts," in Dieter Nörr and Shigeo Nishimura, eds, *Mandatum und Verwandtes: Beiträge zum römsichen und modernen Recht*. Berlin: Springer-Verlag, 39–51.

Wolf, Joseph Georg. 1993. "Haftungsübernahme durch Auftrag? Eine Urkunde aus dem Jahre 48 n. Chr.," in Dieter Nörr and Shigeo Nishimura, eds, *Mandatum und Verwandtes: Beiträge zum römsichen und modernen Recht*. Berlin: Springer-Verlag, 69–91.

Wolf, Joseph Georg. 2001. "Der neue pompejanische Urkundenfund." 118 *Zeitschrift der Savingy-Stiftung für Rechtgeschichte: Romanistische Abteilung* 73–132.

Wolf, Joseph Georg. 2010. "Lo stigma dell'ignominia," in Alessandro Corbino, Michel Humbert, and Giovanni Negri, eds, *Homo, caput, persona: la costruzione giuridica dell'identità*. Padua: IUSS Press 491–550.

Zimmermann, Reinhard. 1996 [1990]. *The Law of Obligations: Roman Foundations of the Civilian Tradition*. Oxford: Oxford University Press.

Index